Moral Majorities across the Americas

BENJAMIN A. COWAN

Moral Majorities across the Americas

Brazil, the United States, and the
Creation of the Religious Right

The University of North Carolina Press *Chapel Hill*

This book was published with the assistance of the Anniversary Fund of the University of North Carolina Press.

Set in Arno Pro by Westchester Publishing Services
Manufactured in the United States of America

The University of North Carolina Press has been a member of the
Green Press Initiative since 2003.

Library of Congress Cataloging-in-Publication Data
Names: Cowan, Benjamin A., author.
Title: Moral majorities across the Americas : Brazil, the United States, and the
   creation of the religious right / Benjamin A. Cowan.
Description: Chapel Hill : University of North Carolina Press, 2021. |
   Includes bibliographical references and index.
Identifiers: LCCN 2020035433 | ISBN 9781469662060 (cloth ; alk. paper) |
   ISBN 9781469662077 (paperback ; alk. paper) | ISBN 9781469662084 (ebook)
Subjects: LCSH: Fundamentalism—Brazil. | Fundamentalism—United States. |
   Religious right—Brazil. | Religious right—United States. | Church and state—Brazil.
Classification: LCC BT82.2 .C69 2021 | DDC 322/.10981—dc23
LC record available at https://lccn.loc.gov/2020035433

Cover illustration: Faint silhouette of North and South America
© Shutterstock/Vitalii Barida.

Contents

Illustrations

Acknowledgments

I could exhaust the pages of this book thanking all of the extraordinary people who have made it possible for me to complete it. This is so much the case that I nearly despaired of writing these acknowledgments! First and foremost, I should like to thank the dear friends who have supported me in all senses along the way, and whose indefatigable patience with my ramblings facilitated the creaking wheels of research and writing. Thank you, Bibi Obler, Spencer Rudey, David Sartorius, Christine Tilton, Lera Boroditsky, Paddy Riley, Natalie Carnes, Tobias Wofford, Marianne Cook, Gabrielle Hunter-Rivera, Dan Droller, Roya Fohrer, Christopher Tradowsky, Melanie Arias, Radhika Natarajan, Chris Gregg, Chuck Cushman, Sam Lebovic, Emily Weaver, Scott Larson, Lilly Irani, Julie Weise, Siobhan Rigg, John Taht, Megan Sokolowski, Nick Riggle, Hami Ramani, Mia Hosaka, Erin Glass, Chelsea Coleman, Clinton Tolley, Brett Riggle, Nathan Young, Carolina Bravo-Karimi, Rudy Fabuñan, Marc Nielsen, Dan Navon, Hildie Kraus, and Andrew Costanzo.

Some dear friends are also colleagues, and it has been my extreme good fortune to enjoy their fellowship across national borders and institutional affiliations for nearly ten years. Working and living alongside these titans, how could I not feel buoyed? This list, too, would be exhaustive, but I must mention Cathy Gere, Simeon Man, Claire Edington, Erika Robb Larkins, and Matt Vitz. My departmental colleagues at the University of California, San Diego, as at George Mason, provided indispensable, warm, and caring support for my work. Special thanks to Pamela Radcliff, Leah Tamayo-Brion, Joan Bahrini, Jeremy Prestholdt, Michael Provence, and Jessica Graham for welcoming me so warmly to UCSD; and to Susan Winchester, Gricelda Ruíz, Sarab Aziz, Susan Bernal, Sally Hargate, and Luke Garton for the many times you have stepped in, seen and unseen, to help me out of a jam or just keep the lights on. Before California, in the wilds of Virginia, I would have been lost without Joan Bristol, Alison Landsberg, Meredith Lair, Matt Karush, Cindy Kierner, and Brian Platt.

The list of scholars who have contributed to this project would alone overrun the space I am allowed; I could not have done this work without the feedback and the forums generated by my brilliant fellow historians, Brazilianists, Latin Americanists, and scholars of the Right. I have often felt, over the course of the last decade, that I stumbled, unwittingly, into the richest of fields; this is a function of the people who constitute them. Thank you to Ernesto Bohoslavsky and Rodrigo Patto, and Mariana Joffily and Maud Chirio (super-heroínas), especially for their facilitation of a community of *derechólogxs*, the latter expanding ever more to include so many incredible folks: Janaína Cordeiro, Larissa Rosa Corrêa, Esther Solano Gallego, Gizele Zanotto, Rodrigo Coppe Caldeira, Leandro Pereira Gonçalves, Paul Katz, Craig Johnson, Daniel Kressel, Pablo Piccato, Tanya Harmer, Molly Avery, Luís Herrán Ávila, Liz McKenna, Stèphane Boisard, and the inimitable Margaret Power and Sandra McGee Deutsch. *Muito grato* to my fellow students of Brazil and of Latin America, who amaze and inspire me: Robin Derby—my first mentor, Tori Langland, Sueann Caulfield, Barbara Weinstein, Jerry Dávila, Carlos Fico, Jim Green, Jeff Lesser, Micol Seigel, José Amador, Jaime Delgado, Colin Snider, Renan Quinalha, Andre Pagliarini, Christina Scheibe Wolff, Vera Paiva, Chris Dunn, João Roberto Martins Filho, Mir Yarfitz, Michelle Chase, Zeb Tortorici, Devyn Benson, Kirsten Weld, Julio Capó, Valeria Manzano, and many, many others.

I am deeply indebted to the staff of the many archives and institutions in which I did research, without whom none of this would have been at all possible. Thank you, also, to the people who permitted me to interview them, or who indicated (or gave!) sources to me for this project.

Finally, and always, I would like to thank my family, who have always made everything seem possible. Monica, Chris, Jaya, Dez, Mom, Dad, and Baboon, this is for you.

It Has Become Attractive to Be Rightist and Conservative

Not so very long ago, Brazilian monarchism—the scattered calls for a restoration of Brazil's imperial throne, defunct since 1889—seemed merely a quaint curiosity, convenient for titillating students and animating conversations about the distant past. Those inclined even to broach the subject might have dismissed monarchists as an esoteric, rarely visible manifestation of certain elite resentments. But in late 2018, a descendant of the royal family began serving in Brazil's government for the first time since the fall of the emperor, nearly 130 years prior. By 2019, another would-be Brazilian royal, captaining the most ultraconservative of Catholic and authoritarian factions in Brazil, had gained prominent and vocal supporters in the minister of education, the minister of foreign relations, President Jair Bolsonaro's senior aide for international relations, and outspoken members of Congress. Both royals threw their support behind Bolsonaro and his agenda and combined hypertraditionalist, religious moralism with an idealized vision of a world returned to monarchy, or at least a world cleansed by neoliberal, hierarchalist, antidemocratic purism. As Bertrand de Orleans-Bragança (a current claimant to the would-be throne who styles himself "his Highness") put it, Bolsonaro and his coterie "figured out how to embody Brazilians' discomfort with the politically correct" and how to mobilize "the desire of Brazilians to free themselves from restraints, from a statist and interventionist mentality, influenced by socialists and Marxists who had come to dominate Brazil and plundered the nation." Bragança's disdain for diversity and pluralism, for "the politically correct," encompassed opposition to affirmative action and to gay marriage and abortion, among other sexual and reproductive rights. This disposition accompanied a program for the further dispossession of indigenous groups, historical erasure of slavery, and dismantling of the welfare state in favor of a conservative orthodoxy familiar to free-market evangelists North and South. "The beauty of society," Bragança contended, "does not lie in equality, but in differences which should be proportional, hierarchical, harmonic, and complementary. Exactly like a symphony." In 2019, Bragança and other monarchists felt their moment had arrived, at least in terms of a political agenda that facilitated reinstatement of their organicist, antidemocratic, and antiegalitarian "symphony." His highness reported with no little satisfaction that "it has become attractive to be rightist and conservative."[1]

Amid the victories and near victories of Trump, Bolsonaro, and similar right-wing populists—and in the face of ebullience like Bragança's—neglect and inattention are no longer the primary problems confronting scholars of conservatism. The Right has moved to the forefront of political, popular, and academic conversations in the past year, or two, or three. Across several continents, right-wing ascendancies, accompanied by a variegated series of ethnocentric conservatisms, curious minglings of neoliberalism and economic nationalism, and antidemocratic yearnings for vague, mythic pasts, have generated interest, passion, and fear. In my own corner of the world, I find myself finishing work on this book, which seeks to historicize the New Right as a transnational phenomenon with deep roots in Brazil. In the pages that follow, I illuminate processes that led to what has felt, to many, like a breathtaking resurgence of the Right. I argue that that resurgence, dramatic in its effects and perhaps baffling in its ideological inconsistencies, derives from a history of conservative activism that united strange bedfellows: Brazilians, North Americans, Catholics, Protestants, secular conservatives, neo-medieval fantasists, authoritarian opportunists, and others. Brazilian activists and institutions were essential to making this resurgence possible. Operating across national, denominational, and ideological frontiers, these Brazilians created organizations and nourished alliances that facilitated the construction of today's transnational Christian conservatism, which has become perhaps the most politically and culturally influential phenomenon of our time. Half a century ago, much of what now goes unquestioned as mainstream conservatism was instead the agenda of a reactionary and fundamentalist fringe. Brazilian conservatives, working with counterparts abroad, laid the groundwork for the normalization of that agenda, the tenets of today's religious Right.

For the past several years, discovering the history of these conservatives has felt more and more urgent, given developments in the political culture of Brazil, the United States, and elsewhere. Would-be royals aside, current events have threatened to overwhelm my writing, in ways that both showcase the harvests now yielded by the historical movements I research and confirm that the terrain of "the" Right continues to shift and realign beneath us. Nowhere could the sequelae of the history presented in this book have been more manifest than in the tumultuous first one hundred days of Bolsonaro's presidency. While journalists complained, with marked ahistoricism, that events were happening "faster" than they ever had before, Bolsonaro's performance in the drama that is twenty-four-hour news cycles certainly produced sensationalism and fast-paced plot twists. The splashiest of these adhered firmly to the politics of morality, traditionalism, and opposition to diversity and "political correctness" that had characterized Bolsonaro's campaign and endeared him to figures like Steve Bannon and Donald Trump. Bolsonaro's new minister of women, the family, and human rights, evangelical pastor Damares Alves, declared herself against feminism, against the "ideology of gender," and for the implementation via her ministry of "a new era, when boys will wear blue and girls will wear pink."[2] Bolsonaro himself, idolizing Trump, embraced the moniker "Trump of the Tropics" and appeared alongside the US president at the White House to announce that the two leaders were united in their perspective: "We respect the traditional family, we are God-fearing, we are against the ideology of gender, political correctness and *fake news*," Bolsonaro declared.[3] In Brazil and internationally, Bolsonaro generated myriad controversies—within the space of one week, he made headlines for forcing the Bank of Brazil to retract an advertisement that featured racially and sexually diverse actors, and for proclaiming that Brazil would no longer welcome gay tourists. "Whoever wishes to come to Brazil to have sex with a woman," he announced, "feel free. But [Brazil] cannot become known as the paradise of the gay world . . . for gay tourism. We have families."[4] Then, of course, there was the infamous "golden shower tweet." On 6 March 2019, claiming to "expose the truth" of what "most Brazilian *carnaval blocos* have become," Bolsonaro attacked Brazil's iconic carnival celebrations as depraved and immoral. To make his point, he tweeted a video of two scantily clad men at a São Paulo street party in which one eventually urinated on the other. "What is a golden shower?" the president asked later that day, via Twitter.[5]

In other sectors, meanwhile, confusion and ambiguity brewed. Bolsonaro's relationships with the recognized instigators of certain contemporary right-wing drives in Brazil grew murkier by the day. On the one hand, he remained discursively, socially, and politically linked with Olavo de Carvalho and Paulo Guedes, respective representatives of a shocking politics of antiliberalism and a not-so-shocking politics of neoliberalism. On the other, the importance of these figures to Bolsonaro's campaign and his election seemed to fade into the past. Even more than Trump, Bolsonaro's postelection overtures to economic nationalism (though he stopped short of trade war with China) caused a loss of faith among at least one core element of his supporters: libertarians and neoliberals.[6] In April 2019, his decision to freeze the price of gasoline in order to avert a truckers' strike—a move copied from his Workers' Party predecessors—drew the ire of former Bolsonaro supporters with free-market inclinations, including the (in)famous young Turks of the Movimento Brasil

Livre, who had been instrumental in marshaling support for the impeachment that made Bolsonaro's election possible in the first place.[7]

Despite the tumult, the hand-wringing, and the elements of the surreal in all of this, there is historical precedent for what we are seeing in 2019 in the United States, Brazil, and farther afield. From this perspective, Bolsonaro's presidency thus far represents much of what we might expect, given Brazil's historical relationship with religious conservatism and late twentieth-century neoconservatism in hemispheric and global context. Bolsonaro's rhetoric, the promise he offers to the conservative constituencies that form his core of support, consists in a union of moral conservatism and what now passes for "economic conservatism"—that is, laissez-faire liberalism or neoliberalism. At the same time, he inevitably fails to deliver on that promise, not only because his populism by definition lacks concrete policy content, nor simply because completely "free" markets are more or less an unattainable fantasy born of neoliberal delirium, but because Bolsonaro, as the current incarnation of that union, reflects the nature it has retained across its decades-long history: tenuous, carefully constructed, and never quite stable. The cries of dismay from (neo)liberals in Brazil disappointed by Bolsonaro's failure to be economically "conservative" enough certainly echo those who deride RINOs (Republicans in name only, accused of appeasing the so-called Left) in the contemporary United States. More tellingly, they reiterate the fractious complaints of past right-wing extremists, Brazilians and North Americans who struggled to cobble together an alliance of religious and fiscal conservatives; who forever saw themselves as the underdog in a fight against communism and globalist liberal democracy; and who saw the likes of the Brazilian dictatorship (1964–85) and Ronald Reagan as traitors to the cause of purer, more exclusivist, and sometimes more violent conservatisms. To quote Paul Weyrich, the founder of the Heritage Foundation—and, as we shall see, an admirer and collaborator of Brazil's pioneering Cold War reactionaries: "On one point the various components of the conservative movement are united; they are impatient waiting for the Reagan administration to catch up to them, and many are concluding that they must leave the president and his supporters behind to fulfill the bright promise of [the] 1980 [election] themselves."[8] Weyrich explicitly denounced Reagan's failure to gut the welfare state and eliminate "entitlement programs."[9] How neatly this dovetails today with demands, from those who consider themselves economic conservatives, that Bolsonaro demonstrate more commitment to neoliberal hamstringing of Brazil's public infrastructure and spending—this, even as the president himself has prioritized drastically cutting public pensions, freezing the minimum wage, eliminating humanities departments in public universities, and reducing federal spending on science by nearly half.[10] All of this follows, it bears mentioning, the recent high-water mark in Brazilian austerity measures: a 2016 constitutional amendment to cap government spending for twenty years, passed after the legislative coup against Dilma Rousseff that same year.[11]

Even at the height of Workers' Party rule in Brazil, long before the drama of 2016, the power of religious conservatism had grown undeniable. While Presidents Luiz Inácio Lula da Silva (2003–11) and Rousseff (2011–16) introduced unprecedented social welfare programs, they largely adhered to a politics of trade and open markets that had marked the administrations of their predecessors. Perhaps most remarkably, they made critical pacts with the Christian Right. By 2010, the Brazilian and American Lefts, such as they were, no longer dared even to flirt with overt secularism, much less opposition to religion in politics. In the United States, no leading politicians risked seeming anything other than firmly Christian: Barack Obama's *style* of Christianity metamorphosed from campaign issue to dogged font of suspicion; and the country's culture wars had grown so presumptive, with such hardened battle lines, that gay wedding cakes unironically fascinated policy makers, journalists, and even the Supreme Court. In Brazil, meanwhile, reproductive and sexual rights became the first issues to hit the chopping block of evangelical power. In a country plagued by some of the world's highest rates of homophobic violence, a curriculum entitled Escola sem Homofobia (Schools without Homophobia) failed in 2011, after religious activists pressured the president to cancel it.[12] Notably, the program was derisively labeled *kit gay* by none other than then-deputy Bolsonaro. As early as 2010, Rousseff stopped supporting abortion rights and began peppering her public discourse with mentions of God. A former atheist, the Brazilian president famously sought evangelical support in 2014 by publicly affirming, "Citing a psalm of David, I wanted to say that blessed is the nation whose God is the Lord."[13] According to political scientist Cristián Parker, Rousseff's political moves "highlighted that the religious choices of the leftist political parties and progressive, populist, and/or leftist movements are no longer antireligious. They . . . rely on nondenominational religious values and symbols, something that would have been unthinkable at the height of the Cold War."[14] Unsurprisingly, the very evangelical groups that Rousseff sought to court with her 2014 proclamation (and other overtures, including policy-making) threw their support behind Bolsonaro in 2018.

These latter-day contortions of the religious Right in Brazil and the United States encompass contradictions and variegations both internal and comparative. The contours of the Right, that is, are never smooth, neither domestically nor when considered across the political and cultural landscapes of both countries. This book is not, however, about the antics of Trump and Bolsonaro, nor even about the power politics of right-wing Christians and their neoliberal allies in the 2000s and 2010s. Instead, part of what I wish to do in the pages that follow is address the question, How did we get here? Answering that question, as we shall see, demands a much broader perspective than that which scholars have applied to the history of the contemporary Right; and it requires including Brazil and Brazilians as critical actors in a story that cannot be understood from the perspective of any single nation-state. The current configuration confronts us with a series of right-wing coalitions that share certain basic tenets across national contexts: antiegalitarianism, antirationalism, antistatism, hierarchalism, and variations of antimodernism, anticommunism, mysticism, antiecumenism, and a sense of the besiegement of traditional cultures. In this book I seek, in one sense, to uncover the origins of that laundry list of now-interwoven issues. How, in other words, did national iterations of conservativism come to have such uncannily consonant contours, and such similar abilities to subsume those contours' inherent contradictions? By 2019, of course, those contradictions may seem less glaring, their potency faded by their very longevity and by the presumption that the platforms we think of as "right" and "left" cohere in some naturalized fashion. Hence Bolsonaro and Trump could appear at the White House to mutually advocate expanding the state's reach into private morality and public security, while at the same time shrinking "big government," dismantling social security programs, and deregulating international capital.

The question "How did we get here?" is something of a feint, an irresistible nod to the current climate of Brexit, border walls, Bolsonaro, and Brazil's legislative "Bible, Bullets, and Beef" caucus. At its core, this book is a history of religious conservatism in twentieth-century Brazil. It follows specific Brazilian activists and institutions as they built Christian conservatism into a national and transnational phenomenon, with the power to determine policy and political culture in Brazil and to help shape and support the aspirations of conservatives worldwide. The book is, in some sense, a history of themes—of the critical hopes, fears, animosities, and affinities that coalesced to create the platforms and power bases of Brazil's religious Right. As we shall see in the following chapters, the anxieties and prerogatives of several branches of conservative Christians in Brazil flourished in the midcentury period, both because of the initiatives undertaken by certain Brazilian actors and because these intensely reactionary Christians became the close allies of the repressive military regime that ruled the country from 1964 to 1985.

My research shows that in the context of authoritarian Brazil, these groups saw their agendas flourish. Right-wing Catholics and Protestants alike gained the support of the regime; their progressive rivals among the faithful, on the other hand, faced persecution. Brazil in the 1960s, 1970s, and 1980s, then, became fertile territory for the flourishing of right-wing religious ideas and networks. In this context, far-right Catholics in Brazil, who had long seen themselves losing a war against change in the world and in the Church, found themselves able to more effectively and sustainably champion hierarchies, rituals, aesthetics, and exclusions considered to be ancient—and, eventually, to wed those priorities to ascendant neoliberalism, in a sense replacing long-standing insistence on "private property" with adherence to a modified ideological foundation for capitalism. Conservative Protestants, meanwhile, likewise saw their fortunes thrive, particularly during the latter days of the dictatorship. As the regime's more repressive and recalcitrant elements solidified their animosity toward the Catholic Church—whose national hierarchy visibly championed human rights and, to some extent, social justice—right-wing Protestants gained purchase in politics and public media; they also benefited from the government's outright persecution of their left-leaning or progressive coreligionists.

Domestically, then, the stage was set for the development of a new and powerful politics of Christian conservatism—a politics that could ultimately unite, for example, conservative Catholic politicians with their evangelical counterparts. As one Catholic federal legislator colorfully put it in 2017, "It's better to open an evangelical Church than a cabaret."[15] Yet in this book I seek not only to unearth that story but to nationally and transnationally contextualize Brazil's Christian Left and Right, historicizing the country's culture wars in ways that elucidate how they were deeply imbricated with and deeply influential in processes that transcend Brazil. Brazilian Catholics at and after Vatican II laid the groundwork for global traditionalism within the faith; separate from those efforts, evangelicals entered domestic politics and gained traction for a new conjuncture of moralism and anticommunism. Yet these events did not occur in a vacuum, nor in cultural or political isolation from each other or from international developments. Rather, Catholic and evangelical conservatism in Brazil advanced in ways that demonstrate the complex contours of the rise of a transnational Christian Right. Brazilian activists became hemispheric and even global activists, forging connections with remarkable fluidity, though also engaging in the squabbling and isolationism that could impede conservative cooperation. Despite the latter, collaborative efforts yielded forums for communication and the sharing of ideas and tactics; those forums, in turn, fostered a network of right-wing priorities, agendas, ideological positions, and lexicons, which would furnish a transnational bedrock for Christian conservatism. Brazil's Christian conservatives, in other words, saw themselves as part of a series of global struggles for the soul not only of their country but of the West and the world. They helped form national and international responses to those struggles, drawing both on strategic need and on ideological affinity.

This book, then, intervenes in current literatures in three critical ways. First, it presents the current configuration of the Right (which we might call the New Right, though that modifier has lost its aptness) as a phenomenon with broad roots that are essentially transnational. For a long time, studies of right-wing movements have taken for granted their boundedness by the nation-state, an assumption determined by the nationalism of historical conservatisms. Here I am joining a small cohort of scholars interested in unearthing right-wing networks and exchanges both powerful and marginal.[16] In this sense, what I present in the following chapters forms a part of a larger history whose contours continue to unfold and to rise from the murky depths of hidden or forgotten histories of activism. The transnational history of the Right, especially in Latin America, has of necessity become a collaborative project, and as my colleagues' excellent work demonstrates, the subjects of this book were not the only activists, nor even the only Brazilian activists, engaged in struggles to renew and restore conservative values.[17] This book, in other words, treats a critical core of activists, remarkably influential in both domestic and international arenas, whose activism shaped and illuminated a broader terrain of alliances and affinities.

Second, and given that historiographical context, this book demonstrates the importance of Brazil as a critical locus for the gestation of the transnational Right. I do not claim that Brazilians single-handedly created modern religious conservatism; but I do contend that Brazilian activists played pivotal roles in that creation, and that those roles have thus far gone largely ignored by scholars. Neglect of these activists themselves and even of their collaborators abroad (including, as we shall see, in the United States) has left us with an incomplete, and thus misleading, notion of how the New Right was cobbled together, in terms of local and international forms of reaction. In order to understand the modern Right, in other words, we must include Brazil as an essential platform for—and Brazilians as essential proponents of—the development of cultural, moral, and political agendas now taken for granted.

Third, and relatedly, this book counters time-honored ways of thinking about the emergence of late–Cold War conservatism, particularly in the United States. The historiography of North American conservatism in the latter decades of the twentieth century is better established than that of almost any-where else; a generation of insightful literatures has led to much better understandings of the rise of new forms of conservatism, from so-called kitchen-table activism in Orange County to the transformation of the Republican Party in the 1960s, and up to and including the politics of race and exclusion following the Vietnam War and leading up to the current moment.[18] Yet the traditional way of narrating the history and origins of that series of right-wing processes has focused exclusively on the United States itself, and particularly on domestic movements for civil and sexual rights and for cultural change in the 1960s. The notion that neoconservatism emerged as a backlash to these nationally specific phenomena must be problematized by stories like those I tell in this book. Brazil's importance, and its relationship with central actors in the rise of the American Right, troubles the domestic lens of most scholarship on the latter. For example, race relations and racism in Brazil occupy a different discursive and political space, thus complicating arguments and assumptions that new conservatisms emerged as a response to U.S.-specific racial politics and identities. Differences in the relationships of race and religion compound this complication, not least because unlike their counterparts in the United States—where a legacy of fundamentalist segregationism and overt racism shaped the (largely white) contours of evangelical conservatism—Brazilian Protestants have tended both to be more Afro-descended and not to prioritize or even address racism.[19]

Likewise, while North American scholarship has long flirted with the notion of U.S. conservatism as a "last-gasp attempt to recapture a mythical, premodern past" based in rural and ethnocentric fantasies, this is not a nationally unique characteristic. Instead, it constitutes a point of connection—as we shall see, Brazilian reactionaries also championed returns to mythic pasts, both at home and abroad.[20] To take another tack, accounts from the North tend to ignore the simultaneity of right-wing religious ascendancy in Brazil and the United States. If American historians like Daniel Rodgers can point to the 1970s and 1980s as the "Age of Fracture," in which evangelicals sallied forth to "save" politics in a campaign of "high moral warfare" that also included conservative Catholics, how do we explain the coevality of this process in Brazil?[21] Surely the latter cannot be dismissed as derivative or peripheral, as it occurred at roughly the same time and—as we shall see—in collaboration with similar processes abroad. In other words, the narrative in the United States, of white rage against civil rights, or the explosion of country music and confederate flags as identitarian symbols, or the rapid spread of born-again Christianity as a political force, while certainly part of the story, does not explain everything—just as the current wave of anti-immigrant, anti-black, anti-LGBT rhetoric and violence in Brazil, linked to older histories of those prejudices, does not solely explain the rise of the Nova Direita (New Right).

Let us leave Bolsonaro and Trump for a moment, however, and return to the 1930s and 1940s in Brazil—the turbulent years of Getúlio Vargas's authoritarian and corporatist rule (1930–45), of right-wing Catholicism occasionally at odds and yet often cooperating with his regime, and of a prominent fascist movement (the Integralists). Dom José Maurício da Rocha, bishop of the small city of Bragança Paulista, roughly eighty kilometers from São Paulo, threw his support behind the latter, openly touting the "superiority of Integralism."[22] When I first mentioned Rocha to archivists at episcopal archives in São Paulo and Minas Gerais, his name elicited snorts of laughter and the suggestion that he was something of a joke. No doubt this stemmed from his extremist positions, or from his latter-day activism at the Second Vatican Council (1962–65), where—as we shall see—he fell quite clearly out of step with the majority of Brazilian Church fathers, famous for their advocacy of changes in the Church. (Rocha, by contrast, joined a minority of Brazilian activists advocating for a return to a premodern, theocratic Church and society.) Yet in the interwar period, Rocha marched in lockstep with Brazil's fascists, writing for the Integralist newspaper *Acção*, focusing his efforts on the "moral orientation of the nation," and even trying to start a "nationalist party" to be coordinated under the aegis of the Church itself. This last goal contravened the wishes even of more powerful conservatives in the contemporary Church hierarchy, including Cardinal Sebastião Leme, archbishop of Rio de Janeiro. It also would certainly have challenged the power of Vargas, whom Rocha suspected of indifference to the moral and spiritual prerogatives prioritized by Rocha himself and by the fascists.[23]

In his public pronouncements, however, Rocha showed little concern for anything except the right-wing vision he shared with his Integralist allies: an opposition to "modernity" that synthesized moral panic, anti-Semitism, anti-rationalism, anticommunism, opposition to global liberalism (including the United Nations), a call for a return to a mythic past based in theocracy and the felt presence of the supernatural, and a sense of the besiegement of right-minded moral folks like himself. Anticipating rightists of later years in these themes, Rocha took those "calamitous times" as a point of departure, declaring that "the modern world . . . suffers the most torturous martyrdom, with no one escaping from the strikes of the [devil]." In his pastoral letters, speeches, and collected essays, Rocha deplored "modern discoveries" like "the corrupting cinema" and its contribution to "the current degradation of the family and of society in general." He denounced the United Nations' Universal Declaration of Human Rights in the same breath as the apocryphal Protocols of the Elders of Zion, relegating both to the terrain of anti-Christian plots. Communism and the "Synagogue of Satan" both agitated, according to Rocha's inversion of the infamous counterrevolutionary refrain, for a future "Without God, Without the Pátria, and Without the Family." Perhaps most dangerous, in Rocha's estimation, was an "irritating laicism," as anathema to him as it would be to generations of rightists thereafter. "Materialism," he wrote in 1932, "causes social evil everywhere, because if the supernatural perspective guided government authorities," great calamities would be avoided. "The supernatural principles of Religion," he continued, "direct us to think about the ruin of earthly goods, the transitory nature of life, the ephemerality of status"—but he fretted that Brazil's government (recently taken over by Vargas in the Revolution of 1930) actually *promoted* this "irritating laicism," favoring the material world over the supernatural and doing so in ways that threatened to "nullify" centuries of tradition and hierarchy via changes to education, marriage, and even death (the "secularization of cemeteries").[24]

Rocha, of course, was far from alone in holding these positions; he shared them with conservative Catholics in Brazil and elsewhere, and certainly with his like-minded compatriots in the Integralist movement. Fascism aside, much of what he had to say followed the lead of the conservative popes Leo XIII (1878–1903), Pius X (1903–14), and Pius XII (1939–58). Rocha is not the most important player in our story—he was merely one among many elaborating in this early moment a litany of issues that would survive, in some form, to populate the platforms of later twentieth-century rightists. Yet Rocha's story hints at a key historical truth: that there is something special about Brazil, whose actors and activists we shall follow across the twentieth century through the course of this book. Alongside others in Brazil, Rocha stirred up a heady and nationally specific cocktail that would persist for decades: anti-Semitism, antiliberalism, fascism with a careful distance from overt racism (increasingly considered un-Brazilian in the Vargas years), anticommunism, and a disdain for modernity constructed around coterminous hatred of perceived secularism and distrust of a global order based in liberal democracy. On this last point, Rocha insisted that the United Nations sought a new era characterized by "Man with Rights and God without even the right to speak His Name!"

Again and again throughout the course of this book, we shall see Brazilian leaders and institutions returning to this mixture of ideas, a foundation for conservatisms to come. Perhaps that is because these ideas, and the people who espoused them, would survive in Brazil as in almost no other country. Integralism, though disbanded in 1937, retained influence and adherents at the highest levels of corporatist government in the Vargas years and then of military-authoritarian government in the dark years of Brazil's Cold War dictatorship (1964–85). By the mid-1960s, when extreme conservative Catholics from Brazil were drawing on their decades of activism to build global resistance to Vatican II, the former Integralist headman Plínio Salgado had not only returned from exile but had taken a position in the Senate. If Rocha, in the 1930s and 1940s, had drawn battle lines that centered on a "third way," corporatist, spiritualistic hatred of rationalism and of modernization, he and others would carry forward, across decades, a torch borne in the name of traditionalist virtues, morals, aesthetics, hierarchies, and political and economic forms—and would do so from the corridors of Brazil's government to the floor of the Vatican Council, to the pulpits of evangelical churches, to the foundation of conservative lobbying groups, and eventually to the transnational articulation of a new Right, predicated on the union of preserved hierarchies and renovated economic liberalism.

I do not argue in this book that Brazilians, much less Rocha, invented conservatism, neoconservatism, or the New Right. The answer to the question "How did we get here?" does not lie, of course, solely in Brazil—but then again, neither does the answer to the question "How did Brazil get here?" Two critical points must be made from the outset: First, the contemporary Right, including the religious Right, can only be understood by comprehending the *variety* of Rights, the unity and disunity of conservatisms, as the result of a fundamentally transnational set of processes. In the era of Bolsonaro and Olavo de Carvalho, of new attention to reactionaries, and perhaps most notably of an explosion of self-described "conservatives" or "right-wingers" who make the terms identitarian, we must recognize that what people in the United States, Brazil, and farther afield think of as "the Right" comes from many places and sources, and the story of its emergence wends through coincidence as well as convergence and cooperation. If we seek the origins of a series of movements that combine "economic conservatism" (that is, the revival and radicalization of laissez-faire liberalism) with "social conservatism" (which we broadly understand as a combination of religious and cultural traditionalisms based in myth-making about the past and particularly about the histories of families, gender, race, and social relations), we must explore all of the factors in that emergence, and at the very least the three modalities just noted: coincidence, cooperation, and convergence. Second, as I argue, Brazil played a particularly prominent role in this story—a finding that makes sense, given that it is now home to a religious Right at least as significant and influential as that of the United States; that its politics of deregulation and neoliberalism rival those of anywhere in terms of radicalism; and that it has long held pride of place in world evangelicalism and, as we shall see, the genesis of Christian conservatism, Catholic as well as evangelical. In this book, I show how that role made Brazil a critical and also a complex locus for developing the Right. This history encompasses more than just North-to-South or South-to-North flows of ideas or influence; rather, it hinges on Brazil's positionality in a complex web of concurrence, divergence, and alliance. In the wide-ranging episodes that compose this book, I trace religious conservatisms across the course of twentieth-century Brazil. These episodes reveal Brazilian actors—sometimes in conversation with foreign counterparts—constructing the pillars of the New Right: that is, antimodernism, antiecumenism, mysticism, antistatism, hierarchalist antiegalitarianism, antirationalism, and the sense of besiegement that characterizes late twentieth-century conservatisms. In other words, this book demonstrates the ways in which particular kinds of antimodernism gestated and flourished among Brazil's twentieth-century Christian conservatives, and eventually evolved into precisely the union of hypercapitalism, exclusivism, and traditionalist Christianity that has grown so domestically and internationally visible and powerful. We shall see Brazilian activists building what would become the national religious Right—but also explore the ways in which Brazil-based actors and institutions played a central role in developing a transnational set of right-wing priorities and strategies.

In chapter 1 we shall again encounter Dom José Maurício da Rocha, albeit as a minor member of an alliance of Brazilian bishops and activists who strove to organize conservative reaction before, during, and after the Second Vatican Council. Two Brazilian bishops, Geraldo Proença Sigaud and Antônio de Castro Mayer, joined a cohort of helpmeets from the Sociedade Brasileira de Defesa da Tradição, Família e Propriedade (Brazilian Society for the Defense of Tradition, Family and Property, known as the TFP) to work behind the scenes of the council. These men had worked together in the past, and the council granted their work more urgency. In the face of what they saw as a satanic and communistic threat of modernization within the Church, Sigaud, Mayer, and the TFP laid the foundation for decades of agitation and resistance. Essential to the development of global traditionalist Catholicism, the Brazilian conservatives have long been the subject of reverence and hagiography among traditionalists themselves; yet academic accounts have largely neglected them. Chapter 1 traces their leadership at Vatican II and afterward, focusing on their work, alongside more widely known foreign counterparts, to solidify and highlight an agenda that would come to define Catholic and—more broadly—Christian archconservatism. Their grievances mirrored those we shall revisit among other reactionaries throughout this book: anticommunism; a strident, detailed moralism; antiecumenism; defense of hierarchy per se; antistatist dedication to private property and free enterprise; and vociferous defense of the primacy of the supernatural in a world perceived to be increasingly secularized.

Chapters 2 and 3 turn away from Catholics to examine the emergence of another critical power center in Brazilian and hemispheric conservatism: evangelicals. While right-wing Catholics busied themselves resisting Vatican II and seeking to eradicate progressivism, evangelicals back home engaged in a related process. The explosive growth of evangelicalism in Brazil has already generated volumes of rich scholarship. Here, I seek to trace how and why that explosion took shape in the ways it did politically—why, in other words, Brazil developed a powerful evangelical Right. Chapter 2 unearths the inter-related conditions that empowered conservatives within the burgeoning evangelical population: just as evangelicals began to abandon their long-touted apoliticism and formally enter politics, Brazil's military regime turned away from the Catholic Church to find new allies among right-wing Protes-tants. The regime and the most reactionary elements among *crentes* (evan-gelicals; literally, "believers") shared, albeit for slightly different reasons, a persecutory moralism and anticommunism that set its sights on rooting out progressive Christianity, ecumenism, and those who sought to make the faith an avenue for social justice and democratization. Here we shall begin en-countering both Brazilian conservative pioneers and their collaborations with international activists, including Carl McIntire, a North American fire-brand critical to the story of the evangelical Right in his home country and, as we shall see, in Brazil.[25] Chapter 3 addresses progressive Christians, explicat-ing what happened to the evangelical Left in Brazil. Brazil's role in the devel-opment of reformist and radical Christianity, particularly among Catholics, is well known, even celebrated; this chapter explores the country's Protestant Left and what it stood for in its moments of greatest potential in Brazil—before, that is, evangelical progressivism was marginalized not only by the enmity of conservative coreligionists but also by the stranglehold of the mili-tary state.[26] The road not taken, for Brazil's evangelical politics, diametrically opposed the Christian Right: Protestant progressives, ever a minority (one scholar has called them a "novelty" limited to the "protestant elite"),[27] never-theless gained some visibility and championed ecumenism, social justice, gender and civil rights movements, democratization, and even the plight of those living and dying with AIDS. Set apart from the neoliberalism, pro-authoritarianism, and moralism of the evangelical Right, progressives found themselves confronting a transnational front of conservatism that stretched from Jimmy Swaggart and Pat Robertson to Brazil's own televangelists and to the halls of dictatorial power.

Chapter 4 focuses more directly on the forging of stronger connections between Brazilian and international, particularly US, activists on the Right. It takes up the story of moralistic anticommunism as fodder for the creation of institutions that spanned national and denominational borders. Brazilian churches and media outlets engaged with and republished moralistic evangelism from the North; but they also sent missionaries to "save" the souls of America and Americans. More influentially, organizations like the TFP, the International Policy Forum, the World Anti-Communist League, the Sociedade de Estudos Políticos, Econômicos e Sociais, and others actively created spaces for and lines of communication between like-minded individuals of various national origins and religious persuasions. These organizations, in Brazil, enjoyed the direct support of the military regime's most recalcitrant and antidemocratic elements, benefiting from corrupt patronage even as the dictatorship itself waned. As a result, Brazil became a key nexus, physically and ideologically, in the circuits that gave rise to the transnational New Right.

Chapter 5 locates Brazil and Brazilians in the genesis and maintenance of the ideological firmament of those circuits. The hand-wringing about the state of the contemporary world that "united the Right" (so to speak) across national and denominational divides took a series of perceived scourges as the essence of a hated modernity. These included ecumenism, communism, secularization, expanded government and the welfare state, and a self-perception of traditionalists and traditional hierarchies as the victims of an ongoing, egalitarian spread of liberal democracy. At the heart of rightists' complaints, and in a sense what bound them together, was the notion that a quotidian sense of the divine or the supernatural, the source of the world's rightful, moral, and social hierarchies, had been abandoned, leaving chaos in its wake. Right-wing reactionaries within and outside the Brazilian state, alongside like-minded allies abroad, thus sought to defend or restore that sense, and with it a litany of values they collectively enshrined as the core of the new conservatism: veneration for private property, hierarchy, nationalism, and traditional culture; and rejection of ethnic and religious pluralism, global liberal humanitarianism and cooperation, modernism (whether in theology or popular or moral culture), secularization, and "communism" (generally associated with any interventionist or welfare-oriented state).

CHAPTER ONE

The Beauty of Inequality
Brazilian Activism, Catholic Traditionalism,
and the Makings of Modern Conservatism

In September 1964, with the third session of Vatican II in full swing, Dom José Maurício da Rocha, bishop of Bragança Paulista and a noted conservative, lashed out at certain tendencies in the deliberations. "The devil," Rocha darkly affirmed, "has exerted himself so that the council may have the least success," creating a "fever of novelties regarding the liturgy." Rocha was incensed by the way that even "the celebration of the Sacred Sacrifice of the Mass has been violently attacked, with [the proposal of] one half in Latin and the other half in the vernacular. . . . The intention is to weaken the Church, plunging it into an even greater confusion than that in which it currently finds itself." The bishop reserved exceptional ire for those who would do away with the accoutrements of "priestly vestment" and especially the cassock (*batina*).[1] Rocha's complaints did not go unheard—for starters, they made him the butt of gentle ribbing by his fellow Brazilian Church fathers in an informal newsletter circulated in Rome. *O Conciliábulo*, generated by progressive-leaning Brazilian attendees, mocked Rocha's dedication to the old ways, reprinting an article about him entitled "Bishop Defends Latin and the Cassock." To the original title, the satirists of *O Conciliábulo* added "STILL!" so that the headline about Rocha read, "Bishop (STILL!) Defends Latin and the Cassock."[2]

Fellow Church fathers, however, were not the only party interested in the pronouncements and activities of conservatives like Rocha—and the bishop's supporters proved both more temporally powerful and longer-lived than the editorial committee of *O Conciliábulo*. As we shall see, support for the cassock, and for traditionalism, resided at the heart of the Brazilian state; moreover, Rocha's defense of these accoutrements of traditional priesthood represented the critical activism of a core group of Brazilians working at and after Vatican II to stem the tide of reform. In part for this reason, Rocha himself is still remembered as a hero by ultramontane Catholics. In 2014, the far-right group Fratres in Unum lauded him as "one of the most influential bishops. . . . Monarchist, fiercely antimodernist, anticommunist and antiliberal, gifted with a privileged intelligence, enormous culture and exemplary piety, he wrote innumerable articles and pastoral letters, in which he revealed his love for the Church and his worries about defending the faith and its customs."[3]

This assessment overestimates Rocha's prominence; but Fratres in Unum's encomium is more significant for what it reveals about the bishop's importance to reactionaries. Even as a conservative, his legacy at Vatican II pales in comparison to that of his brethren from Diamantina, Minas Gerais, and Campos, Rio de Janeiro: Dom Geraldo Proença Sigaud and Dom Antônio de Castro Mayer, respectively.[4] And Rocha was certainly nowhere near as "influential" as his *progressista* compatriots who famously helped to coordinate reforms, among them Dom Hélder Câmara. These relative progressives have dominated headlines and scholarship as well as historical memory since the council; Rocha and a handful of other conservatives, including Sigaud and Mayer, have long since been forgotten. Herein lies a fascinating tension: much has been written about Brazil as a source of ecumenist, justice-oriented reform within the Church; yet behind the scenes, in ways that would affect Catholicism and Christian conservatism for decades to come, a cohort of Brazilian Catholic traditionalists also organized and worked to influence the council and the Church. Though often shrouded in obscurity, Brazilians' centrality to this work sometimes entered the spotlight—as when Mayer presided alongside Marcel Lefebvre[5] over the renegade consecration of bishops at Ecône in 1988; or when, perhaps more indicatively, Mayer and Lefebvre, together in Brazil, issued their controversial 1983 attack on the "false notions" encouraged by Vatican II. In an open letter to the pontiff, promulgated from Rio de Janeiro, the two identified themselves as leaders of a global cohort now seeking to publicize their frustrated traditionalism because "the measures we have undertaken in private during the last fifteen years have remained ineffectual." Together they identified the "origin of this tragic situation" in certain "errors" that would become the bedrock of traditionalist outrage: ecumenism, the decline of supernaturalism, and the promotion of various democratic attenuations of hierarchy.[6]

In these moments, Mayer's centrality to the most famous of traditionalist ruptures emerged dramatically; that centrality, however, derived from a cohort of traditionalist Catholics in Brazil who had conspired across decades, even before Vatican II, to set a course for the mutiny at Ecône. Alongside other Brazilian clerics—most notably Sigaud—and organizations (especially TFP, or the Brazilian Society for the Defense of Tradition, Family and Property, founded in 1960 by lay activist Plínio Corrêa de Oliveira),[7] Mayer played a major, in some sense pioneering, role in the national and transnational politics of Catholic traditionalism, in particular during and after the council. Yet Mayer, Sigaud, and even the rather sensational TFP are often marginalized in broader historiography of the global rise of Catholic reaction and archconservatism.[8] On the one hand, partisans of Catholic traditionalism have always acknowledged the Brazilians' role and even pointed out the ways in which this marginalization dates back across the decades.[9] Academic accounts, on the other, seem to have largely ignored these Brazilian actors.[10] In this chapter I seek to write these actors into that broader historiography, highlighting their activism at Vatican II as part of the construction and evolution of transnational Catholic traditionalism.

Mayer, Sigaud, and Oliveira began collaborating in the 1930s, paving the way toward their vigorous, and vital, archconservative Catholic activism at Vatican II. In 1960, the bishops and Oliveira crowned their longtime cooperative relationship by publishing *Reforma agrária: Questão de consciência*, an anticommunist battle cry for Catholic renewal and against wealth redistribution. The book's preface declared its "position radically against the neopagan avalanche of socialism . . . undermining our Luso-Christian spiritual patrimony."[11] Such polemical crusading by Sigaud, Mayer, Oliveira, and TFP reverberated in midcentury Brazil. They made headlines as representatives of social and political conservatism based in Catholic traditionalism and gained political influence with the military regime and among security forces.[12] Yet their activities also had significant repercussions internationally; they helped to shape and sustain global Catholic and Christian reaction to modernization and secularization.[13] In this chapter, I focus on Mayer, Sigaud, and TFP as important leaders in a constellation of protagonists who, at the crossroads of the Second Vatican Council and in its aftermath, sought to set the agenda of international Catholic traditionalism and eventually of Christian conservatism. By no means did the Brazilians treated here single-handedly generate present-day Catholic traditionalism; but they did play a signal, historiographically undervalued role in its genesis. The bishops (especially Sigaud) and TFP organized against changes they feared would come out of Vatican II, even before the council itself unfolded. The council, as is well known, developed into a watershed, a focal point for diverse currents in the Church, revealing the complex, variegated, and often interrelated factions even within the episcopate (none of which, it bears mentioning, truly sought the wholesale secularization feared by traditionalists). In the months and years that followed, through tumultuous Church politics and their own changing relationships (including Sigaud's break with TFP, as well as Mayer's increasing distance from the Vatican), these leading Brazilian reactionaries would continue to agree on a basic set of issues. TFP and the bishops drew on a tradition of prominent Brazilian engagement with Catholic reaction in the first half of the twentieth century, exemplified by traditionalist heroes like Dom Sebastião Leme, Salgado, and Rocha; and based in that history, Brazilians at Vatican II and afterward worked as part of a transnational group of conservative Catholics constructing a common platform of grievances. This platform eventually came to define Catholic and—more broadly—Christian archconservatism. The key grievances included anticommunism; a strident, detailed moralism; antiecumenism; defense of hierarchy per se; antistatist dedication to private property and free enterprise; and vociferous defense of the primacy of the supernatural in a world perceived to be increasingly secularized.

This last element formed a critical node around which Brazilian Catholic reactionaries and their allies coalesced. Like the other themes just mentioned, the loss of enchantment and mystery, of the presence of the supernatural in everyday life, greatly disturbed those who saw themselves as the *baluartes* (bastions) of Catholic traditionalism. At Vatican II and thereafter, TFP leaders joined Sigaud and Mayer in agitating for mystery and magisterium; indeed, the Brazilians were in some ways the prime (and heretofore unrecognized) impetus behind organized conservative resistance at Vatican II. After the council, they carried on with this work and sought to cooperate in this cause across both national and denominational borders. They persisted, at least in part, thanks to the friendliness that Brazil's dictatorial government (1964–85) displayed toward their endeavors; and though their efforts have gone largely unsung by scholars, they are remembered and lionized by generations of traditionalists within and outside Brazil. In this chapter I seek to address several aspects of this story: Brazilian conservatives' orchestration of a reaction at Vatican II and the focus of that reaction around the fundamental issues of magisterium, the supernatural, hierarchy, and nostalgia for an imagined medieval past in which those values reigned unquestioned; the critical place of moralistic antimodernism in that reaction; the Brazilian military regime's productive affinity for Sigaud, Mayer, TFP, and the issues they championed; and the notoriety and admiration these actors gained in Brazil and beyond.

I. "Congratulations, Excellency, Congratulations": Sigaud, Mayer, the TFP, and Organizing Conservative Reaction at Vatican II

An inveterate opponent of religious freedom, Dom Geraldo Proença Sigaud prepared, in September 1965, to speak out against *De Libertate Religiosa*, the schema on religious liberty proposed by reformers at Vatican II. At the heart of his objections lay a concept he feared and hated: creeping, un-Christian modernity—a "modern man" who would signal the death of the traditional Church. Sigaud thus criticized the schema for accommodating an errant "modern sense of human dignity," too ecumenical and secular to reflect the Church's sacrosanct mission. Fascinatingly, Sigaud suggested that such near-godless modernity inhered exclusively in what we might now call the Global North, eschewing the Global South. "This sense" of human dignity, he argued, "this 'modern' man of which the document speaks is a North American, Central European phenomenon," absent in "Iberia, in Italy, in Latin America."[14] While, as we shall see, Sigaud only rarely owned his leadership of conservative Catholicism, he here seemed to locate the pulsing heart of traditionalism and resistance to change in the ancient and populational centers of Catholicism—southern Europe, Latin America. This was not a claim to superiority or exclusivity; but it did reflect Sigaud's sense of himself and his cohort of Portuguese, Brazilian, and Italian allies as a mainstay of the effort to defeat liberalizing measures at Vatican II.

The council's historic proportions were of course evident even as it took place and generated much maneuvering and speculating among participants and observers, all interested in the outcomes of this high-stakes meeting. The most conservative Church fathers, alarmed by the reformist plans of a developing majority, eventually gathered in an umbrella group calling itself Coetus Internationalis Patrum (International Group of Fathers).[15] This rather loose and shadowy coalition had one clear and distinguishing feature: Sigaud was its leader and the person who did the most work to further its cause, in some sense living up to his contention that "homo modernus" had not yet invaded Latin America. In this work Sigaud was supported by close cooperation not only with Lefebvre but—more significantly—with Sigaud's compatriots: Brazilian TFP activists and Dom Antônio de Castro Mayer. Together, they launched a well-organized attack on Catholic progressivism and change within the Church—one that belies contentions that conservatives lacked mobilization and organization.[16] Among other issues, this attack centered on the anxieties mentioned earlier regarding the supernatural and magisterium as key sites for the preservation of tradition.

The phrase quoted in the subtitle of this section—"congratulations, Excellency"—comes from one of many letters from like-minded supporters who, throughout the course of Vatican II, wrote to Sigaud to commiserate or (as in this case) effusively congratulate him for championing conservative causes at the council.[17] These supporters' enthusiasm underscores their recognition of Sigaud as the lead organizer of the Church's conservative wing in Rome. In writing to Sigaud, they referred to the antiprogressive caucus as "your faction."[18] Some conservatives, in Rome and abroad, seem even to have looked to Sigaud as a sort of beleaguered paladin, venerating him as a martyr-cum–spiritual leader of the cause. As one priest wrote to Sigaud in 1963 in hope of spurring his productivity at the council, "I await your guidance . . . I am so worried about the practical results of the Council." Another, expressing solidarity with Sigaud's resistance to impending changes in liturgical guidelines, informed the archbishop of his (the writer's) intent to retain the old ways and appealed to Sigaud as a protector: "In the case of any difficulties I will count on Your Excellency in Rome."[19]

Sigaud had been vital to Coetus from its formative stages.[20] Planning notes for the faction, in Sigaud's hand, show how he laid out schematics for the group's structure, meetings, publications, activities, and finances.[21] Indeed, much of the group's surviving documentation—including invitations and suggestions for membership—appears to have been written by Sigaud; correspondence was often signed "Geraldo Proença Sigaud, Archbishop of Diamantina, acting for Coetus Internationalis Patrum."[22] Despite his centrality, Sigaud did not always proclaim his leadership role in Coetus. This may have been out of diffidence or a politic sense of reserve—Coetus's status at the council was forever uncertain, and Sigaud constantly fretted about tactics. Thus even when he himself wrote Coetus invitations to other council fathers, he sometimes did not include his name as the group's leader.[23] Even so, Sigaud did directly acknowledge his own leadership role from time to time. His sense of the significance of his activities was so strong that he wrote to his friend and collaborator Plínio Corrêa de Oliveira, "It is extremely difficult to bear so much responsibility alone, and I would so like to have Dom Mayer with me in these crucial moments."[24] Sigaud echoed these sentiments rather pathetically in a letter to Mayer himself: "I feel your absence very keenly, you . . . who might give me your counsel. . . . At this moment I am all alone in Rome."[25] These were admissions to intimate collaborators—but Sigaud also considered his own leadership more broadly perceptible and even noteworthy. In a letter to Brazil's foreign minister in late 1965, Sigaud waxed casual, presuming general knowledge of his role as spearhead: "It must be known to your Excellency that by a series of circumstances I saw myself obligated to take the initiative to organize among the Conciliar Fathers a group that the worldwide press has dubbed 'the minority' and which has played a major role in the Third Session. . . . I am the director and general secretary of this group, on which the result of the conciliar work will depend in great measure."[26]

At this point, correspondence with Oliveira and with Mayer represented more than mere idle chatter on Sigaud's part. Mayer, the withdrawn, deeply conservative bishop of Campos, and Oliveira, the leader for life of the newly minted TFP, were Sigaud's intimate collaborators in this critical period of conservative mobilization. The men were longtime stalwarts of Brazil's Catholic Right, whose intellectual substance they had shaped together in the 1930s via their control of the periodical *O Legionário*.[27] This alliance had thus lasted decades when, in 1960, Oliveira founded TFP. A lay organization, the society convened veteran leadership (like Oliveira, Sigaud, and Mayer themselves) and thousands of young, male recruits who were called to defend traditional Catholicism via protest; a cultivated, militaristic monasticism; spectacular pageantry (in medievalesque garb); proselytizing; and even the practice of arcane defense techniques. TFP would eventually spread across dozens of countries, and its full story lies beyond the scope of this book. Critically for our purposes, the organization was in some sense founded as a response to the threats perceived to be impending with the onset of Vatican II; TFP, in 1960, crystallized an antimodern conservatism that Oliveira, Mayer, and other leading *tefepistas* (TFP initiates) had been developing over decades.

In letters to Mayer and Oliveira ("my dear Plínio"), Sigaud sought to confer with each on the unfolding plans to shape the outcomes of the council. Referring to "battles" in Rome over particular schema (especially those on the critical issues that would become the fodder of Christian conservatism), Sigaud was wont to request logistical, strategic, and ideological collaboration. As he put it in a letter to Oliveira on the status of Coetus, "Tell me your [and Mayer's] opinion. . . . What should we do now?"[28] On several occasions, Sigaud even lobbied skeptical administrators to recognize Oliveira in a more official capacity at the council.[29] This closeness with Oliveira extended to several other officers and functionaries of the TFP—and institutionally Sigaud relied on the organization as a source of financial and personnel support. TFP leaders, in turn, saw Sigaud as a leader of their own crusade to set a globally conservative agenda for the future of Catholicism. In 1963, TFP second-in-command Fernando Furquim de Almeida wrote to Sigaud, referring to their shared "chess game" of strategizing at the council. Almeida took the opportunity to celebrate Sigaud's activism as "a sword thrust against the enemies of Our Lady, and your Excellency can imagine how happy we were to see such a thrust . . . made by someone with whom we collaborate."[30] The medieval imagery of sword-thrusting and the reference to the Virgin were, as we shall see, important here—these were, in fact, among the linchpins of the nostalgic traditionalism that TFP and Sigaud wished to promote. In more concrete terms, their partnership included fetching to Rome a cadre of TFP operatives tasked with the legwork of Sigaud's conservative campaign—everything from carrying messages to printing leaflets to conducting secretarial tasks.

Sigaud deemed this cadre essential to his success. "No matter what," he wrote to Oliveira, "Henrique [Barbosa Chaves, a TFP devotee] must come to help us." Affirming that he and Mayer were "studying" potential council sanction for Coetus, Sigaud wrote to Chaves himself of their shared cause: "My Dear Henrique . . . Our Lord distributes his crosses and his gifts. . . . Your coming is indispensable."[31] So indispensable did Sigaud consider the TFP presence that he activated the levers of his influence in the Brazilian government to finance and facilitate it. Writing to Brazil's foreign minister as both a friend and a fellow Catholic, Sigaud stressed the experience, dedication, and trustworthiness of TFP aides, whom he described as a unique core of support for the conservative strategy in Rome. Coetus had, he noted, been counting on them for years as a cohort of "specialist" agitators uniquely capable of this work.

> We cannot resolve the issues of [Coetus] merely with Italian aides. . . .
> First, it is a question of trust. My [TFP] team has been working with me for several years now, and has already done its work with great efficiency and discretion in the past three sessions. It is also a question of economy, because all of the people I have in mind work from sheer dedication [to our cause]. And that I do not find here [in Rome]. And the Brazilian operatives are specialists, each in a different area of the Council. . . . *The backbone of [Coetus] has been and must continue to be these trusted operatives from Brazil.*[32]

These machinations in 1965 were part of a years-long strategy of bringing TFP staffers to Rome. Oliveira, who had traveled to the Vatican at the council's outset, remembered arriving in Italy with ten assistants, who remained for the duration of the first session. The operation grew relatively sophisticated—TFP brought over an accountant to keep track of the finances of this improvised headquarters, and the militants often worked through the night to edit and then distribute the messages of Sigaud and the conservative caucus. Because the conciliar fathers were housed somewhat haphazardly in seminaries and other facilities around the city, there existed no formal and efficient means of reaching them all. TFP's dawn runs to distribute literature thus took on critical importance to the mobilization of a conservative bloc.[33] This importance was confirmed by no less an authority (self-consecrated or

no) than Lefebvre himself, who would become the most internationally celebrated leader of the post–Vatican II backlash. Lefebvre thought of the TFP
members in Rome as a "directorial committee" of Coetus.[34]

The TFP presence drew the attention of other observers as well, who
noted the centrality of this assistance to Sigaud's cause. Henri Fesquet, a journalist who closely followed the council, noted the great divergence between
Sigaud and the TFP, on one hand, and the majority of the Brazilian delegation, on the other. Where "many other bishops in [Sigaud's] country are
working in the opposite direction, for a redistribution of land and reforms
that are urgently needed," Fesquet observed, Sigaud had made "the intervention most hostile" to Schema XIII, on the Church and the modern world.
Fesquet attributed this in part to "the ultraconservative positions of the Archbishop of Diamantina," but also to Sigaud's role in Coetus and TFP. Fesquet's
reporting described Sigaud as "secretary of the Comitatus Episcopalis Internationalis [*sic*]; his personal secretary is a layman, Mr. Enrique [*sic*] Barbosa
Chaves, who calls himself the director of the Brazilian Society for the Defense of Tradition, Family, and Property (Rio de Janeiro Branch)."[35]

While Fesquet and the editors of *O Conciliábulo* felt, as Fesquet put it,
"unsurprised"—if bemused or irritated—by Sigaud's inveterate conservatism,
they perhaps did not understand the reactionary tenor of the TFP activists
backing the archbishop in his efforts in Rome. Ranking among the leadership
most trusted by Oliveira and Sigaud, Henrique Barbosa Chaves worked in
Rome alongside the likes of Luiz Nazareno da Assumpção. A cofounder of
TFP, Assumpção represented precisely the combination of pretension to aristocracy, nostalgia for the medieval, and rejection of modernity that TFP
and Sigaud sought to insert into the conversations at Rome. Assumpção had
participated in the "Legionário group" that also convened Sigaud, Mayer, and
Oliveira, and throughout his life he championed traditionalism in the form of
class and cultural hierarchy. He (and TFP) made much of his lineage, signaling his descent from "illustrious *paulista* families of '400 years'" (a reference
to a supposed landed aristocracy as the ur-society for São Paulo's rightful
elite). Ever "conscious of the high value of his birth," Assumpção sought to
represent the TFP ideal of a "traditional Paulista, whose manners [*cortesia*]
were marked by the glory days of elegant [aristocratic] salons." Most importantly he "fought with chivalric vigor to safeguard Catholic principles from
temporal society." In death, TFP remembered him as a champion of "everything that all the centuries [of tradition] had created, such as the raison d'être
of society [which was] attacked by revolutions silent and loud, but always ferociously aggressive against Christian wisdom."[36] If the "400 years" preten-

sions of Assumpção and Oliveira himself did not fully make TFP's point about traditional nobility and aristocracy as the social structure they wished to restore, another TFP delegate to Rome surely did so. Among the organizers who came under the TFP banner was the heir to the Brazilian imperial throne, the hope of Brazil's monarchists, French-born Bertrand de Orleans e Bragança, then barely twenty years old.[37]

TFP members, including Oliveira, would later claim that TFP was in some ways even more "directorial" than Sigaud himself. The TFP strategy at the council, recalled Oliveira, called for more radical measures to "resolve once and for all the tragedy that the Council was setting in place." For example, according to the organization, Mayer and Sigaud "neglected" to carry out one dramatic strategy proposed by TFP:

> Dom Sigaud and Dom Mayer were to enter fully outfitted in the middle of the session, pass in front of all the gathered prelates and, in front of the dais of Paul VI, break their miters and throw them on the floor in front of the Supreme Pontiff. The members of the TFP would be waiting outside with all of the press, which would be advised of this event or of some impending explosion. Then the two bishops, leaving the session with a . . . speech—prepared most likely by Dr. Plínio—would launch this bomb into the media, turning the eyes of the whole world to the error that was being committed [at the council]. This explosion would do away with the "spell" that had been cast over many at the Council, and the two bishops would leave the event as heroes.[38]

This never came to pass, of course, and the "spell" preventing a conservative takeover of the council remained unbroken.[39] Nevertheless, the record of reactionary collaboration and organization just described is historiographically important. Several versions of this story have suggested that conservatives were taken by surprise at the council's progressive tilt, and thence stemmed the failure of opposition to various changes in the Church.[40] It is true that Coetus as a whole suffered from unsteady and sometimes untraceable membership; but the organization had a dedicated core of activists and leaders, principally Brazilian strategists and operatives. They created a formal organization, complete with schedules, strategies, and, by 1965, a refined series of pamphlets designed to condemn everything from "religious relativism" to "the Hobbes-Locke-Rousseau-French Revolution line" to lack of faith in the Virgin Mary.[41] Indeed, TFP anticipated the council's tenor and began organizing before the meeting commenced. Early notes shared by Sigaud and TFP leadership in advance of the council called for "formal action. . . . It is

necessary to organize on a global level a fight against the [progressive] doctrines and the authors of those doctrines, especially within the clergy and the
religious orders."[42] In part, the conservatives may have seemed less organized
because they felt the need to create the structure for their activism in secret,
fearing sanction from council leadership. Writing to Oliveira, Sigaud noted
the secrecy of their work, then described the fears of Luigi Carli (archbishop
of Segni), who wished to make Sigaud's activities public because, "if we do
not watch our backs, it might happen that one day from the rostrum of the
Council a public announcement or even condemnation of our Secretariat
will be made, and then all our work will be impossible."[43]

II. "The Importance of the Supernatural Milieus": Medieval Mystery versus Modern "Mundanization"

The cause shared by Sigaud, Mayer, and TFP in Rome recapitulated battles
they had engaged in at home in Brazil, crystallizing in the critical context of
Vatican II several extant currents of traditionalism and thus linking a set of issues that would come to define Christian conservatisms across the world:
moralism, antiecumenism (and contradictory varieties of anti-Semitism), antimodernism, defense of hierarchy, anticommunism, antistatist capitalism and
later neoliberalism, and—perhaps most palpably at Vatican II and thereafter—
vigorous defense of the supernatural as everyday reality. Through his work
within and outside Coetus, Sigaud cooperated with, represented, and organized those at the council who shared some or all of these foci. This litany,
stressing the issues that Sigaud, Mayer, and Oliveira envisioned as the core of
the Church's past and future, synthesized traditionalisms past and anticipated
the currents that would define them thereafter. Together, these Brazilian agitators for "Our Lady" (Mary generally, but especially the Virgin of Fátima)
sought a harking back to mythical traditions of chivalric Marian knight-
errantry, idolizing medieval notions of warriorhood, gender, and palpable,
awesome divinity. Accordingly, TFP ideologues, alongside Sigaud and Mayer,
sought to promote a strain of Catholic conservatism that would concomitantly maintain rigid hierarchies and preserve divine mystery and enchantment as the hallmarks of Catholicism and the mainstay of Church and social
authority.

   In other words, Brazilian leaders at Vatican II busily developed a foundation for neoconservatism that drew on decades of Catholic antimodernism
and on Brazil's own recent right-wing history.[44] To Sigaud, as to the tefepistas, the primary zones of contention were those with implications for the

Church's role in what they perceived to be a secularizing world. The Brazilians campaigned for conciliar measures that would at the very least hold the line *against* modernization, secularization, and any yielding of Church primacy and hierarchy in the face of multiple sources of egalitarianism and social change. These measures included vociferous denunciation of communism; papal and conciliar consecration of the world to the Immaculate Heart of Mary; resistance to religious freedom, considered a plot to unravel Catholicism; and the reaffirmation of sexual and moral strictures, not least the celibacy of Catholic clergy. Sigaud saw himself as the point person and to some extent the arbiter of these conservative foci. Thinking categorically on these and other fronts, he informed Oliveira in late 1965 of his (Sigaud's) decision to take a brief rest, to "save" himself for critical "upcoming battles: religious freedom, Schema XIII [on the Church in the modern world], . . . and the Celibacy of Priests."[45]

Among the elements in this foundation for neoconservatism—acting, in some ways, as the glue binding those elements together—lay a fascination with mysticism and with an everyday sense of the divine. Echoing the nostalgic yearnings of diverse Catholics who had struggled with their faith's place in the modern world, Sigaud, Mayer, and their TFP collaborators (and, eventually, the Society of Saint Pius X and other ultraconservative organizations) advocated a return to medieval cultural and religious forms.[46] This logic adhered to a fundamentalist organicism in which spiritual and religious hierarchies, including the constant sense of God's supernatural power and the rightful authority of Church officials, guaranteed ecclesiastical, social, and economic inequalities and quashed protest, strife, and questioning of the status quo. The "perfect" Middle Ages had epitomized this ideal order, based in a worldview that emphasized the spiritual over the physical. TFP therefore spectacularized medievalesque pomp, gaining fame in the 1960s and thereafter for flamboyant street demonstrations that featured its members wearing capes, tunics, knee-high boots, and other elements of a habit designed by Oliveira to evoke the chivalric, monastic, and militaristic orders of the Middle Ages.

The organicist and vaguely all-encompassing (aesthetic, political, spiritual, institutional) yearning for an imagined medieval golden age, however dramatized by the TFP's public displays, had occupied an eminent position among previous generations of Brazilians. From a certain point of view, the "Religious Question" controversy in the 1870s rested on a foundational tension between liberalism and conservative clerics' attempts to carry out a Roman mandate for a return to an ultramontane model of Church-society relations more germane to the medieval period.[47] Some of Brazil's most hallowed (or notorious) conservative thinkers had seamlessly integrated this strain of antimodernism into their oeuvre. In his 1920 masterwork, *Populações Meridionais do Brasil*, sociologist and jurist Francisco José de Oliveira Vianna bridged medieval Europe and Brazil's colonial roots in a romantic vision of chivalric glory. Brazil's founding elite, in his view, consisted in "men of opulent riches, lords who were also men in whom all the best qualities of character joined together. Morally perfect, by dint of dignity, by dint of loyalty, by dint of probity. Descended from the flowers of peninsular nobility and transplanted [to Brazil], they were all decorated by the medieval type of the *cavalheiro* [knight or gentleman], full of manliness and dignity."[48] The Centro Dom Vital (an archconservative Catholic lay organization and sort of think tank founded in 1922) constituted another medievalist high-water mark. In a volume published by the Centro Dom Vital, reactionary Catholic and sometime integralist Everardo Backeuser lamented the passing of medieval glories in typical form: "The moral perfections of the Middle Ages," he wrote, "have been tragically dying as Man's pride leads him to place himself above the voice of God, speaking through His Church."[49] The Centro Dom Vital also published *A Ordem*, a magazine that venerated medieval Europe as a perfect hierarchical and harmonious system; as historian Tânia Salem points out, for this generation of Catholic activists, "the Middle Ages symbolized the ideal to be restored."[50]

Plínio Salgado, the erstwhile leader of Brazil's fascists, likewise exalted a medieval supernaturalism when, in 1945, he turned—with rather questionable authority—to writing about a "Christian Concept of Democracy." Complaining of the "idolatries of the world" derived from the presence of the devil in modern conveniences ("the journals, the books, the plane, and the movie . . . and especially the powerful radio-emitters") Salgado called for a "new order" that would return to a time before science and "materialism [that] conceives of the Universe and Man only according to their physical expressions; [that] denies . . . the existence of God and the immortality of our souls." The place where human history had turned astray, according to this postwar Salgado, could be pinpointed in early modernity, when medieval and supernaturalistic sensibilities had given way to rationalism: "The scientific myth was reborn from its ancient Greek roots, flourishing with the naturalism of the 17th and 18th centuries, and . . . establishing itself definitively with the experimentalism of the 19th century."[51]

Thus the costumery Oliveira designed for TFP in the 1960s was intended to symbolically evoke (and restore) bygone mysticism that other conservative Catholics had likewise sought to reinvigorate in Brazil; but TFP equally agitated for more direct restoration of mystery and enchantment. Semiprivately, within TFP, Oliveira cultivated a mythos of his own supernatural powers, complete with rather cultlike veneration of him and his mother.[52] More publicly, tefepistas propagated zealous veneration of the Virgin of Fátima as a mystical touchstone of "divine origin" for militant anticommunism. The cult of Fátima held coterminous attractions: the Virgin's alleged 1917 warning about the "errors" that Russia would spread across the world, and the deeply felt sense of the Virgin's divine, physical presence in the world.[53] Sigaud sought to propagate the cult of Fátima as a lightning rod for antimodernism, anticommunism, and the restoration of ultramontane Catholicism. As Heloisa Starling points out, Sigaud's personal secretary forged the links between Fátima and the forces of political conservatism in Minas Gerais (where he and Sigaud resided); the Virgin served as a weapon "taken from the arsenal of mystical Catholicism" to grant a "divine origin" to the anticommunist struggle.[54]

If Fátima represented a specific instantiation of the supernatural behind which traditionalists could rally, TFP's, Sigaud's, and Mayer's efforts at Vatican II sought more broadly to buttress the sense of God's miraculous presence, consistent with the philosophical nature of the council's debates. As we shall see, they sought to preserve the supernatural and its everyday reinforcement of hierarchy via a focus on the details—priestly comportment, clerical vestment and self-presentation, liturgical guidelines, the role of the vernacular in celebrating the mass or in missals, and the relative splendor or squalor of episcopal accoutrements. The focus on these issues stemmed, however, from broader alarm and moral panic about materialism and secularization. Both registers of antimodern supernaturalism united the members of Coetus, and Mayer and Sigaud became orchestrators of resistance, before, during, and after the council, to feared innovations in religious thought as well as practice.

Such resistance formed part of the decades-old (if not older) struggle to reconcile Catholicism with modernity, especially industrial modernity, which James Chappel has outlined as the "search for a Catholic alternative to modernity." Popes, priests, and philosophers had long denounced the "materialism" of the modern West. Sigaud called this a "crisis of identity" in "Western human culture" and focused in particular on what he perceived to be the death agonies of spiritually enchanted life. The "crisis," Sigaud argued with increasing vehemence, revolved around "secularization"—an evaporation of faith in the supernatural and a removal of the mysteries of the divine from everyday life. Sigaud continually excoriated this new worldview, despairing in the aftermath of Vatican II that materialism had generated "a world closed in on itself" rather than open to the supernatural mysteries channeled by the Church, such that "the human project does not extend beyond observable and tangible things."[55] Mayer, likewise, lamented this "New Morality," complaining as early as 1953 that rationalism, modernism, and secularization created a "viscerally anti-Catholic naturalism" that negated the "importance of the supernatural milieus" and "hands Man over to himself."[56] For both bishops, as well as for their TFP allies, the antidote to this mundanization lay in championing the supernatural at and after the Second Vatican Council.

At Vatican II, Sigaud perhaps best summarized this orientation in an elegy for "Medieval Man" (*Homo Medii Aevi*), whom he described, with characteristic wistfulness, as possessed of an "extremely robust" sense of the daily divine and of hierarchical authority. Channeling Pope Pius XII (whom Sigaud and TFP venerated above perhaps any other pontiff), the Brazilian archbishop strongly opposed any softening in the Church's attitude toward non-Catholics. Accordingly, he was a principal voice of opposition to *De Libertate Religiosa*, the schema affirming religious freedom, which he tried to defeat both by direct intervention and by organizing the interventions of other conservatives.[57] Denouncing any such measure, Sigaud argued it would further impair "the masses'" sense of divinely granted human dignity and speed a crisis of authority already plaguing "our age." Demonstrating the nostalgia characteristic of the traditionalism Sigaud and Coetus sought to promote at the council, he longed for an enchanted past: "Medieval Man and Man under the so-called 'Ancien Regime' had an extremely robust, living sense of the dignity, both natural and supernatural, of men. Today our materialized and proletarianized urban masses often have absolutely no sense of human dignity. And how strong can that praiseworthy sense of dignity be given that irreligious and insubordinate spirit in the face of paternal authority, civil and divine, which so pertains to our modern age?"[58] For Sigaud, then, the Church's "paternal" authority lay under threat from modernity, materialism, and "proletarianization," which had deadened mass cultural awareness of correspondence between the worldly and supernatural planes. As another Brazilian bishop and ally of Sigaud's at Vatican II put it, the problem was that "today's life" encouraged people to focus on the earthly, on "mundane necessities" where, instead, "spirit and body . . . should be ruled by a supraterrestrial" sensibility.[59]

This opposition to mundanization focused, among other things, on Enlightenment-based rationalism as a source of the problem, thus adhering to a historical line of thinking forcefully articulated in Leo XIII's 1893 *Providentissimus Deus*.[60] At Vatican II, an antiliberal, antimaterial, occasionally anti-Semitic abhorrence of rationalism and "naturalism" linked conservatives' precepts to bygone papal heroes (Leo XIII and Pius XII the most celebrated among them) and to the antimodern reactions of the interwar Right.

Communism, in this formula, joined liberalism, science, industrialization, and material culture as products of a long-term process of moving away from God and a divinely ordered world. In part, this was an antirationalism based in concern about sexuality, the body, and the mysteries of reproduction, prefiguring later Christian conservatisms in this vein as well. As Sigaud and TFP would have it, the council must counter the "naturalism" that demystified and desanctified life and the human body. The message, in fact, must be that "the *living thing is a mysterious entity*, and science can never affirm that it understands [this mystery] perfectly, exhaustively, and that it knows all of its resources and potential forces." Respect for the mysteries of divinely created life must counter a "naturalistic pedagogy" that approached bodily issues (especially "chastity") "without the supernatural." Such thinking not only opposed modernization, mundanization, and laicization but also linked these to the danger of communist subversion. In fact, communism was only the latest in a series of scourges that TFP leadership referred to as "the Revolution"—a centuries-long process that must be combated at Vatican II. Sigaud and his TFP collaborators paraphrased Plínio Corrêa de Oliveira's masterwork, *Revolution and Counterrevolution*, when it came to the relationship between science, communism, and a materialistic politics of the body: "The great weapon of the Revolution is the scientific-methodical use of unregulated human passions."[61]

Anti-Semitism further linked this framework with Brazil's interwar Right, seamlessly subsuming the recent anti-Semitisms of Brazil's most virulent Integralists with those of European conservative Catholics, whose prejudice against Jews likewise mirrored that of previous generations of Church leaders.[62] Sigaud's preparations for the council, elaborated in apparent consultation with TFP leaders Orlando Fedeli and Fernando Furquim de Almeida, casually linked the deplorable emergence of scientific, antisupernatural "naturalism" to "the Sinagogue."[63] "The leaders of the Jewish people conspire against the Church," read one excursus, via a "rationalist order that touches all aspects of human life." Among Sigaud's papers are several tracts, some of them anonymously circulated at the council, linking Judaism to a rationalist materialism that would "transform the society of God into the society of the Devil." Indeed, one of Sigaud's lieutenants in Brazil invoked perhaps the foremost anti-Semitic canard of the interwar period: the Protocols of the Elders of Zion. In a letter forwarded to Sigaud, João Botelho (a priest and anticommunist celebrity in his own right) complained of the "naturalism that, for a long time, has been undermining the Church. . . . I have a very strong inclination toward 'occult forces.' I have read and reread the Protocols of the Elders of Zion and I always read things about the Masons. . . . I believe we are living surrounded by those powers."[64]

Sigaud's attitude was entirely consistent with his close collaboration with
TFP and its leaders, who saw themselves at the forefront of Catholics in the
Americas and Europe who were angling for a return to a mythical, organicist
medieval social order. For tefepistas, Sigaud's "Medieval Man," like his era,
represented the perfection of social, economic, and political order, which had
deteriorated ever since. That deterioration, TFP philosophers argued, derived from modernity's fading sense of the supernatural and correspondent
increase in rationalism, secularism, and related, misguided egalitarianism.
Before and during the council, TFP leaders attempted to channel this message into heavily didactic position papers and talking points designed to or-
chestrate conservative responses to the upcoming schemas. According to one
twenty-two-page exposition, apparently intended to help guide Sigaud's and
others' interventions, the enemies of the Church sought "the destruction of
the Church and the implantation of a naturalist order. This rationalist order
touches all the aspects of human life, and it places all those aspects in conflict
with the order of the Revelation, of the Church, and of Catholic Society. This
naturalist order, radical and universal, is [what we call] the Revolution. This
process began at the end of the Middle Ages, and has continued in the form
of the Renaissance, the Protestant Reformation, the French Revolution, the
destruction of the Papal States, modernism, and communism."[65]

For TFP, the lost sense of wonder, of the Revelation as order-determining
reality, had led to the many, linked evils of the modern world, from "moral
corruption" to "individual, hysterical, sensual dances" to communism itself.
The key, these conservatives argued, lay in remaining true to or restoring a
vision of the world where supernatural power affirmed the rightness of medieval hierarchy; in the words of one preparatory document, modernity and
perceived democratization made it "necessary to teach the beauty of inequality." Responding to ecumenism, to progressive Catholicism, and to egalitarianism at the council, Sigaud and TFP called for "re-Christianization" and
"rebuilding Catholic society" via emphasis on "private property," antimodernism, inequality, authoritarianism, and "reform of customs." This process,
they hoped, would revivify medieval sensibilities, particularly when it came
to the distinction between an obedient, mystically oriented Catholic subject
and a disobedient, rational or modern, democratic subject. (This was despite
the fact that prominent progressives, far from advocating rationalization and
secularization, sought their *own*, devout mode of incorporating the supernatural power of the faith into modern life.)[66]

As we shall see, Sigaud, Mayer, and TFP focused on liturgical and practical
minutiae as a crucial arena within which to reinscribe the rightful inequalities

between priests and laypeople. Yet the bishops and their TFP allies explicitly extended this "re-Christianizing" emphasis on inequality to the material realm—that is, to hierarchies that went beyond the ecclesiastical, though the two were considered inextricable. At the council and over the course of his life in and out of TFP, Oliveira's sometime lieutenant Orlando Fedeli reviled "socialist and liberal egalitarianism" and the threat of "a society without classes" and without private property. Recurring to Leo XIII and Pius XII, Fedeli, like other tefepistas, would affirm that such egalitarianism was not only anti-Catholic and anti-Christian but fundamentally evil: it "deforms the plans of God," who "created men similar but not equal, and that must be a good thing." This line of thinking, advocating the revival and protection of less restricted capitalism, scorned egalitarianism and social justice efforts, which would cause "the perturbation of all the classes in society, a hateful and insufferable slavery for all citizens . . . talent and ability deprived of stimulus, and as a necessary consequence, wealth stagnating at its sources."[67] Oliveira himself drew medievalism further into this celebration of capitalist inequalities. Rhapsodizing about the value lost with the decline of age-old chivalric and hereditary aristocracies, the TFP founder affirmed the rightness of "just and proportional inequalities among men" and "maintaining the distinction of classes."[68] Sigaud, in the aftermath of the council, directly advised the faithful to eschew egalitarianism. Instead, Catholics should cultivate "humility, recognizing one's place and the superiority of others," always remembering that "class belongs to the very nature of humanity."[69]

Democracy itself, in fact, epitomized those "modern errors," which a healthy sense of the divine order of things would cure. The Church, ever the source of that supernaturally based order, must reemphasize its transcendent, ethereal nature in order to guarantee its own authority and the safety of traditional hierarchy. At Vatican II and in postconciliar activism, Sigaud, Mayer, and TFP set out to accomplish this mission, prescribed by generations of Catholic authoritarianists. "It is essential," read a draft of Sigaud's preparations for the council, "that pious persons comprehend the importance of the Catholic Order as the great external grace which guarantees sanctification and salvation to the multitudes"—a role that required constant, vigilant guardianship of the sacred and the sanctified against the worldly. "It is necessary," he continued, "to remind the faithful that between the Church and the world there is necessarily a conflict."[70]

As part of this re-Christianization based on a bygone Catholic order, the Brazilians at the council and long after agitated for a return to a theocratic society in which the Church's temporal order would render moot questions like religious freedom and cultural pluralism. Indeed, both Sigaud and Mayer had made names for themselves long before the council when it came to vague proposals for a return to medievalesque theocracy. As historian Alfredo Moreira da Silva Júnior insightfully points out, Sigaud's excurses in his years as bishop of Jacarezinho traversed the well-trod ground of the body of Christ as an organicist metaphor.[71] As such, Sigaud proposed that the Church, as Christ's representative on earth, must govern earthly matters: "Do not think that His government is limited to invisible, or extraordinary activity. On the contrary, the divine redeemer has governed His mystical body in visible and everyday fashion by means of His representative on earth [*vigário na terra*; the pope]."[72] Mayer articulated this more forcefully in a 1953 catechism that addressed "the relations between Church and State." The bishop essentially argued for reunification of the two powers, asserting that "Christianity is a *temporal* order of things, based on the doctrine of Jesus Christ."[73] By the time of Vatican II, Mayer would be prepared to oppose freedom of religion on the grounds that states themselves should prohibit it, to the exclusive benefit of Catholicism. In an intervention on the schema on religious liberty, Mayer told his fellow Church fathers, "This declaration must be rewritten, because it sins in two fundamental points: . . . It affirms, for example, the equality of rights for all the religions (the true one and the false ones). Now, on the other hand, we know that *only the true religion has the right to be professed publicly*. . . . It is the law of God that everyone must embrace the true religion and no one is condemned except through his own fault. Therefore the State must not encourage false religions."[74]

III. The Devil in the Details: "Episcopal Splendor," "a Character of Mystery," and "a Spirit of Hierarchy Opposed to the Spirit of Revolution"

If Sigaud wished to "remind the faithful" of the Church's supernaturally granted, supernaturally packaged role as guarantor of hierarchy, of order, and of salvation, he, the TFP, and Mayer concurred that this reminder must consist in attention to detail—the little things that were the stuff of everyday ritual and its trappings.[75] When tefepistas wandered the streets of São Paulo in medieval garb, that is, they did so not for pure love of the Crusades or of pageantry, but because costume, corporeal deportment, and symbology *mattered* to their cause. Accordingly, changes proposed at and after Vatican II to priestly vestments, to the liturgy, and to the trappings of Catholic celebrations and sacraments alarmed these Brazilian conservatives not only for sentimental reasons but because such changes must, they argued, doom the world to modern secularization, the Church to irrelevance, and society to socialist materialism. This argument, a fulcrum of Brazilian activism at and after Vatican II, epitomized these activists' central place in postconciliar traditionalism. Like-minded allies also rallied around this view, and the importance of such details would become a tenet of Catholic resistance to the "new" Church for decades thereafter (indeed, even today).[76] At the council, Sigaud, Oliveira, the gathered tefepistas, and particularly Mayer granted special emphasis to this line of thinking; and afterward, from marches in São Paulo and New York to rebellion in Campos to consecrations at Ecône, they continued to make the visual and aural fundamentals of Catholic practice a sort of last line of defense, for reasons they consistently articulated in terms of order, tradition, hierarchy, and supernaturalism.

If it was "necessary to teach the beauty of inequality," this must be done via insistence on Latin mass (never the vernacular), the maintenance of episcopal finery, the preservation of distinct ecclesiastical costume and of sacerdotal monasticism and aloofness—in other words, via constant, intimate reminders of the Church's magisterium, its monopoly on quotidian access to the supernatural. As noted earlier, these fundamentals of Church *practice* captivated the attention of many in the Catholic world who saw proposed changes at and after Vatican II as destabilizing and even shocking. Below, we shall explore the ways in which authorities in military Brazil supported Sigaud, Mayer, and TFP in their positions vis-à-vis the "new" Catholicism— yet let us turn for a moment to the reactions recorded by Brazilian ambassador to the Vatican José Jobim (1968–73) to innovations in the mass and in episcopal comportment. Jobim, a relatively conservative Catholic himself, exemplified the horror with which many of the faithful countenanced threats to time-honored rituals. In a classified missive to Itamaraty in 1969, Jobim attempted to report comprehensively on what he saw as the impending "auto-demolition" of the Church and indicated that "the exterior aspects of worship—conventual habits, the liturgical language, sacred music"—mattered deeply because changes to them reflected "tsunamis and true cataclysms beneath the surface" of Christianity. What Jobim called the "position of protest" within the Church—progressive Christianity—would have "consequences in all the aspects of the manifestation of faith; championing, for example, a purging of the liturgy, the abolition of the sacramental pageantries [*pompas sacramentais*], the formulation of doctrine in terms more accessible to the contemporary mentality, the rejection of emotional content ... and the revalorization of asceticism." Though the report was intended to be informative,

Jobim could not help but let slip his own personal investment in these details. "The Church of the Council," he wrote, was "shaken to its foundations"; more disturbing yet, "the most grave contestations come from a hierarchy in a state of rebellion." Providing examples of these "most grave contestations," Jobim registered his shock at catechistic innovations, but especially at the results of the Novus Ordo Missae when it came to the format of receiving communion: "The European press," he fairly gushed, "divulges photographs of communion-taking in Holland during which the faithful *take the host in their own hands, chew it, and then drink from the chalice*."[77]

These changes, disturbing to Jobim, were anathema to TFP, Mayer, and Sigaud, who thus railed against any and all reforms to centuries-old symbols, accoutrements, and paraphernalia, and did so for years after he left Rome.[78] Sigaud came to look upon progressive Dom Pedro Casaldáliga (bishop of São Félix do Araguaia, Minas Gerais) as a nemesis, and in a 1977 denunciation written to dictatorial authorities, Sigaud accused Casaldáliga of promoting communism by questioning the "Magisterium of the Supreme Pontiff and of the bishopric."[79] Sigaud described the quotidian transgressions by which Casaldáliga robbed Catholic practice of both mystery and hierarchy, thus promoting mundane egalitarianism and—by extension—communism: "In sum, [Dom Pedro] breaks with the Liturgy and carries this rupture to an unbelievable extent. He refuses to use his ring, his crozier and his miter. And at his ordination, which was done on the banks of the Araguaia River, in place of a miter he used a straw hat; in place of a crozier, a simple oar was used. This is supposed to signify his option for the poor and the oppressed. Such is the extremity of the doctrinal position which Dom Pedro Casaldáliga defends: socialism tinged with communism."[80] In a letter to no less an authority than Brazilian president Ernesto Geisel (1974–79), Sigaud homed in on liturgical detail as the weapon of choice for "subversive" agents like Casaldáliga. Where Casaldáliga, like other progressives, sought to mitigate hierarchies by dressing like his flock and thus "abandoning the cloak of pride and power," Sigaud saw this as a threat tantamount to revolution. "Thus," wrote Sigaud to Geisel in 1977, "the very liturgy itself is taken advantage of to promote class warfare, hatred toward landowners and Government functionaries and to exert moral pressure on the squatters, . . . in order to create an explosive situation that the communists exploit."[81]

TFP lobbyists in Brazil and in Rome agreed wholeheartedly, likewise focusing on the details of Church life as the essence of institutional sanctity and authority. Fedeli, for example, argued that proposed changes to priestly vestments and living arrangements were not "reforms" designed to "adapt the

Church to the times, but [were] the Revolution." Among these measures he listed not only major questions like priestly celibacy but also the more minute issues of tonsure, votive candles, cloistering, and what Fedeli generally called the "secularization of priests."[82] The crux of the issue, according to a late 1960s TFP pamphlet, was that such changes constituted a "Revolution within the Church"—one that sought the concomitant dissolution of enchantment, episcopal and ecclesiastical pomp, and the Church's power. It was, the pamphlet underscored, "an annulment of the authority of the bishopric."[83]

It was Mayer, however, who became the most visible exponent, before, during, and after Vatican II, of attention to detail in preserving both enchantment and magisterium. Indeed, he summed up this relationship in the clearest of terms: opposing the council's potential opening to ecumenism and non-Catholics, Mayer wrote to Sigaud that they must together reaffirm exclusivity, hierarchy, and ritualistic tradition. "We must reprove [the schema on ecumenism] as an attack on the spirit of social hierarchy which *is* the spirit of the Church . . . *it is necessary that this social hierarchy also [continue to] be reflected in the solemnities of the Church.*"[84] In other words, social hierarchy must not only be preserved but also be constantly performed in order to be preserved. Incensed by proposed changes to costume, to ritual practice, and especially to the language of the mass, Mayer inveighed against any and all "innovations" in the details of ecclesiastical and liturgical paraphernalia. As early as 1953, he had passionately defended "legitimate inequalities" as part and parcel of the Church's coterminous strengths: its authority and its everyday supernaturalism. Alarmed at suggestions that the Church should become "egalitarian in its organization, simple and democratic in its discipline, liturgy, customs, and in the ways of being of the members of the Hierarchy," Mayer denounced such thinking as a "laicization of the clergy." He saw this threat emanating from "young clergy," among whom Pope Pius XII had rightly reprimanded, a "desire for novelty . . . which harms ecclesiastical authority." Insisting on the fundamental role of retaining the cassock, Mayer issued a call to arms: "Let us not fear an exaggeration of precisely that traditional spirit" that liturgical vestments and ancient practices corporealized. Barring such "exaggeration" of visible traditionalism, Mayer put it to the priests of his diocese in 1953, they enabled communist victory. Indeed, Mayer's rationale involved a rather frank and frontal attack on *equality itself.* Rather than recurring to the more violent and sensationalist of anticommunist imaginaries, Mayer simply reaffirmed the *rightness of hierarchy and inequality* as natural, merited, and timeless elements of human social organization. Marxists, to Mayer's eyes, erred in their principal goal of achieving "complete egalitarianism," which meant not only "the destruction of the Church" but also the destruction "of authority, and of social hierarchy." He clarified: "The final objective of the sectarians of Marx is, thus, total leveling, the abolition of classes, and egalitarianism. That egalitarianism is the essence of communism, and it is by dint of being egalitarian that it destroys and suppresses the right to inheritance, the family, private property, the social elites, and tradition."[85]

The bishop of Campos contended that the proper response to this egalitarian outlook lay in ritual details: the reaffirmation of priestly and episcopal pomp and circumstance, as well as the preservation of Latin as the language of mystery and of exclusive access to supernatural truths. Defending priestly vestment, he wrote that "it is highly appropriate and consistent . . . that [the clergy] have a habit which is totally distinct from that which the simple faithful customarily wear." With yet more verve, he affirmed the rightness of the "ambience of majesty and aristocratic distinction which surrounds the Hierarchy" of the Church. Bishops, he acknowledged, might "be pastors and not princes," but "exteriorities reveal the nature of institutions [and] therefore the higher the position, the more solemn must be the atmosphere which surrounds it. The bishop occupies princedom in the Church of God, . . . a dignity more eminent than that of temporal princedom. Thus, the Bishop has the obligation to surround himself with the splendor appropriate to his office."[86]

In order that "social hierarchy . . . be reflected in the solemnities of the Church," Mayer invoked one of the issues that would become the heart of traditionalist Catholic reaction worldwide: the Latin, or Tridentine, mass. Coetus responded to the reformist suggestion that Latin bewildered most congregants, who might even confuse the mass with the "profane rites" of pagans, witches, and other non-Catholics.[87] Mayer agreed that Latin was impenetrable to most contemporary Catholics but argued that this constituted one of its *virtues*; it made the mass *rightly* incomprehensible to the laity. In some sense, he became the most visible champion of this position at Vatican II. In a well-publicized proclamation at the council, he contended that "the use in sacred affairs of a language that is not vulgar and, therefore, not accessible to everyone, adds to the dignity of the mass, conferring upon it a certain character of mystery." This air of mystery and sense of the sanctity of Catholic Latin would explicitly serve the purpose of reminding lay Catholics of their place in the institutional and cosmological hierarchy. They must be reminded, in daily practice, of the supernatural capacity conferred by ordination, and thus their own spiritual subjugation to the power structure of the Church itself. As Mayer put it, "The use of the sacred language pedagogically aids the faithful to assimilate the essential difference between themselves . . .

and the priesthood conferred by the Sacrament of Ordination, uniquely capable of genuine sacrificial action."[88]

IV. "Observable and Tangible": Morality, Gender, and Sexuality as Particularly Devilish Details

The "beauty of inequality" and the necessity for reinforcing everyday people's sense of supernatural power and order via visible hierarchies extended to an area of particular concern for the Brazilian activists, linking them with like-minded antimodernists and anticommunists in Brazil and abroad. A focus on morality and sexuality, with strong notes of antimodern moral panic, located the Brazilian activists within an arc of Christian conservatisms past and future. In the early 1960s, Sigaud, Mayer, TFP, their conciliar allies, and their supporters in Brazil's military made moralism, with special attention to gendered behaviors, forms of dress, entertainment, and sexuality—especially, as we shall see in chapter 5, the question of priestly celibacy—a central column within their agenda. Much of the "spirit of the revolution" that they so feared, in other words, appeared in the form of deviant moral, gender, and sexual behavior.

True to form, tefepistas excelled at this sort of moral and anticommunist panic, seeing in progressive Catholicism an element of the all-encompassing "Revolution" their founder had set out to combat. Concurrently denouncing what today's Right would call "big government" (*estatização*), communism, threat to "private property," and the abandonment of time-honored Church traditions, the draft of talking points that TFP prepared for Sigaud at the council dedicated page upon page to a perceived moral and sexual crisis, visible in everything from popular dancing to divorce and from ballet to movies to swimsuits. The document denounced "naturalism" as the source of a conspiratorial desire to abolish celibacy and introduce divorce, but also noted (in note form) a host of other horrors: "Dances. Fashion. Condemnation of dancing in a close embrace, where the couples hold onto each other. Warning about the dangers [even] to those who go to such dances, without dancing. Rock-and-roll: in Catholic [milieus] and the carelessness with which it is approached. Carelessness with the state of one's spirit. Ballet. A form of adoring the body.... Cinema... *a fortiori*, even the best cinema will not do [*não presta*] ... the cinema ... dissipates horribly; it cannot be favorable to religious life. Television: cinema at home." Repeating these themes, the TFP guidelines for action at the council included the "moral corruption" of swim- and beachwear and focused quite obviously on women's behavior. After specifically attacking "limiting birth by illicit means," the document recommended "radical condemnation of all the dances in which a man dances with a woman in a close embrace. Condemnation of the individual hysterical and sensual dances like Rock-and-Roll. Warn against Ballet, a form of deifying the body.... Formal condemnation of 'bikinis,' two-piece maillots.... Condemnation of dance clothing 'tomara que caia' [tube tops]."[89]

Mayer stressed and restressed these themes across decades, linking sexuality to modernity, to the dissolution of the Church, and even to proposed changes in doctrine and liturgy. For years before the council, Mayer had complained about the "new" approach to the human body as evidence of "anticatholic naturalism." In 1953, he attacked "décolletages, swimsuits, and other ways of dressing that show too much of the body"; in Mayer's view, these reflected a misguided progressive Catholic notion that "the body is good in and of itself, it was created by God, and it does not need to be hidden." Such ideas, alongside teenage "flirting"—"a stimulus to sensuality and indiscipline in the high schools"—constituted a "viscerally anticatholic naturalism."[90] Like other anticommunists, Mayer was convinced that such naturalism, particularly in the form of sexual media and behavior, actually formed part of a communist conspiracy. In *Warning Parishioners against the Ruses of the Communist Sect,* Mayer warned of this conspiracy, and how it worked through the immoral, "truly diabolical propaganda . . . that is done by means of leaflets and magazines, in the cinemas, in the theaters, on the radio, in the schools and even the universities."[91] At and after Vatican II, Mayer went so far as to draw a line of equivalence between liturgical changes and sexual deviance, in terms of unacceptability. In a 1970 letter to fellow bishop João Batista Przyklenk, Mayer complained about the Novus Ordo Missae and linked it conceptually with a host of other changes, which Mayer and the TFP saw as evidence of a grand conspiracy: "Now, currently, it has even reached the words of the Consecration. That, when everything else around—in terms of morality and even of Doctrine—is changing in a scandalous way, has become much more acceptable to the *povo* [people]. The man of faith, at least here [in Campos] has a sense of very refined and stable sense of Tradition. There are other changes that he will accept. *Issues, however, like the Mass, and birth control, he will not.*"[92] In other words, the true faithful, led by Mayer himself in Campos, might accept some modifications in Church doctrine and practice—but those that would remain off-limits included, seamlessly, the new liturgy and the pill, details of doctrine and behavior that Mayer saw as part of a singular whole.

The bishops' collaborators weighed in in similar fashion, limning sexuality, and especially the questions of marriage, celibacy, and reproduction, as core elements in the fight for tradition and against "Revolution." As a body,

Coetus expressed strong disapproval of Schema XIII, complaining simultaneously that it did not do enough to defy communism or to reinforce conventional marriage. The group produced circulars (often signed by Sigaud himself), one of which deemed communism "the greatest danger of today" and in nearly the same breath objected that the schema must be discarded because "the Church's traditional doctrines on the ends of marriage and the intrinsic hierarchies therein are insufficiently propounded."[93] Dom José Maurício da Rocha, with whom this chapter began, collaborated with Coetus and epitomized the way in which these complaints were a refined version of the more wide-ranging anticommunist, antimodern, antirational, and anti-Semitic moral panic of years before. In a pastoral letter in 1949, Rocha had denounced each of these enemies as part of a linked "torturous martyrdom" of Christianity in the "modern world." The scourges included not only "the synagogue of Satan" and the ersatz Protocols of the Elders of Zion but also "modern discoveries," "atheistic and diabolic communism," and, most pronounced, the ways that these evils proliferated in a world of marital, moral, and sexual dissolution: "babies are assassinated before even being born" and "married couples watch their homes fall apart [because of] sinful affairs," contributing to "the current degradation of the family, and of society in general, fruit of the corrupting cinema with its entourage of immoral and equally corrupting radio."[94] Keeping track of these debates, Henrique de Souza Gomes, Brazilian ambassador to the Vatican, noted in the context of the Coetus circular that the sanctity of traditional marriage "was the question most hotly discussed in the course of the debates on . . . familial relations." Ironically, Gomes's missives to Itamaraty confirmed the conservative stance of *most* of the Church fathers and of the pope himself—"the overwhelming majority of the conciliar fathers remain faithful to the [marital] doctrine . . . laid out in the Encyclicals *Arcanum* by Leo XIII and *Casti Conubii* of Pius XII"—but his awareness (and the Brazilian diplomatic corps' overwhelming support for this conservatism) did not seem to faze the members of Coetus, who, like Sigaud and Rocha, remained panicked about a morally and doctrinally murky future.[95]

The TFP, especially its adherents in Mayer's own diocese, made plain the connection between sexual and gender comportment, liturgical traditionalism, and the rejection of modernity and of Vatican II that bound these together in the vision of the organization's leadership and many of its practitioners. The latter themselves famously followed house rules that forbade not only contact with women but all forms of sexuality, opting for a monastic lifestyle that, in some cases, included avoidance of seeing one's own body, for fear of "corruption." Accounts from the 1970s onward have emphasized this insistence on

TFP's part that devotees abjure a world in which the "Revolution" held sway, as "sexual sins today are practiced with almost the same casualness with which one eats an ice cream." Tefepistas were expected to attend lectures with titles like "Chastity! Ah, Chastity!" encouraging them to make themselves "humble and pure" in order to combat the "pride and sensuality" of the so-called revolution.[96]

Tellingly, the TFP attempted to extend this requirement to those beyond its direct control, and particularly, at least in Campos, to the arena of the Church itself and the mass. Prelates who, like Mayer himself, were part of or admired the TFP attempted to regulate the details of their parishioners' sexual and gender lives at a level that drew attention and even protest. In 1978, for example, in the parish of Miracema, controversy erupted over TFP and traditionalist influence, especially the activities of Father José Olavo Trindade. Trindade appears to have been an intransigent reactionary linked to TFP and perhaps leading its local adherents. The priest, described as a thirty-five-year-old who insisted on the traditional cassock, had infused the parish with reactionary aesthetic and practice. He instituted a series of reforms, linked in his mind, to combat the TFP's conflated foes: the priest prohibited wedding receptions, forbade women from entering his church without extensive covering (including their hair), eliminated youth masses that featured "sensuous" popular music, and of course restored the Latin or Tridentine mass, celebrated with the officiant's back to the congregation.[97]

Though the priest undoubtedly had the support of some in the parish—and certainly had that of the bishop—others chafed at such conservatism, and their discontent erupted into public protest. By the winter of 1978, anti-TFP parishioners staged demonstrations and began collecting signatures for a petition to Pope Paul VI. The situation developed into something of a local crisis, with dozens of tefepistas descending on Miracema to support Trindade. They made for an intimidating presence, arriving in a *caravana* of nearly thirty vehicles and bringing along their customary banners, standards, costumes, and megaphones. The protesters, meanwhile, made signs and spoke to the press, complaining of the "sick traditionalism" of Father Trindade, who "among other attitudes, does not allow married women, young women, or girls to attend church in pants, a dress with décolletage, or without sleeves." As one discordant voice put it, referring both to Trindade and to Bishop Mayer, "We are in the twentieth century and we cannot allow a bishop to keep us in the medieval era."[98] Protesters and journalists alike focused on Trindade's barring young women from church if they did not dress with anachronistic modesty. The priest's new rules—posted on the door of the church in a medievalesque script—barred from mass females of any age wearing clothing "without sleeves; which does not descend beneath the knee (at least two fingers); excessively low-cut; excessively tight; made of transparent cloth; with mini-skirts"; or who appeared "in masculine attire, trousers, etc."[99]

Observers recounted one particularly striking episode, a shadow of the gendered regulation of bodies that would characterize certain right-wing Pentecostalisms in decades to come. TFP activists, acting on Trindade's orders or with his blessing, purged the congregation of offending unchasteness. Miracema's congregants had tolerated TFP, the story went, "until [TFP activists] closed the lateral Church doors before the mass and, taking up posts in the principal doorway, began a screening of the faithful, beginning with the dress of the young women. And they have rigid criteria, even if a young woman simply dares to show part of her shoulder using the . . . sleeve that has been out of fashion for many years now."[100]

No one, it seemed, was exempt from Trindade's and TFP's crusade against revealing attire. A visiting reporter wrote that she herself had been prohibited from attending church while in Miracema because she was wearing pants; and local businessman Luiz Silva alleged that the priest had refused to baptize an infant because "she was only wearing a diaper."[101]

V. "Laicizing Cultures" and "Unchristianized Christians": Itamaraty, Security Forces, and the State Support for Brazil's Homegrown Catholic Traditionalists

In the face of such local upset and even of national media interest in the TFP as eccentric or vaguely sinister, representatives of Brazil's military regime remained staunchly in the organization's camp. As I have elsewhere noted, various agents and agencies of the dictatorship, particularly within the hard-line and repressive ranks of security forces, expressed solidarity with the TFP and even outrage on its behalf.[102] "It is obvious," read the annex to one secret Ministry of Justice (DSI/MJ) report, "that TFP and Dom Antônio de Castro Mayer (the Bishop of Campos and a staunch supporter of TFP) are being attacked so harshly for their recognized anti-communist positions, and for their unabashed combativeness against the progressive current that is expanding more and more in Catholic circles."[103] The Air Force Intelligence Center (CISA), meanwhile, gathered any and all negative press on TFP—in the interests of countering the journalists, because, as agents put it, "diverse press organizations persist in their campaign against TFP . . . to discredit the Society by means of untruths, insinuations, elisions, . . . omissions, and other tactics, useful for defaming the entity, which is genuinely Christian and a defender of Christian ideals and premises."[104] This support and solidarity extended beyond the incident in Miracema to a more general concurrence with TFP, Mayer, and Sigaud—one that showed security and diplomatic agencies not only defending the conservatives but agreeing with their positions on specific issues of antimodern religiosity and culture war.

While I was unable to ascertain whether Foreign Minister Vasco Leitão da Cunha actually released the funds requested by Sigaud to bring TFP members to Rome, the minister exemplified a general desire, on Itamaraty's part, to serve Sigaud's interests—indeed, Cunha even secured a place for Sigaud's nephew in a diplomatic post in Zurich.[105] More importantly, Sigaud and his agenda enjoyed the enduring support of Brazil's postcoup diplomatic leadership and its representatives in Rome. Brazilian ambassador to the Vatican Henrique de Souza Gomes (who survived the 1964 coup, formally congratulated the new military government and continued to serve until 1968) seems to have retained more ambivalence than his successors, who, as we shall see, roundly rejected the "innovations" of Vatican II.[106] Yet even Gomes seems to have looked upon the council with marked conservatism and seen it as a road to trouble in precisely the terms that Sigaud, Mayer, and TFP did. "The truth is that, as a consequence of the decisions made at the Second Vatican Council, some of them radically innovative, an accentuated disequilibrium can be felt, which can easily lead to disobedience." To provide an example of the kind of "disequilibrium" emerging, Gomes recurred to the very issue that had so concerned Sigaud, Mayer, and TFP: the priestly habit. In a conversation with Antonio Samorè, Gomes recounted, he had learned that during an ordination ceremony at which the presiding cardinal had rightly sported a *ferraiolo* (formal ceremonial cape), the gathered priests had not shown the same formality: "Some came in their cassocks, others in a *clergyman* [simplified habit, or just a collar], but among them came, as a mere spectator, in an unbelievable outfit, in shirtsleeves or even rolled-up shirtsleeves, a Spanish priest."[107] Gomes concurred, then, that the devil was in the details, so to speak. Moreover, he did so because he shared his conservative compatriots' focus on the need for the supernatural as a component of everyday Catholicism. Though he did not often mention individual Brazilians in his correspondence, the ambassador made a point in late 1965 of sympathizing with Sigaud's position that the deliberations on the Church in the modern world failed to "distinguish sufficiently between human progress and *supernatural* salvation."[108]

We shall return in chapter 5 to Itamaraty's general support of Brazilian Catholics' conservative activism outside Brazil, particularly during the Vatican tenure of Ambassador José Jobim, mentioned earlier; but it is worth noting here that Gomes's successors proved yet more pointed in their hostility toward the council and everything that Sigaud, Mayer, and TFP accused it of representing. In a 1969 message to the ministry in Brasília, Vatican business attaché Augusto Estellita Lima expressed his outrage about the "revolutionary" changes under consideration by the pope. "This mentality," wrote Lima, "has given rise to la-icizing social and cultural structures, which make themselves felt above all in the fact that society [is] forcefully permeated by atheism's domination of inter-national organizations, financial institutions and the media." The "mentality" that had reigned at the council and thereafter, Lima wrote, had led directly to a great "number of Christians who are practically de-Christianized [*descristian-izados*] and who mix Marxist ideas with religious belief."[109]

The state's more shadowy elements, and regime hard-liners generally, ex-ceeded Itamaraty in this support for Sigaud, Mayer, and their agenda. Just as security forces held the TFP in high esteem, so they exhibited admiration for and defensiveness of the conservative bishops. This stemmed, in no small part, from those same forces' remarkable concordance with Sigaud's and Mayer's positions, not only on the rather predictable issue of progressives' "defamation" of Brazil (that is, criticism of the regime's human rights record) but also when it came to the generalities and even the minutiae of Vatican II, as well as the council's major figures, debates, and legacies. Significantly, Brazilian security forces closely monitored the council and its aftermath; and they bris-tled, just as Sigaud and Mayer had, at perceived threats to tradition, to Catho-lic supremacy, and to capitalism. One lieutenant in the National Intelligence Service (SNI) went so far as to call John XXIII, who had convoked the coun-cil, "um velhinho senil" (a senile little old man).[110] This general hostility to Vatican II stemmed from the same anticommunism, antiecumenism, and tra-ditionalism that characterized Sigaud's and Mayer's approach. An extensive commentary from the Army Intelligence Center compiled in 1981, clarified this even in its unwieldy—if revealing—title: "Subversive Activity of the Progressive Clergy; Utilization of Ecumenism and of the Bible; Integration of the Revolutionary Process in Latin America." The Army Intelligence Cen-ter traced the titular "revolutionary" developments to "the spirit which preside[d] at the Second Vatican Council (1962–65), which . . . introduced some modifications. These included . . . the incentivization of ecumenism. The newly opened spaces, of course, facilitated the physical and ideological infiltration" of the Church by communists.[111] As early as 1967, with the council barely ended and its legacy still unclear, some Brazilian army analysts had al-ready focused their surveillance on individual clergy suspected of sympathy with the "reformist directives" of Vatican II. The security agents associated such sympathy with "guerrilla-priests" like Camilo Torres and with ecumenism, which in their view, as in Mayer's, "considerably widens the penetration and capacity of communist activity with its base in the so-called Christian Left."[112]

Other agencies echoed this perspective and intensified it, making clear that the Brazilian state's hostile vigilance concerning the council and its aftermath stemmed from a highly wary conservatism closely linked to that of Sigaud, Mayer, and their allies. As we shall see in chapter 5, security forces reacted with vexation to the broad notion that "Catholicism was distancing itself from its traditional standards"—but they saw Vatican II as the root of that distancing, or at least its watershed. To some, the council had mainly granted communist conspiracy an opportunity to flourish. Intelligence agents from the Ministry of Education wrote to their colleagues working within the University of Brasília in 1979 to warn that, while "subversive organizations" had largely been eliminated from Brazil earlier in the decade, they had returned, thanks to the council itself: "Availing itself of the new orientation of the Church with the directives of Vatican II, and of the militancy of infiltrated clerics and laypeople, subversion has initiated a process of re-implanting itself, and . . . is completing its plans with accentuated success."[113] Through the late 1960s and 1970s, air force intelligence officers circulated a manifesto purportedly demonstrating the Brazilian Communist Party's intent to take advantage of the weakness that security forces felt Vatican II had created. Agents quoting from the document stressed the party's delight at "the antagonism between the orientation of the dictatorship and the position defended by the most modernistic wing of the Church, the partisans of the progressive decisions of the Vatican Council."[114] The Justice Ministry, meanwhile, received reports from its secret agents that confirmed the reverence for Pope Pious XII—adored, here and elsewhere, by traditionalists as a bastion—and described his successors and the hated council as affiliating with or at least serving the ends of communism: "Pius XII having died after a long and prestigious pontificate, . . . Vatican II took place. It is not difficult to point out in the [following] two Pontiffs, as well as in the correspondent attitudes of the Council, the progressively sharper outlines of this collaboration with communism [and] . . . ambiguity with relation to socialism, the constant servant of communism."[115]

The SNI, for its part, unequivocally dismissed Vatican II as Marxist, engaged in "changing the image of the Church, of Christianity and even of the figure of Christ."[116] Security agents came to share the despair of traditionalist Catholics in this regard, writing of the council and its aftermath in terms of the "grave crisis confronting Catholic theology . . . aggravated by the 'opening' determined by Vatican II" and bemoaning the weakness of "conservative attempts to restore the . . . stability that the Church represented before the Council."[117] By the 1980s, agents would treat as received wisdom the notion that the Church itself had grown corrupt, "starting with the renovation enabled by John XXIII and by the Second Vatican Council, which culminated in the position taken against the [Brazilian] government." Though much of the conflict between the regime and Brazilian Catholics (of various political stripes) stemmed from issues surrounding human rights, these concerns did not necessarily dictate security forces' antipathy toward Vatican II. Indeed, when the Rio de Janeiro SNI reported on the "position taken against the government" as the "culmination" of Vatican II, agents did not even mention reports of torture or the so-called defamation of Brazil by activist prelates; rather, their report attributed the "accelerated conflict with the government" to the council's empowerment of "followers of Liberation Theology" and its alarming social justice accoutrements: critiques of "the monetarist neoliberal economic system"; "the participation of women in the liberation of the people"; and the denunciation of women's "mode of oppression [as] similar to that which has for centuries affected the Indian and the Black."[118]

The various agents of the state enforcement seemed so closely in sync with the brand of antiecumenism, anticommunism, traditionalism, and general opposition to Vatican II that they essentially identified with Sigaud and Mayer, making judgments based on their authority, quoting them extensively, and taking the bishops' friends (and enemies) for their own—that is, for those of the state and its most ferociously authoritarian and anticommunist, self-appointed guardians. At a basic level, this meant that security forces closely followed any criticism of the bishops and presumed that the critics were themselves subversive malefactors. A 1971 report from the Belo Horizonte office of the SNI, forwarded to several other agencies, left little doubt of where its loyalties lay. Major Pedro Cândido Ferreira Filho lauded Sigaud as a "leader, a man of culture and intelligence who exercises great influence" in the region and clearly resented the way in which Sigaud's "prestige" suffered alongside that of the "public authorities" sanctioned by the regime.[119] This resentment of any criticism of Sigaud extended well beyond the SNI and certainly beyond Sigaud's home state. In 1977, the Brazilian military attaché in Caracas reported with outrage on the "bad faith" with which Sigaud had been portrayed in Venezuelan media, which were the "vehicle of information favorable to the Left and against the Brazilian government."[120]

Other agencies further elaborated this vision of Sigaud, Mayer, and the Brazilian government as embattled allies in the fight against progressive Catholics and their Marxist agenda. By 1968, the CISA saw Mayer and the military state itself as victims of the same progressive Catholic calumnies. In a memorandum to the other security agencies, the air force spies remarked, "It appears that in Campos, [Mayer] is considered by the 'progressista' priests to be a highly reactionary element, since he disagrees openly with [leading progressive bishops], an element that never tires of criticizing the Revolution of March 1964."[121] The Justice Ministry's intelligence service, covering the meeting of the Latin American Episcopal Conference in 1978, specified why Sigaud's foes could likewise be considered those of the Brazilian state. The ministry's spies lamented that the gathered bishops' "disposition . . . is to preserve the directives of the Medellín Conference in 1968, which presupposed the growing involvement of the Catholic Church in matters which go beyond the bounds of the purely religious, with radicalisms presented as solutions to social, political, and economic problems." Sigaud, by contrast, appeared as the voice of reason, regrettably drowned out by these radical, irreligious foes: according to Justice Ministry spies, Sigaud advocated against the "impetus of radical ecclesiastics of the Left and [for] returning the South American episcopate, notably the Brazilian episcopate, to doctrinal orthodoxy"—but in this he stood alone, as "all the declarations, with the exception of Dom Sigaud," took against him and against the Brazilian government.[122] Two years later, the CISA sought to inform intelligence colleagues in the SNI, the navy, the army, and the federal police of the admirable work Sigaud and Mayer had attempted at the February 1980 meeting of the National Conference of Brazilian Bishops (CNBB), the country's relatively progressive Catholic leadership—and how that work had been foiled by "Marxists." The CNBB's general assembly, agents recounted, "was not influenced as had been hoped by the traditionalist and conservative voices of Bishops Dom Geraldo de Proença Sigaud . . . and Dom Antônio de Castro Mayer . . . the authors of the book *Agrarian Reform: A Question of Conscience*." Air force intelligence agents bitterly noted what had been lost here, praising conservatives' coterminous defense of "capitalist ownership of the soil" and attacks on global Catholic unorthodoxy. As Sigaud's and his allies' efforts failed, the agents blamed the progressive bishops, whom they accused of association with "guerrillas," of construing themselves as a "fifth column," and of exceeding even the undesirability of Sebastiano Baggio, "the former Nuncio in Brazil (considered by the Brazilian government as 'persona non grata' because of his . . . leftist and communist activities in Brazil)." The report noted with no small satisfaction that Sigaud, Mayer, and their followers appeared to have the sympathies of the new pope, John Paul II, who had responded coldly to certain priests' desire to marry and who "has been acting with great firmness and determination when it comes to liturgical practices [and] has decreed the prohibition of a sort of communitarian mass, which the CNBB had approved."[123]

If conservatives within the Brazilian state looked on Sigaud as a champion, during and after the council, they oozed enthusiasm about Mayer, echoing the core of traditionalists from across the globe who would come to lionize the bishop of Campos. Even as the diocese itself was enveloped in the scandals and turmoil evinced by Mayer's welcome of extremist elements in the TFP and his increasing alienation from the Vatican, intelligence officials praised the bishop and his domain as islands of tradition and sanity in a sea of destructive, godless Marxist ferment—a desecration of the Church and the clergy, whom communism had caused to forget their spiritual mission. The Army Intelligence Center praised Mayer and the "traditionalist priests of his diocese, who oppose the Marxistization of theology, identifying as subversive that which characterizes the actions of [progressive clergy]: ample distribution of Marxist orientation, masses with adulterated liturgy, religious ceremonies transformed in public acts of protest, the instrumentalization of the faith, and of the faithful, for the purposes of subversion."[124]

Campos, agents of the CISA enthused, retained "a traditionalist current" in its clergy, "aimed at the 'traditional teachings of the Church,' with participation only in the spiritual plane (without interference in the temporal plane), with social [issues] addressed by 'Christian charity,'" rather than revolution or reform. The CISA dismissed opponents of Mayer—including his successor, sent by the Vatican to bring Campos back in line—for their "acceptance and introduction of Marxist philosophy" and concomitant "vision oriented toward the poor" and toward "greater participation of the Church in social issues" (as opposed to adhering to the traditional Catholic doctrine of promoting charity without structural change).[125] In missives to central headquarters in Brasília, the Rio de Janeiro SNI waxed even more fulsome in its praise of Mayer. In a 1975 "Summary Evaluation" written from Campos, agents lauded him as "an ardent adversary of leftism, having . . . condemned the Manifesto of the Bishops of the Northeast. He maintains an attitude of support for the activities of the TFP. His position in the municipality has been fundamental for the extant climate of tranquility."[126] (Given that Mayer would resign in five years and be excommunicated in thirteen, this last claim seems unfounded.) The SNI credited the bishop's stand against reform for the fact that "the north of Rio de Janeiro state has become known as a refuge for the conservative clergy, called traditionalist . . . who have remained conservative, impervious to the growing tide of innovations in the Church, pastoralist in name only." Demonstrating telling familiarity with the notion of the new liturgy as one of the principal transgressions of Vatican II, the Rio SNI described Campos as a stronghold and Mayer as a hero, especially after he resigned rather than discontinue the Tridentine mass: "D. Antônio de Castro Mayer, conservative, ex-bishop of the Diocese, extremely lucid at 76 years of age, has always had, together with his followers, a very clear position against the modifications introduced, by [Vatican II], to the centuries-old traditions of the Church." They limned Campos itself, meanwhile, as "an upscale rural area, with a solid middle class, also profoundly conservative." As we shall see in chapter 5, security forces extended their sympathy for Mayer and Sigaud to the nitty-gritty of doctrinal and liturgical issues—here, as elsewhere, they framed that sympathy in terms of a shared horror of the aforementioned "modifications" in the "centuries-old traditions of the Church." According to the SNI, Vatican II and progressives heralded a "new morality," "profanation of the Churches," "Liberation Theology," "veering toward socialism and communism," "the secularization of the clergy," "assimilation to the spirit of the world," "the dilution of spirituality," "compulsive preoccupation with the promotion . . . of ecumenism," and "horizontalism in religion and among men, the democratization of the Church."[127]

Revealing the depth of their support for and even dependence on the conservative Brazilian bishops, state agents recurred to Sigaud in order to identify potential "subversives," relying on the archbishop's "information" (that is, his prejudicial assessments) in determining whom to surveil. In 1974, after Sigaud had appeared at a meeting of the Latin American Anticommunist Confederation, a regional branch of the extremist World Anti-Communist League, agents of the CISA took note of the Catholic organizations indicated as subversive by Sigaud and forwarded these to other branches of the Brazilian security forces. The archbishop had indicated the danger posed by lay apostolates geared toward workers, wherefore the CISA informed other agencies that those involved with such groups should be targeted for arrest and repression: "As the majority of the militants of the MPL (Movimento Popular de Libertação) . . . are engaged, currently, in these so-called Worker Apostolates, we suggest that the attached report be diffused [among security forces] and forwarded to the presiding officer of the [dictatorial tribunal] investigating the MPL."[128] Police even demonstrated a more intimate relationship with Sigaud in this regard, drawing on his accusations to scrutinize particular individuals. In 1976, for example, federal police in Paraná took Sigaud's denunciations of a progressive priest as evidence of his subversive intent. "From our initial investigations," they wrote, "it has been found that in

1955, according to the accusations of [Sigaud], the [suspect] was provoking religious unrest." The report even included a years-old letter written by Sigaud detailing the "illegal preaching" of the purported subversive and warning against any other priests' collaboration with him.[129] This kind of collaboration between Sigaud and security forces added a classified dimension to the archbishop's very public support of positions coincident with the hard line in the military state. Moreover, Sigaud performed a rather breathtaking defense of security forces themselves, openly mocking claims about torture in Brazil and defending the regime's reputation with what can only be seen, in retrospect, as callousness. According to one report of a press conference in 1970, Sigaud began by decrying a campaign of "defamation against Brazil" and denied that there was torture, persecution of progressive Catholics, or a "supposed genocide against indigenous people." He then launched into a shockingly explicit screed: "He said there were no political prisoners in Brazil. . . . He asked the audience why—if according to the European press there have been cases of assassination and torture of political prisoners who have had their testicles and fingernails ripped out—when the terrorists present the government with a list of their comrades to be freed in exchange for kidnapped persons, they only include in those lists comrades who are still alive and with their nails and testicles intact."[130] Further demonstrating his support for the forces of repression—and their methods, even though he had just denied them—Sigaud facetiously asked his audience whether European terrorists "had had their confessions pulled out of them by the police . . . using caramels and chocolate." Sigaud went on to deny the report that a Brazilian nun had been subjected to "electric shocks on her genitals and being publicly stripped." Instead, he said, "prisons in Brazil are frequently more of an overnight boarding house, as happens in his diocese, where prisoners condemned to up to five years of jail continue to work and to study, returning to the prison only to sleep."[131]

Outside the ranks of security forces and their secretive work, Sigaud in particular also enjoyed the patronage and admiration of known hard-liners and putschists. Marshal Juárez Távora, an eminent anticommunist (whose aspirations to become the dictatorship's first president were eclipsed only by the victory of Humberto Alencar de Castello Branco), had a conservative, Catholic, and antidemocratic past dating back decades.[132] Little surprise, then, that he developed an admiration for Sigaud's ideas. In 1956, before the coming tumult had begun in earnest, Sigaud sent a copy of his work condemning agrarian reform to the marshal, with the inscription, "To Your Excellency General Juarez Távora, Geraldo, Bishop of Jacarezinho respectfully offers [this text]." Távora went on to highlight parts of the essay he deemed particularly relevant, presumably for their consonance with his own religious anticommunism.[133] Artur da Costa e Silva, who *did* serve as military president (1967–69), met and corresponded with Sigaud, in some sense the most visible Church official to support the government. In 1968, as repression increased, Sigaud attended an audience with the president, to whom he lent "an embrace of solidarity." The meeting itself marked the occasion of the TFP's signature campaign, designed to solicit the pope's intervention in the Brazilian Church because, as Sigaud himself said in his appearance with the president, "the problem of communist infiltration cannot be ignored by the bishops of Brazil and it requires on the people's part the clear awareness that communism is incompatible with Christianity."[134] Carlos Luís Guedes, among the principal conspirators in the lead-up to the 1964 coup, waxed particularly eloquent in his appreciation of Sigaud. Raging against the "terrible progressive wing" of the clergy, Guedes lauded Sigaud as the undisputed leader of resistance to it:

> But great names, above whom floats the White Dove illuminating the [Holy] Spirit for them, remain alert and pray for the intangibility of the traditional church, that which was founded under the authority of Peter, against which the gates of Hell will not prevail. One of these, above all, stands out for the courage and frankness of his attitudes: Dom Geraldo Proença Sigaud, the Archbishop of Diamantina. . . . Preoccupied with the faith and likewise with the destiny of the Pátria, they form a first line of combatants, lucid, strong, and unafraid, illuminating, inspiring confidence, generating the kind of dedication, that leads, if necessary, even to the [ultimate] sacrifice.[135]

VI. "The Brains of Their Movement, Their Guiding Intelligence": Brazilians and Global Catholic Traditionalism

As the foregoing passages indicate, regime insiders saw in Sigaud not only an ally but a leader, someone who had taken a prominent role in fighting for traditionalism. General Augusto Moniz de Aragão—a notorious hard-liner and president of the Clube Militar—put it thus after Sigaud delivered an incendiary speech at the Escola de Aperfeiçoamento de Oficiais (a military officers' training academy): "Dom Sigaud's message is a bit of peace, an encouragement, a solace so that we go on fighting for Brazil. . . . We must not leave the initiative to the enemy. We must act."[136] This attitude extended beyond such military leaders and indeed beyond Brazil. Among Catholic traditionalists, especially among the more extreme and those willing to break with more mainstream Catholic institutions, Sigaud, Mayer, and even TFP itself stood for decades as beacons of hope and guidance.

Mayer's decisions in and beyond his diocese served as a famous and broadly intelligible example of radical resistance to change. His visibility, both as a renegade at Vatican II and as leader of the holdout priests of Campos, made him something of a hero, locally as well as globally—he eventually gained the moniker "The Lion of Campos."[137] Within the diocese, of course, priests and laypersons who valued the traditional mass and other accoutrements of the Church's past heralded Mayer as an embattled warrior for downtrodden conservatives, marginalized by a tide of progressivism and institutional sea change. Indeed, even after Mayer was replaced by a new bishop who more diligently obeyed the Vatican, a holdout segment of renegades honored the former's wishes by refusing to submit to the new bishop's authority, even risking legal action against them.[138] The memory of Mayer as a model of stalwart resistance lasted decades, continuing to today. When I interviewed Dom Fernando Arêas Rifan, Mayer's successor as leader of Campos's traditionalists, Rifan spoke of his former mentor in terms similar to those used by reactionaries in and beyond the diocese. Belying the complexities and contradictions of Rifan's own reconciliation with the Vatican, he described Mayer as "brilliant," "learned," and "faithful to the magisterium of the Church." In Rifan's retelling, as in that of other admirers, Mayer appears a humble servant of the Church who only took action because he found himself "perplexed" by the "apostasy of the priests [who adopted the new mass]," by "the new doctrines," which were "errors."[139] Jonas dos Santos Lisboa, a local parish priest who faced arrest in 1982 for refusing to either submit to episcopal authority or vacate his church, precisely articulated these sentiments about Mayer's legendary humility, theological prowess, and importance beyond Campos. In an interview decades later (2008), Lisboa demonstrated the ongoing hagiography of the former bishop, a formidable historical memory that provides ongoing inspiration to traditionalists:

> Dom Antônio, a renowned theologian, whose fame is well known, distinguished himself by his upright character, by his love of the Holy Church, and by his confidence in doctrine. He wrote innumerable pastoral letters, which when published *surpassed the borders of the diocese and even of the country*, given the interest that they awakened. . . . We priests who were trained by him learned submission to the magisterium of the Church from him. . . . He [gave] all the documents of the Second Vatican Council . . . their true interpretation according to the tradition of the Church and not that of the modernists. He denounced abuses and as an

attentive pastor, he warned against the modernist dangers that were destroying the faith and good customs [morality].[140]

By the time of this interview, Lisboa had found a home in the Personal Apostolic Administration of São João Maria Vianney, a unique formation within the Church and to my knowledge the only Catholic jurisdiction set aside specifically for the purpose of celebrating the traditionalist (pre-1969) mass. He granted the interview to Fratres in Unum, an extreme traditionalist group that takes figures like Lisboa and Mayer for heroes.

As Lisboa indicates, however, the former bishop of Campos gained fame and renown that extended far beyond Brazil. He came to be internationally celebrated as a champion, even a martyr, of traditionalism. My point here is not that Brazil, nor Mayer himself, was the *only* source of such fall-on-your-sword opposition to the "new" Church. Rather, I wish to make clear a critical discrepancy: while scholarly accounts of global traditionalism have tended to exclude these Brazilian actors, traditionalists *themselves* regularly acknowledge the centrality to their cause of Brazil, Sigaud, Mayer, and Plínio Corrêa de Oliveira. Traditionalist Catholic and self-published historian Griff Ruby's account of the last several decades of Church history (revealingly titled *The Resurrection of the Roman Catholic Church*) epitomizes this view. Ruby lauds "bishops who held the line and remained Catholic despite the pressure from all sides to get in step with the new religion" and adds, "Most heroic of these bishops was Antonio de Castro Mayer, who along with another holy bishop, Dom Geraldo Proença Sigaud, who was Bishop of Jacarezinho, and their political ally Plínio Corrêa de Oliveira, kept parts of Brazil faithful during the years that the rest of Latin America was falling for the heretical 'Liberation Theology.'"[141]

The sense of Brazil as just such a redoubt is echoed in the *Remnant,* a Minnesota-based publication that claims to be "the oldest Traditionalist Catholic publication in the world." The management of the paper—and associated video and internet ventures—sees it as part of a venerable legacy of religious neoconservatism, "fighting against the revolution in the Church for over fifty years, just as it has been fighting against the errors that infect the modern state—Liberalism, Socialism, Communism, the New World Order, a degenerate youth culture, the abortion epidemic, euthanasia, sex education, etc."[142] As such, the *Remnant* holds Mayer and Sigaud in high esteem. In 2015, editor Michael J. Matt spoke against any concessions to the new mass, invoking Mayer's legacy: "We cannot declare a truce with that about which Bishop Antonio de Castro Mayer said back in January of 1978: 'It seems to me preferable that scandal be given rather than a situation be maintained in which one slides into heresy. . . . I am convinced that one cannot take part in the New Mass. . . . We cannot collaborate in spreading a rite which . . . leads to heresy.'"[143]

Indeed, the *Remnant* lamented the 2002 rapprochement between Rifan and the Vatican precisely *because* Campos had represented a last bastion of traditionalist ritual—a home for the twenty-five priests, legendary to those who favored the old rite, whom Mayer had led in refusing the Novus Ordo. In conjunction with *Catholic Family News*, a traditionalist monthly headquartered in Niagara Falls, the *Remnant* released a statement condemning the move. "The priests of Campos, Brazil, once a body of opposition to Vatican II, are now a spent force," the editors wrote. "Campos' Bishop Rifan takes part in the New Mass and the clergy's public resistance to post-Conciliar modernism has fizzled." To underscore this point, they quoted an Australian leader of the fundamentalist Society of Saint Pius X (SSPX), the priestly fraternity founded by Lefebvre in 1970:

> How is it that these 25 priests from Campos, who for 33 years refused all collaboration whatsoever with the New Mass, who put together these famous reasons for refusing to assist at or collaborate in the New Mass, who so well defended the canonical status of traditional priests, persecuted precisely because of their refusal to celebrate the New Mass, have suddenly changed their tune? It was not the death of Bishop De Castro Mayer. . . . It truly was the devil's tail. Not only were they forbidden all missionary work outside the diocese, . . . but now they are forced to positively cooperate in the New Mass, and to justify it as well. . . . This is nothing less than a complete victory for modernism.[144]

Swiss bishop Bernard Fellay, himself responsible for the posthumous (2009) rescinding of Lefebvre's and Mayer's excommunications, likewise bemoaned the new mass in Mayer's former domain. In 2004, Fellay denounced the appearance in Campos of the "New Mass where you have really scandalous happenings: ladies giving Communion in the hand, a ceremony of crowning Our Lady conducted by a woman in the presence of all the cardinals and bishops attending, and so on."[145] From Australia to Niagara Falls, then, the fall of Campos could be construed as a "complete victory for modernism," given what Mayer, his stewardship, and the diocese had come to represent.

The SSPX, while dedicated to the memory of Lefebvre, has continually and perhaps increasingly venerated Mayer. It published and promotes the hagiographic *Catholic, Apostolic, and Roman*, an anonymous (attributed to "the Priests of Campos") companion volume to an adulatory biography of Mayer. As the SSPX's description of the book would have it, "This is the story of the

epic battle against Fideicide [faith-killing] in a humble corner of South America."[146] When the bishop emeritus died in 1991 (still formally excommunicated),
the organization's magazine the *Angelus* fulsomely celebrated his legacy—not
only his cooperation with Lefebvre, but Campos itself: "The majority of the
priests in the diocese of Campos (336 of them!) resisted the Modernist orientations of the new bishop and remained faithful. Bishop Antonio was thus
able to maintain a completely traditional 'diocese' within a diocese, [with]
parallel chapels to protect the faithful from the enemies within."[147] Such an
elegy on the SSPX's part generally occurs within a transnational web of like-
minded reactionaries, stretching from Brazil to Europe and North America.
For example, the reactionary French *Courrier de Rome*, founded in 1967 to
combat the "conciliar revolution," carried an article drawing on Mayer as a
paradigm for defining missal rectitude—which the SSPX itself then reprinted
in separate English and Spanish publications.[148]

Today's traditionalists, even as the established narrative foregrounds Lefebvre, nevertheless maintain that Brazil's conservative bishops played leading, essential parts in the drama of Vatican II and its decades-long aftermath. John
Vennari, editor of *Catholic Family News* from 1994 to 2017, described the formation of Coetus, rightfully, as Sigaud's initiative. This "substantial force resisting
the liberal revolution at Vatican II," Vennari wrote, "accomplished a great deal."
Moreover, "it was formed by Brazil's Bishop Proença Sigaud, who wanted to
organize the scattered conservative prelates who were resisting the liberal alliance, and Archbishop Lefebvre was a major player in this conservative group."[149]
Ever dedicated to Lefebvre as founder, the SSPX nevertheless acknowledges
the Brazilians, describing the French archbishop as "backed by two combative
Brazilian bishops, Antonio de Castro Mayer and Geraldo de Proença Sigaud."

Yet even Lefebvre himself acknowledged the preeminence of Sigaud and
Mayer in conciliar and postconciliar traditionalist movements. Though now
referred to (particularly by the SSPX, whose adherents see themselves as his
heirs) as the primary force behind Coetus and conservatism at the council,
Lefebvre recalled these events differently: "The soul of Coetus was Bishop
Proença Sigaud as Secretary, I myself . . . was the 'public face' in the role of
chairman. Bishop de Castro Mayer was vice chairman and 'the thinker.'"[150] If
Lefebvre thought of Sigaud and Mayer as the "soul" and the brain of Coetus,
he also acknowledged their specific roles as collaborators in the various
conservative campaigns at the council, such as petitioning the fathers to denounce communism.[151] What is more, he made much of the tefepistas' role,
noting that the work of the conservatives at the council would have been impossible without them. In this regard, Lefebvre went further even than Sigaud

himself—the French prelate referred to TFP as a "directorial committee" of Coetus and also described the ways in which their legwork served as the organization's lifeblood: "Brazilians, members of the TFP, helped us with great abnegation, working during the night delivering the texts that five or six bishops would have redacted.... With the aforementioned bishops [Sigaud and Carli] and ... Mayer ... we would edit these texts which were printed during the night; in the wee hours some of these Brazilians would go to distribute our pages in the hotels and mailboxes of the conciliar Fathers, just as IDOC [a Dutch-founded informational apparatus at the council] did in an organization twenty times as large as ours."[152] Lefebvre thus not only recognized the Brazilian bishops and their TFP helpmeets but saw them as core adjutants in the conservatives' against-the-odds battle against the progressives' much more impressive onslaught.

When it came to Lefebvre and Mayer in particular, there was, of course, *o óbvio ululante*: the unavoidable fact of their spectacular cooperation in making the pronouncements and laying the groundwork for their eventual rejection of Rome. As noted at the outset of this chapter, the two issued a watershed joint statement in 1983 from Rio de Janeiro. In it, they denounced the "principal errors" that led to the "tragic situation" of the Church, which was fast leading the two of them into the territory of schism and excommunication. This list of "errors" hewed closely to Mayer's basic notions of the value of inequality and hierarchy, denouncing various egalitarian initiatives: "a 'latitudinarian' and ecumenical notion of the Church," "a collegial government and democratic orientation in the Church," "a false notion of the natural rights of man," and the end of the Inquisition.[153] After hotly debated negotiations between Lefebvre and the Vatican, Mayer traveled from Brazil to join his friend and collaborator in Switzerland in June 1988. Together, and contravening the will of Vatican authorities, the two consecrated four bishops, meant to serve as the inheritors of Lefebvre's and Mayer's legacy—that is, to continue rejecting the "new" Church and its rites once the two renegade bishops had retired or died. As Mayer put it in his remarks at the ceremony, "The two of us [Mayer and Lefebvre] have drunk at the same source, which is that of the Holy Catholic Apostolic and Roman Church."[154] The men consecrated (in the view of Lefebvre and Mayer and their supporters) in 1988 were to serve as the future leaders of the SSPX; but they also consecrated a bishop to lead "Mayer's order of priests," the Society of São João Maria Vianney, after Mayer's death.[155] (This was not recognized by the Vatican until 2002, when Licínio Rangel became an "auxiliary bishop" within the special formulation of the Apostolic Administration, discussed earlier.)

Perhaps the most telling testament to the ongoing veneration of Mayer among adherents of traditionalism is the hagiographic book *The Mouth of the Lion*, referenced by Catholic reactionaries of various stripes as a masterpiece. The book is the work of Naval Academy literature professor and Catholic convert David Allen White, a devotee of traditionalism and enemy of the new mass, which he dismisses as "lousy music, lousy literature, putrid liturgical dancing."[156] White admires Mayer and his legacy as the strongest, desperate antidote to such hated innovations—the book's subtitle is *Bishop Antônio de Castro Mayer and the Last Catholic Diocese*. White epitomizes the sense of Campos as a symbol, a final battleground carved out by Mayer and his compatriots as a beacon of hope to traditionalists everywhere. *The Mouth of the Lion* argues that the Brazilians (Mayer, but also Sigaud and Oliveira) "caught the whiff of rot" in progressive Catholicism before any of their future allies.[157] As a result, they created in Brazil one of the most lasting bastions of "true" Catholicism. The book limns Campos as a place where the dreams of traditionalist Catholics meet those of neoconservatives in the preservation of hierarchy, capitalism, and venerated cultural and moral touchstones:

> Campos may, in fact, be the last Catholic City. . . . The Sabbath is respected, obscenity does not spill onto the streets, human beings are content with their God-given lot in life and fulfill their appointed tasks. Charity is public and exists in individual acts of kindness, not in contributions or payroll deductions. Young people exude innocence and retain their purity until their marriage day. . . . Thousands turn out to publicly honor the blessed Sacrament. Within the limits of the city can be found four Traditional Catholic churches and three Traditional Catholic Chapels, a Traditional Catholic seminary, Traditional Catholic schools.[158]

White, as a representative of contemporary traditionalists, wrote this book precisely to redress the sense that Brazil and Mayer have not been given their due. The book argues that Mayer and Oliveira had laid the groundwork for their roles at Vatican II long before the convocation of the council and had in fact "spent two decades wrestling with the heresies of the Revolution in the forms of communism and socialism and modernism and progressivism." In Rome, therefore, Coetus "named [Mayer] publicly as the 'brains' of their movement, their guiding intelligence." And while the "TFP saved Brazil from communism," Mayer alone bucked the worldwide trend of obedience to Vatican II. It is thus, to White, inconceivably wrongheaded that the press "largely ignored" Mayer's role at Ecône, and that this error has continued to the present day.[159]

Conclusion

Traditionalists' present-day reverence for Campos and for Brazilians' role in the foundational moments of resistance to the "new" Church that emerged after Vatican II mirrors the awareness of that role held by Mayer, Sigaud, and Oliveira themselves as well as by their contemporaries. As we have seen, Marcel Lefebvre and his surviving followers are among those who have seen the Brazilians as critical actors, even heroes, in this regard. This view, however, generally does not extend beyond traditionalist Catholic circles, outside which Sigaud and Mayer have passed into relative obscurity, and Oliveira's legacy is not seen to include his activism at Vatican II.

Yet if Catholic traditionalism is the milieu in which these activists can be said to have had the most direct and recognized effect, their impact also extends to the broader terrain of modern religious conservatism. In the chapters that follow, we shall meet other Brazilians and non-Brazilians who likewise adhered to a platform that would increasingly gain coherence as that of a renovated, late Cold War Right that crossed national as well as denominational and ideological divides. Here, we have seen Brazilian Catholics, on a world stage, espousing an early version of that platform—combining, with seamless presumption, anticommunism; moralism; antiecumenism; hierarchalism; animosity toward the state and particularly toward state-led largesse; triumphal organicism regarding birthrights, private property, and capitalism; and a woebegone affinity for the supernatural in the face of perceived secularism. As Brazil's archconservative Catholics, led by Sigaud, Mayer, and Oliveira, worked to create ways to build support for that platform, they would eventually find allies within and outside Brazil, and within and outside the Catholic Church. In the meantime, their midcentury activism made Brazil an important locus for the development of a specific brand of religious conservatism. That brand, as this chapter has explored, blended affinity for hierarchy (earthly and divine) with a nostalgia for a glorified medieval past; it appended an overweening moralism as a central component of that antimodernism; and it enjoyed support among the most conservative and indeed dangerous elements of the Brazilian military regime. Given the tension between the regime and elements of the Church seen as more progressive, Sigaud, Mayer, and the TFP enjoyed a unique position during the decades in which they built their opposition to the changes that followed Vatican II; at and after the council, they were recognized by observers and particularly by admirers as important leaders and proponents of a reactionary fringe that increasingly symbolized an alternative for dissatisfied Catholics.

CHAPTER TWO

Guardians of Morality and of Good Behavior

Morality, Dictatorship, and the Emergence of
Conservative Evangelical Politics in Brazil

By 1969, Reverend Joá Caitano, like many of his Pentecostal coreligionists in the Assemblies of God, was deeply concerned. In "A Patient Condemned to Death," he made clear that the titular "patient" was humanity. "The world is sick!" Caitano wrote, "and the name of the sickness is Sin! Yes, Sin, which means disobedience, transgression, iniquity, prevarication, and rebelliousness!" He explained that the two primary aspects of this moral plague were "rebellion" (as "sons rebel against their fathers [and] daughters no longer respect their mothers," leading to worldwide inklings of "Revolution") and "sex." "Sex," Caitano railed, "has become the primary stuff of the world in which we live. Free love is the most common thing. . . . Respect for morality no longer exists. Theaters . . . exploit the masses with sex as an attraction. . . . Sexual orgies are growing frighteningly across the world. Houses of prostitution have grown into veritable agencies of sin that destroy the body and soul of man!"[1]

In some ways, this excursus may seem straightforward, even familiar—an example of time-honored evangelical moralism and millenarian apocalypticism. Caitano's words would harmonize with (if not mirror) conservative Christian reactions in other parts of the Americas and the world; indeed, these reactions developed in dialogue with each other.[2] But in the Brazilian context, "A Patient Condemned to Death" represented the stirrings of a key development in Brazil's ongoing military rule and the first blush of a new chapter in Brazil's religious and political history. Five years after the coup that inaugurated the dictatorship, evangelical moralists like Caitano stood poised to construct a formidable Christian conservatism, which the dictatorship fundamentally enabled and encouraged, and which would change the face of Brazilian politics and culture.

A cursory look at Brazil's current politics demonstrates the lasting legacy of this process. Long the fastest-growing religious groups in Brazil, Protestantism and particularly Pentecostalism have come to occupy an increasingly dominant position in Brazil's politics—religious and secular—a position some have called the Nova Direita, the New Right.[3] By the year 2000, little more than a decade after the return to democracy, conservative forces were in some ways reclaiming even those mainline denominations, where evangelical progressivism had once made inroads. Among northeastern Presbyterians, for example, progressive communities seemed to evaporate, leaving in their wake a fundamentalist revival that rejected the reforms of yesteryear: social justice agendas, human rights, the ordination of women, and most especially interreligious and ecumenical initiatives, alongside all manner of "modernistic practices."[4]

Yet the rise of this Right, and particularly its evangelical component, was in evidence long before the solidification of the country's return to democracy.[5] By the 1980s and 1990s, moralistic mass prayer meetings led by conservative pastors had garnered not only national attention but the warm support of leading government authorities, including presidents both military and civilian.[6] In the mid-1980s, as a constitutional assembly gathered in Brasília to debate and codify the promises of democracy made in the 1970s, an emergent cadre of evangelical politicians began laying the groundwork for the *bancada evangélica*, an ideologically congruent "evangelical bloc" in Brazil's legislature. The contours of this bloc made themselves manifest early, as evangelicals in the constituent assembly sounded off on the issues they claimed justified their participation in the process. Congregationalist and soon-to-be federal deputy Daso Coimbra generalized, declaring that "the group of evangelical deputies will react against the agenda of the delegates from the Left"—but other evangelical deputies expressed their goals much more explicitly. Costa Ferreira, an Assembly of God member from Maranhão, opposed protections against discrimination on the basis of sexual orientation, on the grounds that such protections would deepen a patent moral and sexual crisis: "If the expression 'sexual orientation' should remain [in the constitution], there will be total debauchery. Even without it, debauchery is already here! The whole world has [excessive] freedom! Male homosexuals run around dressed like women, with blonde wigs, high heels and everything else! . . . Lesbians go out dressed like men, cut their hair, and wear beards! Who is discriminating against these people? . . . Constitutional prevention of discrimination for reasons of sexual preference would . . . bring to Brazil the curse of other countries. It would be a curse equal to that which took Sodom and Gomorrah."[7]

João de Deus, a delegate from Rio Grande do Sul and an Assembly of God pastor, focused less on homosexuals than on abortion, railing against its legalization even as he reasoned that Brazil's "economic crisis is a reflection of its moral crisis." Curitiba delegate Matheus Iensen, meanwhile (also of the Assembly of God, as were fourteen of the total thirty-four evangelical delegates), explained that he and his fellow evangelicals were at the convention to defend the family. "The radical Left," he said, "wants to liberate everything. The family is the basic unit of society and must be preserved."[8]

In what would prove to be seminal developments for the religious and political history of Brazil and the hemisphere, the dictatorship witnessed and facilitated the politicization and empowerment of conservative evangelical Christians. In this chapter and the next, I trace this process, uncovering the ways in which the dictatorship itself and the transition to democracy incubated the religious Right in ways both overt and covert. This chapter will identify ways in which a developing evangelical Right drew closer to the regime and gained power and favor; the next chapter will investigate the ways in which these conservatives and their allies decisively foreclosed the possibility of a different kind of evangelical politics in Brazil, that of progressive Protestantism. Here I seek to temper certain current wisdoms about Brazil's religious politics. First, I challenge the notion that the Catholic Church's alliance with prodemocracy and pro–human rights forces during the regime meant a unilateral triumph for postdictatorship Catholics when it came to these issues; instead, as I demonstrate, alliance with the military, even with the most repressive elements of the regime, constituted quite as viable a path to postregime power for evangelicals.[9] Second, whereas some have noted the Sarney government's cozying up to evangelicals, I date the alliance to an earlier process, a politicization that began with the likes of Caitano in the 1960s and built to a crescendo in the 1980s and 1990s.[10]

The conflation of Cold War and culture war, which I have outlined elsewhere, formed a broad matrix, home to an array of moral panic–based approaches to countersubversion.[11] Within this latticework, Brazil's evangelical rightists shared a particular language of moral crisis with powerful members of the military regime, who in turn recognized and supported certain allies among Brazil's Protestants. This was a religious demographic that had theretofore eschewed formal politics as "mundane" and inconsistent with dedication to the things of God. Evangelicals' alliance with the regime thus reshaped Brazil's politics during the dictatorship; perhaps more importantly, this novel regime-religious axis, founded on morality, anticommunism, and opposition to left-wing Christianity, marked the formative years and ultimately the shape of Brazil's current democracy.

As a result, the Right, which gestated in dictatorial Brazil, developed outsize domestic influence. Furthermore, it prefigured the global religious Right of today—in ways that constituted a pivotal departure for evangelicals themselves, and a critical development in Brazil's antimodernist politics and culture. That development, briefly put, was the empowerment of an evangelical

Right based in a series of agreements. These agreements bound such evangelicals together with conservative Catholics and, far more importantly, with members of the regime eager to combat liberation theology by promoting archconservative, antimodern, often fundamentalist versions of Christianity. Progressive evangelicals, though always a minority, engaged with liberationist political and theological currents also moving through midcentury Catholic circles; a few such progressives even gained national visibility.[12] The emergent conservative coalition, then, agreed on a set of issues whose amalgamation forged an engine of conservative outrage: overweening moralism; hand-wringing about modernity (the cultural accoutrements, that is, of economic and infrastructural modernization); and ferocious opposition to ecumenism and to communism, which were themselves conflated with each other and with liberation theology and progressive Christianity.

I. Battling the Prince of Shadows: Everyday Moralism and the Mundane

Morality had, of course, always been a part of evangelical narratives in Brazil and beyond. The crisis-mongering of the 1980s—Costa Ferreira's and Daso Coimbra's avowals of dissolution in the here and now, for example—differed, however, from previous incarnations in that the latter condemned the terrestrial world out of hand as the site of an eternal battle against Satan. Earlier evangelical moralisms, that is, reacted not to a perceived spike in immorality so much as to an ongoing, timeless struggle against all things mundane, including (or especially) politics and politicians. Such moral reckonings and preachings represented, above all, a traditional evangelical rejection of worldliness—a deliberate focus on the things of God and His kingdom, well in keeping with historical evangelical and fundamentalist traditions in Brazil and abroad.[13] Thus the injunctions of yesteryear differed markedly from those that developed during the dictatorship and especially *abertura* (gradual redemocratization)—the latter variant militated against an acute crisis, the former against the sins of the ages.

Hence, in early 1961, *Mensageiro da Paz*, the official newspaper of the Assemblies of God in Brazil, neglected moral panic–mongering in favor of reminding readers that waywardness and evil inhered in this world. Human beings simply needed to recognize the spiritual "poverty" of the world and the necessity of rejecting the mundane in favor of "divine grace."[14] Pastor Vandir Henrique da Silva made this message more proscriptive, affirming that the world itself, in the most general terms, was the root of deviance: "To love the world is to become deprived of spiritual vision. It is to conform or grow accustomed to the world's practices and customs, contrary to morality of the bible[,] ... to the intoxicating effects of carnal passions, which do battle against the regenerated soul of the Son of God. Spiritual weakening is the fruit of conforming to the world."[15] Da Silva's conception of worldliness, rooted in the Bible, transcended time and did not revolve around a current or exceptional crisis of moral standards or practices. A chorus of admonishments from across the denominations echoed this perspective, taking worldliness for their principal enemy. The message that earthly life, pertaining to Satan, lay beneath the notice of good *crentes* pervaded evangelical cosmology, reflecting decades of strict doctrinal abstention from the mundane.[16] The world was but a "battlefield" in the age-worn struggle against the "prince of shadows"—so much so that, according to prominent pastor and sometime missionary to the United States Geziel Gomes, "the ways of this world are the doctrine of Satan."[17]

According to traditional evangelical prescriptions, crentes must studiously, even obsessively, avoid the things of this world. This avoidance mandated explicit disavowal of politics and the political. For most of evangelicals' history in Brazil, that is, worldly politics elicited not only disapproval but visceral aversion. The dictum "to Caesar the things of Caesar and to God the things of God" appeared as a frequent, almost reflexive refrain, indicating the automatic quarantining of the faithful from the low and meaningless management of terrestrial affairs.[18] Methodists in São Paulo, for example, rejected the idea of redistributive reform in 1969—not because they opposed such reform, but because they refused to contemplate such political issues. One preacher complained that structural reforms were "so much talked of," when "reform of the inner man" (that is, of the soul) should trump the mean issues of inequality and injustice.[19] In 1978, when, as we shall see, opposition to political involvement had already relaxed in some evangelical quarters, *assembleiano* (Assemblies of God) leader Joanyr de Oliveira had to recognize that "a considerable parcel of the evangelical community is hostile to [politicians]" such that "no other class is so attacked and maligned" by evangelicals.[20] In some ways this narrative continued long past the point when evangelicals had become political, a sort of identitarian residue of bygone apoliticism. As late as 1988, Independent Presbyterians—latecomers to the political table—still read "os nossos na política" (our kind in politics) as a sign that "new times are arriving."[21] Though the Assemblies of God supplied fourteen of the thirty-four evangelical delegates to the 1986 constitutional congress, the faithful retained a sense of the traditional reticence toward politics, insisting in the early 1980s that overt politicking must give way to the inviolability of ordination. "As a pastor," Oliveira affirmed, "I am extremely careful not to involve the church in political struggles. The sanctity of the Church must not be marred by anything in this world."[22]

Indeed, before the *abertura* period, the merest hint of politics drew ire from readers of evangelical publications. In 1968, for example, the *Jornal Batista* was forced to issue something of a defensive apology for straying but a little into terrestrial issues. When the *Jornal*'s editors opined on student activism and massive antigovernment protests in March, readers wrote in to complain that the journal had "done something political." The editors' response, testy though it was, rather hypocritically eschewed political writing: "To say that our article was political just because we affirmed that we are not living in a dictatorship is . . . excessive."[23] Lutheran pastor Jost Ohler, meanwhile, editor of that denomination's *Jornal Evangélico*, admitted that the newspaper had reported on national politics—and noted reader reactions that demanded he "clearly separate" the *Jorev* (its abbreviated name) from secular publications. Some readers, in fact, went so far as to call for independent, preemptive censorship that would keep politics out of the Lutheran biweekly, as "a journal of that kind has no place in our Church."[24]

II. A "Wave of Immorality"? Moral Panic and the Politics of Antimodernity

Even as some *Jorev* readers staunchly held the line on politicking, however, other evangelicals had grown decidedly more open to morality *as politics*. The way in which this happened determined the fate of evangelical politics for decades to come. Indeed, the fact that Brazil's evangelicals forged a Nova Direita has much to do with the late authoritarian moment in which they entered politics. Conservatives, seizing on morality and discourses of moral panic as "nosso terreno" (our territory), combined those with antiecumenism and anticommunism, and simultaneously made common cause with and gained the support of regime insiders. As part of this process, conservative evangelicals in the 1970s and 1980s abandoned their studied apoliticism and dominated the debut of self-identified crente politicians. Led by Baptists and assembleianos, these politicians championed remoralization as their point of entry into the "dirty" world of national politics. They oversaw the emergence of evangelicals in the national legislature as a self-appointed vanguard against imminent moral calamity.

As a first step toward this moralizing politicization, the vague denunciations of worldliness described earlier evolved into an *acute* sense of a crisis in

Brazil's and the world's moral, gender, and sexual culture: that is, a moral crisis engendered by modernity and modernization. The embryonic evangelical Right adopted a sustained moral panic that would become an axis of commonality with the military government. Through the 1970s and 1980s, conservative evangelicals came to see traditional morality ("nosso terreno") under unprecedented attack. Thus whereas Ebenézer Cavalcanti had, in 1968, insisted on the constancy of sin and the unimportance of change—even going so far as to say that changes in young people's comportment should not be seen "in terms of a *problem*"—by the late 1970s moralists' concerns had grown increasingly sharp when it came to youth, delinquency, "modernity," and sexuality. Contributors to *Mensageiro da Paz* previously adhered to the conviction that "carnality" and "moral laxity" were symptoms of Satan's everyday and eternal temptation of the faithful—but by the 1970s, the newspaper and its readers stood at a crossroads. While a few pastors still presented sin as a transcendent and apolitical reality, many fellow assembleianos took a different tack. Adauto Edson Dourado, for example, touched one of rightists' most sensitive nerves when he addressed working women as a scourge of modernity. In "Where Is Sarah, Your Wife?," Dourado reminded crentes of the "biblical principles that a woman should marry and be a good housewife." He lamented the fact that, unlike the biblical Sarah, wife of Abraham, "many today disregard this principle in favor of following the new course that modern teachings urge upon families who seek to follow the world and its evolution of customs." Dourado expressed particular angst about *this moment* in which so many women had left the home and, worse yet, the government contemplated legalizing women's right to work night shifts. "May Christian women," he concluded, "very prudently not abandon Christian principles but know to stay in their true and correct place."[25]

Mensageiro contributors moved beyond this single issue to a larger panic that encompassed a much-ballyhooed "wave of immorality"—a phrase that in itself indicated the perceived temporality of this phenomenon. In 1980, the newspaper reported that "sectors of society remain apprehensive in light of the wave of immorality that inhabits the mass media, with open corruption of customs, by means of texts and photos exposed to the whole public, and not just to pornography aficionados." The article "Morality in Decadence" argued that these acute developments had caused "national grief," partially assuaged by the presence of evangelicals in Congress who "roundly denounced this calamitous state of Brazilian morality." The piece quoted Congregationalist deputy Daso Coimbra's horror-struck pronouncements on the "industry of pornography and depravity reaching heights never before

"Conferências de Vida Abundante" (Conferences of Abundant Life), advertisement, *Mensageiro da Paz*, March 1977, 16. Photo taken by author and used by permission of Casa Públicadora das Assembléias de Deus.

seen, including . . . incitement of couples to practice collective libidinousness." Coimbra called for "a brake [*freio*], in the name of morality, and of good customs, and indeed, in defense of the family, today invaded by this type of literature that is distributed with no impediment."[26]

Mensageiro readers appear to have shared, if not exceeded, the moral anxieties of their newspaper. Letters to the editor in 1977 complained about everything from *Mensageiro*'s failure to adequately oppose divorce legislation to "photographs with *cabeludos* [long-haired youths] and . . . sporty clothing combated by a considerable portion of our leadership" to the issues of women's hair, makeup, and long (or not long enough) skirts.[27] Indeed, even advertisements seemed to target reactionism among rank-and-file assembleianos. A promotion for "Conferences of Abundant Life," a prayer meeting led by Pastor Édino Fonseca, "International Evangelist," drew on ambient fears about young people and moral, sexual, and national crisis. The advertisement depicted a well-groomed young man—probably the pastor himself, and certainly not *cabeludo*—in a smart suit with glasses, holding a bible. Beneath the photo, text encouraged potential attendees to reach out to the pastor for help in dealing with the "crises" afflicting Brazilians. Fonseca promised, "Messages that will transform your life. Wars. Abortion. Drugs. Witchcraft. Economic crisis. Spiritual hard-heartedness. Homosexuality. If these issues shock you, come to hear the servant of God, Pastor Édino Fonseca."[28]

Other right-wing evangelicals also weighed in on these heady issues. Abel Amaral Camargo, the leader of the Independent Reformed Presbyterian Church of Brazil—a conservative dissident branch of Presbyterians who, influenced by Pentecostalism, broke with the main line in 1972[29]—told his followers that the moral crisis of the 1970s was so acute that it *must* represent the "last hour." For evidence he pointed to the bugbear of many cultural rightists: modern mass communication. "Television," he wrote, "is a tool that the devil uses . . . to dirty the hearts of parents, children, and guests. . . . He is wise and wily. Television has caused the corruption and degeneration of many families."[30] *O Presbiteriano Conservador*, meanwhile, the outlet of another conservative Presbyterian group, teemed with admonishments on proper marriage, "the death of modesty," and "the virtuous woman."[31] The Evangelical Council on Religious Education, meanwhile, published *Revista da Mocidade*, which warned young readers about "the moral crisis of our days," summed up in the admonition that "all things conspire . . . to favor a climate of moral degradation that touches all the levels of society." Vaguely blaming "the communists," articles addressed "sex and sexuality" and "the family in danger," because "sexual comportment . . . has come to permit everything and impede nothing," including "'collective marriages,' that is, a 'family' constituted by various husbands and various wives, living promiscuously . . . in fornication."[32]

Perhaps most visibly, Pastor Nilson do Amaral Fanini, the "Brazilian Billy Graham," took up the chorus of moral panic in the late 1970s and early 1980s.[33] His sermons, journal, radio addresses, and television program (all called *Reencontro*) took an increasingly strident tone about critical threats to youths, the family, gender, and sexuality. In 1977, Fanini's sermon "Let Us Evangelize" appeared in the July issue of *Reencontro*. Fanini professed acute shock and horror at "seeing so much sin." Young people's "revolt against authority, against their parents," seemed based in a "revolt against God." According to Fanini, "The Devil has poured the acid of hell—drugs—into the lives of millions of people. Pornography has invaded literature, theater, and even day-to-day language."[34] From here *Reencontro* moved into classic moral panic about "Sodom and Gomorrah" and heavily gendered anxieties about women's "bodies given over to the desires of the flesh."[35]

At this point (1983–84), *Reencontro* brimmed with articles marking nationally visible Baptists' transition into a politics that centered on moral panic. The sense of an *acute* crisis (rather than a transcendent, consistent state of worldly sinfulness) suffused these pieces. As Delcyr de Souza Lima wrote in August 1983, "Immorality, permissiveness of behaviors, are assuming proportions *never before seen*, helped along by the mass media. Pornography has become an industry ... without society reacting at all. Homosexuality puts on airs of being a mere option of human liberty and is accepted with indulgence, when not with actual appreciation. The family is deteriorating and producing an immense number of traumatized children. . . . Vices enslave ... in Brazil, destroying health, morality, the work force, and the family. Drugs reach even children of school age."[36] A year later, João Bernardes da Silva—a fellow Baptist and president of the evangelical Trans-World Radio in Brazil— made this sort of panic even more classically about children, whom "defective, so-called progressive education" exposed to "comic books ... obscenity ... pornography, television and movies filled with violence and sex."[37]

Few evangelical outlets reached the heights of moralistic outrage regularly produced by the Publishing House of the Assemblies of God in Brazil (CPAD). CPAD eventually became Brazil's, then Latin America's, largest evangelical publishing house, and in 1997 it even established a new outpost in Miami to cater to Latinos in the United States.[38] In the 1970s, the outfit's Portuguese-language books, magazines, journals, and glossies targeted youths with the message that modernity meant moral—that is, gender and sexual—cataclysm. Nels Lawrence Olson, a Wisconsin-born missionary who served in Brazil for over fifty years and became a key part of the national assembleiano landscape, published several books, including *O lar ideal* (The ideal hearth, 1983). Drawing on Billy Graham, Olson first denounced "the feminist movement that insists that ... woman be 'liberated' from the position that God has given her as wife, mother, and homemaker [and from] her vocation to occupy the second [subordinate] place in the household." Olson complained of the "great moral decadence that is apparent today" and moved on to discuss youths in terms redolent of the moral panic of ten, if not fifteen, years past.[39] Bemoaning the generation gap and a general revolt against "law and order" among young people, he pointed to "youths who revolt against work and study: they sit around on corners, all *cabeludo*, experimenting with drugs. [G]roups of them, boys as well as girls, rent apartments and pass the time playing guitar and singing in their way. They are in revolt even against corporeal cleanliness: they stop washing themselves and combing their hair." Clarifying the transnational nature of the problem, Olsen made reference to "hippies" and to Berkeley's countercultural "provos."[40]

CPAD's *Jovem Cristão* (Young Christian) directed this message at young crentes themselves. Writing in early 1979, soon-to-be editor Abraão de Almeida managed to condemn young people, feminism, pornography, substance abuse, mass media, masturbation, and hippies in a two-page article. "SEX," he wrote. "The appeals [to it] are overwhelming. Movie posters . . . try to disarm the moral reserves of passersby and draw them into the quagmire of low sensuality, of vile pornography." Worse yet, he added, was "the new product for consumption: the sexual liberation of women." The visit of North American sexologist Shere Hite—whose books were nationally banned—to Brazil in 1978 left Almeida and his fellow pastors near apoplectic. Almeida quoted one of his colleagues on the "theses put forth by the sociologist from the other America: 'She has come to teach Brazilian women to be prostitutes.'" He rounded out his diatribe with the assertions that "hippies confused liberty with libidinousness" and that true "Christian liberty" mean "liberation from the claws of sin and, consequently, from the ephemeral vices and pleasures of this life."[41]

Contemporary and later *Jovem Cristão* articles drove these points home even more stridently. Geremias do Couto's "Delinquent Youth: The Problem of the Century" argued that "human behavior has degenerated" especially vis-à-vis young people's sexuality. "Prostitution . . . the illicit and immoral commercialization of sex," he wrote, with notes of incredulity, "even involves young homosexual males, initiated in that practice when they were very young."[42] The editorial "Infamous Passions," in 1980, execrated sexual "iniquities" and "abominations" alongside the idea that homosexuality, ever "recognized as an abomination before God[,] . . . is become tolerated, admitted, forgiven."[43] Articles from the next several years had such revealing titles as "Flirting Seen in the Eyes of God," "Sexuality, Rebellion, and Dressing Yourself," "The Prostitution of Sex," "Modern Sexuality and the Bible," and "The Curse of Rock and Roll."

The fierceness of such CPAD publications appeared most vituperatively in Claudionor de Andrade's *Há esperança para os homossexuais!* (There is hope for homosexuals!), which had much less to say about hope than about the wages of sin. Lamenting "a generation that has come to breathe sex" because "today, everything is saturated with sex," Andrade made the sensational claims that homosexuals "rejoice in sodomizing our children" and that "those in the know affirm that at least seventy percent of the performers of that filthy and perverted rhythm [rock and roll] are homosexuals." Homosexuals, he wrote, deserved the "plagues" that God sent to punish them for their sins: "degeneracy," exemplified by Oscar Wilde; and AIDS, a "deserved punishment" and the "divine response" to the unprecedented moral crisis Andrade perceived. Indeed, he implied that readers should, in some way, rejoice in the death of icon Rock Hudson. Reveling in the visceral details of Hudson's last days, Andrade lapsed into metaphor: "Ulcerated, giving off an unpleasant order, [Hudson] staged the final act in his own tragic play which was, at the same time, funny."[44]

It is important to note that these outpourings of moral panic simultaneously reflected a long tradition of doctrinal and moral antimodernism among fundamentalists in Brazil and in the United States (dating at least to the emergence of fundamentalism itself) and an unprecedented foray beyond mere pulpit millenarianism—an adoption of politics as politics-of-moralism. Indeed, the linkage of historic, doctrinal antimodernism and fundamentalism with contemporary moral panic occasionally grew explicit, as when *O Obreiro*, in an issue that railed against ecumenism and immorality (putatively linked), took time to denounce theological "modernism." An eponymously titled editorial ("Modernism") featured the cautionary tale of an Icelandic minister who, "imbued with his modernist ideas (and how many of these exist today!)," had contradicted the core beliefs of fundamentalists by straying from biblical literalism. "Modernism," here, meant in part what it had meant since the turn of the century, connecting the antimodern pulpits of New Jersey to those of Rio de Janeiro: the grievous sin of declaring that the Bible was "just a myth" or a set of parables.[45] In *A Seara* (a Christian lifestyle magazine also published by the Assemblies of God), meanwhile, Pastor José Apolônio further clarified the interdependent relationship between doctrinal antimodernism and moral panic, in an interview whose headline read "We Need to Save Our Doctrine." Asked about the "biggest problem facing the evangelical family today," Apolônio held forth about modernism in both senses. The "biggest problem" was that "the evangelical family is undermined by an avalanche of innovations, that is, the tendency toward change in doctrine and in customs. . . . Today there is so much laxity, *and* so much modernism."[46]

Conservative evangelicals in this moment thus wove together historic antimodernism and an acute sense of moral crisis. As may be partially evident from the foregoing references, they did so with relentless attention to seemingly minor, repetitive aspects of everyday life. The devil, in other words, lay in the details: women's behavior, sexuality, family life, pornography, homosexuality, music, television. Vague, general catchphrases about the "wave of immorality" or "today's permissiveness" gave way to detailed laments about

N. Lawrence Olson, "A mulher virtuosa" (The virtuous woman), *A Seara*, May 1983, 11. Photo taken by author and used by permission of Casa Públicadora das Assembléias de Deus.

rock 'n' roll, birth control pills, miniskirts, divorce, free love, sex work, adultery, and other devilry ranging from substance abuse to posture to hairstyles to reading material.[47] As in other evangelical communities, for example, women's hair received a disproportionate share of anxiety. As early as 1969, *A Seara* warned against "the snares of Satan," foremost among which stood women's hair, clothing, jewelry, and makeup. In another nod to the ways in which the specifics of the New Right transcended national borders, Brazilian evangelical conservatives mirrored North American religious rightists' obsessive focus on what one historian has called "women's acts," on gender and the control of women as the linchpin of traditional culture.[48] Referring (as was the custom) to women with short hair as "nude," the magazine launched into a lengthy, but representative, screed: "Hair was given to [Woman] as a veil.... How many women, who have natural beauty and become deformed by the lack of composure with regard to hair!... How many women have disobeyed the law of the Lord, for the law of the scissor! Yes, now I am pretty! For whom? Certainly for the world, for the devil and the flesh. [P]ainting the face [also] insults God.... Disguised females go about painted in the churches, at the cinema, on the sidewalk and all around. Beware of them, young *crentes*!" An article in the same issue denounced—alongside "socialism" and "rebellion"—the "apostasy" of "nudism, beginning with a woman's hair."[49]

III. "Nosso Terreno": Abandoning the Apolitical

Conservative evangelicals unerringly supported the military regime, even as its repressive excesses alienated moderate Christians who (like many) had initially supported the coup. I will discuss this overt support presently, and in chapter 3 we shall see security forces further reciprocating this support, after a fashion. First, however, it is worth noting that as the dictatorship ground on, moral panic became an avenue by which these conservatives not only reconciled themselves to secular politics and the formerly forbidden things "of the world" but also drew close to the regime itself. Political activity crept into evangelical life and media beginning in the 1960s, though the idea of crente politics as new and alien remained present well into the democratic transition. As Presbyterian Humberto Carlos Parro (himself the mayor of Osasco, São Paulo) noted with evident surprise in 1983, "There are many honest [politicians], more honest ones than corrupt ones, even though evangelicals have the opposite impression."[50] Such mistrust, however, had already been on the wane for years, as Protestants in Brazil took increasing interest in the secular world. By the late 1970s, *Mensageiro da Paz* had commenced printing a regular "Informação" segment, which brought news of the mundane into the denominational newsletter—and continued to do so despite complaints from some readers that such political news belonged strictly in "secular publications."[51] Notably, as "Informação" became a fixture, it too revealed the tendency toward moral panic as a point of entrée into worldly engagement: the segment regularly featured news about moral and sexual misconduct. The January 1980 edition, for example, juxtaposed news of rampant prostitution and "moral crime" in Iran; descriptions of a protest held by three hundred "women of 'nighttime activities' and *travestis*" in São Paulo; the contention that pornography worldwide reflected "wrongheaded sexual liberation"; and an alarming report on syphilis and other STIs in the United States, with the editorial comment that "the results of the permissiveness represented by 'free love' are apparent: deformed children, blindness, paralysis, insanity ... and countless moral costs."[52]

Attention to the "news" of the world, however, was just the beginning; crentes also began taking a much more active role in electoral politics. To the surprise of some observers, Baptists and Assemblies of God enjoyed disproportionate representation in the opening salvos of the newly redemocratized Brazil. Of thirty-four evangelical delegates at the national constitutional convention in 1988, twenty-two came from these two denominations alone.[53] The decade before the convention, in fact, had presaged this readiness of *batistas* and assembleianos to take the political plunge. It was in these two denominations that the strongest voices of politicization emerged, arguing that the faithful must enter politics for the express purpose of defending evangelicals' moral interests.

By the late 1970s, *Mensageiro da Paz* had begun to suggest to the Assemblies that the nonsacral world demanded their attention after all. The "Informação" segment digested news of the world and revolved around conservative moral and political anxieties, from Carnival ("known for the participation of men disguised as women") to abortion to Soviet relations.[54] In 1978, admitting that many evangelicals were still "hostile" toward the idea of political involvement, *Mensageiro* director and leading assembleiano spokesperson Joanyr de Oliveira exemplified advocacy of politics for morality's sake. "We must consider," he wrote, "authentic evangelicals are in Parliament as interpreters of our points of view," acting merely as rightful mouthpieces of evangelicals across Brazil to "combat gambling," "condemn alcoholism," and generally "expose to public opinion that which any 'born again' man has in his heart" in moral terms.[55] Here Oliveira trod a thin but increasingly common line—one that divided the proscribed politics of the mundane from what some conservative evangelicals called "nosso terreno": the public politics of private morality, spirituality, and sexuality. In the waning years of dictatorship, Baptists and Pentecostals routinized this approach, such that by the time of the constitutional assembly, there were open calls for evangelical political dominance.

Nemuel Kessler, sometime editor of *A Seara*, perhaps best exemplified this trend. In an editorial titled "Our Candidates at the Constituent Assembly," Kessler urged readers to form a block of moralistic voting. Notably, he foregrounded a slate of issues galvanizing religious conservatives in Brazil and abroad: "combating abortion, a war against pornography, the fight to stop the legalization of gambling ... and constant vigilance to avoid the subversion of order." As if to demonstrate the transnational scope of this emergent evangelical sense of political self, Kessler directly cited the example of the United States as a "lesson" in how to moralistically politicize evangelical faith. Kessler admired the "braking action brought into effect by evangelicals in [the United States] regarding the moral degradation, the tendentiously degenerate behavior of various segments of the American people," and the "open Bible and God-given authority" by which Jimmy Swaggart, Pat Robertson, and Oral Roberts "vehemently combated abortion, drugs, prostitution, adultery, Satanism, Rock, and other evils."[56] Accordingly, he called for the same kind of pressure in Brazil. "We can help President José Sarney to moralize this country," he urged.

> What the North American preachers are doing constitutes a great lesson for us, Evangelicals of Brazil. . . . Let's fight against the liberalization of Brazilian censorship, which has permitted the television to be used as a vehicle of adultery, violence, and pornography. Let us fight against the flood of erotic magazines in all the newsstands of the country, and against the advertisements spiced with sexual appeals. Let us reprove . . . those who are attempting to drown this country in rottenness and immorality. . . . *Let us not forget that we are the guardians of morality and of good behavior in this country.*[57]

Engineer-turned–federal deputy Arolde de Oliveira, an adult convert to Baptism, gladly kept that guardianship in mind; in what would become a typical attitude, he argued that he had become a politician precisely to represent the moralism at the heart of the new evangelical politics. He had run for office, he said, because "the political path," guided by evangelical "moral values, constitutes the most sure way to overcome . . . the difficult time through which we are passing." Representing his "evangelical community" and its interests, he assured crente and noncrente listeners, formed his primary mandate in government.[58] Writing in the *Jornal Batista*, José dos Reis Pereira crystallized the "nosso terreno" claim, arguing that Baptists had a duty to step into public conversations about morality and religion. Notably, he and others maintained that this did not invalidate their coreligionists' heretofore vehement apoliticism. During the constitutional convention, Pereira observed, "We [Baptists] have maintained the reserve that has characterized Brazilian Baptists with relation to manifestations of a political character . . . we do not opine with respect to deliberations of a political character; we do not fail, however, to speak out when those deliberations enter into the moral or religious realms. Then we publish editorials and collaborations denouncing officials' exploitation of gambling and their excessive tolerance with respect to eroticism or even pornography. . . . *Morality and religion we consider to be our territory.*"[59]

Pereira left very little to the imagination when it came to the role of Baptists and like-minded evangelicals in this, "their territory." He made claims to a quasi-Falwellian moral majority status, in which pernicious "minorities" of liberals were "extremely active" in trying to derail the constitutional priorities of a "conservative majority." Though in this schematic Pereira placed Baptists at the "center" of the political spectrum, his description of their position belied this claim. Baptists, he wrote, had entered politics in order to quash "ecumenism," "theological liberalism," and "so-called 'theology of liberation' and of its closest relative, international Communism." As we shall see, these were precisely the fault lines that divided conservative from progressive evangelicals and drew the former into the orbit and favor of the regime.[60] Importantly, Pereira demonstrated the ways in which evangelicals were making a claim not only to moralism-as-politics but to avowed conservatism as a quasi-identitarian position. In Brazil, where identifying as "conservative" had long fallen out of favor, Pereira advocated an emergent, if tellingly defensive, willingness to *call oneself conservative*, paving the way for today's identitarian conservatism.[61] Making the case for conservative politicization of the Baptist Church and its press, he contended that "the position of this journal has always been conservative. *There is no shame in being conservative*. Is the great Margaret Thatcher not conservative? Was the greatest statesman that England produced in this century, Winston Churchill, not a conservative? *I don't know why conservatives are afraid to affirm their position.* They let themselves be intimidated by accusations of radicals who call them retrograde, rightist, and reactionary. The Brazilian Baptist *povo* [people; community] is conservative and [this] journal could not be any different."[62]

IV. The Politics of No: Against Ecumenism, against Marxism, against Modernism, against Liberation Theology

This burgeoning conservative identity would prove determinative, not least because it materialized in the context of a military regime that hated and feared (by the mid-1970s, almost above all else) what it perceived as a conspiratorial amalgam of progressive Christianity, ecumenism, Marxism, and moral deviance. As we saw in chapter 1, the regime ferociously opposed Catholic progressivism and supported conservative holdouts. This attitude not only extended to evangelicals, whose debates security forces avidly followed, but influenced a turn away from the Catholic Church and toward conservative evangelicals on the part of officials. These, then, were the fault lines that would divide the evangelical New Right from its left-wing counterparts and create a crucial common ground with the reigning military, which retained not only authority but of course formal control of Brazil's governing apparatuses until 1985. (It is important, that is, to remember that the outgoing military regime, though discomfited by multiclass, popular demonstrations and organizing, ultimately relinquished power over the course of a decade, and based on debates and decisions made *within* the regime.) Opposition to ecumenism, to democratization, to progressive politics, and to social justice initiatives drew the formative evangelical Right closer to the regime—and closer to its fearsome dungeon keepers, for whom, it appears, the enemy of an enemy was a friend. Significantly for the fate of both conservative and progressive Christianity in Brazil, the shared enemy took the amorphous and often conflated shape of the amalgam just mentioned: ecumenical cooperation, progressive Christianity, suspected moral and sexual deviance, and putative Marxism. What might have been an embattled conservative evangelical fringe, in other words, shared this conflated foe with the most powerful forces in the land, both recognized and covert.

The moralism just outlined cannot in fact be separated from correlative antiecumenism, antileftism, and anti-Marxism on the evangelical Right.[63] As we have seen, Baptist pastor José Pereira denounced "moral" dissolution, gambling, and "the excessive tolerance of eroticism and pornography" right alongside "ecumenism," liberation theology, and what he called "its close relative, international communism." In this he was far from alone, as evangelical conservatives across Brazil made similar connections and ferociously demonized ecumenism, reserving—like their allies among North American evangelical conservatives and within Brazil's police state—particular vitriol for the World Council of Churches (WCC).[64] By 1980, for example, *Mensageiro da Paz* presumed enough familiarity with the WCC to refer to it by its acronym in routine, vehement denunciations of the organization as the point of a dissolute, ecumenist, Marxist, modernist spear. A headline article in May 1980 typified the ways in which conservatives' attitudes and language echoed long-standing anticommunist tropes and the counterintelligence jargon of regime insiders: "The tentacles of the WCC insinuate themselves in practically all the evangelical denominations, even the orthodox Assemblies of God in Brazil, because, in surreptitious and indirect ways, . . . we hear among us talk of ecumenical services and ecumenical social events . . . and all in a way that is strongest among our youth." Careful to make complete the sin-ecumenism-modernism-communism circle, the article clarified that "yes, what we are seeing in the modernist ecumenist position is the preparation of religious people for the manifestation of the first Beast of the apocalypse: a worldwide political-religious government. . . . All that interests ecumenists now is the practice of 'theology of liberation' which is nothing more than complete Marxist socialization."[65]

Counseling other pastors, Abraão de Almeida rhetorically asked, "Where is massified ecumenism heading?"—and came up with answers that were, by this point, standard. Dismissively presuming the "Marxification of the Catholic Church," Almeida reported on the WCC's "total rejection of evangelical doctrine and more and more effective rapprochement with the worldwide Marxist movement." Worse, to Almeida's mind, ecumenism's world leaders had engaged not only in "open combat against capitalism" but also in gender-based activism and women's liberation, with a focus on "women in a changing world and the economic exploitation of women."[66] The preoccupations of reactionaries, then, encompassed modernist doctrine, cultural upheaval (especially when it came to gender and sexuality), ecumenism, and progressive theology, all bound up in staunch anticommunism.[67] This reflected broader trends in most of Brazil's Pentecostal and certain of its mainline denominations, where demonization of social justice–minded Christianity led not only to fissures but to the active persecution of coreligionists perceived to be progressive. Purged from important positions in their churches and affiliated institutions, many of those who had opted for openness to liberationist Christianity found themselves further betrayed when conservative crentes cooperated with security forces to facilitate the detention, torture, and even disappearance of progressives.[68] This repressive atmosphere developed perhaps most infamously in the Presbyterian Church, where Pastor Boanerges Ribeiro, styling himself as a "hard-line President," ruled the denomination with an iron fist from 1966 to 1978, or for the bulk of the dictatorship.[69]

V. Cozying Up to the Regime

Such cooperation in marginalizing and even persecuting progressives, as we shall see, formed a key component of approximation with the regime, based in this common enmity. But nearness to the dictatorial agenda, cemented by the stamping out of progressive evangelicalism (the subject of chapter 3), consisted also and importantly in conservatives' anticommunism and authoritarianism. The nascent right wing of evangelicals, that is, maintained a reflexive anticommunism alongside staunch support for military government and repression. At least in part, this related to evangelicals' traditional veneration of hierarchy and institutions—a cultural and doctrinal tendency that grew more pronounced among conservatives over the course of the dictatorship. In the context of national autocracy, pastors extolled the virtues of "authority" from the domestic home to the nation's metaphorical family, linking "domestic insubordination and disrespect for teachers" with the sin of "rebellion" and lack of due respect for governing powers.[70] Even more commonly,

Church leaders invoked an identitarian sense of evangelicals as people who respected extant hierarchy, the phrases *autoridades constituídas* and *poderes constituídos* [established powers and authorities] often serving as shorthand for the naturalization of conservative support for the regime. As Joanyr de Oliveira put it in 1977, the faithful must be careful "not to injure the good relationship that there has always been between the Assemblies of God and the established authorities" and to "preserve among us the principle of respect for the institutions of the Country."[71]

Others voiced more enthusiastic support for military rule. The *Jornal Batista* embraced the coup of 1964 with representative gusto—and, unlike some other Christian publications, the *JB* never repented of that support. "It's about time!" opined the journal in the aftermath of the putsch, drawing on classic anticommunist discourses to condemn the "savvy and opportunist ... communist minority" that had purportedly threatened the country's youths and its stability.[72] In 1968, Baptist leaders insisted that "we are not living in a dictatorship" and supported government repression of student protests ("a political movement in which the Government was attacked while the failed guerrilla 'Ché' Guevara was exalted") and of activist clergy involved in social justice and human rights campaigns, to whom the *Jornal Batista* referred as "guerrillas."[73]

The Assemblies of God and conservative Presbyterians likewise stood behind military government and anticommunist repression. In 1980, with democratization on the horizon, *Mensageiro da Paz* linked into hemispheric networks of fundamentalist anticommunism, reproducing the antimodernist warnings of famed Canadian firebrand Oswald Smith: "Sinister forces operate all around us. False religions proliferate everywhere. Communism, the most powerful weapon yet forged by the satanic mill, threatens to make Christianity disappear."[74] Three years earlier, reflecting the ongoing climate of persecution against progressive Christians, the assembleiano editorial board raised the alarm about communist terrorism *among Brazilian evangelicals*. Uncertain whether the Assemblies of God themselves had been affected, they reported with no little horror the concerns of Saulo de Tardo Baptista, president of the Baptist Convention of Pará and Amazonas, who "denounced the 'frightening infiltration' of Marxism in Latin American seminaries" and affirmed that "the great majority of terrorists still in activity are children of evangelical households." (By this point in the dictatorship, there were very few armed combatants still struggling against the government—most had been decimated in the early 1970s.) While the Presbyterian Church of Brazil (IPB) under Boanerges Ribeiro rooted out progressivism and any hint of "subversion," the even more right-wing Conservative Presbyterians (IPC) drew anticommunist language directly from J. Edgar Hoover. Reviewing a translation of Hoover's *Masters of Deceit* in late 1964, Alceu Moreira Pinto lauded the book's demonstration of "the danger of communism that seeks to subtly infiltrate in the Churches of Christ"—indeed, he noted, among communists' six principal objectives was that of "making contacts with the youth" of religious organizations.[75] Moreover, the Conservative Presbyterian Church wholeheartedly supported the 1964 coup as a "victory of democracy" over the "diabolical [Communist] regime" that "was trying to turn Brazil into Russia's front parlor." Church authorities also openly celebrated repression itself. As the newly empowered military swept aside lives, liberties, rights, and dignities, Conservative Presbyterians rejoiced in political violence against "these puppets of Nikita Khrushchev" and crowed that "for a long time now, Brazil has needed to be expunged."[76]

Endorsing the coup, of course, was not in itself unusual—many individuals and organizations greeted the reality of 1 April 1964, with an enthusiasm (or at least a lack of condemnation) that they would later regret. For conservative evangelicals, however, this support remained constant until the very last days of the regime, and even beyond. The Presbyterian Church of Brazil oversaw what João Dias de Aráujo recalled as an "integration of various sectors" of the Church with the regime, including, in the 1970s, exchanges with institutions of military higher education.[77] Indeed, conservative evangelicals from several denominations made important inroads at one of the intellectual nerve centers of the military-bureaucratic state: the Escola Superior de Guerra (ESG), or National War College. Sprinkling the ranks of students and professors in Brazil's top training program for budding technocrats, evangelicals made a point of spreading the Word at the ESG. As *Jovem Cristão* reported, assembleiano pastors Túlio Barros and João Frazão de Oliveira had, "during the completion of their course at the Escola Superior de Guerra, distributed our literature to professors and students, who had, thus, their first contact with an evangelical publication." Guilhermino Cunha, a conservative Presbyterian (IPB) nabob, not only studied at the ESG but became a lecturer; he held forth on the demonic influence of Cuba and the brilliance of repressive military president Emílio Garrastazu Médici.[78]

The ESG created a peculiar confluence of civilian and military elites who, in the crucial years of the dictatorship, officialized a narrative in which moral-sexual crisis and communist subversion (putatively inseparable phenomena) justified military government and repression.[79] Cunha's work at the school articulated this logic quite precisely, casting him and his brethren as guardians of morality who, naturally, upheld military rule. He directed a working group whose alarm about teenage pregnancy, sex in the media, and "deteriorated" families—in which mothers were no longer "chaste, pure, a saint, a champion embroiderer, baker, and cook"—led to the conclusion that "Brazil, today, is living the greatest crisis of its existence."[80] In his individual work, he wrote in classic ESG form about the relationship between anticommunism and remoralization. "The period before" the 1964 coup, according to Cunha, "was marked by an accentuated decline in the standards of behavior due principally to communist infiltration. This deviation from healthy . . . moral principles was responsible for the weakening of national morality. A strong nation is not built with a morally weak people."[81]

Joining Cunha at the ESG in 1980–1981 was another of the school's most illustrious evangelical scions: Cunha's future ally, Baptist celebrity, and soon-to-be federal deputy Arolde de Oliveira. Oliveira had already accrued power and influence before his stint at the ESG. Originally trained as a military engineer, he earned a degree in economics in Rio de Janeiro before working for the state communications corporation, Embratel. By 1978 he had served two years as the station chief of Embratel's permanent offices in Washington, D.C.—a position he left to work for two further key military-bureaucratic organizations: SUDAM, the Amazon regional development agency, and the National Department of Telecommunications (DENTEL), one of the bodies formed to support the military's broad effort to create an integrated, nation-building communications network. He brought these experiences to the ESG, where he wrote and spoke in institutionally consistent fashion about "Mass Electronic Means of Communication (from the psychosocial to the political)" as well as "Social Communication, Public Opinion, and Censorship." Oliveira favored the latter because, as he saw it, the government must protect "the simple man . . . educated in the Christian Word" from the "noxious messages," the "bigamy," the "human hedonism," and the "destroyed family" that mass media so freely exhibited.[82]

The Word had come to Oliveira himself, in fact, *during* his time at the ESG—via no less a personage than Nilson Fanini, soon to be a Baptist celebrity and a conduit of the regime's power into the hands of a moralistic evangelical Right. A fellow ESG student, Fanini, too, wrote of Brazilian families laid waste by "women's leaving the home to work" and "a whirlwind of [mass] communication that . . . grows perverse."[83] Fanini later recalled his conversion of Oliveira as perhaps his most important interaction at the military school: "By the grace of God, . . . at the Escola Superior de Guerra, we won Dr. Arolde de Oliveira for Christ. At that time, Dr. Arolde was director of DENTEL. Today, he is a member of our Church and a Federal Deputy. Ever since he converted, Dr. Arolde and I began to pray and to fight for [control of] Television Channel 13."[84] This last was a fight, as we shall see, that Oliveira and Fanini would win, cementing the cultural and legislative ascendancy of conservative evangelicalism—what Oliveira called the "evangelical community's . . . important role in the heart of Brazilian society."[85]

That important role, to many evangelicals, revolved around the notions of moral guardianship previously outlined, constructed on behalf of what Antônio Pierucci, in a contemporary analysis, called a "moral majority [*maioria moral*]."[86] Moral guardianship, to conservatives, included the maintenance of one of the military government's most powerful and oft-used repressive arms: censorship. Oliveira himself supported government censorship, and many right-wing crentes shared this view. In the late 1980s, as progressives sought to wrest Brazil's constitutional culture from two decades of military-authoritarian repression, rightist evangelicals strove to preserve censorship. Nostalgic for the days "we all remember, when during the Geisel [military] government, pornographic magazines were prohibited," *Jornal Batista* editor Nilson Dimarzio bemoaned constitutional opposition to censorship. His editorial ("Censorship Censored") called the potential elimination of government censorship "profoundly lamentable for persons of good sense and equilibrium, who seek to fight for the preservation of morality and good customs."[87] Pastor Alberto Blanco de Oliveira argued that crentes must advocate for "liberty without anarchy"—that is, for liberty *with* censorship. Of those who wished to permanently exclude government censorship of mass media, he said, "No, that is not democracy, nor liberty, but libertinism." He continued, "Those who like pornography [and] those who think the exploitation of sex by publicity agencies is beautiful need to respect those who want to see something else in magazines and on their televisions. Another grievance is that of homosexuality. The homosexuals who want to see their abnormality respected need to respect the sensibility of those who are normal. . . . Is it necessary to lose good upbringing and manners in order to establish the New Republic?"[88]

Fanini, characteristically, defended the censorial policies of the last two military administrations. In 1977, as he worked to gain national visibility, he exhorted listeners to combine evangelization with promotion of censorship—which he construed as a point of commonality with the military government: "We must evangelize Brazil because the devil is trying to destroy man with . . . pornography. Let us pray for and support our authorities . . . to avoid the pouring out of this acid from hell."[89] Daso Coimbra, whose fears of rampant group sex we witnessed earlier, made clear that "freedom of the press and liberation from censorship" were to blame for the explosion of "pornography and depravation."[90] Without effective moral censorship, asked Claudionor de Andrade (he of the "hope" for homosexuals), "why are we paying taxes?"[91]

VI. "Good Standards": Embracing Fundamentalist Evangelicals

Conservative evangelicals, then, maintained support for the military regime and for repressive policies, and did so even as the dictatorship shed domestic and international allies. Antiecumenism, moralism, and anticommunism drew the regime and the reactionaries together; yet this was just the beginning of a fruitful relationship for both parties. The regime's desire to lean away from (or perhaps even punish) the Catholic hierarchy, seen increasingly as a source of criticism, opposition, and subversion (see chapter 1), led to key developments in the relationship between the state and evangelicals: persecution of Protestant progressives, which we shall investigate in chapter 3, and the direct and active promotion of religious conservatives to positions of power and influence. There was an exchange of favors and resources here—conservative evangelicals backed the regime publicly and privately, and the regime in turn granted favors and aid to conservative evangelicals, most notably in the form of media platforms and electoral assistance. To put this another way, the state leaned *toward* conservative evangelicals, empowering what might otherwise have remained an extremist fringe in Brazil's politics and culture.[92] The configuration of the New Right that emerged at this moment did so in large part under the auspices of the dictatorship; and did so in such a way that, for the first time in decades, made conservatism respectable as such. As José dos Reis Pereira tellingly affirmed, "There is no shame in being conservative."

Evangelicals and the overt and covert forces of the state acknowledged the definitive turn away from the Catholic Church and concomitant support for conservative evangelicals. In chapter 3, we shall investigate how this turn also entailed repression of left-wing evangelicals. When it came to rightist Protestants, however, agents of the state moved from ambivalence to unreserved celebration. State agents, who formerly tended to ignore Protestants, began to seriously evaluate crente theological and political positions, and to describe them as "good standards," possessed of "a balanced line of pastoral activity, where the social aspect is prioritized *without*, however, diminishing the spiritual side." Agents from the Naval Intelligence Center, surveilling the First World Baptist Congress on Urban Evangelism, in 1983, could scarcely contain their enthusiasm. Delighted by the congress's general anti-Marxism, they took its theological underpinnings seriously, galvanized by "severe criticisms of 'progressistas' and the teachings contained in Liberation Theology." [93]

By 1981, security forces considered conservative evangelicals a viable alternative to working with the troublesome "progressistas" of the Catholic Church. Gloating about "defections" from the ecumenical movement, the Rio de Janeiro branch of the National Intelligence Service (SNI) explained that "differently from what occurs in the Catholic Church, where disagreement [with liberation theology] is prohibited from being made public by the hierarchy, the dissidences among the protestants have begun to take the form of diverse publications." As examples of such antiprogressive "dissidence," the report contained issues of *Mensageiro da Paz* as well as the propaganda of the missionary William "Bill" LeRoy, himself a disciple of infamous North American reactionary Carl McIntire. The agents noted appreciatively that, while Catholics were lost to left-wingers embraced by the Church hierarchy itself, eminent and vocal Protestants, including the internationally acclaimed likes of Billy Graham and the Salvation Army, had attacked the progressive alternative in Christianity. Two years earlier, the Porto Alegre SNI had taken a similar tack, dismissing the Catholic Church as utterly subverted and thus, with any luck, likely to lose out to the "seitas" (sects—a contemporary term for Protestants, still considered somewhat cultish). This, the SNI explained, was merited because the Catholic Church had shown itself pervaded with "exaggerated preoccupation with temporal concerns" and neglectful of spirituality.[94]

Evangelical conservatives themselves displayed a general awareness of this—that is, of themselves as the inheritors of the mantle of "guardians of morality" and of their ascendancy as favored by the regime. In 1977, assembleiano Samuel Escobar wrote in "The Christian and Politics" that evangelical conservatives were poised to eclipse not only Marxist-tainted Catholics but even Catholic conservatives, who could not help but be affected by the weaknesses of their coreligionists.[95] The ever-vocal Joanyr de Oliveira, meanwhile, was more direct, articulating the transition he saw happening from Catholic to evangelical power: "These days, the voice of the Catholic Church no longer influences the government ... above all because the [Catholic] clergy and [the federal government] are experiencing one of the most serious crises in the history of their relations.... It's the hour and the turn of the evangelical churches to have their say."[96]

Confident pronouncements like these began to proliferate among the brethren, and not without good reason.[97] As we shall see in chapter 5, titular authorities as well as security forces threw their support behind not only Brazilian conservatives but also international conservative celebrities and organizations. Indeed, Bill LeRoy, whom the Rio de Janeiro SNI praised in 1981, was just one of several agents working at the behest of Carl McIntire. Among McIntire's Brazilian allies supported by the regime was the fundamentalist, conservative Presbyterian firebrand Israel Gueiros and his family. For the Gueiroses, dialogue with McIntire had led to exchange with conservative missionaries and trips to the United States in the 1940s and 1950s, which had borne spectacular fruit.[98] The family, led by Israel and his uncle, Jerônimo, embraced fundamentalism, then broke with more mainstream Presbyterians and carved out their own peculiarly antimodern fiefdom in their native Recife.[99] At the height of the crisis, in 1954, Israel Gueiros taxed Brazilian Presbyterians as "adulterous" and "modernistic," then dramatically departed the denomination with certain members of his congregation.

Gueiros might be considered the most reactionary of Brazilian mainline Protestants, cut from the same cloth as McIntire himself. Gueiros's personalistic leadership, generally intemperate behavior, vicious attacks on other ministers, and lifetime of vitriolic anticommunism and antimodernism gained him a reputation that would last decades.[100] Yet he received the endorsement of central SNI authorities in Brasília, who cited Gueiros, alongside Nilson do Amaral Fanini, Leivas Macalão, José dos Reis Pereira, and Abraão de Almeida as conservative evangelical counterbalances who might stymie a putative international Catholic conspiracy (fed by the WCC) to found a subversive "popular Church" in Brazil.[101] Indeed, like other conservative Presbyterians, the Gueiros clan thrived under military rule, from persecuting their enemies to expanding their power base in the North and holding formal and lucrative political office. Nehemias Gueiros helped craft a decree-law consolidating military rule in 1965; Evandro Gueiros became a powerful government attorney; and Eraldo Gueiros even rose to the governorship of Pernambuco (1971–75).[102]

Israel Gueiros represented an extreme form of antimodernist fundamentalism, akin to that of US counterparts with whom he closely collaborated (see chapter 5). Yet his warm reception among regime spies—alongside the ongoing power of the Gueiros clan in the North—was but one example of the dictatorship's alliance with extremists. The eyes of the regime closely tracked the movements and ideas of conservative evangelicals and tended to look on them with surprising approbation, given the fire-and-brimstone tenor of these individuals and communities. *Mensageiro da Paz* brimmed with violent millenarianism, vitriolic appeals to repent, and the print equivalent of pulpit thumping or "holy rolling." Yet because this apocalypticism took the form of antimodernist antiecumenism, it won the favor of officials. They didn't like *everything* they saw; in fact, SNI agents rather held their noses at what they evidently considered *Mensageiro*'s poor taste and cheap tactics: "In its headlines, such as 'Does the Bible Defend Prostitution?' it seeks to stir up . . . doubt and sensationalism . . . using a technique long abandoned by more honest publications." Yet in general, these agents rated *Mensageiro*, alongside other CPAD publications, "a newspaper of good standards."[103]

Furthermore, the SNI used *Mensageiro* as a source of *reliable information* about the WCC and the supposed machinations of ecumenists. That is, even if the agents held their extremist, Pentecostal allies in some measure of disregard, they embraced even the wildest theories about shared enemies. This meant that officers of the regime made common cause with sensational extremists, such as Abraão de Almeida. When *Mensageiro* reprinted an excerpt from his *Babylon, Then and Now* (CPAD, 1982), which concluded that the ecumenical movement was the awful fulfillment of the biblical prophecy, SNI agents in Rio de Janeiro forwarded it to central authorities as evidence of evangelicals' allied position in the fight against subversion. Indeed, the agents apparently underlined key passages from Almeida's description of the WCC, including the assertion that ecumenists "seek to impose this new Babel. . . . They appeal to political measures, and demand collective solutions, . . . facilitating Communists' seizure of power."[104] To SNI officials, this constituted worthwhile intelligence, not on the religiosity (then extraordinary, less so today) of Almeida and his ilk but also on the progressive enemy and the merit of evangelical conservatives as allies.

If they embraced outlets like *Mensageiro* with some tepidness, members of the dictatorial government nevertheless warmed even to the most questionable of allies among conservative evangelicals. Intelligence analysts in Brasília, by 1980, were willing to rule favorably on the likes of Paulo Maciel de Almeida, a little-known pastor who had taken to writing long, colorful, rather delirious letters to General João Figueiredo, then president of Brazil. The letters displayed a penchant for the supernaturalism common in evangelical circles but far outside the mainstream. In one letter, Almeida informed Figueiredo, "Mr. President, in the early morning of the 30th of September of 1979, I dreamed that your Excellence was my father." The missive prophesied a "great social convulsion" that would surely take place the next month unless "avoided by a divine intervention to be done through me." The agents acknowledged Almeida's "good dose of eccentricity" but took care to note his "great aversion to the progressive clergy" (which they underlined in their report). They further recounted his bizarre habits *insofar as those involved opposition to or harassment of progressive Christians*. He had challenged the papal nuncio to a theological debate in which Almeida sought a declaration, in the name of Pope Paul VI, that the Catholic Church was "not a true Church of Christ [and] no more than a commercial organization, camouflaged as religious"; and Almeida had the "habit of collecting . . . a dossier of the activities of Catholic priests." All of this led to the agents' conclusion: Almeida, whatever his oddities, was a solid ally. In their words, he "seems to be committed

to the Revolution of 31 March 1964" and "has good ideas." Perhaps most notably, they affirmed that he "is a mentally balanced person."[105]

Almeida was an outlier in terms of his tactics; but ideologically and theologi-
cally, he represented the variety of conservative pastor with whom agents of the
regime made common cause in the 1970s and 1980s. Repeatedly, they took note
of conservative Christians for their helpful opposition to *progressistas*, and the
government eye for cooperation ranged from small-time preachers to nationally recognized leaders, like Robinson Cavalcante, Israel Gueiros, Nilson Fanini,
Leivas Macalão, José dos Reis Pereira, and Abraão de Almeida.[106] As we shall
see in chapter 4, they also lavished praise on the national and international
organizations these men helped form, including the reactionary groups the
Latin American Evangelical Confraternity (CONELA), the Confederation of
Fundamentalist Evangelical Churches of Brazil (CIEF), the Latin American Alliance of Christian Churches (ALADIC), and its parent organization, McIntire's International Council of Christian Churches (ICCC or CIIC).

Importantly, this kind of favorability on the part of regime functionaries
extended to the explicitly political. In the 1980s, the police forces of the regime, fearing and resenting democratization itself, wrung their hands at the
potential for what they called "malicious," left-wing co-optation of the return
to electoral politics. In an effort to prevent this, security officials gathered massive amounts of data on candidates for elected office, openly aligning themselves with "those labeled of the Right."[107] Promoting legislative conservatism,
intelligence officials could scarcely contain their enthusiasm for moralistic
evangelical pastors as candidates. With many new faces on the political scene,
intelligence agencies tended to presume the suitability and reliability of those
who fit a certain mold: conservative, moralistic, and evangelical, especially
Baptist or assembleiano. Archconservative Daso Coimbra appeared as the
"conservative, discreet, virtuosic connoisseur of legislative works." Of Jeremias
Soares de Oliveira, an assembleiano already accused of having misused public
funds, the SNI wrote that "he is possessed of the most wholesome democratic
principles" and clarified that he "has a favorable position . . . toward the federal
government." Pastor Matheus Iensen, soon to be made infamous by accusations of corruption, was among those political partners whose electoral fate
worried SNI officials—in part because they considered him a friend not just of
conservative government but of the intelligence agency itself, whose future
seemed dubious in the face of a new constitution. A report that purported to
"evaluate the degree of trustworthiness" of politicians "in the sense of their
potential actions in the defense of the interests of this agency [the SNI]" included Iensen in a list of those considered "trustworthy." A separate report that

same year fretted about the electability, given redistricting, of several allies of the former regime, including Iensen, other "pastores evangélicos," and former military officers themselves.[108] In 1986, the head of the Army Intelligence Center expounded at length about the prospects for the new constitution, exhibiting ongoing hostility toward "so-called 'progressives'" and concern that the convention might serve "the interests of the Left, by allowing it its always-plotted seizure of power." The general took comfort, however, in the presence of conservative Protestants who might "guarantee the [constitutional assembly] with an evangelical 'lobby'" and ensure that the convention's proportions be, "numerically, conservative."[109]

João de Deus Antunes, supported by the Assemblies of God, combined two traits that would come to form hallmarks of early evangelical politics: corruption and homophobic moralism. When progressive evangelicals met to try (in the words of Zwinglio Motta Dias) to "rescue the term evangelical, because it means so much to all Christians" from the clutches of conservatives who were basically co-opting it, Antunes showed up at the meeting uninvited, essentially to champion corruption. He agreed that he was a "cronyist" (*fisiologista*) and insisted that "everyone who goes to the national legislature does so to engage in cronyism (to trade votes for personal favors). . . . I just do it on a higher moral plane." Perhaps that "moral plane" referred to his homophobia, an element in Antunes's pronounced moralism. He had denounced (as "the curse of Sodom and Gomorrah") legislation that would prevent anti-LGBT discrimination. Despite all this, the SNI judged him "of the center in the ideological field" and added that he "has a very good relationship with the Intelligence Community"—that is, with the SNI itself and other policing agencies.[110]

Intelligence observers often noted the moralism of their favored candidates: they found Antunes "possessed of great religious convictions, and [he] advocates social peace, morality, and good behavior"; while Iensen was said to have the support of several other religious denominations, not least because he was "considered 'extreme' in his defense of religious doctrines." Authorities exuded praise for other candidates and politicians described as "conservative," such as Antônio de Jesus Dias, who "was elected with the votes of the conservative wing of . . . society because he presented an anti-communist, moralistic language" and because he was a "tireless fighter for the principles of Christianity and of good behavior, against the presentation of scenes of nudism and sex on Television." And they described Pastor Altomires Sotero Cunha as a "rookie in political life" who had the support of Baptists and Pentecostals. "Being a conservative, evangelical, and businessman, he will defend . . . propositions favorable to private initiative as well as social issues. He has pronounced himself in favor of the political economy of the Federal Government."[111]

Indeed, at this juncture, backing the federal government marked a major opportunity and a turning point in the history of evangelical politics—one of the keys to the religious Right's ascendancy in Brazil. This was part of what government officials privately acknowledged as a "troca de apoio"—a trading of favors—between evangelicals and the presidency, in which conservative evangelicals would gain power and patronage in direct exchange for their opposition to more popular forces in late authoritarian and then newly democratized Brazil. This was especially true during the administration of José Sarney, whose doubtful legitimacy marked a fault line in Brazilian politics; by this point, however, evangelicals had grown adept at cozying up to the regime in exchange for favors and resources.

VII. Trading Favors: The Regime, the Reactionaries, and the Platforms of the Religious Right

Sarney remained a force in Brazilian politics in the 2010s. When he retired from the Senate, he was the longest-serving member of Congress and dubiously distinguished as the only surviving ex-president not to have been elected by direct vote. By that time, too, Sarney had something of a mixed record when it came to evangelicals in politics. In 2011, Sarney (alongside Brazil's president, Dilma Rousseff) was honored at the National Meeting of Evangelical Leaders for his role in granting cultural patrimony status to evangelical music. Just a year before, however, in October 2010, Sarney joined former Brazilian president Fernando Henrique Cardoso in denouncing the entrée of religious and moral issues (particularly abortion) into politics. "I think," opined Sarney, "that when we have religion participating in politics, we inevitably have a path that will end in fanaticism."[112] But Sarney's relationship with evangelical, moralistic politics began rather more auspiciously—in 1988, when Sarney himself was president of the republic. Early that year, Sarney became the first Brazilian head of state to grace the general assembly of the Brazilian Baptist Convention with an official visit. The visit, during which Sarney paused for photographs with Baptist leaders, was emblematic of the ascendancy of right-wing evangelicals in the Brazil of redemocratization, a time in which they not only supported the military regime and its legacies but traded on their newfound connections to garner a firm foothold in Brazil's political and media cultures.

From the late 1970s onward, as conservative evangelicals politicized and drew closer to the regime, they developed channels of communication and support with centers of authority, and these channels would prove both lucrative and generative of influence. During the long transition to democracy, the burgeoning evangelical Right achieved a sort of lockstep with the outgoing military regime, laying the foundations for right-wing evangelical visibility and influence in the postmilitary period. That lockstep hinged on negotiation not only around the moralism explored earlier but also on more mercenary relations with the government. In other words, rightist evangelicals shared, and championed, the demobilizing military state's moral agendas, then reaped further benefits by leveraging moralism and backing those forces within the state that sought as conservative a transition to democracy as might be contrived.

Rio de Janeiro's television Channel 13, mentioned earlier in Fanini's reminiscence about converting Arolde de Oliveira, epitomizes another critical way in which rightist evangelical power coalesced. As individual deputies from various denominations formed the incipient *bancada evangélica*, crentes gained national visibility and institutional strength, particularly via tax status and broadcasting concessions from the federal government. When Oliveira recounted his victories on behalf of evangelicals, foremost among them was the achievement of tax-exempt status for *Reencontro*. Oliveira and fellow right-wing evangelical deputy Igo Losso lobbied "in innumerable audiences with the President of the Republic and other Ministers of State" to have *Reencontro* declared a public utility.[113] Via similar processes, other evangelical media outlets added their voices to the tax-exempt chorus—Matheus Iensen, whose company had acquired two radio stations in the 1970s, laid the foundations for a radio empire when he secured Radio News of Peace as a public utility in 1988.[114]

Reencontro's star, like those of other evangelical media organizations, only waxed brighter. In 1979, organizers claimed that this was the single television program capable of reaching the most Brazilians, with sixty-five broadcasting stations and 480 syndicated broadcasters.[115] State interest in and support for this and other programs increased as Fanini and his colleagues brought their programs in line with the moral agenda of the Figueiredo government. By 1982, these links had grown strong enough that Figueiredo appeared prominently in Fanini's famous, and then-unprecedented, *lotação* (selling-out) of Maracanã for a prayer meeting. The event, entitled God Save the Family, featured Fanini himself, flanked by the president and several ministers of state, before an audience of 150,000 people, demonstrating evangelicals' growing

President João Figueiredo speaking at Maracanã at Pastor Nelson Fanini's historic prayer meeting in the Rio de Janeiro stadium, 1982. Photo available at https://www.flickr.com/photos/32341837@No5/6166485942.

power. Beyond sanctioning the event with his official presence, President Figueiredo took to the podium himself. "My dear, dear friends," he told the gathered throng, "the teachings of the Gospels, which for seven years now *Reencontro* has transmitted to us, are the most secure guide for Man to develop his talent. . . . In a world thrown into tumult by the constant change, those teachings preserve the elemental values of human beings, of their dignity and their spirituality."[116]

Each of the parties involved recognized the significance and the mutual benefit of this landmark moment. Months prior, the possibility of a presidential appearance had been researched and recommended by the Rio de Janeiro branch of the SNI, at the behest of central authorities. Intelligence officials waxed eloquent about Fanini, presenting him as a close ally of the state and seeking to deepen that alliance. The report recalled his politics of conservative morality, his status as an ESG alum, and his *already* privileged access to state resources. Fanini had secured funds from the Ministry of Health, via back channels, to provide a food program to potential converts, "mechanized by the State." The agents strongly recommended that the president make an appearance at the Maracanã event, despite the fact that Figueiredo already had another commitment that afternoon. They further advised the president to follow the Baptist leader's directions as to what to say: "Fanini suggests, for the presidential speech, the topic 'Condemnation of Pornography—Defense of the Nation's Moral and Spiritual Values of the Family.'"[117] Speaking for all evangelicals, Arolde de Oliveira affirmed this moment as a landmark. "Never," he observed, "has the evangelical *povo* been granted so much prestige by the federal Government."[118] Even nonevangelical conservatives, supporters of the regime who opposed *progressistas*, praised the Maracanã crusade as a bold, worthy move on the part of authorities and evangelicals. One prominent conservative praised the president's speech and half complained that "in this moment of ecumenism, the Catholic hierarchs probably won't recognize the importance of this achievement [the Maracanã prayer meeting], at which the President of the Republic appeared."[119]

The prayer meeting, however, marked just one milestone in Fanini's rise. Government support for *Reencontro*, based on the common focus on "tumult" and the need for reaffirmation of family-based morality, reached a new high-water mark at the end of 1983, when Fanini's and Oliveira's hard work—and their relationship with Figueiredo—paid off. In November of that year, the president chose Fanini's corporation from among thirteen applicants to control Rio de Janeiro's Channel 13, a platform that would lead to even greater national visibility for *Reencontro*.[120] This kind of media access, from Fanini's television show to Iensen's radio holdings, granted conservative evangelicals critical access to developing markets at a time of expansion in Brazil's mass media and laid the foundations for evangelical conservatives' sway over Brazilian media today. Exchanges like these gave conservative evangelicals good reason for their enthusiasm about Figueiredo (and, later, Sarney) and for their optimism about their own ascendancy. In the early 1980s, Fanini and others were ebullient about the rising influence of evangelicals, going so far as to proclaim a "new era" in Brazil's religious and political cultures. As *Reencontro* put it, events like the Maracanã triumph and "the growing space occupied by Pastors, leaders, and issues pertinent to our evangelical community in the mass media, are evidence of a new era for this important segment of Brazilian society."[121]

Closeness to the regime's moral agenda and to postauthoritarian political agendas drew conservative evangelicals into the halls of power, sometimes literally. In 1982, celebrating a planned crackdown on pornography, Figueiredo welcomed a group of evangelical pastors into his office for a public moment of prayer and solidarity. In a videotaped ceremony archived and distributed by the presidential press secretary, the pastors presented Figueiredo with a bible and praised his courage in "taking a stand" against pornography and immorality. Emphasizing "just how much it repulsed me, my government, my friends—the [material of a sexual nature] that I was reading, that I was seeing, that I was hearing," Figueiredo responded that he was taking action against "indecency" because he "just could not stand by." He then thanked and praised the pastors as pillars of Brazil's moral community: "You, sirs, ... defend with intransigence ... the interests of our Christian society. You cannot imagine just how much you are giving to our homeland [*Pátria*]. In particular ... you are serving as a stimulus for me. The generous words that I have just heard; ... I confess, they will serve as a model."[122]

This was, then, indeed a new era—and one that did not, as Sarney's appearance at the Baptist convention indicates, end with military rule itself. In fact, the horse-trading, back-scratching comfort between evangelicals and the government intensified during the Sarney administration and the drafting of the new constitution. Given the president's unelected status and his unpopularity, officials were eager to identify legislators and constitutional assembly members on whom the government might count as allies. The Sarney administration looked to consolidate the president's control and to weaken his opponents. Many among these opponents had envisioned more radical democratization, a promise that seemed likely to be fulfilled upon the election of Sarney's predecessor, Tancredo Neves. Neves, however, died before taking office, leaving Sarney to take power. Intelligence documents provide a clear picture of the way in which officials cultivated the developing relationship between Sarney and conservative evangelicals as an exchange of favors—what SNI documents called a *troca de apoio*. In apparent approbation of the newly minted Evangelical Parliamentary Bloc, a report compiled by SNI officials in Brasília took stock of the bloc's support for the government. Admiring the emergent caucus of evangelical conservatives for its "firmness of principles" in denouncing the hated National Conference of Brazilian Bishops (CNBB) and "clero progressista," the report noted that the conservatives had offered "unrestricted support" to President Sarney in his quest to maintain himself in the presidency. As the SNI observed, this support was obtained in exchange (*troca*) for the president's favorable attitude toward the group, including not only "the interests of the evangelical group (against abortion ... in defense of the family, of morality, religious freedom, and the maintenance of censorship)" but also more tangible patronage: control of the Bureau of Fisheries Development (SUDEPE).[123]

The SNI was confident that this arrangement would "present agreeable features for both parties: the Government and the Evangelical Parliamentary Bloc" and prove to the detriment of "the political component more to the left" in the legislature. Evangelicals, aside from having their moral issues backed by the administration, "would have in hand an organization of national reach (SUDEPE), which will encourage the pastoral work of this group" and—the SNI noted with ill-concealed glee—thus "prevent the ideological preachings of the pastoral commission on fishing, that *progressista* organization tied to the CNBB, which has been building its proselytizing action in this very area." The president, it was understood, "will be able to count on the group of evangelical parliamentarians, who will support him in an unrestricted form." In other words, the Sarney administration and the conservative evangelicals would both win in terms of shared moralism, stymying of progressive Christian efforts, ongoing authoritarianism, and the empowerment of conservative Christians and their agenda. Moreover, the SNI assessed this proposed deal as all the sweeter given the very nature of the participants: "The inherent posture of evangelicals should also be kept in mind—the group spirit, maintained by the very faith that they profess."[124]

This favoritism toward conservative evangelicals by the government was *so* pronounced, in fact, that public outrage and demand for accountability followed. In 1988, representatives of the Brazilian Press Association, the Evangelical Confederation of Brazil, and the Catholic Church met to denounce conservative, evangelical assembly members "accused of receiving favors in exchange for their support of the projects and individuals of the very Government."[125] As various press outlets reported at the time, legislative and juridical commissions investigated the provision not only of favors but also of federal funds in exchange for conservative evangelical votes in support of the Sarney regime.[126] As the *Jornal do Brasil* put it, "A good portion of the evangelicals make preparing the new Constitution a great and lucrative business, trading votes for advantages and benefits for their churches and, many times, for themselves. The new Constitution ... has already furnished ... a television channel, at least a half dozen radio stations, important government posts, benefits of the most varied types, and above all money, lots of money."[127] Paul Freston's nearly contemporary study of evangelicals' entry into politics, published in 1994, affirmed that the *bancada evangélica* had done extremely well when it came to the "political currency" of television and radio concessions.[128]

Outspoken Lutherans and representatives of the Protestant progressive Ecumenical Center for Documentation and Information, frustrated with the increasingly conservative tone of evangelical politics, became the first of many to accuse Matheus Iensen of graft.[129] In the aftermath of Neves's death, with Sarney dubbed a military continuist and lacking the public's confidence, Iensen had floated the parliamentary bill guaranteeing Sarney's presidency for the remainder of Neves's term. Persistent reports in Brazil chalked up

Iensen's media acquisitions to his willingness to cozy up to the conservative forces still linked with the military regime.[130] Indeed, two decades later, the bill was remembered as the "Matheus Iensen Amendment"—reflective of the fact that, as one commentator put it, "at the time, Deputy Iensen was the symbol of the politics of 'you only get when you give.'"[131] Fellow evangelical conservatives, meanwhile, came to Iensen's aid, lauding him as a champion of evangelical morality and visibility, operationalized via music and mass media. As fellow assembleiano deputy Salatiel de Carvalho put it (echoing the defiant tone of Antunes on "cronyism"), "If the President wanted [a mandate of] 100 years in exchange for 100 radio concessions, if it was to disseminate the Gospel, I would do the trade."[132]

The ascendant Baptist conservatives, too, faced criticism that attributed mercenary underpinnings to the Figueiredo-Fanini axis, including criticism from less conservative evangelicals. The progressive bulletin *Aconteceu no Mundo Evangélico* had derided evangelical adherence to censorship; now it took a sharp-tongued approach to Fanini's successes at transforming moralism into celebrity. In 1986, when Fanini spoke of "a New Being" for the New Republic, *Aconteceu* doggedly reminded readers of Fanini's ties to the ESG. With undisguised sarcasm, the newsletter remarked that "the 'Billy Graham of the Third World' [Fanini] now does not seem so constrained in demonstrating his esteem for the New Republic, even though he has long supported the military governments, a stance which earned him the concession of a television station."[133]

Such criticism prompted Arolde de Oliveira to a telling defensiveness about himself, his pastor, and the president just weeks after the Maracanã event. Proudly expounding on the visibility and power accruing to the "evangelical *povo*" based on its ever-closer ties to the presidency, Oliveira fretted that there were those who would detract from this prestige, who "received . . . the news of the President's appearance with a certain cynicism."[134] These views, he insisted, were beyond unwarranted—they were nearly sacrilegious.

> Frivolous analyses might mistakenly construe a correlation with the electoral politics of the moment in the nation. To interpret [the Fanini-Figueiredo relationship] that way is to broaden the hosts of anti-Christians. . . . In truth, the President came [to Maracanã] moved, solely, by the Christian sensibility of the event [and] preoccupied with the necessity of strengthening the family; convinced that the destruction of moral and ethical values . . . cries out for a firm attitude from the government. In short, President João Figueiredo, who is a religious man and

who fears god, decided to participate in the Fanini Crusade because he understands, also, that the perversity manifest in society in our days, has its origins in the loss of spirituality.[135]

Conservative evangelicals, in short, drew close to the centers of governing authority in political spaces where the glacial pace and nonlinear form of the democratization process, combined with antidemocratic and clientelistic machinations, left power in the hands of those who had supported, or continued to support, the military-authoritarian agenda.[136] Moreover, the conservatives did so via a path that linked their moralistic prognostications and reactionisms to those of the outgoing regime and its partisans, while (as we shall see in the next chapter) outspoken progressive evangelicals eschewed this route, embracing social justice and *not* moralism. In the critical years of the late 1970s and early 1980s, conservative crentes shared the language of panic about the family, sexuality, and morality with the Figueiredo and Sarney administrations—and gained a proximity to government that would reward them handsomely.

CHAPTER THREE

Paths Taken, Paths Repressed

Dictatorship, Protestant Progressives, and the
Rightward Destinies of Brazilian Evangelicalism

By late 1988, Pastor Caio Fábio d'Araújo Filho, a liberal Presbyterian and president of the ecumenist evangelization group National Vision for Evangelization (VINDE), had had his fill of the new variety of conservative Christianity,
particularly in its latest, insidious form: televangelism. Reacting to what, by
this time, constituted an onslaught of North American and Brazilian media,
Araújo critiqued the form and the style of these "plastic" pastors. In an interview with the ecumenical journal *Aconteceu no Mundo Evangélico*, Araújo
denounced the "Jimmyswaggartization" of Latin America, including Brazil.
"Jimmy Swaggart," the journal summarized, "is just the tip of the iceberg
which is today's North American Church, which represents what is ultraconservative in the religious scenario of that country."[1] Araújo himself directly
critiqued conservative moralism as false, and a cover for graft. Asked about
TV Rio, controlled by Nilson Fanini, Araújo responded,

> All asceticism which posits lifestyle practices of the "don't touch
> this"/"don't touch that"/"don't drink that" variety has the appearance of
> morality . . . but at the moment of great life decisions, it has no value
> against corruption and sensuality. . . . I hear people talking about evangel-
> ical TV, but it is not [evangelical]—as far as I know, evangelicals have not
> gained a television station and if they have, well, something in the inter-
> nal politics of broadcasting must have been arranged. . . . "Evangelical
> TV" represents a false marketing that does not coincide with reality. . . .
> The only thing different about [TV Rio] is that its proprietor, being a pas-
> tor, has the intention of doing a religious program between 7 and 11 A.M.[2]

On why Pastor Fanini had been favored with the television station, over and
above other desirous candidates (like the *Jornal do Brasil* and Editora Abril
Cultural), Araújo was unequivocal: "It was that rally in Maracanã, the *Reencontro* prayer meeting, which relied on the presence of then-president
Figueiredo—the biggest rally that [the military regime's institutional party]
held. . . . *At that time, evangelicals of that line were the last political support that
that defunct government had recourse to. So, [the TV Rio concession] was a prize*

for Pastor Fanini's perseverance and loyalty. Reciprocal loyalty, bearing even into our days the ramifications of positions favorable to the government."[3]

Many years later, Araújo would come under scrutiny and even face prison for a political scandal of his own. Yet at this moment, in 1988, he gave voice to a well-developed alternative to the Christian Right we encountered in chapter 2. In his rejection of moralism, his opposition to mega-televangelism, his accusations against Christian conservatism, and his choice of a venue—the leftist *Aconteceu*, rooted in ecumenism and supportive of causes from agrarian reform to Afro-Brazilian enfranchisement—Araújo was not alone. Instead, he represented a politicized evangelicalism whose potential, as his complaints about rightist power and graft indicate, was already being foreclosed on.

This chapter sheds light on a critical road not taken, explicating the fate of progressive Christianity in Brazil. The history of Brazilian left-wing Catholicism, its global importance, and the military regime's complicated relationship with the Church is of course quite well known.[4] But what of social justice–minded *evangelicals*, Protestants who turned to liberation theology, ecumenism, and cooperation not only with each other but with Catholics? There existed, in the Brazil of dictatorship, a left-wing Christian world in the making—the potential for a broad and inclusive community of progressives from a variety of churches. Yet this world never truly emerged, certainly not in a form as influential as that of the Christian Right. Progressive Protestants gained some visibility in Brazil, across decades; a handful of left-wing Protestants even served in the national legislature, Lysâneas Maciel and Benedita da Silva the most famous among them. Yet, by 1990, such figures could only seem more exceptional than ever, as conservatism dominated among evangelical clergy and politicians—a state of affairs that has, in most ways, persisted to now.[5] The deeply committed and hardworking activists of today's Christian Left in Brazil—Koinonia and the Ecumenical Center for Documentation and Information (CEDI), the National Council of Christian Churches (CONIC), the Ecumenical Center for Services of Evangelization and Popular Education, and others—have an important and distinguished history, much of it dating to the period in question. Yet quite obviously these are not the most powerful evangelical forces in today's Brazil, nor in the hemisphere. This chapter relates the story of how and why the ascendancy of Brazil's evangelical Right accompanied the frustration of its burgeoning evangelical Left—how and why the road to a powerful progressive Protantism in Brazil was, by and large, not taken.

There was—and is, as the foregoing list of organizations indicates—a notable and active nucleus of leftist Protestant activists and organizations that

developed out of midcentury Brazilian Christians' interest in liberation theology and in cooperation with like-minded Catholics. This included radicals
alongside moderates, anticommunist reformers together with those who incorporated Marxism into their theological and practical approaches. Here we
shall explore what that emergent Left looked like, especially when contrasted
with its alter ego, the ascendant Right. In a sense, the broad, allied progressive
goals set by Protestant liberationists and ecumenists existed in a relationship
of mutual, if antithetical, construction with the reactionary priorities of the
Right. That is, in the days before identitarian conservatism, the Protestant
Left's development in late authoritarian Brazil, and its alliances with ecumenism and with rights movements, formed a basis against which rightist evangelicals would prioritize moralism, neoliberalism, antagonism toward minority
groups, and isolationist dogmatism. This last, ironically, led to something like
an antiecumenist ecumenism. In a sense, what I aim to do in this chapter is to
destabilize the assumptions that have been built into the phrase "culture
wars." Popular and scholarly usage has made this a term of long record, one
whose familiarity naturalizes and elides its contradictions. But these "wars"
do not in fact make logical, or intuitive, sense. Why should people oppose the
death penalty but favor abortion? Or promote moralism while ignoring corruption? There was a moment when these battle lines were drawn. How did
that happen?

In general terms, the Protestant Left tended to promote ecumenism, social
justice, and (eventually) a variety of identitarian causes, including racial-
and gender-based rights movements. Beyond this, progressive Christians eschewed the moral panic displayed by their rightist counterparts; and the
former, ultimately, sided *against* the military regime, opting for positions that
diametrically opposed the right-wing approximation with the dictatorship
described in the last chapter. That approximation, certainly based in the
factors just discussed, also depended on security forces' enduring hatred of
progressive Christianity and their hypervigilant repression of it. State agents
feared ecumenism and liberation theology so much that in the terminology
of the intelligence community, these became slurs, little more than epithets
for "communism" or "subversion." Amid theories of grand, global conspiracies, conservatives within and outside the state feared a leftist amalgam that
prefigured the fault lines of today. Security forces and conservative rightists
could agree on the threat, that is, of an alarming, well-articulated and well-
heeled, international agglomeration of ecumenism, theological Marxism
masquerading as social justice, rights movements (including black rights and
feminism), gender deviance, and communist machination. On the Right this

perceived threat led to the emergence of a rather contradictory phenomenon: antiecumenist ecumenism, or rather multidenominational organizations that sought to counteract interdenominational cooperation.

I. The Protestant Left, Such as It Was

Excellent scholarship has unearthed histories of interaction between evangelical Christianity, the Cold War, and military authoritarianism; indeed, the connections between American evangelical missionaries, local congregations, and the terrorist states of 1980s Central America pervade historiography as well as popular knowledge.[6] Brazil, however, is something of a special case in the history of evangelical Protestantism in Latin America. In the 1970s, Brazilian Protestantism stood on the verge of an explosion of visibility and of popularity, with new adherents flocking to Pentecostalism and to a glittering new televangelism industry. By 1972, the first evangelical preacher had appeared in a telenovela, an oft-heralded sign of the times; and in the decade or so following, evangelicals of several stripes forsook a studied, even doctrinal apoliticism and entered formal politics.[7]

In this context, even more than in decades past, evangelicals could be found inhabiting points throughout the political matrix. Nationally, Brazil saw the rise of prodemocracy organizing and of social movements for several key, often identitarian causes (such as feminism, black power, and gay rights). By the late 1970s, these social movements, alongside social justice, antipoverty, and human rights advocates (including representatives of the Catholic Church), garnered both attention and increasing success in their demands for democratization. As the military regime grew more and more unpopular—its demise would be cemented by massive street demonstrations in São Paulo and Rio de Janeiro in 1984—the stage was set for a schism among evangelicals. In the simplest of terms, this can be understood as a face-off between conservatives we encountered in chapter 2 and an alternative with a very different, if somewhat doomed, promise: that of a unified Christianity focused on social justice and something resembling liberation theology. Brazil's Christian Left included intellectual and activist pioneers, some of them quite famous; and it briefly represented a distinct, possible future for the politics of evangelicalism in Brazil. These relatively left-wing sectors of Brazil's evangelical population formed a tenacious opposition to the religious Right that we have begun to see coalescing in the 1970s and 1980s.

What, then, were the contours of this quashed Christian Left? Summary is a dubious exercise here, given the great variety of approaches to Christian activism and to theology in this moment; progressive Christians tended to come from mainline communities, but they traced their paths across denominational, doctrinal, and even national borders. Significantly for our purposes, though, the positions of evangelical progressives, and the promise they offered of a more compassionate Christianity in Brazil, diametrically opposed those of their conservative counterparts, precisely when it came to the fault lines just noted: moralism, ecumenism, doctrine (including liberation theology), and social justice (including rights movements). On Marxism itself, the progressive field was somewhat ambiguous, with certain famous exponents of liberation theology collaborating with Marxists or adopting Marxist positions and others remaining staunchly anticommunist.[8] Yet social justice–minded evangelicals tended to lament and even deride the moralism of conservatives, to oppose the military regime itself, and to champion a broad swath of issues—doctrinal and social—that would come to form the litany of right-wing anxieties.

Moral Calm: Eschewing the "Terreno" of Protestant Conservatives

As the battle lines were drawn, moral panic became the "nosso terreno" we have seen naturalized in right-wing discourses; but progressive Protestants did not share in the moral panic–mongering. Instead, they voiced relative calm on all the issues that had so inflamed the Right. Progressive pastors, congregants, and activists supported women's work outside the home, did not decry calamity in mass media, and even (in marked contrast to the Claudionor de Andrades of the world) expressed solidarity with sex workers and victims of AIDS. Moreover, they directly opposed (in some cases ridiculing) the moral panic of rightists.

Exemplifying the *lack* of moral panic, Reverend Gessé Moraes de Araújo, a Presbyterian minister from Ribeirão Preto, spoke of the changes—principally urbanization, industrialization, and an increase in female-headed households—that so preoccupied the Right, *crente* (believer) and non-*crente*. These changes, he acknowledged, "have, in a very accentuated form, been causing a strong impact on familial structure.... Women as well as men, today, pass the greater part of their time working far from home for the sustenance and maintenance of the family." He even admitted that this might have enabled a "generational conflict"—but none of this, he emphasized, constituted cause for undue concern. "The occurrence of all those changes that might suggest the disaggregation of the family," he said, "have [instead] worked toward its fuller integration. The fact is, this divine institution, created for the happiness of the human species, and which has perpetuated itself across the years, derided as outdated by some, categorized as 'disintegrating' by others, is a [permanent] reality."[9]

The General Council of the Methodist Church likewise acknowledged changes in family and societal structure and relations—but did not point to contemporary morality and sexuality as disastrously or apocalyptically gone awry. In the pronouncement "The Family and Its Problems," the council, like Araújo, noted the sense of "rapid and profound transformations, where the norms, values, and basic principles of life are constantly moved." Yet the council also did not condemn such changes out of hand. Indeed, it supported forms of birth control and "family planning," and, in stark contrast to the antifeminism of rightists, viewed women's liberation as a positive change. "Woman," the pronouncement observed with approval, "no longer considers herself a mere baby-maker and guardian of household chores, but has become a person, a companion, an active part of the social process, sharing with her husband the responsibilities of formation, direction, and sustenance of the family. All of these factors have led women to seek their fulfillment outside of the home."[10] When it came to "the problems of youth," and those of mass media, the council likewise took a progressive stance. Rather than balk at young people's sexual or political comportment, the document commended young people for taking the "most active" role in confronting "the demands and oppressions that the people are suffering." Its critique of mass media, while acknowledging the "exploitation of sensual attraction as a weapon of propaganda," did not focus on sex so much as on materialism ("having instead of being"), on violence, and, significantly, on sex*ism*. Mass media, in this view, were less problematic for their exploitation of sex than for their reinforcement of restrictive ideas about women's bodies and sexualities—for "standardizing types of feminine beauty as if they were ideals."[11]

Throughout the 1980s, progressive outlets echoed and even intensified these positions. The Methodist teenage magazine *Flámula Juvenil*, far from condemning so-called hippies, featured an illustration of a young man making the peace sign, with the explanation that "lifting two fingers means peace and love."[12] *Flâmula* also echoed the message that sexism, rather than sex, was the troubling new development in mass media, as images perpetuated the "objectification of women," "machismo," and women's "secondary roles in professional and familial life."[13] Determined to rectify this imbalance, progressive Methodists, Lutherans, and Presbyterians undertook serious conversations about the ordination of women—and women pastors emerged in the former two denominations in the 1980s, with the support of *Flâmula* and *O Estandarte*.[14]

The latter, in fact, insisted that "woman has the same capacity as man to acquire knowledge of any sort. The erroneous idea of some . . . who affirm that women are inferior to men . . . was left behind, and a long time ago."[15] Indeed, some Presbyterians' gender and sexual liberalism extended even to consideration of abortion, which was the bugbear bar none of Christian rightists in Brazil and the United States. In 1984, *O Estandarte* published the opinions of Portuguese pastor João Neto, who favored the legalization of abortion so that it might be "realized under humane conditions . . . with safety for the woman."[16] So notable were such positions in Independent Presbyterian Church of Brazil (IPIB) publications, in fact, that some laypersons wrote in to complain of the leadership's failure to adopt moral outrage. As one letter to the editor put it, "It is lamentable to belong to an institution like our [Independent Presbyterian Church] of Brazil, when, confronted by . . . so much immorality and indecency that predominates in telenovelas, commercials, and other TV programs . . . [the church] presents total omission, with no position or protest that could impact society. . . . Couldn't our synods and presbyteries orient themselves against this awful situation?"[17]

If Presbyterian leaders and publishers, like their Methodist and Lutheran counterparts, conspicuously failed—in stark contrast to rightist counterparts—to panic morally, they did so in ways that tended toward support for a constellation of left-wing political causes that will sound familiar to present-day readers. As the foregoing examples indicate, progressives, largely from the mainline groups, demonstrated relative support for women's rights, youth activism, and social justice in various forms. For the ecumenists of CEDI, such support extended even to outreach to sex workers. The Mary Magdalene Project, a Presbyterian charitable program from the United States, received CEDI's glowing review for its work assisting female sex workers—assistance designed less to stigmatize public sexuality than to attenuate the traumas of a population that regularly "suffered sexual violence, abandonment," and abuse. The program, according to the approving CEDI reporter, "does not discriminate religiously in its assistance. It merely helps the prostitutes in the reconstruction of their lives and does not engage in proselytizing."[18]

Perhaps most striking, Lutheran and Presbyterian ministers involved themselves in solidarity-based activism with Brazilians living with AIDS. Whereas Claudionor de Andrade had celebrated the death of Rock Hudson and the spread of the "gay plague," Reverend Assir Pereira, president of the General Assembly of the IPIB, went on record calling for mercy for those suffering from AIDS. This is not to say that he—or any Presbyterians—openly called for toleration of homosexuality. Indeed, Pereira denounced "apologia of homosexuality and sexual promiscuity"—but, more centrally and more forcefully, he took to task those who read AIDS as the punishment of sinners reaping their just deserts. "There is great ease on the part of the Church in casting judgment about AIDS. 'It's [because of] sin! God has sent His punishment because of sin!' Thus bellow the preachers and laypeople who think themselves mouthpieces of God. This reveals a total lack of knowledge of Biblical theology and of human suffering."[19] In the spirit of ministry and solidarity, Pereira attended a "working group on AIDS," convened by the São Paulo State Secretariat of Health. Shocked by what he heard (at this point, statistics showed 300,000 Brazilians and 1.5 million U.S. Americans living with AIDS), Pereira was perhaps more distressed at the inhumane treatment of "the sick." He blamed "fear and ignorance which discriminate against the sick; . . . the abandonment of the patient by health professionals, by religious leaders, and even by their families, [abandonment that is the] fruit of prejudice and condemnation of that which we judge to be the consequence of sin." As president of the IPIB, Pereira issued a call for mercy, for "the evangelical message of love and forgiveness," and for education, "because the [level of] ignorance among young people and adults is . . . frightening."[20]

Lutheran pastor Ricardo Wangen went even further, supporting efforts to build solidarity around the multiple problems confronted by AIDS sufferers and their families. Wangen, who was also a professor at a prestigious Lutheran divinity school, sat on a panel with Ubiratan da Costa e Silva, then perhaps São Paulo State's most well-known gay activist.[21] While Costa e Silva affirmed that AIDS was not the exclusive province of gay men, "Wangen also emphasized that the Christian [must] assume a position of compassion and solidarity, along a path not of condemnation, but of help and succor." Wangen's attitude was emblematic of those evangelicals who helped create the Evangelical Association in Support of and Solidarity with Persons with AIDS and Their Families, which sought to maintain a Center in Support of Life—a refuge for those AIDS patients who had been otherwise abandoned.[22]

By this time, then, the lines of evangelical politicization had been drawn—moralism represented something of a wedge separating right from left in forums where evangelicals felt increasingly comfortable voicing political opinions. In fact, evangelical progressives did not just eschew the moralism described—they decried it as distracting, if not cynical and even un-Christian, insofar as Christianity could be interpreted as an agenda for compassion, equality, and charitable abnegation. Facing the conservative, moralist onslaught in national politics, progressives criticized the preoccupation with morality and proposed that Christians should focus on the "real" problems facing Brazil—those of equity, human rights, and resistance to authoritarianism. Lamenting the fact that Brazil "remains the same, structurally" (that is, highly unequal), the liberal, ecumenical journal *Aconteceu no Mundo Evangélico* called for better vetting of candidates who "are basically elected by the votes of [fellow] crentes." *Aconteceu* added that these crente politicians, obsessed with moralism, stagnated the national legislature, since "they only know how to present bills against alcoholic beverages, smoking, and gambling, and to gain donations for evangelical charities."[23] In other words, evangelicals who envisioned a less reactionary, more humanitarian religious politics raised an alarm about the right-wing tendencies of moralist politicization: yes, the brethren should enter politics, but *not* for the express purpose of moralism, as was presently the case.

As early as 1975, these differences had evolved into jeering, as leftist evangelicals derided religious reactionism in various forms. The relatively ecumenist *Jornal Evangélico* reported that year on the ultra-right Catholic organization the Brazilian Society for the Defense of Tradition, Family and Property—and focused less on its Catholicism than on its moral rigidity. Drawing on a recently released exposé, the *Jornal* derided the society's attitudes toward sex and the body: "Even the sight of one's own body is considered a terrible sin."[24] By the 1980s, as noted earlier, *Aconteceu no Mundo Evangélico* would openly criticize conservative evangelical politics as solely focused on reactionary morality.[25] When the *Jornal Batista* pressed the government to prohibit the exhibition of Jean-Luc Godard's *Je vous salue, Marie*, an *Aconteceu* editorial mocked the "wave of permissiveness" decried by the Baptists and suggested that the latter were narrow-minded bigots who blindly associated morality, sexuality, and the Left: "*Even without having seen the film,* [the *Jornal Batista*] feels authorized to judge it 'a grotesque parody of the life of Mary, in which there are those erotic scenes so favored by decadent intellectuals, indecent and blasphemous.'" The Baptists, continued *Aconteceu*, hoped to use the morality issue as a wedge between religious and nonreligious progressives.[26] (Notably, it was the Baptists who came out on top here, as the film was, indeed, banned.) While left-wing denominations criticized the moral reactionism of the Right, their conservative counterparts supported each other. In 1988, for example, the *Jornal Batista*, having successfully campaigned for the censorship of the Godard film, wrote favorably of the work being done by the Publishing House of the Assemblies of God. In particular, the Baptist journal praised *The Occult Message of Rock*, a moralistic diatribe coauthored by none other than Claudionor de Andrade and Geremias do Couto.[27]

"Opening the Windows" of the Churches: Ecumenism

Not all progressives dismissed moralism in these terms, of course; and certainly no prominent progressives advocated the kind of dissolution of which they stood accused by conservatives.[28] The former *did*, however, advocate ecumenism, which thus formed a very real line separating the divergent currents in midcentury Brazilian evangelicalism. Ecumenism—both among evangelicals and across other (Catholic and non-Christian) faiths—had long nettled fundamentalists and other conservative crentes, but it began to attract an increasing contingent of moderates by midcentury. In the 1960s and 1970s, a debate on whether to create cross-denominational linkages raged between those who opposed ecumenism—especially Baptists, Pentecostals, and conservative Presbyterians (the Conservative Presbyterian Church and the Presbyterian Church of Brazil [IPB])[29]—and those willing to at least entertain ecumenism in some form, among them Independent Presbyterians, as well as Lutheran and Methodist Church officials. Antiecumenists would become the backbone of the 1980s religious Right, while the pro-ecumenists moved steadily to the left, advocating the morality of equitable reform in opposition to conservative evangelicals' newly politicized moral panic.

The stirrings of worldwide ecumenism had quickened with the founding of the World Council of Churches (WCC) in 1948 and with the Vatican's moves toward cooperation before and during Vatican II. The WCC, emerging out of postwar globalism and favorable attitudes toward international cooperation, remained largely North Atlantic in terms of funding and leadership for most of the twentieth century.[30] Yet as the council—the world's largest ecumenical organization—set its sights on redistribution, democracy, and equity, links with the Global South proliferated. In Brazil, those evangelicals who would tend leftward had likewise grown remarkably more open to denominational exchange. Brazil's Methodists and Lutherans joined the WCC in 1948 and 1950, respectively, and by the mid-1960s, the Episcopal Anglican Church of Brazil and the Independent Presbyterians had affiliated via the International Council of Missions, a related interfaith organization.[31] Other progressive Presbyterians would refer to interdenominational dialogue using the catchphrase "opening the windows" of the Church.

There was a certain tenuousness here for some of Brazil's Christians. As one Methodist pastor put it in 1970, "If you asked me if I *espouse* ecumenism, I would say partially. I still don't have a really clear definition of the word."[32] Yet the Lutheran hierarchy more openly approved of the WCC and the ecumenical project, while *Aconteceu no Mundo Evangélico* unreservedly advocated ecumenism.[33] The most prominent and active Protestant progressives, meanwhile, formed institutions and publications designed to promote cooperation with other denominations in the name of Christian unity and of promoting peace, equality, and even radical reform or revolution.[34] *Aconteceu* emerged under the publishing auspices of CEDI, which by the 1980s (with the support of important representatives from several major denominations) would declare that "ecumenism is irreversible."[35] In a display of just how divided evangelicals had grown, when federal deputy and Conservative Presbyterian Francisco Dias attacked the National Conference of Brazilian Bishops (CNBB), *Aconteceu* came to the aid of the CNBB, siding with the Catholic and ecumenically minded hierarchy *against* the reactionary Dias, who had accused the CNBB of "religious spying."[36]

"Military Men Who Dishonor the Uniform": Opposing Military Rule, Upholding an Emergent Left-Wing Agenda

Ecumenism, then, formed a definitive rift between the developing left- and right-wing branches of Brazilian evangelicals. Perhaps more divisive still were the issues of anticommunism, guerrilla struggles, military government (in Brazil and abroad), and social justice itself. As we have seen, those evangelicals who would eventually form the rightist anchor of the *bancada evangélica* (evangelical bloc) tended to maintain staunch anticommunism, support for authoritarian regimes (including the national government), and a relative neglect of social justice concerns; whereas the precise opposite characterized the evangelical sectors that would, eventually and unsuccessfully, seek to counterbalance the *bancada*. What began with opposing the brutalities and restrictions of dictatorship ended, for certain evangelical progressives, with dedication to a series of causes that resembled a litany of the New Right's bugbears: wealth redistribution, antiracism, feminism, environmentalism, and even activism against the AIDS pandemic.

Whereas conservative evangelicals remained staunch supporters of the military regime from its inception until (or past) its demise, progressive Christians had a different set of relationships with the dictatorship and with authoritarianism more broadly. For many, the politicization of the 1960s and 1970s involved a process, shared with a wide swath of Brazilians, of gradual disaffection with the regime and eventual opposition to it, even among those who had originally supported the coup. For others, the regime sparked immediate opposition, facilitated links with other antiregime sectors, or led to radicalization. Whatever the case, progressives by and large did not maintain the unwavering enthusiasm for the regime that so benefited conservative evangelicals.

The IPIB exemplifies a pattern in which initial endorsement of the 1964 coup gave way to ideological and political disaffection and then opposition. *O Estandarte*'s reflexive anticommunism led journal editors to support rather breathlessly the coup itself and even some subsequent repression.[37] However, these were relatively minor political notes in a time when many Presbyterians maintained a doctrinal abstinence from politics. By the time politics became more appropriate fodder for evangelical discussion, the IPIB had mainly repented of its former pro-coup stance. In 1987, the journal even issued an apology for its support of the 1964 putsch, admitting that the dictatorship had been brutal and murderous and lamenting publicly the involvement of evangelicals in the military state's fearsome torture apparatus.[38]

The Lutheran *Jornal Evangélico* opposed military regimes—in Brazil and abroad—more forcefully and consistently. In 1971, the *Jorev* sought to make such opposition an evangelical issue, excoriating the government's tolerance of death squads and noting that a courageous Methodist policeman had come forward to expose one such squad.[39] In subsequent months and years, the journal would support calls for an end to the regime's repressive Institutional Act Number 5 (the legislative architecture for much of the repression between 1968 and 1978); highlight democratic activism that protested the government's privileging of economic development over civil and human rights; compare the regime—"military men who dishonor the uniform"—to Pontius Pilate; and roundly upbraid National Security Ideology, the Brazilian variant of a hemispheric intellectual framework for human rights abuse.[40] In 1972, the *Jorev* risked censorship and worse by openly supporting the left-leaning regime of Salvador Allende in Chile—a regime that would soon thereafter, of course, be toppled by yet another military government.[41]

Aconteceu no Mundo Evangélico, meanwhile, represented the institutionalization of progressive ecumenism in Brazil. Accordingly, it furnished progressive Christians' most vociferous opposition to the dictatorship and to right-wing authoritarianism more broadly—a sharp contrast from the prohierarchy, pro-authoritarian ideas that suffused conservative thought at this time. Throughout the 1980s, the ecumenical newsletter celebrated the victories of the Brazilian military government's adversaries; repeatedly and openly criticized military state torture in allied Uruguay and Argentina; cheered Chilean Methodists' opposition to Augusto Pinochet while condemning religious support for Argentina's dictatorship; and disowned those rightist evangelicals in Brazil who supported military government at home and in neighboring countries.[42] Indeed, as *Aconteceu* noted, it was a liberal Presbyterian pastor, Jaime Wright, who founded and administered one of Brazil's most famous and influential antiauthoritarian and antitorture organizations, Brasil Nunca Mais.[43]

Progressive evangelical outlets, notably for our purposes, denounced the very dictatorial censorship that their conservative counterparts celebrated (and, once it ended, mourned).[44] An outraged *Aconteceu* editor ridiculed the censoriousness of conservative evangelicals as closed-minded bigotry and expressed incredulity at brazen advocacy of "a return to censorship."[45] *O Estandarte*, in an outpouring of antidictatorial sentiment, referred in aggrieved tones to the years in which "iron-clad censorship" had prevented the airing of various kinds of truth, but "was even greater within the church than without."[46] As early as 1975, the *Jornal Evangélico* opposed preemptive censorship, government or otherwise.[47] The Geisel and Figueiredo administrations already shared their predecessors' suspicion of and hostility toward left-wing Christians, and the opposition to censorship did not stand the more progressive sectors in good stead with the latter two military presidents.[48]

Worse still, from the perspective of conservatives and the regime, progressive evangelicals did not hold the line on the kind of all-encompassing anticommunism that undergirded cohesion on the Right. Famous Christian progressives denounced the reflexive anticommunism of the Right as paranoid, counterproductive, and even conspiratorial.[49] Even as those who would constitute Brazil's evangelical Right came together on the issues of anticommunism and antiecumenism, more left-wing evangelicals joined forces to support the emergent, increasingly linked causes of social justice—from poverty and inequality to environmentalism, and from feminism and antiracism to AIDS visibility and treatment. Hence when the Methodist youth journal *Flámula Juvenil* fretted about "the world in which we live," it was not to denounce communism or the moral "crises without precedent" that filled right-wing forums; instead, the Methodist publication focused on "some things that worry us, even in the midst of the beauties of our land: inflation . . . [that] has been mistreating our ever-suffering people . . . lack of adequate food, and consequently of health, clothing, and education." When the journal did mention "prostitution and even crime," it blamed "impoverishment which leads to unemployment and underemployment." Sin, in other words, might constitute a critical and ongoing problem, but only a progressive agenda could furnish real solutions. Structural problems, colonialism, and multinational capitalism were the roots of the crisis: "Our [natural resources] are transferred to other countries, while our environment is destroyed. Swaths of our land are taken from their true owners, the Indians, and retained by powerful Brazilians and foreigners. Racism, though hidden in various forms, does exist."[50]

O Estandarte (which had, after all, supported João Goulart's precoup literacy and land reform programs) also called directly on ordinary evangelicals to dedicate themselves to social justice activism. Drawing on liberal Harvard theologian Harvey Cox, Reverend Odair Mateus exhorted Presbyterians as follows:

> It falls to each of you to decide how to fight for life against death. . . . Some will be able to make their contribution by engaging themselves in the movements for the defense of the environment . . . protesting against the sacrifice of the Amazon [to foreign investment]. . . . Others will . . . choose the path of political militancy. They are called to fight more and more and more so that the State exists for the good of the people and not the people for the good of the State. Still others will manage to engage in pacifist movements and those of disarmament. Others, finally, will be able to leave the best neighborhoods of the city and join, in the slums, the movements of popular consciousness-raising.[51]

To these general calls for democratization and equity, left-wing evangelicals added sundry progressive issues, from gender equality to anti-imperialism. Lutherans called for an "energetic" labor day in May 1975; by the 1980s, the *Jornal Evangélico* was publishing cartoons of Ronald Reagan and an anonymous friend (wearing an "I Love the IMF [International Monetary Fund]" button) under the heading "The United States: Embodiment of Capitalist Imperialism"; and environmentalism reached the nuanced heights of concern about toxic pesticides that might decimate the world's bee populations.[52] Lutheran writers also expressed solidarity with the International Year of Women (1975), celebrating women's work outside the home and even sexual liberation. One article ("Enough of Submission") went so far as to assert that "the sexually repressed woman is the consequence of repressive social order. . . . It is impossible for women to be free, it is impossible that the man/woman relationship be pure, clean, and honest, when the social order pushes men to be poor in spirit."[53] Perhaps the most telling testament to this kind of evangelical activism lies in the disaffection it drew from certain readers—similar in spirit, if not in tone, to the criticism faced by the Assemblies' *Mensageiro* when it began publishing (conservative) political articles.[54] A Blumenau, Santa Catarina, reader of the *Jornal Evangélico* complained not only that the journal had grown too political, but that its politics were too left wing. The reader condemned the journal's antiapartheid and pro-agrarian re-form articles.[55] While other readers came to the defense of left-leaning editorial decisions, the turn to the left had clearly been noted, including both its national and international implications.

II. "The Social Aspect Has Become More Important than the Idea of Religion Itself": Targeting Protestant Progressives for Persecution

The evangelical left that *Jorev* represented, however, developed into something of a road *not* taken, given the history we are exploring here. The positions taken by progressive Protestants, beginning with ecumenism and linking into identitarian rights and social justice movements, earned them the enmity not only of conservative Christians but also of the state. Formal authorities, alongside overt and covert security officials, drew closer to conservative evangelicals while concomitantly persecuting progressives. As we saw in chapter 1, the regime and its enforcers execrated Catholic progressivism, which they saw as one of the likeliest sources of communist subversion. Rather logically, given the evangelical Left's criticism of the regime, its enforcers extended their hatred of Catholic progressives to like-minded Protestants, lesser though the latter may have been. Thus, even as a vocal minority of Protestants in midcentury Brazil (following the lead of Brazilian Catholics and foreign Protestants) contemplated or adopted the just-described focus on social justice and something that resembled liberation theology, the crosshairs both of security forces and of Brazil's evangelical conservatives shifted sharply onto this emergent Protestant Left. The future they envisioned never materialized largely because, as we shall see, the dictatorship and conservative evangelicals joined forces to disempower, if not eliminate, Protestant progressives.

Police archives abound with records of massive and, as the 1970s wore on, increasing surveillance of Protestants. It is worth noting certain complexities of using these sources—classified, often reflecting internecine and bureaucratic concerns, and generated in some cases by individual security workers with motives of their own, the records of dictatorial enforcement are riddled with contradictions. Often, the "information" they contain reflects very little of the realities of their subjects and much more of the prejudices, misconceptions, and myopias of their authors. Yet it is in this final respect that they are most useful to us here, as they demonstrate attention to and anxiety about progressive Protestants mounting across security agencies. Long aware of

Catholic progressivism, Brazil's fearsome security forces appear, in the main, to have discovered Protestant progressivism in the waning years of dictatorship. That is, while there were certainly examples of early suspicion and hostility, the vast majority of the available documentation dates to the 1970s and 1980s, after the onset of *abertura* (gradual "opening" of the dictatorship) and especially as democratization loomed—in other words, precisely the period in which the regime was drawing closer to conservative Protestants.[56] In 1979, local National Intelligence Service (SNI) agents in Rio de Janeiro forwarded a report titled "Activities of the Protestant Church in Brazil" in which they affirmed that "in the same way that there is leftist infiltration in the bosom of the Catholic Church, this is happening in the Protestant Church."[57]

A chorus of reports from the time echoed this sentiment, often with accompanying denunciations of ecumenism and of the WCC in particular. The São Paulo SNI observed that "contrary to what had been happening to this point, it is not only Catholic religious groups" that were taking up leftist "issues of a political, economic, and social character." The agents ominously and erroneously concluded that "since these Protestant groups are only now broaching social and political themes, it is still early enough to assess the potential repercussions that this new attitude may have."[58] Just a few years later, however, the "new attitude" seemed old hat (as indeed it was) to these hostile observers. A 1984 report written by the commandant of the Second Army exemplified the routine approach that intelligence agents had adopted by this point, his prose peppered with phrases like "once again" and "yet another." As the commandant put it, "One more time, it is confirmed that the so-called 'theologians of liberation' are much more interested in the political aspect than in the religious one, as if they were active militants of a populist party of the left and not religious people [who should be] concerned with the connection between Man and the Divine."[59] Likewise, he grumbled about "yet another entity . . . that serves as a tool for the progressive clergy" and "yet another Organization of the Masses" that "links intellectuals and politicians of socialist tendencies, from the most radical leftists to the so-called liberals."[60]

Beyond merely accusing these progressives of communism and potential subversion, security officials tended to deride their theological positions and even their religiosity itself. Open, scornful critiques of liberationist Christianity suffused the state's tabs-keeping records on it; foremost among these was the idea that progressive Christians were irreligious, having subordinated spirituality to politics. As early as 1973, SNI agents in Rio de Janeiro accused several groups of mainline Protestants of concomitantly abandoning true religion and subverting democracy. The agents alerted their colleagues to "adverse propaganda" designed by ecumenists to "persuade people to accept ideas, symbols, and values that the communist regime, adapting to their doctrinal interests, has transformed into an ideological battle-flag." To the agents' minds, these Protestants played a subtle game of sneaking this "ideological battle-flag" into what should have been a religious space. Here was "a common effort where the social aspect has become more important than the idea of religion itself. It is observed that the [progressive Protestant groups] are not interested in elaborating a text which would address religious anxieties, but instead have assumed a position of preserving human rights, precisely in the moment in which that universal proclamation [of human rights] is used as a standard for communist political propaganda."[61]

This became, in fact, the refrain of security forces, who seemed undecided as to whether progressive Protestants were active, dissimulating conspirators, foolish dupes, or a combination thereof. Police described progressive Protestants as subversive enemies who took their cues from liberationist Catholics and forsook religion itself for activism that tended to promote communism and weaken Brazilian national security. This, intelligence documents made clear, pertained both to Catholic subversion and to its putatively emergent Protestant shadow:

> The manifestations of the . . . progressive tendency of the Catholic clergy continue to be directed essentially at temporality and, by choice, to favor the poorest strata of society and those that understand themselves to be marginalized, like the black, the Indian, and the tenant farmer, the very strategy of the "liberation theologians," inspired by Marxism, who hope to inspire a "new society" and a "new Church," both explicitly based in those social strata. [Lutherans, Methodists, and CONIC], continue distancing themselves from the spiritual plane and assuming, after the example of the progressive current of the Catholic Church, a position more exclusive of other social strata and more politically engaged.[62]

This, intelligence agents argued, was religion "running radically away from the goal to which it is dedicated," and in a way that threatened the state itself.[63] In 1981, the Porto Alegre headquarters of the SNI singled out certain local denominations—Methodists and especially Lutherans (or IECLB), of whom they wrote, "Like the behavior of the 'progressive wing' of the Catholic Church, the pastors of the IECLB have been emphasizing issues of a temporal character, leaving those of a religious nature on the back burner." The spies sharply noted progressives' turn away from the regime and associated it more or less with sacrilege: "The disposition of these [Protestant] religious sectors to publicly oppose the Government and the current regime, as well as the political interest manifested by these religious ministers, reveals the intent to act politically, leaving the spiritual and religious aspects in the background."[64] A 1984 report added that progressive Christians, "who are always gaining more followers, have begun constituting a parallel power structure, insistently confronting the Government and the extant political regime."[65]

Making no secret of their antipathy for democratization, security forces conflated prodemocracy political activity with subversion. They saw this "distancing from the spiritual plane" as a ploy for bringing down the government, especially via the restitution of direct elections: "In the activities of the above-indicated religious groups, their uniformity stands out in clamoring for direct elections . . . as soon as '84, associating themselves with the fight of those who oppose the current government."[66] The Rio de Janeiro SNI, meanwhile, put a finer point on the irreligiousness argument, affirming that "the current leaders of the 'theologians of liberation' are politicians of the left (socialists and communists), supporters of the class struggle prized by Marxism, more than they are religious."[67]

Beyond these generalities about progressive trends and presumptive Marxism, state agents engaged in extensive and hostile surveillance and repression of left-wing evangelicals.[68] Indeed, an astonishing wealth of archival documents attests to the steep learning curve that secret police followed, not only to inform fellow authorities about the nitty-gritty of ideological and theological conflict among evangelicals but also to watch, control, and—in the most egregious cases—wreak violence on specific evangelical activists and thinkers. As several scholars have noted, internal repression within the churches (especially the IPB) went hand in hand with conservatives' cooperation with security forces; that internal repression and cooperation not only empowered conservatives within the denominations but also created climates of fear and suspicion about progressivism itself. What has not been elaborated is the resulting wealth of intelligence data that security amassed, and just how deep hostility toward progressive evangelicals ran. The monitoring was extensive and fearsome, ranging across all of Brazil and all of the potential denominations involved. I have elsewhere elaborated the ways in which this monitoring often focused on Protestant educational institutions, young people, and suspected immorality as anticommunism.[69] But all facets of evangelical life and activity were fair game, and virtually any Protestant engaged in or contemplating liberationism or social justice might expect to encounter suspicion, surveillance, and perhaps detention. Progressive publications (and especially, as I shall discuss momentarily, ecumenist ones) came under especial scrutiny—as in the case of a 1981 report shared between the Rio de Janeiro and federal SNI agencies, which listed nearly all of the major leaders of progressive and ecumenist evangelicalism in Brazil at the time and denounced them in the strongest of language. They "seek to stir up the class struggle," the SNI warned; "using Bible passages, those responsible for this magazine transmit discontentment, inconformity, hopelessness, and revolt to their readers." They concluded that "it is rational to infer" that this was a group "profoundly permeated by the Socialist International, for which the World Council of Churches is a Front Organization."[70]

Intelligence reports regularly included lists of individual "progressista" enemies to be watched, alongside estimations of the potential subversiveness of whole denominations. "In the protestant religion, the 'progressista' wing is formed by the Methodists, Lutherans, Episcopalians, and part of the Presbyterians, grouped together in the National Federation of Presbyterian Churches (FENIP)," according to São Paulo agents in 1982. These and other agents monitored emergent schisms, with an eye to identifying individual and institutional allies and enemies. Among Presbyterians, they judged "the fundamentalists and conservatives are 'on the Right,'" the IPB "in the 'center,'" and the IPIB "on the Left," adding that "on the left, in addition to the Independent Presbyterians are listed the Lutherans, the Methodists, and the Anglicans."[71] Even in the early 1960s, security forces were aware of and gathering information on leftist evangelicals and the denominational fault lines that they revealed. By 1965, the Naval Intelligence Center could confidently report that Waldo César, who "passes himself off as a protestant pastor," had raised the hackles of fellow Presbyterians as well as of dictatorial spies themselves. In his background dossier ("ideological antecedents"), it related that between 1962 and 1965 he was "highly engaged in the process of communization of the evangelical Brazilian milieus. Suspected of being financed by a clandestine communist entity based in the United States of America. He maintains contacts with Richard Shaull . . . considered the greatest agitator in the evangelical milieus in Brazil."[72]

Several years later, in the heart of dictatorship, various agencies deepened the state's knowledge of and partiality in the growing crisis among Brazil's Presbyterians. The São Paulo SNI monitored left-wing Presbyterians, insistently accusing them of promoting communism within their Church. Of one suspect, for example, the agents wrote that he championed a "program in which he preaches disobedience to the authorities, on the pretext that one only owes obedience to god. He has facilitated the penetration of communist ideas in the Presbyterian Church." Showing themselves to be remarkably well

informed about the putative connection (drawn by conservatives themselves) between "modernism" and communism, the SNI sided with the fundamentalists and against "modernistic and socialist ideas."[73] Indeed, the SNI
and DOPS (the political police) both expressed heightened awareness of the
"problem" of modernism—which at this early date was becoming the rallying
cry of antimodernist fundamentalists, perhaps most famously of conservative Presbyterian strongman Boanerges Ribeiro. The São Paulo DOPS, in an
undated report likely from the late 1960s, targeted Richard Shaull as the
spearhead of a Presbyterian conspiracy "interested in the destruction of evangelical Churches for the implantation of an anti-democratic regime." In other
words, "the finality of the movement [is] the DESTRUCTION OF CHRISTIAN
PRINCIPLES, for the sake of destroying the Churches, in order to implant a
socialist regime of the left. This would be obtained by the abatement of
Christian faith, which has always been an impediment to materialist and leftist ideas [and by] theological 'modernism,' which tries to destroy all the traditions of the Church, bearing it into enfeeblement."[74]

FENIP, the left-leaning Presbyterian association noted earlier, drew exemplary attention as a hotbed of resistance to conservatism within the Church.
SNI officials apparently read the organization's journal assiduously, keeping
tabs on individual members as well as on the threat they posed to conservative
fundamentalism within the Presbyterian faith. Decades after their reporting
on Waldo César, SNI officials closely monitored individual "elements" in the
left-wing evangelical world as a matter of course, including those of FENIP.
This monitoring generated voluminous reporting, with titles like "Synthesis of
the Activities of Protestant-Evangelical Elements, Linked to the Leftist Current Active in Brazil." Two such reports affirmed that "FENIP is nothing more
than a schism provoked by Presbyterian elements with a leftist tendency, bitter
about the sanctions imposed on their political activity by the Supreme
Council of the . . . IPB." In a moment when the *Jornal da FENIP* did indeed
advocate departure from what it called the "intolerant sect" of conservative
Presbyterians, the agents added that FENIP was a hotbed of "theological
modernism and ecumenism," and thus clearly a threat to national security.[75]

The watchers continually cited Methodists and Lutherans as problematic
groups and carefully tracked individuals and internal debates within these denominations. The Ministry of Transportation's Intelligence Service singled
out Methodists as particularly compromised by subversion and listed particular transgressors. "One of the most infiltrated Protestant Churches," the
agents confirmed, "is the Methodists [*sic*], particularly by dint of the action,
national and international, of Professor Warwick Estevam Kerr."[76] They like-

wise accused Lysâneas Maciel (not, in fact, a Methodist) of "continuing to act in politics and in Protestantism in favor of the International Communist Movement."[77] As early as 1970, the secretary of public safety of Rio Grande do Sul affirmed the danger of "communist infiltration in the Lutheran Church" and listed the "communist elements" therein. Confusingly, the list included some non-Lutherans but presumed, with all the authority of intelligence work, the presence of a "subversive movement in the heart of the Lutherans" and concluded with the assertion, "Aside from those listed, Richard Shaull and Paulo Wright are also subversives."[78]

Liberationist celebrities like the latter, of course, faced intense scrutiny. Security agents carefully tracked the movements and activity of progressive activists and intellectuals domestic and international, especially Shaull, Hugo Assman, Rubem Alves, Jether Pereira Ramalho, Waldo César, and others. The extant documentation fairly brims, in fact, with individual surveillance reports as well as with various "syntheses" of the Protestant Left's activities, nearly all of which list the major figures of Protestant progressivism as "communist agitators," "subversive elements," and so on.[79] What is more, the state's spies created and shared lists of anyone who interacted with or attended the lectures or sermons of such activists—which the spies referred to as "subversive linkages" on the part of "religious and lay people" not otherwise clearly "involved in contestation."[80]

III. Ecumenism as Enemy

As some of the material we have seen thus far indicates, security forces and conservatives joined forces to demonize not just Protestant progressivism in the abstract but also the associated threat of ecumenism. Overt and covert authorities within the regime developed hyperawareness of ecumenism as a wedge issue within evangelical communities and came to see it the way rightists did: as part of an international conspiracy, fronted by the WCC and other organizations, that would bring Catholics, Protestants, and sundry progressive rights movements together to subvert Brazil and the West. Suspicion, in some sense, began at home, where all of Brazil's ecumenist organizations were prime targets of surveillance. Indeed, various outlets of Brazilian statecraft made "ecumenical" something of an epithet in their internal discourse, indicating the level at which antiecumenism (as anticommunism and countersubversion) was operating within the state. In this, the government's spies, in Brazil and outside it, very nearly matched the ire and the paranoia of their conservative ecumenical allies.

By the late 1970s and early 1980s, security forces exhibited a familiar, even routine assumption that the WCC and ecumenism generally equated to plots against Church, state, and society. Indeed, though some have supposed that the language of their reports meant these documents were written by Church personnel themselves, the evidence demonstrates that agents themselves had gained extensive knowledge of religious individuals, institutions, and terminology, always with the presumption that ecumenism was an evil.[81] Accordingly, one 1981 intelligence synthesis provided the following bulleted list of "initial ... premises" for any agents who, inexplicably, did not yet know these equivalencies:

- "Ecumenism," as it is conceived of by considerable Protestant and Catholic sectors, that is, based on the teachings of the Theology of so-called "Liberation," has been gathering various parties into the same ideological trench;
- the inexistence of strong orthodox leadership, among either Catholics or Protestants, leads us to believe that Liberation Theology will continue its constant conquest of new initiates among the faithful of both creeds;
- the current leaders of the "theologians of liberation" are politicians of the left (socialists and communists), supporters of the class struggle prized by Marxism, more than they are religious;
- by dint of its unmatched economic power, the WCC has been coordinating, directly or indirectly, the propaganda of "Liberation Theology," even though its creators are, in the main, Catholic.[82]

As this list of supposed preliminaries indicates, denunciation of ecumenism and of the WCC had become de rigueur among secret police as much as among conservative evangelicals themselves. Alarmed at an array of proposals made at an interfaith meeting in 1982, the Rio de Janeiro SNI reported on a jumble of issues raised, especially the idea that a subversive "popular church" stood poised to explode across Brazil and Spanish America. In the words of the report, "Christianity is dying in Latin America and the People's Church is being born." Whatever the dizzying issues addressed at this meeting, the agents were certain of one thing: "In all of this, there remains the certainty that the followers of Liberation Theology, be they Catholic or Protestant, are pursuing the goal of creating a Popular Church (PC), of an ecumenical character, subordinated to the World Council of Churches (WCC), in the Latin American Countries."[83]

Hostility toward ecumenism dated at least to the Médici government (1969–74), when agents from the Army Intelligence Center actually elaborated a rationale for their theories of ecumenist conspiracy. They limned ecumenism as a pathetically transparent veil for subversion:

> As far as the current euphoria for the topic of ecumenism is concerned, it must be considered that a true believer, whatever his creed, could not accept with satisfaction an inferior position for his religion in relation to any other. . . . By nature, one religion repels any other, because it is enough that they are different for one of them (which would be the true one) to be automatically antagonistic to all the rest (which would be the false ones; the errant ones). In theory, then, no Catholic could ever think that it would be better to have a [Protestant] President. . . . By this logic we can see the true intentions of the "progressista" clergy.[84]

Ecumenism, then, had little chance of impressing state agents with its drive for inclusion and human rights. Indeed, the latter issue (considered a humbug by the military regime, whether propounded by Catholic, Protestant, or lay spokespersons) was one of many ways in which ecumenically minded individuals and pro-ecumenist organizations fell afoul of the dictatorship. In part for this reason, "ecumenical" became, by the late 1970s, less a descriptor than a slur in the lexicon of the state's intelligence and repression bureaucracies. Phrases like "has ecumenism as a philosophical base" or "of an ecumenical character" coded the disqualification of individuals and organizations as, in the words of one 1979 report on the WCC, "an element of a radical line contrary to the Revolution of 31 March 1964."[85] These bureaucracies homed in on Brazilian and international organizations committed to cross-denominational cooperation, denouncing them as "fronts" for what state agents called the "International Communist Movement" (abbreviated "MCI," the intelligence community's doctrinal, always-capitalized vision of a global conspiracy).

Constant surveillance and harassment of the leftist CEDI, for example, convinced spies from the Air Force Intelligence Center that this largely social justice–oriented organization "by its activities . . . all of important social penetration . . . is yet another vehicle of the so-called 'progressive clergy,' a sector that, right now, serves to support the activities of various subversive organizations."[86] Another report confirmed that "it is licit to infer that the CEDI and its mouthpiece *Tempo e Presença* are profoundly penetrated by the Socialist International, of which the World Council of Churches is just a Front Organization."[87] Other ecumenical organizations faced the same assumptions on the part of secret police. Though agents in São Paulo admitted the "closed" nature of the Ecumenical Center for Services of Evangelization and Popular

Education, they nevertheless investigated it based on its name and "the participation of religious and lay people involved in contestation and subversion."[88] This attitude meant that agents' hyperawareness of ecumenism as a threat placed religious cooperation in the same dangerous zone as syndicalism and collaboration with Russians. As the 1982 report titled "Linkages in the Subversive Process" (a secret report created by intelligence at the Ministry of Foreign Relations) would have it, Dom Paulo Evaristo Arns's trip to Sweden to engage in ecumenical dialogue was thus "linked" (via subversiveness itself) to sundry other suspicious activities. (These, apparently equivalent, included Italian trade unionism and Brazilian citizens' participation in Russian celebrations of the anniversary of the Bolshevik Revolution.)[89] The sensitivity to ecumenism as a threat to the state trumped even other indications of countersubversive probity: Benjamin Moraes was a Presbyterian pastor who had collaborated in creating the military government's legal machinery and served the regime as secretary of education in Guanabara. He had also been welcomed at the Escola Superior de Guerra, where he held forth on ethics and morality.[90] Yet, in 1975, he came under suspicion for his dealing with ecumenism. A SNI report from that year imputed "solidarity with the Counter-Revolutionary thesis" to him, noted with disapproval his support for certain opposition-party candidates, and explained that "he is a pastor with ecumenical ideas and he follows the religious orientation of the WCC, an international outfit, with strong communist influence." The report even claimed that Moraes's church in Copacabana was "the principal agency, in Brazil," of the WCC, linking him to other, more radical, younger Presbyterians, some of whom Moraes had worked with in previous decades. Moraes responded to these accusations. In a letter to the Ministry of Justice in September 1975, he protested, "I will always fall into formation at the side of those who defend the principles of the Revolution of 1964: against corruption and subversion."[91]

The WCC suffered a near-constant barrage of such accusations, "front organization" becoming the catchphrase that operatives of the SNI and other intelligence agencies invariably used to denote it. Any Brazilian individuals or organizations associated with the WCC thus fell under the rubric of "communist front organizations subordinated to the WCC."[92] The idea was fairly basic: the WCC stood behind a far-reaching, cleverly disguised plot to establish a dictatorial World Church or "People's Church," which would be a stepping-stone to communism across Latin America and beyond. Dozens of domestic groups associated with ecumenism were thus taxed as "front organizations of the World Council of Churches"; individual activists would be derided as false prophets "shielded by that international organization: the World Council of Churches."[93]

From the presidency to the various ministries to the secret police, dictatorial authorities appear to have been unified in their antiecumenism and in their attitude toward the WCC. Suspicion and alarm stretched across government circles, including the Foreign Relations Ministry, and as far away as the Brazilian embassy in Vatican City.[94] Indeed, Ambassador José Jobim, himself a staunch Catholic, mirrored not only the anticommunism but also the doctrinal traditionalism and even disgust of Protestant conservatives when he spoke of ecumenism creeping across world Christianity. When Dom Hélder Câmara met with WCC representatives in the Vatican, Jobim indicated his mistrust not only of the WCC but of its permanent relationship with the Vatican and the latter's openness to ecumenism itself, which Jobim associated with theological modernism and the dilution of the faith: "I will go so far as to say that the Church is already seeking to establish points of understanding even with Spiritism."[95] A letter to the SNI top brass from concerned agents, meanwhile, asserted—with characteristic directness—that the WCC "has as its philosophical base ecumenism" and warned of the "communizing activity" of its members. If the watchword "ecumenism" was not enough to raise hackles, the agents continued, "As an efficient ally of the International Communist Movement (MCI), the WCC has supported communist campaigns, financing liberation movements in Black Africa and cultivating pastors within the 'modernistic theology.'"[96]

Intelligence agents assured themselves and their colleagues that the WCC was the wealthy, maleficent backer of various ecumenical organizations in Brazil, bent on socialism in the guise of religion. In a report entitled "Action of the World Council of Churches (WCC) in Latin America and in Brazil," Rio de Janeiro agents described the council as "based on Liberation Theology. This, in turn, interpreting the continent's reality through a Marxist lens, devolves into Marxism on the part of its adherents, who are trying to form a Popular Church, divorced from any religious Orthodoxy. To reach such an objective, Catholic and Protestant 'progressives' align with each other, and they count, for this, on a web of organizations that enjoy plentiful financial resources. . . . The political choices of the WCC, by dint of its senior leadership, make it a natural ally and privileged partner of the Socialist International."[97]

A similar report a year earlier, from central headquarters in Brasília, used nearly the same language, reflecting the uniformity of opinion (disseminated via these reports themselves) that had already come to dominate the security establishment's stance toward ecumenism and the WCC in particular.

"Possessed of plentiful financial resources," the WCC was said to "influence decisively the behavior of various Protestant Churches or their dissidents, aside from constituting a center of orientation for . . . Catholics engaged in Liberation Theology." These reports, like a host of others, listed the individuals and organizations in Brazil thought to be "fronts" or "elements" in the WCC conspiracy or who "follow the orientation of the WCC." These included churches (the IECLB, the Methodist and Episcopal Churches, the Pentecostal Brasil Para Cristo), and ecumenical organizations: the Ecumenical Center for Services of Evangelization and Popular Education, CEDI, the Association of Evangelical Theological Seminaries, the Institute for Religious Studies, FENIP, the Latin American Council of Churches, CONIC, *Aconteceu no Mundo Evangélico*, and others—the lists often went on for pages, even tens of pages.[98]

IV. The Specter of a Vast, International Conspiracy

It would be difficult to overstate the certainty with which state agents envisioned a grand conspiracy—or a series of grand conspiracies—here. The WCC, from this perspective, was simply (to use the term of art) "the point of the spear," a managerial or front outfit for an international, wealthy, expertly planned, multifaceted, and ongoing plot. Domestic ecumenists, institutional and individual, were thought to receive funds, training, and personnel as part of this scheme, directed from either the shadowy halls of Geneva or those of Moscow, or both. A 1984 summary of intelligence on CEDI epitomized this attitude:

> Just like so many other ecumenical entities of the progressive line, CEDI has been, is, and will continue to be the recipient of substantial resources originating with foreign assistance entities [that] persistently advocate civil disobedience and try to convince the *povo* [people] that the solution is to oust the current regime, if necessary by force. The support, including financial support, given by CEDI to CUT-São Paulo [a major labor confederation] demonstrates [CEDI's] real political position in this country. Its links with communist front organizations affiliated with the WCC . . . characterize its objectives together with the popular movements.[99]

Brazilian government officials unerringly fixated on the supposed affluence of this shadowy conspiracy, coupled with its global links and its liberationist orientation. The WCC stood accused of "coordinating" the plot, financially and ideologically, via its "unmatched economic power"—but some reports envisioned direct Soviet control.[100] An army primer on liberation theology (undated, but most likely from 1979–1982) contended that "the Soviets, comprehending perfectly the value of the religious element in Latin America, have utilized the religious factor as the point of a spear for the USSR's penetration of the continent. Liberation Theology has been (and continues to be) the instrument utilized." The primer affirmed that this plot stretched beyond Brazil—indeed, the "most active focal point of that radicalized Christian intellectual elite has been concentrated in the north of the Continent, in Colombia and Central America." Nevertheless, domestic "'progressive' penetration, by way of TL [liberation theology], has become even more dangerous, because of the convergence . . . with the materialist doctrine of Marx-Engels." Moreover, the danger was explicitly "geo-strategic": as army officials explained, "With the Caribbean dominated, the South Atlantic will come to constitute a vital route of commerce and navigation, whose security depends fundamentally on Brazil. This country becomes, necessarily, the next target and key objective, presupposing a greater radicalization of the progressives of Liberation Theology."[101]

Some of the concerns exhibited by state agents in Brazil were not unfounded; at the very least, they became self-fulfilling prophecies. Brazil's security forces were not alone in denouncing the WCC nor were they entirely wrong about the anticapitalist potential of liberation theology and of the WCC itself. By the late 1970s, the organization *was* an opponent, on a global scale, of regimes like Brazil's and a sometime supporter of radical organizations abroad (though not in Brazil itself). Internationally, the WCC attracted the ire of conservatives far and wide—many, like Ernest Lefever, accused the WCC of funding guerrillas and undermining Western security.[102] Controversy intensified during the tenure of the organization's third general secretary, Philip Potter (1972–84). Born in Dominica, Potter's own blackness and his staunch support for antiapartheid movements in southern Africa fueled the flames of conservative reaction—particularly when, in 1978 and 1979, Potter headed delegations that granted thousands of dollars in aid to Zimbabwean and South African liberation fighters.[103] Though the grants were part of the WCC's long-running Program to Combat Racism, the fact of collaboration with nationalists was of course not lost on Brazil's spies: "It should be noted," wrote SNI agents in Rio de Janeiro, "that liberation movements in Angola and Mozambique received the support of the WCC."[104]

Likewise, security forces rightly saw religious activists as mouthpieces of a burgeoning international human rights network. The WCC and other ecumenical and left-leaning Christian organizations were among the many voices across the world taking up the growing cry for human rights in the face of late

Cold War atrocities. In Brazil, champions of human rights famously included Catholic authorities, something that put the Brazilian regime in a difficult position vis-à-vis no less an interlocutor than the Vatican.[105] Protestant groups, too, critiqued the dictatorship's excesses from inside and outside Brazil; and the WCC supported both the Latin American Council of Churches and the Brasil: Tortura Nunca Mais project.[106] The former took a lead role in opposing abuses region-wide, while the latter, headed by Presbyterian activist and ecumenist Jaime Wright, proved critical to revealing and combating atrocities within Brazil. In the face of such religious activism, the increasingly glaring contradiction between the state's democratic rhetoric and its human rights abuse meant that government agents would brook no criticism of Brazil's human rights record. By the late 1970s, covert and formal government authorities had in fact come to see agitation for human rights as a conspiratorial cover for antiregime agitation and, by extension, communist subversion. Hence the links maintained by ecumenists with the WCC and other organizations appeared to police forces in Brazil as alliances with a worldwide leftist plot designed simply to defame and depose the regime. As one brigadier general put it, "Of particular importance are links . . . with international entities, which links give [human rights organizers] the possibility . . . of achieving the goal of divulging news of the so-called 'Brazilian reality' [of authoritarianism and human rights abrogation], according to the leftist lens."[107]

The projected grand conspiracy, however, was little more than a chimera; global interfaith articulation fell far short of the "world church" feared by anticommunists. As ecumenism evolved nationally and internationally, it continued to spark debate and disagreement even among those inclined to collaborate. Certainly the WCC's support of liberation movements in Africa—the activity that most exposed it to charges of radicalism—caused controversy *within* the organization itself. The Salvation Army famously withdrew from the collective in 1981, much to the delight of Brazil's conservatives. (The Salvation Army nevertheless continued to accept grants from the WCC after this point.) As the renowned historian and priest Adrian Hastings wrote in *African Affairs*, "right-wing attacks on the WCC might well give the impression" that "by the late 1970s churches and liberation movements were . . . walking hand-in-hand," but in fact "there was . . . on each side a wide spectrum of attitudes."[108]

Accurate assessment of enemies, however, was rarely the province of Cold Warriors on either side of the global divide; and Brazil's establishment adhered to the rule in this case. In part because they drew on the ideas of right-wing Christians friendly to the regime, spies maintained the fiction of a well-planned ecumenical-communist plot. Convinced that a wealthy cabal of globalist and globalizing subversives stood poised to promote communism in Brazil's religious communities, officials took steps to control access to those communities, and to Brazil itself. Documents show a concerted effort on the part of the SNI and other agencies to promote immigration and visitation from conservative Christians, alongside explicit plans to exclude foreigners suspected of espousing left-wing or pluralistic versions of Christianity. This effort began with stepped-up surveillance of religious travelers, including evangelicals, from the North Atlantic. This harassment, it should be noted, did not rise to the level of repression (detention and worse) of domestic activists. Nevertheless, by 1970, the watchers began taking particular note of religious travelers deemed "suspicious," based on links with ecumenical groups, visits to Eastern bloc countries, and social and racial justice activism.[109]

Over the course of the decade, this monitoring blossomed into hostility toward religious migrants who were not explicitly right wing. When a Quaker delegation planned to visit São Paulo in 1980, the local SNI worked up a report on the American Friends more generally. The report noted the visitors' likelihood of meeting with local ecumenist groups and, worse, revealed "links in the United States with the local Black Movement." The combination of ecumenism and civil rights activism did not portend well, from the agents' point of view: "In the same way, the AFSC [American Friends Service Committee] has been involving itself in work with Latin and American Indian minorities. Currently there exists in the AFSC a tendency to seek to fabricate and connect problems felt by minority groups in the United States and in the Third World."[110] Likewise, when representatives of the United States National Council of Churches (NCC) visited Brazil, intelligence agents fretted not only about their attendance at meetings of CONIC but also about these international visitors' more general history of progressivism. When Reverend Arie Brouwer—head of the NCC and a leader of the world ecumenical movement—spoke in Brazil in 1985, SNI watchers feared the influence he might have on domestic ecumenists who called for an "autonomous, sovereign, truly democratic [constitutional convention], representative of all the social strata." The SNI further profiled the visitors and the NCC itself. "NCCUSA," they recorded with alarm, "is made up of thirty-one churches, including those of the blacks and excluding the religious groups of the extreme Right."[111]

Around this time, progressive Catholics and evangelicals complained that their international counterparts were being denied immigration to Brazil in an opaque process that favored conservative Christians and particularly fundamentalists from the United States. Dom Ivo Lorscheiter complained that "the worst part is not receiving a reason for the denials [of entry of progressive missionaries]. You ask here and there, but the SNI is who has the last word, and we just remain without an answer." Other members of CONIC, including Lutheran pastor Sílvio Schneider, complained of the "discrimination" reflected in "difficulties created for the coming of certain foreign missionaries to Brazil." Those who gained access, it was said, were "certain types of missionaries . . . from the United States, with more fundamentalist theories, and not linked to local issues."[112]

Right-wing visitors, meanwhile, were welcomed and even encouraged. In 1977, intelligence officials sought to facilitate the visit to Brazil of Richard Wurmbrand, the famed anticommunist crusader and author of *Tortured for Christ*. Noting that Wurmbrand might offer speeches to "military organizations," Air Force Intelligence Center (CISA) operatives enthused that "the anti-communist spirit of Pastor Wurmbrand, and the objectivity with which he presents his speeches, have awakened great interest among the Security Agencies, by dint of the plentiful material that is presented in his lectures, like films, documents, slides, etc." They referred vaguely to impediments and difficulties encountered by the Brazilian man (apparently a friend of the regime) seeking to coordinate Wurmbrand's visit—impediments that the CISA itself intervened to mitigate: "This agency, via the Ministry of Justice Division of Security and Intelligence (DSI/MJ), solicited the intervention of [Justice] Minister Armando Falcão." The CISA saw to it that Wurmbrand was not only admitted but granted permission to speak at Maracanã in April 1977.[113] This support for anticommunist evangelicals put state agents right in the middle of a struggle over the tenor of missionary and evangelical outreach in Brazil; and the agents sided with conservative Brazilians and their ilk among foreign visitors. Well aware of progressives' concern about the admittance of right-wing evangelicals and their media representations, security operatives calmly looked on as fundamentalist missionaries entered the northeast of Brazil and as U.S.-style fundamentalism gained adherents, in no small part because of the broadcast popularity of Jerry Falwell, Rex Humbard, and Jimmy Swaggart.[114]

Various security agencies joined the effort to bar progressive Christian visitors, citing the threat of communist conspiracy. In a 1970 report, naval intelligence agents fretted about the "International Communist Movement" (referred to as "MCI," a shorthand) targeting youths, an international plot "to reframe the so-called 'generational conflict' by granting it political-ideological content based in Marxism." The agents sought to prohibit the "activity of International Organizations of Marxist Ideology," among them the WCC, the YMCA, the Red Cross Youth, and UNESCO. Furthermore, they sought to monitor individual Brazilians and to prohibit the entry into Brazil of foreign "elements" linked with these organizations.[115] Known leftist or radical Christians—from Richard Shaull to Camilo Torres—meanwhile, were of course cause for particular concern. Cuban socialist pastor Sérgio Arce Martínez, for example, was well known to security forces and fretted constantly about his and other activists' potential plans to visit Brazil.[116]

V. The Politics of No, Redux: Prefiguring Present-Day Politics

What is perhaps most interesting and most significant about these antiecumenist and antiprogressive conspiracy theories is that they combined a litany of issues that will sound familiar to present-day observers. Security forces, that is, envisioned the vast conspiracies just outlined as composed of a perfect storm of subversive tactics that included Protestant ecumenism, progressive Christianity more generally, rights movements (especially black rights in the vein of the U.S. civil rights movement), communism, gender and sexual change (especially feminism but also changing sexual mores), and guerrilla warfare. They envisioned, then, a transnational, transdenominational plot whose outlines contained the precise sparks that would ignite New Right outrage. The emergent conservative coalition, represented by conservative evangelicals who held the sympathies of the state's hard-liners, responded with a "no" to all of these potential changes: no redistribution, no liturgical innovation, no ecumenism, no change to existing social and cultural (especially racial, gender, and sexual) hierarchies, and certainly no communism. In a sense, then, this was the birth (or a birth) of the New Right.

As briefly noted earlier, security forces associated almost any attempt at solidarity with the downtrodden to be a tactic of subversion. This meant that progressive Christians who sought to assist or even recognize the "marginalized, like the black, the Indian, and the tenant farmer," were accused of employing "the very strategy of the 'liberation theologians,' inspired by Marxism." To some extent, this reflected security forces' previously noted concurrence with conservatives of both Catholic and Protestant origin: all parties, that is, could agree that progressive questioning of the principle of hierarchy itself represented dangerous communistic anathema. Thus when pastor João Dias de Araújo preached that "the Kingdom of God has arrived, it is present . . . within men, [it] belongs to the children, to the poor, to the humble in spirit and to the persecuted," security forces and conservatives heard at least two things: a threat to time-honored hierarchies, celestial as well as earthly, and a related, subversive attempt to religiously sanction class warfare.[117] Moreover, subversive threats to hierarchy were observed to have crossed national as well as denominational borders, from the perspective of police. Quaker and NCC visitors from the United States, for example, seemed particularly suspect because of their links with black churches and the "local Black Movement." A 1982 SNI report illustrated security forces' conflation of these and other issues on a domestic and international scale. Broadly critical of any Christians (including progressive Catholics) who could not be called "traditionalists," the report demonstrated equal, undifferentiated outrage about Marxism, black liberation, and birth control, raised rather indiscriminately. By way of example, the report made a point of "citing, in passing, the 'Quilombo mass' celebrated by four Bishops in Recife, in the rhythm of candomblé; . . . and pronouncements of [progressive Bishop] Ivo Lorscheiter, favorable to the birth control pill."[118]

The military's intelligence and security organizations not only concurred with conservatives in identifying progressive Christianity as a danger; they likewise associated it with sexual deviance, all wrapped up into one plot against state, society, and civilization. In 1981, for example, the general then commanding the Second Army (himself an inveterate Cold Warrior) made clear the way that this association was already bound up with incipient culture war—along battle lines that resembled those of the New Right. Commandant Sérgio Ary Pires demonized all manner of progressive Christianity, from Vatican II to Hugo Assman, Richard Shaull, and the WCC, as fulcrums of communist "physical and ideological infiltration." According to Pires, such infiltration included disrupting the "traditional standards" of youth, alienating children from their parents, attacking priestly celibacy, and other "distortions of the 'New Church.'" Indicating the detailed level at which these conflationary visions operated, Pires crowed with knowing triumph at what he presented as evidence of Dom Paulo Evaristo Arns's implication in this subversive wave. Arns must be engaged in "anti-Christian evangelization" and "political-ideological instrumentalization" because he had "gone to watch *Jesus Christ Super Star* and personally greeted the lead actor."[119]

Military officials, like conservative religious people more generally, were alarmed and even incensed by changes to rituals or liturgy. This was especially the case when those changes seemed to indicate evidence of the amalgam conservatives envisioned themselves facing off against: social justice, rights movements, cultural change, communism, and subversion. When, for example, CNBB representatives organized a *Via Crucis* based on the theme "Land and Work for Everyone, So That Everyone May Have Life" (the CNBB's slogan for the year 1984), SNI officials in Porto Alegre listed this act among "Activities of the Progressive Line of the Clergy, Demonstrations

Against the Regime's Politics in the Political, Economic, or Social Fields."
The watchers noted with knowing apprehension that the presentation not
only drew attention to democratization efforts and "the suffering of the workers" but also "paid homage to the Brazilian black man. . . . The discrimination
suffered by the black in society was also shown." Another scene, they noted,
"was dedicated to the Brazilian Indian" and suggested that "Brazil in 1500 was
robbed from the Indians, who are the real owners of this land."[120]

Moreover, when officials summarized their "conclusions" about "religious
people of this political line, who are always gaining more adherents, [and
who] now constitute a parallel power, insistently confronting the Government and the current political regime"—in other words, progressive Christians as enemies of state and society—they made special note of the multiple
"positions" that justified this view of religious activists. Among those was action "in favor of the poorest sectors of society and those that are understood
to be marginalized, like the black, the Indian, and the tenant farmer." Worse,
to the minds of the agents of the SNI, progressive Christianity was gaining "a
broader character insofar as its battle flags are concerned, since it has come to
focus on urban social struggles, principally the problem of unemployment, of
wages, of housing, and of the black in society."[121]

As if to round out the litany of issues sparking alarm on the Right, surveillance of an international ecumenical meeting in Caxias do Sul resulted in a
casually damning report from agents of the SNI. Singling out critics of "police and military repression" who concomitantly promoted various forms of
social justice, the document repeated what had by this point become plati-
tudes about the dangers of ecumenism, "the new Christianity," the "popular
Church," liberation theology, and the WCC, especially in Latin America. The
oft-quoted phrase "Christianity is dying in Latin America and the Church of
the People is being born" appeared in the report's conclusions. Perhaps most
interestingly, however, the agents zeroed in on two issues that would come to
form the backbone of the New Right: feminism and government regulation
as social justice–linked bugbears. The state agents dwelt on the opposition to
"neoliberalism" on the part of their (perceived) internationalist ecumenist
antagonists (including inveterate regime opponent Carlos Alberto Libânio
Christo, known as Frei Betto). Emphasizing the dissenters' origin not only in
Brazil but in Argentine and Chilean delegations, the agents described a
wholesale dismissal of "the economic model implanted in the Southern
Cone" based on the idea that state regulation and equitable industrialization
were being "replaced, inexorably," by "a monetarist, neoliberal economic system." The SNI emphasized, with no small measure of disdain, the role of

women in this struggle to preserve the "opportune protections of the State." Indeed, the role of women generally, taken up at the conference, seemed to alarm the agents based on its combination of feminist and class-equity themes: "The participation of the woman in the task of liberating the people was one of the themes of the conference. Two expositions fell to Brazil: 'analysis of the situation of the peasant woman' and 'analysis of the religious life of Catholic women in the country.' . . . The conclusion was that woman has been suffering a 'model of oppression similar to that which has affected blacks and Indians across the centuries, and that recognized rights and values are not attributed to her.'" The idea, in other words, of minoritarian opposition (women, Afro-Brazilians, and indigenous-descended Brazilians) cohering, understanding itself as collectively and individually oppressed, and engaging in a struggle against deregulatory capitalism formed the primary anxiety elucidated in this report.[122]

Indeed, the amalgam went further than just the linkage of social justice, rights movements, and opposition to late Cold War neocapitalism. In keeping with long-standing practices, security forces and their conservative evangelical allies tended to focus intensely on "dangerous" women and on sexual or gender deviance—beyond ideological feminism itself—as symptoms of a broader progressive threat to order, religion, and the state. In a summary investigation of one famous Protestant activist, a formal Military Police Inquest concluded that the man combined several leftist dangers: student activism, the (defunct and largely ineffective) "Movement Against the Dictatorship," social justice agitation, and marriage to a "north American leftist" wife who had imbibed some "liberated" ideas while studying in Moscow.[123] Another exemplary investigation, this one initiated in 1965 by the Naval Intelligence Center, linked several prominent progressive evangelicals in what intelligence officers considered, even at this early moment in the dictatorship, to be an expansive, international conspiracy. One activist was described as "highly engaged in the . . . communization [*sic*] of the Brazilian evangelical milieus," actively fomenting continent-wide guerrilla activity, constantly in contact with a cosmopolitan coterie of suspected subversive malefactors (including Richard Shaull and other progressive evangelicals from Princeton, Chicago, and elsewhere), "financed by a communist/clandestine entity based in the USA," and, perhaps most worryingly, associated with one Laura Magalhães, known to security forces as a force for the concomitant communization and seduction of university students. This assessment was thus consistent with a broader tendency among security forces to see gender-deviant women as particular threats.[124] This is not to say that *men's* gender and sexual deviance (real or imagined) lay beyond the purview of the antiecumenist, antimodern banner taken up by security forces and conservative evangelicals. In one particularly notable incidence, air force intelligence excoriated no less an authority than the apostolic nuncio in Brazil, Sebastiano Baggio, perceived as a progressive. His conduct, they said, was injurious to every country where he had been stationed and also to the Vatican itself. The salient facts came in list form, accusing Baggio of "stirring up leftist agitation, sustaining it, and honoring it in all ways"; of carrying contraband for "leftist syndicates" and perhaps for "his own profit"; and of "liberated attitudes in his ways of dressing, frequenting beaches and entertainment venues."[125]

VI. United against Union: Antiecumenist Ecumenism

Another element of the antiprogressive, antiecumenist groundswell bears mentioning here. If security officials and conservative evangelicals reached an alliance based in opposition to ecumenical, social justice–oriented Christianity, this alliance incorporated a further, consequential, and somewhat ironic development: the linkage of different conservative denominations based on that opposition—that is, a sort of antiecumenist ecumenism. As we shall see in chapter 5, this cooperation to stymie cooperation took on international dimensions and spread across continents; here, however, I wish to point out that within Brazil itself, conservative forces collaborated, ironically enough, in their efforts to prevent and demonize collaboration itself. In order to oppose ecumenism, Brazil's conservative Christians formed institutions designed to unite the Right across denominations—again, in the name of combating interdenominational cooperation.

Catholic conservatives concurred with their Protestant brethren when it came to these issues. Indeed, the reactionaries we met in chapter 1 could not have been more emphatic in their rejection of proposals for reconciliation between the Church and other religions. Bishops Geraldo Proença Sigaud and Antônio de Castro Mayer were particularly caustic in their censure of those who contemplated any sort of appeasement of "false religions." This was evident at the Second Vatican Council itself, where they spearheaded opposition to any such opening toward other religions—especially the schemas on ecumenism, religious freedom, and the Church in the modern world. As Mayer argued in 1965 in a statement on the declaration *De Libertate Religiosa,*

> The declaration must be elaborated entirely anew, because it sins in certain fundamental points. (A) It affirms . . . the equal right [to practice] all

religions (true and false). Now, on the other hand, it is known that only the true religion has the right to be professed publicly. Thus the rights of the true religion and of the false ones are *not* the same. (B) Human nature only perfects itself with adherence to the true and the good; human dignity is not safeguarded from error even when accompanied by good faith. (C) It is the law of God that everyone embrace the true religion and no one is condemned unless it is through their own fault. Thus the state cannot encourage the false religions.[126]

Observers from Brazil could not help but note the ferocity of this opposition. Nearly all the Church fathers favored a declaration on religious freedom (the final vote was 1,997 to 224); yet as one bishop noted in his daily bulletin, Sigaud denounced the proposed schema as philosophically errant, "based on principles of modern phenomenology," and likely to further "the danger of . . . Marxism." Sigaud's confederates, including Ernesto Ruffini, Marcel Lefebvre, Mayer, and Luigi Carli, were among those few who argued that "the declaration should be absolutely rejected."[127] Likewise, Brazilian diplomats ranked this as among the biggest items of contention at Vatican II generally, but especially among conservatives. In a 1965 report to the minister of foreign relations, the Brazilian ambassador at the Vatican wrote that "the document which aroused the most attention" at the council was "that about the relations of the Church with the non-Christian religions. . . . Its promulgation led to an unbelievable number of interventions, letters, visits, pamphlets and all manner of threats in the last three years to the Secretariat for Unity of Christians, charged with this matter, to impede first the discussion and later the approval of any text in this regard." Even after the approving vote, continued the ambassador, "there were extremely strong objections made to the text by bishops from Arab countries and by those of strongly conservative tendencies."[128] Ten years later, as the details of implementing Vatican II decisions continued to be hashed out, then-ambassador Antônio Borges Leal Castello Branco listed the relatively minor issue of celebration of Church rites for "the non-catholic deceased" alongside abortion, birth control, priestly celibacy, the ordination of women, and "sexual comportment" as a major pronouncement of concern to Brazilian Catholics.[129]

As we shall see in chapter 5, such Catholic antiecumenism, combined with anticommunism, even led to cooperation with evangelicals in international milieus.[130] A first step toward that cooperation, however, was the creation of a domestic forum to unite conservative evangelicals across denominations— based on (and oddly in spite of) these conservatives' shared opposition to cross-denominational cooperation in the form of ecumenism. This forum was the Confederation of Fundamentalist Evangelical Churches of Brazil (CIEF), created at least in part by extremist missionaries from the United States.[131] Founded in 1959, CIEF brought together Baptists, Presbyterians, and Pentecostals under an umbrella of ferocious anticommunism and anti-ecumenism.[132] Announcing a national congress in 1981, the organization defined itself as follows: "CIEF is a national movement of religious clarification, Christian confraternity . . . on behalf of Biblical and historical Christianity, and of combat, without quarter, against all the forms of theological and moral apostasy in the bosom of the Church of Christ in our days. [CIEF] fights to ensure our theological patrimony and the autonomy of each Christian denomination and of each local Church [as a] biblical alternative against the spurious and anti-Biblical ecumenism of the World Council of Churches. Spiritual Unity—Yes! Ecclesiastical Unity—No!"[133] Insuring "patrimony" against the assault of apostasy, then, allowed for some vague sense of Christian "spiritual unity" while unilaterally rejecting ministerial, hierarchical, or doctrinal merging. (Though most ecumenists did not, in fact, envision a "World Church," this was the bugbear of conservatives, and it was to this perceived threat that they responded when they decried "ecclesiastical unity.") Distrust and execration of doctrinal changes were, in fact, old hat for CIEF—the organization's founding statutes brimmed with such language, notably in its first two preambular "considerations":

> Considering that it is the sacred duty of all the true churches of the Lord Jesus Christ to bear witness to their faith, especially in these dangerous times of apostasy, in which the fundamental doctrines of Christianity are being openly denied;
>
> Considering that the apostasy of the last few years, of which Paul spoke, have [*sic*] been characterized in our times by theological modernism, which denies the fundaments of "the faith once delivered to the saints."[134]

The document went on to refer to the threat of an ecumenist, communist "Super-Church, apostate and Babylon-esque," and to the "doctrines of the devil" spawning across Brazil and the world via progressive and modernist theology.[135]

Security forces exuded pleasure at the emergence and ongoing cantankerousness of CIEF. Agents attended the organization's conferences, kept track of its publications, and sang the praises of its members and mission. One report, parroting CIEF's own language as though it were the SNI's own, described the mission of "religious clarification" and "combat against all forms of theological and moral change" and so on. The report editorialized, appreciating how "CIEF places itself frontally against the leftist orientation that is being given by the World Council of Churches (WCC), against Marxism in all its modalities and against Liberation Theology which [CIEF's] initiates define as being 'a form of infiltration of communism in the Protestant and Catholic Churches.'"[136] If anything, the political police wished CIEF's actions were *more* forceful and more effective at discrediting and even eradicating progressive Christianity. Another report, relating a planned CIEF congress, appreciated the organization's representation of "dissension [from progressivism] among protestants, which . . . takes form in various publications."[137]

Conclusion

Within a few years of CIEF's founding, conservative evangelicals would be cooperating in ways far more influential, at least as far as the lives of nonevangelical Brazilians were concerned. Though scattered evangelicals had cropped up in electoral politics across the decades, it was in the 1980s that they cohered into a recognizable and even auto-denominated group. By 1986, when delegates gathered to form a new national constitution, evangelicals from different denominations had banded together in what would come to be known as the *bancada evangélica*. To this day, the *bancada*, also known as the Frente Parlamentar Evangélica, is somewhat amorphous, consisting in an ever-expanding constellation of Christian legislators. What has always been clear, however, is the group's conservative nature and its inclusion of reactionaries from across the denominations. Today's *bancada*, dominated by the Assemblies of God, Baptists, and the Universal Church of the Kingdom of God, reflects the early strength of the former two denominations, whose antiecumenist ecumenism in the 1980s at the very least allowed them to cooperate to stymie the fuller democratization envisioned by more progressive delegates to the constitutional convention.[138]

CHAPTER FOUR

Preach the World, Reach the World

Authoritarian Brazil and the Organization(s)
of a Transnational Right

Baptist pastor Nilson do Amaral Fanini, whom we met in chapter 2, became
Brazil's first mega televangelist. As we have seen, his close ties to the
Figueiredo regime helped him build *Reencontro* into a Christian media jug-
gernaut, in ways that were unprecedented in the Brazil of that time. The "Brazilian Billy Graham," however, lived up to his moniker in multiple, complex
ways that exceeded pioneering mega-evangelism. Like his North American
namesake, Fanini rose to fame and fortune championing a conservative, moralistic, and anticommunist evangelistic revival—then tempered his vim and
vitriol in later years. Before that tempering, however, Fanini—like Graham—
constructed a legacy of right-wing evangelism that transcended national borders and national identities. In their peak years, the two shared a penchant for
global Christian conservatism, personally and institutionally. They represented, individually and via associations, the ways in which such conservatism
would become ascendant by dint of its potential for translation, transposition,
and transnational collaboration.

Fanini, in fact, had begun his career by crossing borders. A 1958 graduate of
the Southwestern Baptist Theological Seminary in Fort Worth, Texas, he
would later recall, "Right here [in Texas] is where I got my vision for the
world."[1] As if taking the school's motto ("Preach the World. Reach the
World.") literally, Fanini eventually delivered sermons in some eighty-seven
countries, including postrevolutionary Mozambique and Angola. In 1995 he
crowned these achievements with his accession to the presidency of the Baptist World Alliance, becoming the first Brazilian to hold this position. By this
time Fanini had had something of a change of heart—during his tenure he
would meet not only with Fidel Castro but with the Pontifical Council for
Promoting Christian Unity. Yet in his heyday as a televangelist, a decidedly
anticommunist and antiecumenist Fanini brought together Baptists internationally for very different reasons.

As early as 1977, Fanini warned anyone who would listen that "there are
already more communists than Christians in the world"—an impetus, in his
view, to evangelization and moralization.[2] In 1984, as president of the Brazilian

Baptist Association, he remained staunchly opposed to cooperation with Catholics and even more so to social justice–oriented Christianity or the "preferential option for the poor."[3] In the final week of June 1983, he and a close-knit group of Baptist pastors from the United States organized a global meeting at Fanini's power base in Niterói. Calling it the First Worldwide Baptist Congress on Urban Evangelism, they gathered five hundred religious and academic leaders from more than thirty countries. Asking, "What can the Baptist Church do to save the city?" the delegates eventually concluded that they must seek "new doctrines for work in the social field"—yet the overwhelming tone of the conference seems to have been criticism of just such work. Special attention was paid to "evangelizing the Marxist world," with the reminder that Marx sought to eradicate religion; and the congress featured Argentine pastor Samuel Libert, who affirmed the worst fears of right-wing Christians in this moment. "The Theology of Liberation," Libert declared, "is an ideological movement and not a theological one, which seeks to secularize the Church." He execrated the "progressive wing" of his and other churches, accusing this so-called wing of a conspiracy to suborn political and spiritual leadership. Fanini himself presided over the congress's organizing committee, which comprised Libert and other allies, including several conservative Southern Baptists from the United States.[4]

Fanini, as we have seen, played a critical role in the rise to power and visibility of politicized evangelicalism in Brazil. As moralistic and anticommunist alliance with the military regime facilitated his mass televangelism, the Baptist leader laid the groundwork for generations of similar, nationally famous pastor-celebrities in decades to come. Yet Fanini's story illustrates the ways in which the ascendancy of such players and their platforms both depended on and reinforced an *international* context of conservative evangelism. At Maracanã and on Channel 13, Fanini demonstrated how right-wing Protestantism had acquired considerable influence in domestic politics and culture; at the First Worldwide Baptist Congress on Urban Evangelism, Fanini demonstrated something else—the ways in which Brazilians participated in international networks that created a playbook for right-wing Christian activism *beyond Brazil*.

Earlier, I argued that Brazilian Catholics at and around Vatican II laid the groundwork for global traditionalism within the faith, while back at home an ascendancy of evangelical politics in late dictatorial Brazil drew on support from the government to construct a budding, national New Right. These events did not occur in isolation; rather, they happened in ways that showed the complex contours of the rise of a transnational Christian Right. Brazilian activists, who became hemispheric and even global activists, formed connections that simultaneously showed the facility of transnational linkages and the ongoing fractiousness that could always impede conservative cooperation. Despite the latter, individuals and institutions did create forums for communication and collaboration—eventually, these would constitute a web of shared right-wing priorities, agendas, ideological lexicons, and strategies.

Moralistic anticommunism, in a sense, lay at the heart of this web, historically and discursively speaking (that is, in terms both of antecedents and of the ongoing right-wing lexis). The Christian Right itself has of course outlasted the Cold War—yet anticommunism lingers on, implicitly and explicitly. As I shall discuss in chapter 5, the shared agendas mentioned here comprised a specific litany of issues that fused that web into a coherent, transnational Right: antimodernism, antiecumenism, anticommunism, mysticism, antistatism, hierarchalist antiegalitarianism, antirationalism, and the sense of besiegement that characterizes late twentieth-century and early twenty-first-century conservatisms. In this chapter, we shall begin to trace Brazil's development as a key nexus in the circuits that gave rise to the transnational New Right. Here, I explore the ways that moralism and anticommunism can be seen as fundaments on which the rest of that litany was to be built. Opposition to communism—or, more precisely, a culture of anticommunism that interpreted various (nearly limitless) perceived evils across decades as the fruit, proof, or threat of communist subversion—provided an early link between diverse national and denominational groups that would come to adopt the rest of the issues from the now-familiar New Right platform as a sort of common ground. Anticommunism also served as the fulcrum that gained these groups the support of Brazil's military regime—making Brazil a key locus for the gestation and empowerment of right-wing actors and institutions whose legacy would transcend the country itself.[5]

This chapter and the next, then, reconnoiter the ways in which what has become the Christian Right of Brazil, the United States, and elsewhere emerged transnationally—by which I mean that it developed not only in several national contexts but via and because of the people and institutions that connected those national contexts and drew on their specificities to advance what came to be seen as a common series of causes. Chapter 5 will elaborate the marriage of disparate issues, later naturalized under the moniker "right-wing" but in fact cobbled together as the common priorities of a set of international actors and activists. In this chapter, I wish to begin sketching the formation of a network uniting different Christian and even non-Christian groups around moralism and renovated anticommunism. Various participants from this network received the approval and support of Brazil's authoritarian government—which made Brazil the "key locus" described earlier, not only for Brazilian conservatives but for their counterparts abroad.

I. "Total Decadence": Brazilian Evangelicals, Moral Crisis, and Hemispheric Revival

In October 1977, subscribers to *A Seara* received an edition with the cover story "'Free Love,' That Poor Slave." In an introductory editorial, Joanyr de Oliveira seemed to wring his hands at moral changes wrought of late: "Today . . . the 'love' that is most talked about is . . . a practice in which physical attraction predominates, [with] cynicism and mockery." Family and marriage, he moaned, were treated with scorn as "stuff for squares."[6] The issue's main attraction, however, was doctor and university professor José Maria Nascimento Pereira's full article, "Free Love, Slave Love." Pereira trod well-worn paths of evangelical moralism and moral panic, even acknowledging that "the thesis of 'free love' is not new among the youth of Brazil." He likewise carped about the casting aside of traditional morality: "Everything that is institutionalized has come to be violently attacked and repudiated. Among those values . . . marriage, the family, and other things have been considered anti-human, inhuman and unnatural. . . . Values like fidelity, virginity, chastity, stability, and responsibility have become taboos."[7]

In some ways, Pereira's screed reflects precisely the climate of moral panic we have seen gripping—and fortifying, and enabling—Brazil's conservative Christians in this period. Yet two further, salient points are worth noting: Pereira linked this putative moral crisis to global events, and he did so in ways that signaled right-wing links across denominations. "Free Love, Slave Love" limned "free love" as an international concept, but perhaps more impressively opened with references to Erich Fromm ("psychoanalyst and atheist philosopher of international fame, living in the United States") as well as to "hippies" and "Jean-Paul Sartre and Company." The upshot of these philosophers and their "movement," from Pereira's point of view, was nothing short of utter chaos and the failure of "civilization." Strikingly, he drove this point home citing yet more images from abroad: "What was seen in the 'hippie civilization' was total decadence . . . of which the Woodstock festival, the singer Jimmy Hendrix, who committed suicide, are saddening examples."[8]

Pereira's article thus invited Brazilian readers to marshal defenses against a threat that transcended Brazil. Sinful decadence, which required the urgent attention of moralistic Christians, emerged in this vision as a conspiracy that did not itself respect the boundaries of nation—hippies in the United States elicited free love and the collapse of the family in Brazil. Indeed, Pereira seemed to see an unbroken fabric of sinfulness among "university youths" stretching across the North and South Atlantic, from Paris to Berkeley to Rio de Janeiro. This was not unique to Pereira, of course, nor to evangelicals, as I have illustrated among moralists of other stripes.[9] What was special here was the notion that Christian conservatives must unite, politically, against moral threats; that those moral threats were transnational in nature; and that a united conservative response must convene the right-minded faithful across denominational lines. Pereira's article had originally appeared in *Mocidade Batista*, a Baptist youth publication, and had been adopted by Oliveira as a call to arms for *assembleiano* (Assemblies of God) readers. The message, then, was that conservative evangelicals of *various* (generally antiecumenist) persuasions must unite around this transnational moral imperative.

As if in answer to this message, conservative Christians in Brazil rallied not just around domestic moralistic initiatives—like Fanini's "Deus Salve a Família"—but also around foreign celebrities, especially those from the United States, who thus solidified their position as leading lights of a transnational mobilization of moralistic and anticommunist Christian conservatism. Indeed, there developed something of a love affair, among Brazilian rightists, with mega-evangelist extremists who had gained fame in the United States and would, in the course of time, successfully promote the migration of political discourse toward the New Right: Jimmy Swaggart, Jerry Falwell, Pat Robertson, Rex Wade, and others. Broadcasting from Ohio, Rex Humbard was for some years Brazil's most popular televangelist.[10] Swaggart graced the cover of the October 1987 issue of *O Obreiro*, whose editors could barely contain their enthusiasm for the man they called "Our Worker" (Nosso Obreiro). Swaggart had just completed an "Evangelistic Crusade" in São Paulo and in Rio de Janeiro, where by some estimates he drew more than two hundred thousand admirers to Maracanã stadium.[11] And according to *O Obreiro*, Swaggart was the "most popular evangelical musician of our time," deservedly beloved by more than five hundred million viewers in 145 countries, and leader of the single "greatest evangelical work related to helping minors in the entire world."[12]

By this time, Swaggart's program could be seen daily in the television listings of major newspapers in Brazil, and the country's evangelicals made much of his empire and its messages. *A Seara*, for example, published a May 1986 article entitled "A Wall of Fire Will Protect the Family." This direct translation of a David Wilkerson sermon in Swaggart's *Evangelist* represented the

Jimmy Swaggart gracing the cover of *O Obreiro* (October–December 1987). Photo taken by author and used by permission of Casa Públicadora das Assembléias de Deus.

seamlessness with which Swaggart's moralistic anticommunist message, originally directed at the United States, could be adopted by Brazilian counterparts. A *Seara* praised Swaggart for showing "how God will save the faithful and their families from the uncontrollable avalanche of immorality in these days." The article itself, meanwhile, cobbled together the moralism and anticommunism that were fast becoming a familiar playbook—one that here transcended the nation. Sex, drugs, and rock and roll (alongside "violence, Satanism, sadism, impiety[,] . . . divorce," and sundry other moral panic–buttons), via translation, were presented as just as pertinent in the Brazilian context as in the American one for which these admonitions were intended. The translated sermon began by interpreting a recent music video as "a veritable vision of hell" and continued into further "images of the tragic moral decadence of American society." The article culminated in a state-of-the-art condemnation of AIDS as God's punishment: "Will our grandchildren have to attend schools where they teach that homosexuality is a decent—or even preferable—way of life? Can it be that God, no longer tolerating that, liberated this curse to punish these perverts?"[13] The article showcased the conflations that defined Christian neoconservatism from the United States to Brazil: "Let the homosexuals and sadists exalt their ways. Let the rockers mock society with their crazy and malicious ways! Let the Devil come to Earth with his great fury. . . . Let the impious rage! Let the Communists . . . preach and practice their atheistic doctrines! Let society love sin, just as Rome did in the past!"[14]

What is salient here is not just Wilkerson's and Swaggart's cobbling together of moralism and anticommunism, packaged in a tenor of millenarian urgency; rather, it is the way in which this precise version of politicized evangelism could strike such a deep chord among Brazil's burgeoning evangelical Right, then (in 1986–1987) just bursting onto the national political scene at the constitutional assembly. Evangelicals in Brazil, as we have seen, had themselves politicized "nosso terreno"—and the issues raised here would concretize into the platform of a unified Christian Right, so much so that the bugbear of homophilic primary education remains at the center of Christian conservative politics in Brazil today.

This celebration of and even identification with North American megaevangelists of the New Right extended far beyond Swaggart and even beyond denominational loyalties. *A Seara*, itself an Assemblies of God publication, warmed up to celebrities from Billy Graham to Jerry Falwell to Pat Robertson and Oral Roberts. In a televised 1983 interview with Pastor Ielon Nascimento, Graham hinted at the ways that alliances across denominations and institutions had become important. The interview, published in the October issue of *A Seara*, insisted that the "majority of evangelicals" in the United States "are not involving themselves in politics" but displayed sympathy for Falwell's Moral Majority. "I am not a member of the Moral Majority," Graham affirmed, "but they have some good objectives." Most impressive, Graham articulated a Christian conservative identity that transcended nationality *by dint of moralism itself*. Graham explained that he felt himself almost a "citizen of Brazil" and "of the world" because of his faith and his battle against "problems" like "crime and pornography": "I consider myself more a citizen of the world than an American. I feel as though I were a citizen of Brazil. . . . When I began to preach, I used to almost identify the North American way of life with Heaven. But I don't think that way anymore. There are many great problems in the United States, a lot of crime and pornography. I am ashamed much of the time. We Christians have to get worried." Graham's words, reso-nant with the editorial staff of *A Seara*, thus constituted a call to arms, a trans-national vision of evangelical Christian consciousness-raising in a unified battle against "pornography and crime."[15]

Swaggart, Wilkerson, and others received the fulsome praise of outspoken conservative Christians in Brazil, especially when it came to moralistic anti-modernism and anticommunism. Claudionor de Andrade, for example, who had celebrated AIDS (and even reveled in the death of Rock Hudson) as just, divine punishment for homosexuality, admired Wilkerson as a pioneer of suppressing rock music—a "diabolical" rhythm designed to "incite sexual ex-citement," "hypnosis," and "rebellion."[16] Few, however, could exceed the en-thusiasm for North American evangelists elicited by Pastor Nemuel Kessler. In a column entitled "Let Us Preserve Morality and Good Behavior," Kessler fretted that redemocratization would impede moral censorship—and rather ironically cited the example of U.S. evangelical conservatives as an (antidemo-cratic) model to be emulated. Kessler lauded the "braking action brought to bear by the evangelicals of that country when it comes to the moral degrada-tion, to the degenerate behavior of various segments of the North American people." Citing a recent article in *Time* magazine, Kessler reported that "to the surprise of many, the magazine found that North Americans have been greatly influenced by the preaching of men like Jimmy Sweggart [*sic*], Pat Robertson, Oral Roberts, and others, who with their Bibles open and their authority given by God, have vehemently combated abortion, drug use, pros-titution, adultery, Satanism, rock, and many other evils that have long af-fected the North American nation." This, Kessler insisted, should serve as a model for Brazil's Christians: "What the North American preachers are doing in the United States constitutes a great lesson for us, the evangelicals of Brazil. May our evangelical programs also have the same efficacy.... Let us fight the liberalization of Brazilian censorship.... Let us not forget that we are the guardians of morality and good behavior in this country." The "lesson," in Kessler's view, should be a playbook for bringing moral-religious pressure to bear on government and making alliances with center-Right leaders (them-selves of dubious moral authority). Despite José Sarney's questionable legiti-macy, and perhaps because of his ties with the outgoing military regime, Kessler expressed confidence that "we [conservative evangelicals] can help President José Sarney to moralize this country."[17]

Even lesser-known U.S. evangelicals made the grade in terms of publica-tion and circulation by Brazilian conservatives, demonstrating not just the facility of transnational collaboration but also the adoption of tactics from abroad. James Dobson had by this time become a household name—but even Dobson's less popularly known mentor, Clyde Narramore, saw his advice translated into Portuguese for conservative Christian readership. (Narramore, a psychologist who dedicated himself to fomenting stable marriages within the faith, also counseled now-familiar self-reliance, stressing God's contempt for the "lazy.")[18] Pastor and Sunday-school teacher Miguel Vaz translated a series of essays for *A Seara*, including the arguments of one Peggy Musgrave. Via the technique—then developing in the United States—of drawing on scripture to discredit second-wave feminism, Musgrave tweaked the nose of "Elizabeth Caty [*sic*] Stanton" and others who sought to challenge Christian traditionalism in gender roles. Since women had been present at the Last Supper, Musgrave argued, "the feminists of the 20th century" took entirely the wrong tack when it came to "women's emancipation."[19]

The flow of evangelism, it bears noting, was not one-way. Brazil in this period also generated a coterie of "reverse missionaries"—Christians leaving Brazil to minister to communities in the United States and Europe. Beyond defying national borders, this project seemed to ignore them completely, as though the work of confronting moral crisis trumped any sense of local or national boundaries. Discussions of these missions did not, for example, even mention Brazil's formerly subordinate position in this regard; nor did they deem it necessary to justify the massive expenditures necessary to support missionaries in faraway New England when there were lost souls to be found at "home" in Nova Iguaçu. Though the Universal Church of the Kingdom of God is the oft-cited example of Brazil's (and Latin America's) contribution to this phenomenon, the story in fact encompasses a broader time span and range of institutions.[20] As early as 1949, Carl McIntire himself wrote (with no little smugness) that Brazilians he met had written off the United States as taken by sin and modernism: "One national said, 'The American people are sitting on a volcano and do not know it.' . . . They explain that modernism has made it possible!"[21] Across the decades, this sentiment would persist, leading to Brazilian-based missions to the North. By 1980, the Assemblies of God newspaper *Mensageiro da Paz* ran a recurrent report entitled "Missions." Amid moralizing and anticommunist fodder for Brazilian *assembleianos* ("Gambling: That Social Cancer"; "Abortion: A Doctor Wants to Liberalize the Laws"), the newspaper related the arrivals, successes, and status of missionaries like Geziel Gomes, an emissary in Hartford, Connecticut, and Elpídio Santos, then serving in New Bedford, Massachusetts. Gomes, notably, had been a champion of moralism and of fundamentalism in Brazil in the few years before he established himself in Connecticut.[22] Assemblies of God missionaries had also been sent to Peru, Bolivia, and other Latin American destinations. These missionaries, while seeking principally to save Latinx and especially Lusophone souls, saw themselves as enacting a response to the decadence that affected not only Brazil but *also the United States*. Gomes in particular "pointed out that in the United States the necessity of Workers is great" because the immorality-inducing "material facilities of American society grow with every day," making the "Work of the Lord" both increasingly urgent and increasingly "difficult." So dangerous was the atmosphere, affirmed Gomes, that even the missionaries themselves might "involve themselves too much with the things of this world, forgetting the Work of the Lord."[23]

II. "Gatherings of People of Real Substance": The International Policy Forum

Evangelists' physical and televised border crossings may have created a sense of common purpose and mitigated the notion of separate communities of the faithful. But the heavy lifting of constructing a transnational New Right happened in organizations specifically dedicated to this purpose. A constellation of institutions, new and old, layered individual connections atop a sort of clearinghouse approach to right-wing organizing: activists seeking to combat the threat of global Marxism, moral dissolution, and modernism looked to extant organizations and leaders from around the world, including standout connections in Brazil. The International Policy Forum was one such organization, perhaps the example par excellence (though, as we shall see, its key players also populated other key arenas). The IPF has received comparatively little scholarly attention, yet this group brought together a hemispheric coterie of right-wing celebrities and power brokers and created the space in which these actors could create a common agenda.

The IPF came into being as the brainchild of Paul Weyrich, a vital but relatively unsung hero of the Reagan-era Right in the United States. In the late 1970s and 1980s the burgeoning Christian Right made something of a darling out of Weyrich, a tireless and seemingly omnipresent force who secured the various ideological and operational joists of the New Right. Far-right celebrities appeared to depend on him; and conservative publications of the 1980s fairly worshiped him. By his own account, Weyrich arrived in Washington in 1966 and noted with dismay, "Contrary to what I had assumed, conservatives here showed almost no sign of being organized." As a result, he took the task upon himself, with great success. By 1984, *Free the Eagle*, a far-right publication founded by eccentric Mormon economist and author Howard J. Ruff, proclaimed Weyrich a hero: "Americans all owe him a great deal."[24] A Catholic, Weyrich became a major supporter of evangelical conservatives, offering advice, moral and tactical support, and even financial assistance to fundamentalists.[25] As such, he virtually brokered the antiecumenist ecumenism necessary to link conservatives across the lines of faith in the United States. This was so much the case, in fact, that Weyrich is in some sense responsible for the emergence of Jerry Falwell's (in)famous Moral Majority. When Falwell balked at joining hands across denominational lines (doctrinal differences worth, in Falwell's words, "shedding blood"), it was Weyrich who suggested to the Baptist leader that he must lead an interdenominational "moral majority" of Americans.[26]

At the heart of Weyrich's vision of this North American "majority" were the very topics we shall see binding the transnational New Right in chapter 5. Weyrich admired libertarians' commitment to economic liberalism but wished to wed that ideology to a social, cultural, and religious archconservatism. Limning Reagan and his ilk as "establishment" conservative disappointments, Weyrich ferociously opposed homosexuality and abortion; liberation theology; "neo-modernists" within and outside the Catholic Church; the weakening of faith and of mysticism brought on by modernization; women who did not "put the family first"; and a host of other issues.[27] These issues, of course, now constitute familiar planks in a right-wing platform. Weyrich, however, pioneered that list, putting in place those individuals, think tanks, and publications that would *launch*, for example, the New Right's attack on homosexuality.[28] Founder of the United States' most important New Right organizations—the Heritage Foundation and the Free Congress Foundation (FCF), among others—Weyrich served as something of a domestic clearinghouse, uniting such figures as Phyllis Schlafly, Fred Schwarz, John Singlaub, Morton Blackwell, Ronald Reagan, Enrique Rueda, Connie Marshner, Tim LaHaye, and—as noted—Jerry Falwell.[29] His FCF represented the point of the spear, operationalizing Weyrich's goals of reinvigorating conservatism in a new form that took sexual morality, cultural traditionalism, fiscal austerity, religious rigidity, and supernatural mysticism for its interrelated cores. Like the evangelicals we met in chapter 2, the FCF called on the right-leaning faithful to overcome apoliticism, "to match the demands of faith with the pressures seemingly inherent in the political arena," and to overcome the "almost instinctive reaction . . . to hide from political responsibility lest one contradict the call of holiness."[30] And like the Catholics we met in chapter 1, Weyrich and the FCF popularized the central goal of fighting the "leftward drift" of the Catholic Church and of Christians in general. Within the FCF, Weyrich developed the Catholic Center for Free Enterprise, Strong Defense, and Traditional Values. Claiming to be "known to Catholic activists throughout the United States," the center sought to combat "the progressive movement to the left . . . of the Church"—principally by mobilizing the conservative faithful. Via publications, public programs, and workshops, the center would "prepare the average conservative Roman Catholic to change from a passive complainer to an activist capable of helping to reverse the leftward drift of the Church," of Christianity, and of pluralistic Western democracies.[31]

Weyrich's remarkable career as a—if not the—linchpin of the North American New Right lies beyond the scope of this book. That career, though mentioned by certain scholars, has remained mired in some historiographical shadow. Yet more shadow covers Weyrich's direct facilitation of a transnational neoconservative movement. Alongside his better-known projects, Weyrich founded the IPF, designed explicitly to consolidate right-wing leaders across national borders in just the way Weyrich had sought to unite them domestically. From Weyrich's point of view, disunity on the Right constituted the most pressing problem; and the IPF would address that problem hemispherically, if not globally. Gathering in Washington in January 1985, the group's board of governors tellingly titled its meeting "Liberty in the World: Can the Forces of Freedom Cooperate?"—combining hawkish New Right anticommunism with an expanded geographical scope. A prospectus from the previous year made the group's objectives plain, again signaling the notion that right-wing forces must unite against a powerful leftist threat. "The Problem: Our Lack of Solidarity" presented IPF as a much-needed solution:

> For two centuries the world's *leftist* intellectuals and activists have built their own global networks. . . . This international solidarity is a source of enormous advantage to the Left. . . . Conservatives, on the other hand, are woefully ignorant of each other across the world. Pro-freedom leaders rarely work together across international boundaries. They seldom even are personal friends of those who would be natural allies in other countries. The problem is simple. While the Left has successfully built a network of activists around the globe, conservatives have been isolated from one another. What should be a worldwide conservative movement is almost totally divided by national boundaries. . . . IPF proposes . . . to get key conservative leaders and activists meeting and working together on a regular basis.[32]

Weyrich and Morton Blackwell (the IPF's first president) planned to include business and religious nabobs, prominent lobbyists, politicians, and "media leaders" and "intellectual leaders." These members would meet twice a year—

once in the United States, and once in another country. As the plan made clear, the core values established as common ground for all members would mirror the neoconservative platform then developing among activists like Weyrich and his counterparts in Brazil and elsewhere. The IPF would oppose big government, communism, immorality, and secularism and would provide a communicative space in which members could train together and share tactics. The biannual meetings would "provide members with information to help them combat excessive government in their own countries. Attendees will learn from each other new ways to halt the spread of Marxist totalitarianism." A list of "principles and beliefs" included "limited government," "limited taxation," "free enterprise," "traditional family moral values," and "rights" as "God-given, not government-given." Each of these, like anticommunism itself, seemed threatened by "secular humanism in education."[33]

From its early days, the IPF was designed to impress and even intimidate potential members and enemies alike, using a combination of calculated exclusivity, propagandistic promotional material, and associations with power and influence. As the organization's 1984 plan put it, *"The IPF Board of Governors meetings will be gatherings of people of stature and real substance.* Members will personally get to know international leaders with major resources who share their values. No one will be involved who is not a real 'mover and shaker' in his or her own country. We are an organization of movement-oriented, conservative leaders."[34] In its "Benefits to Members" section, the IPF promised that those who joined would "develop personal friendships with pro-freedom leaders," would "gain advance knowledge of business trends and political prospects in other countries," would "keep abreast of the problems of conservatives in other countries," and would "plan joint action with like-minded people from other countries." All of this, the leadership clarified, would be by invitation only. "Invitations to membership are extended only by the IPF Executive Committee upon nomination by IPF members." Those who *did* join would have to pony up a US$5,000 membership fee, making the elite and exclusive feel of the organization more pronounced—and more profitable.

Membership was advertised as an entrée to glamorous, elite jet-setting and hobnobbing; this networking, in other words, could scratch ideological itches alongside those of social and political ambition. The board of governors' meetings sought to entice those who wished to "travel abroad" and "meet in renowned hotels and excellent conference facilities in the United States and abroad." To embellish this luxury approach to transnational lobbying, all travel arrangements would be made by the IPF itself, whose annual budget for the meetings was a dazzling $250,000.[35] The organization billed

Morton Blackwell and Ronald Reagan in the IPF publication "International Policy Forum Prospectus, 1984–1985." Photo taken by author.

these summits not just as meetings of like minds but as star-studded influence mills. The "people of stature and real substance" honored with invitations would encounter famous IPF leaders and collaborators from North America, among them Weyrich himself, Phyllis Schlafly, V. Lance Tarrance, Reed Larson, Congressman Vin Weber, Oliver North, and former Ku Klux Klan leader Richard Shoff. Beneath a large photo of IPF president Morton Blackwell with Ronald Reagan, the group's literature touted the former's appointment to the White House Office of Public Liaison, where, as a special assistant to the president for public liaison, he had "helped thousands of conservatives get jobs in the Reagan administration."[36]

Whatever the dubious merits of lunches with Vin Weber, the IPF reaped early rewards from its efforts to link like-minded conservatives "of substance" across the world, especially in the Americas. "Conservative and pro-freedom leaders outside the United States are enthusiastic about the IPF concept," boasted one report. "In recent months, IPF has received pledges or cooperation from prominent leaders and key activists" in nearly a dozen countries. By 1984, the group was active in Argentina, Canada, Brazil, Guatemala, El Salvador, Israel, Austria, France, Great Britain, Taiwan, and Australia. Schlafly herself addressed an audience of some two hundred at a meeting in Australia that year; in the coming half decade, the group would hold meetings in Buenos Aires, Santiago, Córdoba, São Paulo, and Bern and establish a Paris-based "school" for direct-mail programs. Bernard Cardinal Law, Richard J. Neuhaus, John Singlaub, and Australian-born Fred Schwarz all addressed the group, alongside Reagan administration functionaries, including Ambassador Faith Whittlesey; these Americans were joined by an ever-increasing coterie of international speakers from the Americas, Europe, and eventually the Middle East and Asia.[37] The group's membership and its directorial board deliberately transcended nation, region, and denomination. A few years into its tenure, the IPF proudly trumpeted the international and multifaith provenance and prominence of its leadership and followers, the inner circle of which included ferocious anticommunist and apparent Reagan favorite James Whelan as well as Paige Patterson, the head of the Foreign Mission Board of the Foreign Baptist Convention.[38]

The IPF also partnered with foreign think tanks to achieve the central goal of fomenting an international conservative "movement." In Córdoba, the IPF joined the Institute of Contemporary Studies in welcoming 170 members from across the Americas and as far away as Monaco, South Africa, South Korea, and China.[39] The conference aimed to induct members into means of utilizing modern mass-media techniques for conservative goals—exploiting, that is, "the most modern techniques and organization of political campaigns." In fact, that had by this point become the IPF's principal pedagogical focus. The group's leadership, rather in keeping with its alliance with the likes of John Singlaub and other counterinsurgency hawks, saw itself as a "school" for conservative mobilization, complete with tactical classes like "Media of the World: Dangers and Opportunities."[40] To promote "internal strength and international cooperation among freedom-loving people," the "faculty of each Understanding Politics Conference consists of experts in the main areas of modern democratic political technology, e.g. direct mail, media relations and polling analysis." At the Córdoba conference, the "faculty" covered topics ranging from "Mobilizing the Business Community" to "Organizing Young People" and "Creative Use of Radio, Newspapers, Television, and Video Cassettes."[41]

Beyond the IPF meetings, Weyrich and Blackwell trotted the globe as individual foot soldiers of right-wing visibility and coalition building. Weyrich gave interviews, made speeches, and arduously courted the far-right groups of the Americas, including Brazil. In Argentina, he told journalists of the need for a sharp, domestic, and international turn to the right. Weyrich described the "so-called conservative revolution" as "exaggerated" and complained of Reagan's complacency. He insisted that "very few fundamental reforms have been made" and thus "much remains to be done on the conservative agenda," especially when it came to government spending, the Great Society, anticommunism, abortion, and "those who propitiate policies favorable to the growth of state functions." Blackwell, meanwhile, led a deputation of IPF observers to Chile, where they alleged that "leftist" counterparts sought to pervert the 1988 referendum on the Pinochet regime. "To counteract the leftist bias against Chile" and "the anti-communist Pinochet," the IPF sponsored a "high-level delegation" that included Senator Carl Curtis and Ambassador David Funderburk.[42] Via the Council for National Policy (CNP), Blackwell and Weyrich (a founding member) fostered hemispheric right-wing women's cooperation. At a forum in Guatemala in September 1988, "more than 40 women" from the United States and Central America gathered for "Women in the Hemisphere Achieving Together," an event attended by a delegation of women referred to as "CNP wives." Blackwell also enacted plans to internationalize the Right by a different route—ironically, via "big government" itself—seeking to flood the foreign service with right-minded acolytes. He offered what he called a "Foreign Service Opportunity School," which was "designed to help young conservatives pass the foreign service exams."[43]

Significantly for our purposes, Weyrich represented himself (and was received) abroad as the point of the New Right spear—not only an innovator and a pioneer but also a collaborator. As he told Argentine journalist Luís Álvarez Primo in 1988, "In general we think of the North American conservative movement as a movement of people who believe in limited government, free enterprise, strong national defense, and traditional values. *I like to believe that we were the first to add the concept of 'traditional values' to that equation.*" In what may have been one of the earliest articulations—certainly the earliest transnational articulation—of "I want my country back," Weyrich told Álvarez that he and his partners wished "to recuperate the type of country that made the United States a great nation."[44] With the support of the Reagan administration, Weyrich traveled as far afield as Bahrain, where he addressed a group of "senior members" of the government, apparently winning them over. As U.S. ambassador Sam Zakhem rhapsodically recapped, Weyrich "represents the caliber of speaker that is needed at this post—and ... most posts in this area—in addressing political concerns." The IPF founder combined "academic" knowledge of the Right with his role as a "practitioner." He thus, in Zakhem's words, "brings a wealth of experience, enhanced by knowledge, to his audiences. The audiences note and appreciate the difference."[45]

Weyrich established a fond and productive relationship with his Brazilian counterparts in the Brazilian Society for the Defense of Tradition, Family and Property (TFP)—or, better put, with the transnational series of organizations that the TFP was becoming. This relationship is remembered with particular warmth by TFP members in Brazil and abroad. Upon Weyrich's death in 2008, the American TFP (TFP-USA) remembered him as an "outstanding leader and mentor of the conservative movement" whose "efforts were of paramount importance in uniting conservatives for many decades." Weyrich, as TFP-USA rather bluntly put it, "moved moral issues into the forefront of the Cultural War." In this work, he collaborated closely with the TFP in its various national and domestic iterations: "Mr. Weyrich was also a good friend of the American TFP. Since the early eighties, he regularly met with Mr. Mario Navarro da Costa of the TFP Washington Bureau, with whom he traveled on several occasions to Latin America and Europe, visiting the local TFPs and being introduced to their networks of friends. He also visited the Brazilian TFP in 1988, and met with its founder Prof. Plinio Corrêa de Oliveira. Over the years, Mr. Weyrich had proven to be an invaluable friend."[46] Weyrich had, as early as 1985, traveled to São Paulo to give what would become a series of talks to the parent cell of all the TFPs; the global TFP's official history recalled him as "one of the principal political strategists of the American 'New Right.'"[47] In August 1988, Weyrich returned (for at least the fourth time) to Brazil, this time as part of an IPF delegation intended to increase collaboration with Brazilian IPF members, who were in fact the leaders of the TFP: Plínio Corrêa de Oliveira, Mario Navarro da Costa (the TFP's man in Washington), and Adolpho Lindenberg. Blackwell and Weyrich, along with Henry Walther, each addressed some one thousand assembled TFP members in São Paulo. The TFP magazine *Catolicismo*, evincing major enthusiasm, published what it called "significant excerpts" of Weyrich's speech. Weyrich hit on the salient, current points of American neoconservatism, from pointing out the strategic importance of "appointing conservative Federal Judges" to discrediting "the terrible liberal Michael Dukakis (in the United States, liberal in politics is equivalent to leftist)" to complaining of a legislative deck stacked against the Right, such that "Congress has many communist sympathizers." If *Catolicismo* loved Weyrich, the feeling was mutual. Indicating the success of the effort to link arms ideologically across the hemisphere, Weyrich remarked,

Allow me to say, in conclusion, that I consider it a great privilege to be here. *The conversations I have had with your leader have been the most extraordinary of my entire political life.* And I thank you for being here because you all honor me with your presence. In our battles, both in the United States *and in the world, the TFP is one of the few trustworthy and truly coherent organizations with which we can associate.* And we thank God for your existence, and hope that you continue in this great struggle. And we will continue to collaborate with you in our country.[48]

As Margaret Power has pointed out in her landmark study of American links to the TFP, Weyrich was matched on this front by Blackwell, whose ties to the organization in the United States and Brazil developed both breadth and depth. Convinced that "what they [the TFP in Brazil] were doing was compatible with what we were doing—building a conservative movement in the United States," Blackwell visited Brazil "hoping" to adopt the Brazilian TFP's techniques.[49] Particularly impressed with the TFP's recruitment and training programs, he developed a closeness with Mário Navarro da Costa:

I do training programs abroad and Mário would keep track of where I was going and in a number of countries . . . he would ask me if I would be willing to meet and talk with TFP members in that country. In several countries, I think I did it. . . . Let's see. In the early days I did it in England, and Scotland, and France, and Spain, and South Africa. . . . I've done it in Argentina . . . when I took my wife to Buenos Aires, and I talked to some of the Argentine TFP people.[50]

Following in the footsteps of the Schlaflys, Blackwell offered advice and support to the TFP in Brazil, which he also visited and addressed.[51]

III. The TFP: Brazil's Own IPF?

The IPF and its strong connections to Brazil indicate the ways in which major figures in the conservative movement were actively building transnational linkages as a means of simultaneously strengthening domestic efforts and constructing international coalitions in defense of traditional Christianity. Brazil's centrality here surfaced again in Plínio Corrêa de Oliveira's position on the IPF Board of Governors—a position that the TFP gleefully touted, just as Weyrich and his associates publicized *his* connections with the TFP in Brazil and the United States.[52] When Oliveira, at the 1985 IPF board meeting in Dallas, spoke on the importance of Latin America in resisting global Marxism, the TFP crowed that "the eminent Brazilian Catholic thinker made a profound impression on the participants."[53]

Nevertheless, this chapter's foregrounding of the IPF is in some ways a feint, as the Brazilian TFP itself acted with equal eagerness and alacrity to create a transnational web of anticommunist neoconservatism, one that overlapped and interlinked with the work of people like Weyrich and Blackwell in the United States and elsewhere. As I and others have elsewhere elaborated, the TFP proliferated geographically, establishing chapters across the Atlantic world. Yet perhaps more remarkably, the TFP cultivated and maintained relationships with the most active New Right and extremist organizations of the 1980s and 1990s, placing itself at the center of efforts to foster cooperation. Oliveira himself traveled and spoke abroad, but the organization also dedicated particular agents to planting its seeds across the world. Among these was Mario Navarro da Costa, the TFP's aforementioned agent in Washington, who was still resident in the capital's suburbs as of 2017. Navarro da Costa had counterparts elsewhere. Carlos Eduardo Schaffer, for example, served the TFP in Canada, Austria, Germany, and Lithuania. Born in Curitiba in 1942, Schaffer joined the TFP in 1961, then spent decades raising funds, visibility, and chapter presence for the organization. The TFP credits him with founding the Canadian and Austrian divisions, which he directed in the 1970s and 1990s, respectively. True to form, he introduced direct-mail systems similar to those promoted in the early 1980s by the IPF. He also popped up as an "Austrian correspondent" for the American TFP.[54] As of 2018, Schaffer was apparently living in Vienna and still affiliated with the national TFP there.[55]

Others, too, assisted in the work of linking the TFP to like-minded conservatives around the world—as far away as the Philippines, but particularly in the United States.[56] TFP-USA became one of the organization's strongest and most vocal chapters—surviving, in fact, the major schism that rocked the Brazilian TFP in the 1990s. In part, this must have been because key players from Brazil visited and collaborated with the leadership and rank and file of TFP-USA. As early as 1966, just as Weyrich was arriving in Washington, D.C., the Brazilian TFP was already cultivating links with other rightist Catholics in the United States. In that year, the group sent a representative to the five-hundred-strong conference to promote conservatism sponsored by the traditionalist publication the *Wanderer*. The TFP was "among the few foreign entities invited," and its presentation sought to demonstrate a "living image" of the TFP's tactics and strategies in Brazil. Brazilian *tefepistas* (TFP initiates) were careful to note that this was important because the forum included "various personalities of distinction in North American conservatism." Two years later, the TFP representative at this same annual gathering was José

Lúcio de Araújo Corrêa, who led a delegation from the Rio de Janeiro TFP.[57] By late 1971, Corrêa was on a tour of twenty Canadian cities, at each stop addressing interested crowds of fifty to three hundred people. He capped the tour with an overture to nearly a thousand Pilgrims of Saint Michael, a Catholic patriotic group.[58] Corrêa also visited Boston, promoting TFP-USA there in 1971 and 1972 and representing the Brazilian TFP at that city's Rally for God and Country, which in 1971 "gathered nearly 1000 representatives of conservative and anticommunist organizations in Boston." Corrêa stationed himself at the entrance to the rally, where he proselytized on behalf of the TFP as a worldwide effort.

Perhaps most impressively, Corrêa's legwork saw the TFP seeking to take the lead in establishing transnational *and* transdenominational linkages. In 1974, some years before Weyrich's outreach to Jerry Falwell and before the recognizable rise of a religious Right in the United States, Corrêa initiated contact with one of the pioneers of that Right: Carl McIntire. McIntire was an inflammatory, even infamous figure in the United States and (as we shall see) in Brazil. The founder of several far-right organizations and a succession of fundamentalist Presbyterian communities, he represented a fringe in American religious politics that, in part because of McIntire's own antics, grew closer and closer to the mainstream and helped create the modern religious Right.[59] Most strikingly for our current purposes, McIntire had built a reputation as a ferocious anti-Catholic. Yet in 1974, Corrêa wrote McIntire a letter in English, enclosing a glossy pamphlet (also in English) plugging the TFP's achievements as a transnational organization. Such propaganda was critical, as Corrêa aimed to expand the TFP's reach and its global leadership of "the" conservative movement—expand it, that is, to include *evangelicals.* He flattered McIntire, indicating at the outset that he "would like to çongratulate with you [*sic*] for publishing such an interesting and informative Newspaper" (McIntire's incendiary *Christian Beacon*). The letter introduced the TFP as a "network of loyal patriots who got together to defend our menaced Christian Civilization," then immediately acknowledged, and explained away, the potentially insurmountable difference between writer and recipient: "We are militant Catholics," Corrêa admitted to the vitriolically anti-Catholic McIntire, "but we are firmly opposed to the rampant liberalism going on in the Church." Essentially what he proposed to McIntire was an alliance, in spite of their presumed enmity, in the name of a new, common platform designed to combat progressive Christianity, secular modernization, and communism. As we shall see shortly, the letter enumerated precisely the building blocks that were fast becoming the pillars of the religious Right: nostalgia for a mythic (sometimes medieval) past; mysticism and supernaturalism; anticommunism; antimodernism; moralism; antiecumenism; defense of hierarchy; and antistatist dedication to private property and free enterprise. Remarkably, too, Corrêa presented a further element of commonality between himself, McIntire, and their respective organizations. In Corrêa's vision, the TFP was a lead player in the promotion of the neoconservative cause across the region and the world. Just as McIntire's International Council of Christian Churches (ICCC) sought to transnationalize *his* version of Christian fundamentalist traditionalism, the TFP kept its finger on the pulse of religious, cultural, and anticommunist politics throughout the Americas. If the pamphlet did not make this clear, Corrêa made reference to the TFP's recent intervention in Venezuelan elections, to elect "the 'lesser evil.'"[60]

McIntire's response to Corrêa was cordial, if not enthusiastic. Nearly a month later, through his secretary, the New Jersey firebrand replied to the Brazilian leader that "we are happy to know that you enjoyed reading the *Christian Beacon*" and suggested that they exchange publications. Corrêa would subscribe to *Christian Beacon* and in turn send copies of *Catolicismo* to the São Paulo branch of the ICCC. More interestingly, Corrêa received an invitation to the next meeting, that July, of the Latin American Alliance of Christian Churches (ALADIC)—the right-wing network that McIntire and Bill LeRoy had successfully spawned in Latin America.[61] The cordiality, and willingness to welcome not only *Catolicismo* but Corrêa himself, constitutes a surprise in and of itself, given that most fundamentalists' (but *especially* McIntire's) caustic anti-Catholicism should have meant an utter rejection of the TFP based on doctrine and denomination alone. (McIntire, as we will see, had a strong, perhaps predominant streak of opportunism.)

From the TFP's perspective, however, McIntire's opportunism, opposition to Roman Catholicism, and sluggishness in responding did not seem to constitute major stumbling blocks or cause for concern. McIntire, in fact, was only one of many avenues that the organization pursued in its drive to transnationally lead a united religious Right. TFP agents like Mario Navarro da Costa and Carlos Schaffer fanned out across the hemisphere and the globe and created links with other countries and other organizations, some of them notable—or notorious. Active in the United States, Canada, and Europe in the 1970s and 1980s, Brazilian *tefepista* Nelson Ribeiro Fragelli made speeches in New York, Boston, Los Angeles, Miami, Toronto, Berlin, Baden, and elsewhere. He also reached out to Catholic organizations where he might find a sympathetic ear, from the Pilgrims of Saint Michael to groups of Catholic refugees from Eastern Europe.[62] By 2006, Fragelli had taken charge of Italy's

Luci Sull'Est (a Marian brainchild of Plínio Corrêa de Oliveira) and was, along with Luiz Antônio Fragelli and Prince Bertrand de Orleans-Bragança, a regular fixture at TFP events in the United States.[63] Luiz Fragelli and his wife and son had in fact left Brazil to serve TFP-USA as early as 1974; Fragelli served as the North American chapter's director.[64] These agents were Plínio Corrêa de Oliveira's close, even intimate, collaborators. Nelson Fragelli, at the least, was among the "slaves of Dr. Plínio," a secret society or inner sanctum of TFP members dedicated to worshiping the master and his mother.[65]

Such individual ambassadors notwithstanding, the TFP also sought to establish links with various right-wing institutional allies abroad. By the 1980s, these included Italy's Alleanza Cattolica, a lay organization founded in 1960 that has sought to combat the "modern secularization process, that is, society's estrangement from God and His law."[66] In France, the group partnered with Lecture et Tradition, a self-described "humble army of the soldiers of Christ, in those Legions of the Counter-Revolution that Heaven is preparing for the hour of triumph." Lecture et Tradition mirrored Plínio Corrêa de Oliveira's vision of a grand "Counterrevolution" to restore traditional, medieval Catholicism. In keeping with this global vision, the TFP and the French organization shared a refusal "to enter the partisan and fratricidal struggles that have divided 'the Right.'"[67] An ocean and a continent away, California-based John Steinbacher gained national fame for his opposition to sex education in schools, which he denounced as a communist plot in his "factual exposé of America's Sexploitation conspiracy."[68] To the TFP, Steinbacher was a valued ally, "the well-known North American writer" whose preface to the 1972 English edition of Oliveira's *Revolução e Contrarevolução* "honored" the latter in ways that could hardly be matched.[69] The translation was published by the far-right Educator Publications in Fullerton, California, whose list included several of Steinbacher's own works (including *The Child Seducers*, his magnum opus) as well as titles like Erica Carle's *Hate Factory* (which attacked godlessness in public education) and Joseph Bean's *Source of the River Pollution* (appreciated by one right-wing pamphleteer for denouncing public schools as "body snatchers" and a "war against society, which is directed by the federal government").[70]

Perhaps the TFP's most sensational alliance, however, was with the fearsome World Anti-Communist League (WACL), whose activities in the second half of the twentieth century ranged from panic-mongering to covert and overt support for right-wing terrorism. Secretive and often disreputable, the league has been alternately fueled by and the subject of (divergent) conspiracy theories across the decades. WACL maintained ties with some of the world's most notorious extreme rightists—from neofascists to anti-Semites to counterinsurgent war criminals—as part of a network that also centrally featured the TFP and its globe-trotting ambassadors. By 1979, WACL chapters were active in scores of countries, and TFP members working with WACL rubbed shoulders with the likes of John Singlaub (implicated in the Phoenix Program and the Iran-Contra affair), Suzanne Labin (the celebrated French anticommunist and regular in Brazilian right-wing circles, whose exploits I have detailed elsewhere), Phyllis and Fred Schlafly, Jesse Helms, Roger Fontaine, Billy James Hargis, Carlos Penna Botto, and Vernon Walters, former U.S. military attaché in Brazil. Institutionally, WACL was associated (or synonymous) with Interdoc, the Inter-American Confederation of Continental Defense, the Latin American Anti-Communist Confederation (CAL), Singlaub's Western Goals Foundation, the American Council for World Freedom, Le Cercle Pinay, Mexico's Los Tecos, and eventually the Mexican Anticommunist Federation—all extremist organizations sharing the TFP's flair for anti-Semitism, anticommunism, and medievalist nostalgia. By the 1980s, WACL had become an avenue for supporting Central America's brutal dictatorships, with money and tactical aid coming from as far afield as Mexico, Argentina, and the Knights of Malta.[71]

Corrêa and the Brazilian TFP cultivated alliances with WACL and with several of its notorious members. As Margaret Power has noted, the Brazilian and Argentine TFPs sent delegations to WACL's 1971 conference in Manila. In 1974, the São Paulo headquarters of the TFP held a special event to welcome "anticommunists from various parts of the world," who came to fraternize and exchange audiovisual presentations and tactics. The attendees included Fred Schlafly, then president of WACL and of the American Council for World Freedom; Suzanne Labin; and Shim Hyunjoon, WACL's secretary general.[72] Brazilian participation swelled to proportions significant enough that WACL's 1975 annual meeting was held in Rio de Janeiro. For the occasion, the TFP provided key logistical support: Plínio Vidigal Xavier da Silveira (an intimate friend of Oliveira, something of a cofounder of the TFP, and another "slave" of the founder) helped secure visas for the international crowd of right-wing celebrities descending on the marvelous city.[73] This relationship did have its limits—as if to prove the validity of Weyrich's dire diagnosis of right-wing disjointedness, the TFP apparently refused to participate in a 1972 meeting of a WACL affiliate group because of a difference of opinion about the protofascist Argentine priest Julio Meinvielle.[74]

Where the TFP could not represent Brazil as a right-wing clearinghouse, however, other Brazilian extremists were quite willing to step forward. As assiduous members of a transnational far-right community, Brazilians had been key WACL activists even before its inception, via the institutions that preceded it. Suzanne Labin organized the meeting that "prefigured" WACL itself; and Brazilian Carlos Penna Botto (whose very name, to quote historian Rodrigo Motta, became a "synonym for fanaticism, for exaggerated and irrational anticommunism") was present at each of these, in 1960 and 1961.[75] Perhaps most mysterious among those Brazilians supporting WACL was Carlo Barbieri Filho. Rumors continue to swirl around Barbieri, whose entanglements seem to have ranged from São Paulo banking scandals to WACL itself to Central America's civil wars and even to Operation Condor.[76] By some accounts, Barbieri, who was reputed to tote a pistol on his hip at all times, struck even *tefepistas* as too "volatile."[77] Yet when he was not serving as the treasurer for Condor—a fearsome cross-border kidnapping operation shared between several South American dictatorships—Barbieri maintained contacts with some of the Brazilian dictatorship's highest authorities, and he successfully founded and presided over right-wing institutions of his own. Barbieri served as a Latin American agent for WACL, thus connecting it with the shadowiest of anticommunists in the hemisphere. He traveled the world to its conferences, including the Mexico and Taipei meetings; founded the Sociedade de Estudos Políticos, Econômicos e Sociais (SEPES) (which did, at least occasionally, collaborate with the TFP), the Brazilian chapter of WACL; and he was instrumental to the development of CAL, whose 1974 conference he organized and presided over at the Copacabana Palace.[78] The next year, he would serve as WACL's president. By 1976, the National Intelligence Service (SNI) headquarters would describe him as "a democrat who enjoys an excellent relationship with national and international anticommunist organizations."[79]

In some sense, Barbieri's "excellent relationship" was overdetermined—WACL, his pet project, made him a key player in and point of contact for an organization designed to connect extreme anticommunist activists from across the globe. Yet it also made him a focal point nationally, as right-wing Brazilians of various stripes flocked to the cause—demonstrating, if nothing else, the willingness of Brazil's leading conservative activists to support network building across national and denominational borders. When Barbieri organized the meeting of CAL in 1974, Geraldo Proença Sigaud was among those who answered the call to speak. Sigaud, whose sometime connection with the TFP stemmed from his own penchant for medievalesque Catholicism, informed the gathered delegates that progressive Catholic enemies of his government (including high school students) were the enemies of all anticommunists.[80] Alongside the bishop of Diamantina, steadfast in his own support of CAL and WACL, famed reactionary journalist Gustavo

Corção stepped to the podium to denounce progressive Catholicism and doctrinal pluralism.[81] Ideologically aligned, Corção and Sigaud were not exactly friends—but as two of Brazil's most celebrated conservatives, they provided powerful sanction for Barbieri's open invitation for the region's and the world's extremists to come to Brazil. The 1975 WACL conference drew global right-wing celebrities like Jesse Helms and Fred Schlafly to Rio de Janeiro, where the latter complained to his fellow WACL members about "the appropriation of funds, the elaboration of big social welfare programs, and the confiscation of private property." Helms added, notably, that he and Billy Graham had privately agreed that South America alone contained the future's promise when it came to evangelical conservatism: "Europe is, spiritually, almost dead," while South America, "in a full process of religious awakening, produces the leadership of the strongest anti-communist movements."[82]

Helms, Schlafly, and Graham aside, the meeting also saw the participation of a motley crew of domestic conservative stars, including the two highest-ranking reactionary ministers: Armando Falcão and Alfredo Buzaid. The former considered delivering the meeting's keynote and ended up delivering closing remarks, in which he expressed his and the president's "obvious solidarity" with WACL. The league, he declared, "is very important because the democratic universe is poor in combat leadership."[83] By the late 1980s, Falcão would have passed the baton to another, rising star in Brazil's government and its renovated and reenergized conservatism: federal deputy Daso Coimbra. In 1987, Carlo Barbieri Filho—the head at this point of the Latin American Democratic Federation, yet another regional right-wing alliance—represented Brazil at WACL's world conference in Taipei. Alongside him stood Coimbra—an ascendant celebrity of Brazil's fledgling democracy, and perhaps the most visible leader of a new crop of conservative evangelical politicians laying the groundwork for a Christian Right in the new Brazil.[84]

IV. At the Crossroads of Dictatorship and Democracy: State Support for the Right in Brazil

Such links, the cross-pollination of powerful state authority with extremes of right-wing anticommunism, were in fact very much the rule in the Brazil of the 1970s and 1980s. I argue that this is one of the historical contingencies that sets Brazil apart as a center for the germination and nurturing of the world's New Right. As scholars of Central America have long and astutely pointed out, the story of atrocity-ridden civil war and state violence in that region depends not only on the involvement of North American evangelicals in local politics and culture but also on the late Cold War brand of Christianity that some of Central America's power brokers came to share with missionaries and Reaganites. In Brazil, I contend, we are looking at a different and perhaps more broadly determinative configuration. Brazil's homegrown Christian conservatism, bound up in organizations like the TFP and in more hybrid organizations like ALADIC (discussed shortly), made for a ready landing pad for American evangelical celebrities. Perhaps more importantly, however, the nation's ambitious Nilson Faninis, Plínio Corrêa de Oliveiras, and Barbieris had, in their own right, created international organizations of right-wing agitation. Sometimes, as in the case of Barbieri, or that of José Corrêa de Oliveira and Carl McIntire, Brazilian rightists pioneered collaboration with counterparts from the North Atlantic—collaboration that would erect the pillars of the transnational New Right. Part of what lent these individuals and their institutions the leverage to create a stronghold in Brazil was the cozy welcome they received from Brazil's governing authorities—the outgoing military regime and the residual military and security apparatus it left behind.[85] From the TFP to WACL to Fanini to Sigaud's and Mayer's efforts at Vatican II, key individuals and agencies of Brazil's sprawling, authoritarian and postauthoritarian state lay virtually at the service of antimodern anticommunism's Brazilian-born foot soldiers. This mattered because it made Brazil a special locus of support for right-wing extremists—putting Brazil in the dubious company of Paraguay, dictatorial Argentina, apartheid South Africa, and Ronald Reagan's United States. If extreme rightists wanted to build a movement, Brazil was one of the safe havens where they could hope to avoid prying journalists and post-Vietnam protest movements.

I have elsewhere detailed the ways in which the TFP enjoyed closeness to and power within Brazil's military regime.[86] This not only meant rubbing shoulders with the regime's highest authorities (including the generals in the presidential palace); it also extended to friendship and protection offered by the state's abusive security forces. A 1968 SNI memorandum, reproduced for other agencies over several years, concluded with no little satisfaction that the "TFP is in the ascendancy . . . impelled by the idealism of its young militants" and that the government should look on the group as an ally.[87] A federal police report to the minister of justice echoed the notion that the TFP must be considered a friend of the military state, precisely because of its focus on youth culture: "TFP, in its objectives, in its methods, in its structure, and its activities, is identified with the politics and purposes of the Government, which is evident in the integration between the leadership of the Society [the TFP] and civil and military authorities. . . . That identification acquires special importance in the Society's persistent struggle against communism, detecting and denouncing its most insidious infiltrations, for the good of safeguarding the values of Christian Civilization in Brazil." Reemphasizing this endorsement, the deputy enthused about TFP's combination of religious and cultural traditionalism with youth inculcation: "The services that TFP lends to society . . . are innumerable, from courses it teaches in its various sectors to denunciation of any initiative that . . . might come to threaten the values of Christian Civilization in Brazil."[88]

The support did not end with warm wishes and glowing reports; as we shall see in the next chapter, state authorities shared many of the transnational Right's views on the nitty-gritty of antimodernism, supernaturalism, antirationalism, and other New Right priorities. But the Brazilian state also went out of its way to locate, protect, promote, and even fund conservative causes, at both a national and international level. As I described in chapter 2, the dictatorial and postdictatorial state embraced the nascent evangelical Right, granting Christian conservatives access to media platforms. This was part of a broader trend that included Itamaraty's support during and after Vatican II for containing progressive Catholicism worldwide (see chapter 1). It encompassed direct financial support for the magazine *Permanência*, a font of right-wing anticommunist moralism. The magazine, a mouthpiece for Gustavo Corção and other traditionalists, brought together the famous journalist with like-minded individuals who also participated in the TFP and were instrumental in building Brazilian support for Marcel Lefebvre. The publication received subsidies from the Ministry of Education and Culture as well as the Federal Council on Culture. *Permanência* editor Julio Fleichman— whose son Lourenço remains one of Brazil's leading opponents of Vatican II— and certain of its prominent, archconservative collaborators were cited by the SNI as reasons the government should not only fund the magazine but commission articles from its staff.[89]

These avenues of patronage for domestic rightist outlets paralleled the government's enthusiastic support for Brazilian-based platforms of the transnational New Right. When security forces discovered something called the Confederation of Fundamentalist Evangelical Churches of Brazil (CIEF), founded in 1959 as part of a growing, international network of fundamentalist antimodern organizations, the reactionary spies of the state excitedly affirmed the organization's potential. As indicated in chapter 3, admirers at the SNI described CIEF as "a national movement of . . . Biblical and historic Christianity" that sought to stymie the onslaught of cultural and theological modernism. As we shall see in chapter 5, government agents shared the

Christian neoconservative consensus against theological and doctrinal innovation; yet such nuances notwithstanding, the SNI clarified CIEF's status
as a staunch ally by virtue of its anticommunism and its opposition to the
hated World Council of Churches (WCC): "CIEF positions itself frontally
against the leftist orientation that has been given by the World Council of
Churches, against Marxism in all its modalities and against Liberation Theology, which [CIEF] members define as *'a form of communist infiltration in the
Catholic and Protestant Churches.'*" The authors of the report emphasized the
last phrase; they even more strongly stressed CIEF's solidarity in the broader
fight against "guerrillas" across Latin America. Quoting a speech made at a
November 1981 meeting of the group's leadership, the São Paulo agents informed their counterparts in Rio de Janeiro and Brasília of CIEF's view that
guerrilla fighting elsewhere in the hemisphere "is not happening by chance.
The communists have a plan to dominate Latin America by 1985 (our emphasis)."
The state agents were particularly pleased with a missionary pastor representing CIEF who railed against Marxist interference in gender, sexual, and social
relations, "pitting children against parents, women against men[,] . . . creating
social, moral, and political anarchy."[90] State agents in Rio de Janeiro also gathered data on CIEF, approving it as an ally in the fight against ecumenism (presumed to be a front for communism), a remedy for what the agents described
as "the lack of strong orthodox leaders, either Catholic or Protestant," who
might inhibit liberation theology's "constant conquest of new members."[91]

CIEF, which—as I shall explore presently—was deeply enmeshed in a network of flamboyant extremism linked to Carl McIntire and his Brazilian allies,
was a symptom of the broader willingness of government officials to make common cause with extremist organizations that few other global authorities were
willing to condone. If, as we saw in chapter 2, the regime could embrace the marginal likes of Paulo Maciel de Almeida, it also found itself making alliances with
bigger New Right fish. This should come as no surprise given Brazil's participation as a principal in Operation Condor; what is striking is that this bled over
into widespread covert and sometimes *overt* support for organizations and activists who might otherwise have remained discredited as fringe, too extreme for
recognition by actual power holders. CAL, for example, had become known as a
bastion of extremists; the group lost credibility after successive exposés of its
links to drug trafficking and death squads in Central America as well as to international crime syndicates and to the infamous Argentine Anticommunist Alliance.[92] Yet when Sigaud and Corção stepped to the podium at the 1974 meeting
mentioned earlier, Brazilian security forces were not just present in the audience
but fulsome in their praise of these figures' intransigence. That same year, moni-

toring Corção's bitter dispute with Brazil's Catholic hierarchy, officials at SNI headquarters observed that "nothing of what [Corção] has said is untrue; for confirmation one need only look to what was heard from D. Geraldo de Proença Sigaud, the Archbishop of Diamantina, at the opening of the Second Congress of the Latin American Anticommunist Confederation, in Rio, about the communist infiltration in the catholic clergy and laity, in addition to the obfuscation of the episcopate in general."[93]

CAL, of course, was a microcosm of the global umbrella, WACL—whose reputation worldwide included ties to fascism, racism, death squads, and organized crime. As one British former WACL member put it, "The World Anti-Communist League is largely a collection of Nazis, Fascists, anti-Semites, sellers of forgeries, vicious racialists, and corrupt self-seekers. It has evolved into an anti-Semitic international."[94] Justice Minister Falcão's endorsement of WACL in the speech mentioned earlier was telling, as was the speech itself—an *open* condonation of the organization, which by this point had been forced to purge members in the face of accusations of neo-Nazism and anti-Semitism. Tellingly, when a journalist from *O Estado de S. Paulo* attempted to interview the minister at the meeting, the former was rebuffed by a robust security presence provided by Brazilian secret police.[95] Interestingly, Falcão's and Buzaid's endorsements constituted something of a change from just two years before, when Brazilian government officials (including the president and vice president) had declined to participate officially in WACL's annual meeting (in Mexico City that year) "not by virtue of its ideological content, but because of its relative lack of importance and, above all, because of the possibility of provoking news items that might be manipulated to the detriment of Brazil's image." Brazil's highest officials, then, were tempted to openly embrace WACL, and only did not do so because it *was* embarrassingly fringe. Even at this juncture, while acknowledging that WACL "defends intransigent positions of the extreme Right," Brazilian officials expressed overt and covert support of the league and its subsidiary, CAL. Security forces, of course, heartily approved, and the president's office sent a telegram of support; moreover, the Brazilian embassy in Mexico was instructed to closely monitor and send news of the proceedings. By 1974, Falcão's Ministry of Justice, above and beyond his personal participation, would send out telegrams inviting foreign journalists to witness his WACL appearance; and the ministry sent no fewer than four representatives to the meeting.[96]

SEPES and Barbieri could not have enjoyed fuller support from Brazilian government authorities. The SNI reported that he "enjoys a good reputation with the security agencies" and enthusiastically endorsed his media endeavors (a dubious radio station and newspaper that intelligence agents referred to as the "Carlos [*sic*] Barbieri Filho Group") as "opposed to the leftist scheme that predominates in Brazil's communications media." Meanwhile, intelligence agents saw SEPES as "developing relevant action in favor of the anticommunist cause and ... support for the principles of the Revolution of 1964."[97] SEPES's directorial board featured members of Brazil's long-term political elite, and certain darlings of the moralist dictatorship. The latter most notably included Antônio Carlos Pacheco e Silva (author of the anticommunist screed *Hippies, Drugs, Sex, and Filth*), Theophilo de Azeredo Santos (president of the ESG alumni association), and Eudoxia Ribeiro Dantas (ex-president of the right-wing women's group Campanha da Mulher pela Democracia). Geraldo Proença Sigaud, somewhat unsurprisingly, also took his place on the board; at this point he had already openly condoned torture as a tool for anticommunists, observing that "confessions ... are not obtained with candy."[98] When Barbieri personally invited Falcão to speak at the 1975 WACL conference—where Barbieri himself spoke alongside Fred Schlafly—the SEPES leader took special care to note that the meeting "already enjoys the approbation of the President of the Republic."[99] The covert proof of this might have spoken for itself: the SNI, DOPS (the political police), and CIE provided security and logistical support for the event.[100]

This was significant in the context of WACL's reputation for extremism and deserved isolation. A Brazilian ambassador, observing the WACL conference in Asunción two years later, warned his superiors of the organization's increasing disrepute and political toxicity. Of the major leaders who might have attended, Ambassador Fernando de Alencar observed that only Alfredo Stroessner had made an appearance (albeit with all of his generals). The U.S. ambassador (a Carter appointee) dismissed WACL as "benefiting the communists"; and Alencar dryly noted that "many of those present at the Congress, as far as we can tell, used false names or declined to appear in the attendance lists." Even at this, Alencar—who represented rather a high-water mark of skepticism about WACL among Brazilian authorities—reported with pleasure about Barbieri's role and that "the numerous Brazilian delegation discharged a prudent course of action." In other words, Alencar himself and his government supported WACL; the ambassador's principal qualm lay with WACL's lack of backing from *other* governments. "The Congress," he explained, "lacks the support of the Governments of the majority of the countries represented"—but this did not impede Brazilian government support. Rather, it made WACL's, Barbieri's, and SEPES's home in Brazil attractive and comfortable compared with the relatively cold reception they might have received elsewhere. Indeed, at this point in the late 1970s, Brazil stood alongside the likes of "Paraguay, Argentina, Chile, and South Africa," linked by their support for WACL, antipathy for Carter's putative human rights politics, and what Alencar called "growing international isolation." The list of WACL-friendly countries would, of course, expand by one key member the next year, when Ronald Reagan became president of the United States. Reagan, an ally and apparent personal friend of John Singlaub, wrote to WACL, "I commend you all for your part in this noble cause . . . our combined efforts are moving the tide of history toward world freedom." The Oval Office's support did not go unnoticed by Brazil's representation in Washington, nor by spies from the Foreign Ministry, both of whom observed the organization's encouragement by "President Reagan himself." Brazil and the United States, then, were two states (and the two largest, most globally significant states) that welcomed the likes of the league and its extremist coteries and thus provided a safe haven for incubating the transnational New Right.[101] Little wonder, then, that these decades later, these two are the epicenters of what many have observed as eerily similar Christian neoconservative powerhouses.

V. A "Clear, Uncompromising Stand": Carl McIntire and the Rise of a Cantankerous Christian Right in Brazil

WACL and the TFP furnished institutional homes for a constellation of far-right actors who found a warm welcome in dictatorial and postdictatorial Brazil. Another such institutional home—or series of them—grew out of the endeavors of Carl McIntire and his Brazilian allies, for whom the regime and its legacy also created an affirmative and conducive environment. McIntire's controversial profile can hardly be overstated—an incredibly divisive figure in his native United States as well as across the world, he and his followers were described by a midcentury critic as "organized malcontents who zealously seek to promote hate and disruption under the banner of the Christian faith."[102] Among the earliest exponents of the Christian far Right in the United States—then dismissed as a "half-mad, half-venal and fortunately very small underworld of American Protestantism"—McIntire could never secure the approbation even of mainstream Protestant conservatives, much less of the national political establishment.[103] Rather, as Markku Ruotsila has observed, McIntire's role was that of a pioneer, a "vanguard of the evangelical ascendancy," who would come to "set the terms of national political debate."[104] Indeed, as early as 1950, McIntire had grown so inflammatory as to earn the derision of fellow Presbyterians, mainstream Protestants, and even corporate sponsors. As he complained in a letter to an ally in April of that year, TWA had barred his ICCC from chartering flights to an international conference because the airline "claims we are not a bona fide religious group."[105] Yet the extremes of government anticommunists in the United States and Brazil granted him platforms from which to launch his vitriol and rub shoulders with power brokers. Though many in the U.S. government and lay leadership shunned McIntire, he had something of a sympathetic ear in the person of J. Edgar Hoover. In the mid-1950s, Hoover publicly took McIntire's line of argument—that American Christianity faced implacable subversion: "F.B.I. Head Says Church Faces Greatest Period of Assault from Communists," read one paper's headline.[106] Hoover corresponded amicably with a subscriber to the *Christian Beacon*, exchanging pleasantries about the rightness of their cause. As Hoover put it, in gratitude for an enclosed copy of the *Beacon*, "Thank you very much for bringing these items to my attention. It was indeed thoughtful of you. I also want you to know how much I appreciate your generous comments, which are most heartening."[107]

Hoover (himself a Presbyterian) notwithstanding, most American Protestants, even fundamentalists, held McIntire at arm's length during his lifetime, though his obsessive and megalomaniacal maneuvering did increase the visibility and eventual viability and palatability of his brand of extremism. In Brazil, meanwhile, McIntire's successes were arguably more influential, especially within the country's relatively small (at that time) evangelical population. Collaborating with local fundamentalist reactionaries, McIntire was able to become a principal vector not only for far-right Christianity in Brazil but for fundamentalism itself. Indeed, *mcintiristas* gained outsize sway among Brazilian Protestants. Despite the previously noted national love affair with the far more well-known likes of Jimmy Swaggart, Pat Robertson, and Billy Graham, McIntire cut so much of a figure as to become the face of archconservative evangelicalism in Brazil. His success was immediate: as early as 1949, Émile-Guillaume Léonard—a French religious historian then resident in São Paulo—observed the warm welcome McIntire had received from evangelicals, especially in the North. As the New Jersey pastor visited one Brazilian capital after another in a tour of counterprotest against the work of WCC representatives, Leonard reported that "conservative [Brazilians] dedicated themselves to the reception of the Reverend Mac Intyre [*sic*] with an enthusiasm and devotion, principally financial, that the [WCC personnel] had not experienced." Like-minded Brazilians, including prominent Baptist pastors Adrião Bernardes and Rubens Lopes, then created a "Fundamentalist Coalition" that continued to spread McIntire's message "with redoubled ardor" after he had left Brazil. Within ten years, they would be hosting the ICCC's fourth worldwide conference, held at Rio de Janeiro's Hotel Quitandinha in 1958.[108] According to Leonard, McIntire and these Brazilian allies were "looked upon with much sympathy . . . by innumerable persons of diverse religious denominations" and "warmly welcomed by Presbyterians," especially in northern strongholds like Recife.[109] Sixty years later, historian Elizete da Silva would reaffirm McIntire's splashy determinativeness in Brazil, dubbing him the midcentury period's "principal divulger of fundamentalist principles" on a national scale.[110]

In chapter 2 I discussed Israel Gueiros and the Gueiros clan, indicating their coziness with and spectacular rise under military rule. Gueiros's relationship with McIntire himself was foundational and richly productive on both sides. Anticommunism, antimodernism, and personalistic ambition provided the major links between the two men and their followers. As early as 1949—when he had only just founded the ICCC and begun his career as an international rabble-rouser—McIntire visited Brazil and met with several members of the Gueiros family, among other evangelical leaders. In the aftermath of that visit, he exchanged a veritable flood of rapid-fire letters with these men, especially with Israel, who appears to have returned McIntire's correspondence as soon as he received it, and vice versa. At this early juncture in the extreme fundamentalist trajectory that would feature both men as collaborators for the next several decades, their letters revealed not only the centrality of reaction to modernism and to suspected socialism but the excitement with which they contemplated cooperation across borders as a boon to both. In September 1949, upon his return from Brazil, McIntire wrote to Jerônimo Gueiros, Israel's uncle, recalling a visit to Jerônimo's house and a pleasant theological exchange "on your porch." McIntire gleefully reported that his success at making contacts and promoting fundamentalism in Brazil had benefited him at home: "I have written Israel and want to keep in close tough [*sic*] with him and all the developments in the church. The modernists in this country have been very much surprised by the reception which we received and the turn of events in Brazil."[111] A month later, in one of a succession of letters to Israel, McIntire enthused about the possibilities of partnership. Enclosing copies of his own *Modern Tower of Babel* ("and if this isn't enough we will send you some more!"), McIntire also suggested he and Gueiros might fruitfully draw on John T. Flynn. This (notably) Catholic activist, McIntire related, "has been aroused to the actual condition of modernism and pro-communist, socialistic activity in these larger churches."[112] A separate letter envisaged Gueiros assisting McIntire in his campaign to "open"

Asia and Africa to their brand of far-right Christianity. "So, Israel," McIntire mused, "God is opening doors upon doors and I believe that this movement of the twentieth century reformation will be to our great churches a means of helping to save them and to strengthen the saints for the glory of our blessed Saviour."[113]

This vision, or a version of it, soon came to pass, as Gueiros became McIntire's principal collaborator in Brazil and farther afield, elevating himself and his country to a place of critical importance in McIntire's gambits to "win" Latin America and expand the ICCC, of which Gueiros served as first vice president.[114] Between fund-raising and social trips to the United States, Europe, and Asia, Gueiros led his followers into schism with the Presbyterian Church, establishing his own conservative fiefdom in Recife. He then helped to found, perpetuate, and lead a Latin American subgroup of McIntire's worldwide ICCC. ALADIC, the Latin American Alliance of Christian Churches, became a bastion for McIntire-style antimodernism, fundamentalism, and anticommunism in the region. Gueiros served as its principal organizer and—more than once—its president. In the latter role, for example, Gueiros organized ALADIC's seventh congress, in Recife, in 1967. He arranged for McIntire to give a speech that was broadcast on multiple television channels and as far away as São Paulo. Gueiros authored a list of resolutions for the conference, including a telegram supporting the occupation of "all of Jerusalem"; a message of support for Humberto Castello Branco's regime upon his death; a "Declaration on Customs" that complained of "worldliness with all its evils . . . penetrating in the heart of the Churches, especially via women's fashion"; and a denunciation of progressive Christians across Latin America.[115] Gueiros's brother-in-law, Aggeu Vieira, whom Gueiros dubbed the "Melanchthon of our campaign," spoke at the conference, where he championed the antiecumenist ecumenism (including only "denominations that are genuinely evangelical") outlined in chapter 3. Perhaps more evocatively, he also marked the occasion by writing a near-blasphemous poem about McIntire, entitled "Rev. Carl McIntire, a Trench against Communism." "Thy boldness," Vieira rhapsodized, "thy daring courage, makes true Christianity an ever-lit shining torch. All Brazilian Christians render thee homage. . . . May thy body be a staunch Trench."[116]

Gueiros and the "Fundamental Presbytery" (a group of four pastors who, in addition to Vieira, considered themselves the heart of fundamentalist archconservatism and McIntire-style reaction in Brazil)[117] also played outsize roles in the creation and promotion of CIEF. Though not as expressly transnational as ALADIC—which incorporated fundamentalists from across

Spanish America—CIEF was itself a testament to the impact of cooperation with McIntire in Brazil. The organization, so much beloved of fundamentalist extremists and representative of the antiecumenist cooperation that drew the Christian far Right into security forces' good graces, was more or less McIntire's most ardent and faithful outpost in Brazil. The force of his influence might be surmised from the testimony of Antônio Gouvêa Mendonça, one of Brazil's foremost Protestant historians of religion. Crediting McIntire with "institutionalizing fundamentalism as an international movement," Mendonça noted that the "apostle of discord" had visited Brazil on several occasions, at least contributing to "the creation of a Federation of Fundamentalist Churches."[118] Indeed, McIntire himself continued to visit and participate in CIEF events; but perhaps more importantly he had a North American lieutenant in Brazil. Bill LeRoy became the ICCC's representative in São Paulo, handpicked for the job by another McIntire collaborator, Margaret Harden, who herself spent years living and working in Brazil on behalf of the New Jersey fundamentalist. LeRoy followed her example, first as a McIntirist missionary, then as the principal representative of McIntire and his organizations in Brazil. As such, LeRoy not only promoted CIEF and appeared at its meetings and events but also for some time served as its executive secretary.[119] These efforts did not go unappreciated—like Vieira, other Brazilian archconservative fundamentalists nodded gratefully to the relationship between McIntire, the ICCC, and fundamentalist network building in Brazil. CPAD publications director and archconservative Abraão de Almeida observed in his 1980 *Teologia Contemporânea* that McIntire's leadership had generated fundamentalists' "own ecumenical organization . . . the ICCC, under the leadership of Carl McIntire." Reporting, with satisfaction, that by 1973 the ICCC brought together over 201 denominations from eighty-seven different countries, Almeida went on to affirm that "in our own country, it is represented by CIEF."[120]

Alliance with McIntire generated more than just robust antimodern and anticommunist infrastructure—Gueiros, Vieira, and their friends among fundamentalists found themselves, perhaps not surprisingly at this point, on the right side of the regime. McIntire himself cozied up to Brazilian authorities, fulsomely praising Brazil's dictatorship and others throughout the region and the world that he considered to be staunchly and even violently opposing communism. The New Jersey firebrand ventured to write directly to General Ernesto Geisel when the latter occupied the Brazilian presidency. McIntire sought to convince Geisel that while Jimmy Carter (but recently returned from a state visit to Brazil) had hobnobbed with progressive "Cardinals . . . who are opposed to your government," McIntire himself and his ilk could be trusted to staunchly support the dictatorship. He even enclosed a copy of Malachi Martin's *Final Conclave*, which, as McIntire admonished the Brazilian president, "outlines how the Communists are working in the Roman Catholic Church and speaks of their activities throughout Latin America." Informing Geisel about the activities of Israel Gueiros, ALADIC, and the ICCC, he presented them as allies in a common fight against the WCC and progressive Christians everywhere. He and Gueiros, McIntire affirmed, offered "strongly anti-Communist religious groups which have been challenging Mr. Carter's helping the communists." He closed with a statement of support blended with rather peremptory advice: "We truly commend you for your clear, uncompromising stand. Do not make concessions which will give the Communists any advantages."[121]

McIntire's papers do not contain indication of how (or if) Geisel personally responded to these overtures. But perhaps more importantly for local fundamentalists, state agents and enforcers did recognize and approve of Gueiros, McIntire, and their affiliated organizations. In fact, by the early 1980s, when other, more famous pastors had largely taken the mantle of leadership of the North American New Right, Brazilian police remained vigilantly attentive to McIntire's potential as an ally. A 1982 SNI report, informing fellow agents about the "schism among protestants in Brazil," lamented that those who opposed the hated liberation theology "do not enjoy plentiful financial resources" imputed to the WCC and to Catholic progressives. Yet the report listed ALADIC and the ICCC, alongside the antiecumenist Latin American Evangelical Confraternity (founded in direct opposition to the Council of Latin American Churches), as the beleaguered but important Protestant opposition to progressive Christian politicking. Israel Gueiros and Nilson Fanini, as well as José dos Reis Pereira and Abraão de Almeida, were among the trusted "conservative" pastors listed.[122] A year earlier, spies in Brasília had named McIntire himself (and even given his address and phone number, which was unusual for international subjects) in a report that traced his recent journey across South America. The agents noted that, with the support of CIEF, he had visited Chile, Argentina, and Brazil, where he spoke favorably about each dictatorial government then in power. "Commenting on the international attacks on Chile, he emphasized that these 'are orchestrated by Communism and its allies,' among them . . . the 'World Council of Churches,' an entity which supports the Marxist theory of 'liberation.'"[123] Army intelligence officers, meanwhile, noted McIntire's special interest in Latin America, especially Brazil and Chile, which he visited at least five times. An ally in the struggle against the WCC, McIntire caught these officers' attention for his critiques of the organization as a "front for International Marxism." Indeed, McIntire's opposition to progressive Christianity more generally pleased the army chief of staff's office, which summarized McIntire's mission as that of "denouncing and alerting the Christian Protestant Churches about the religious doctrine known as 'Liberation Theology,' born in the heart of the Catholic Church, as a product of new 'progressive' theologians, which in practice takes the form of activism, class struggle, and support for guerrillas."[124] McIntire's lieutenants, too, merited attention in the struggle against ecumenist progressivism. In a report entitled "The Dangers of Liberation Theology," the Bahia branch of the SNI quoted Bill LeRoy on the execrable infiltration of religion itself: "'Liberation Theology is a form of communist infiltration in the Catholic and Protestant Churches.' This critique and warning are those of North American Pastor William LeRoy, executive secretary of the Federation of Fundamentalist Evangelical Churches of Brazil [CIEF]."[125]

Conclusion

McIntire's affinity for Brazil, justified as it may have been by security forces' ongoing appreciation of him in the 1980s, dated back to a period long before his name was known to authorities in South America. The New Jersey preacher made his first voyage to the continent in 1949, when he spent six weeks visiting Argentina, Chile, Brazil, and Puerto Rico. In letters recounting his exploits, McIntire and his missionaries immediately identified Brazil as a place where he and his ideas could gain a receptive and productive foothold. No fool, McIntire appreciated that "there are more people in Brazil than in all the rest of South America" and was thus all the happier to report that as soon as he arrived in Brazil, he noted an improvement over his time in other countries: "It is almost impossible to realize such a complete turn about between our experiences in Buenos Aires and our reception here [in Brazil]. [Aide] Bill Garman was right when he forecast our welcome. . . . Several hundred people, with the press and photographers, went to the airport. . . . [At] the meeting Saturday night . . . the theater was packed and jammed to its five balconies, with people standing on all sides. Some were turned away. . . . It was thrilling!" Throughout the visit, he echoed this excitement, concluding that "it is impossible to convey to you the reception we are receiving in Brazil. The 'best man' the World Council of Churches has could not have a better hearing. The response is tremendous. The *Beacon* [McIntire's newsletter] has gone before us and is avidly read. My book, *Modern Tower of Babel*, which was sent to some pastors has been read, and we have met those who are 'in line' for their turn when someone else finishes." Beyond being flattered, McIntire began to see Brazil and his allies there (including Gueiros) as a model for other places. Upon leaving Brazil and arriving in Puerto Rico, he admonished, "The developments in Brazil were an encouragement, and the leaders here will want to keep in touch with things there."[126]

While McIntire was falling in love with Brazil (or with the reflection of himself he hoped would emerge there), Brazilian evangelicals remained for the most part apolitical, though that would (as described in chapter 2) soon change. On a national and world stage, however, Plínio Corrêa de Oliveira, Antônio de Castro Mayer, and Geraldo Proença Sigaud were already preparing the way for their decades-long resistance to the progressivism they saw emerging within the Catholic Church. Notably, this was an early moment in *both* the United States and Brazil when it came to politicized Christian conservatism. As the next chapter shows, however, the following decades saw each country's religious Right play a key role in elaborating the platform that would come, eventually, to be known as the New Right.

CHAPTER FIVE

Uniting the Right
Staples of the Transnational Right-Wing Consensus and the Platforms of Contemporary Conservativism

The three pillars of modern conservatism are religion, nationalism, and economic growth. Of these, religion is easily the most important because it is the only power that, in the longer term, can shape people's characters and regulate motivation.

—Irving Kristol, *The Neoconservative Persuasion*

In the early 1960s, as the cantankerous minority of Brazilian Catholic leaders prepared to spearhead reaction to *progressismo* (reformism) at Vatican II, prominent TFP activist Orlando Fedeli furnished Dom Geraldo Proença Sigaud with a draft response to the issue proposals then being promulgated from Rome. Across dozens of handwritten pages, the draft railed against a variety of perceived, imminent catastrophes. Viewed in hindsight, this document reveals an early schematic of several pillars of neoconservative thought: veneration for private property, hierarchy, nationalism, and traditional culture, coupled with rejection of ethnic and religious pluralism, global liberal humanitarianism and cooperation, modernism (whether in theology or popular and moral culture), secularization, and "communism" (generally associated with any interventionist or welfare-oriented state). Like much of the conservatism that would emerge over the next few decades, this document granted special attention to education, youth, and sexuality as key concerns for the future. In a particularly trenchant denunciation of "naturalistic" education—considered a rationalistic scourge of modernity—Fedeli neatly summarized several core New Right anxieties about that future: "Pedagogical naturalism: neither chastity nor the supernatural." What was lost, then, in modernity? Sexual morality and, concomitantly, any sense of the divine.[1]

A continent away from the São Paulo headquarters of the Brazilian Society for the Defense of Tradition, Family and Property (TFP) and an ocean away from Sigaud's activities in Rome—and still somehow, as we shall see, not so distant—Paul Weyrich had not yet moved to Washington, D.C., not yet discovered the weakness and disarticulation of the Right that he later claimed motivated his work. In future decades, as he busily constructed North America's neoconservative infrastructure, its platforms would hew closely to the framework Fedeli had outlined in the early days of outrage about progressive Christianity: property, small government, anticommunism, moralism, and medieval mysticism were the stuff of Weyrich's personal and political banners. As political scientist Jean Hardisty notes retrospectively, Weyrich was among the earliest activists to make the critical link between moral and fiscal conservatism, especially when it came to incorporating homophobia.[2] We shall see shortly how Weyrich brought his moralism and supernaturalism to Argentina and elsewhere, but by the early 1980s these were essential components of his domestic activism. Explaining what he considered the execrable rise of divorce rates, Weyrich pointed to "the declining influence of religion; people who have ceased to look at an eternal picture make decisions based on the here and now." More pointedly, he lamented the loss of something he attributed to a better, more wholesome and orderly, mythic past: constant, widespread, keenly felt awareness of divine authority. Weyrich deplored the putative effect of this loss on education: "The absence of the recognition of God as having authority in all places has been one of the contributing factors to our chaotic and undisciplined classrooms."[3] The trouble with modernity, then, was as clear to Fedeli in 1961 as it was to Weyrich nearly twenty-five years later: a quotidian sense of the divine, which granted the world its rightful moral and social hierarchies, had been abandoned, leaving chaos in its wake.

This, in many ways, lay at the heart of all the conservatisms we have encountered in this book—and thus, logically, at the heart of the transnational neoconservatism they helped to construct. The Christian Right of the late 2010s, having gained so much sway in Brazil and the United States, retains many of the hallmarks of this formative period, in the mid- to late Cold War, when Fedeli and other Brazilians pioneered—sometimes coterminously or cooperatively, and sometimes coincidentally—the hallmarks of a neoconservatism that would in fact outstrip its creators, becoming less the domain of the Weyrichs and Plínio Corrêa de Oliveiras of the world and more that of the Jerry Falwells, Franklin Grahams, Marco Felicianos, Silas Malafaias, and Jair Bolsonaros. Nevertheless, the nuts and bolts were there, from antirationalism to resistance to secularization; and perhaps more determinatively from antimodern cultural traditionalism to neoliberalism that could be both conscious and unconscious of its "neo" qualities (that is, the novelties born of its extreme recommitment to laissez-faire). In a sense, I am tracing a certain continuism, a cycle of conservatism that some scholars have interpreted as a recent tendency to rehash older forms of reaction but that, at a broad level, represents a longue durée pattern of reformulating and repackaging basic initiatives of exclusion.[4]

This chapter sketches the ways in which a recognizable Christian Right began to take its current form, marrying the apparently contradictory ideologies and traditions just mentioned. What, to employ a contemporary phrase, "united the Right" in this period? The blueprints lay in the legacies of Catholic and Protestant activism we have explored in previous chapters. These disparate actors united across faiths and across borders in a coalition based in ferocious resistance to change, both real and perceived. We have already explored some of the changes that incited such reaction, but in general, the transnational Right coalesced around an increasingly clear set of issues and sensibilities: anticommunism; antiecumenism; a vocal, aggrieved sense of besiegement, which we might describe as a persecution complex; pro-capitalist hierarchalism, or a sort of incipient neoliberalism; and antimodernism that demonized science, rationalism, modernization, and secularization, instead favoring supernaturalism and a penchant for mythic pasts. Modernization and secularization were thought to present twin threats, as dangerous to the legacies of private property, anticommunism, rightful hierarchy, and religious or divine order as they were convenient to the putative aims of an ecumenist, progressive enemy envisioned as global and conspiratorial—convenient, that is, to the demythification or demystification of the world and to the dismantling of ancient hierarchies.

As we shall see in this chapter, traditionalists execrated this latter possibility. Individuals and organizations from across the hemisphere, led by some of the Brazilian and American pioneers we have already met, convened, however fractiously, to cobble together and then to address a shared constellation of grievances. They sought to oppose ecumenism; to halt the spread of modernism, particularly when it threatened to alter liturgical details and to bring secularization or rationalism to various areas of religious, social, and economic life; to rescue a supernaturally inflected sense of the world as simultaneously physical and metaphysical; to constantly invoke the specter of venerated, mythic pasts, particularly whimsical medieval pasts; to glorify hierarchy and inequality, and to do so in ways that demonized "big government" and especially the welfare state; to renew anticommunist fervor; and to present themselves and their cause as underdogs, as persecuted minorities hounded to the brink of inexistence by liberal and progressive oppressors. Brazil and Brazilians had a special place in the construction of this agenda, not only because of the actors we have already met, but because conservative allies within the Brazilian government *also* recognized these issues as central problems. From the presidential palace to the musings of security forces and the secret cables of Brazilian diplomats, the loss of the "old"—traditional culture, traditional hierarchies, traditional inequalities, traditional rituals and details—seemed a threat that mandated support for neoconservative institutions, however fringe, and the undermining (sometimes covert) of progressives.

I. "True" and "False" Ecumenisms: Antiecumenist Ecumenism Goes Global

In chapter 3 we explored the ways that the antiecumenism at the heart of Brazilian Catholics' reaction to theological "modernism" grew complicated and contradictory when it engendered its own brand of cross-denominational cooperation. Though Antônio de Castro Mayer execrated the "false religions" that might benefit from a Vatican declaration of religious freedom; and though the Confederation of Fundamentalist Evangelical Churches of Brazil, following other antiecumenists, invoked the threat of a coercive "Super-Church, apostate and Babylon-esque," the enemies of progressive ecumenism in Brazil nevertheless found themselves, rather awkwardly, cooperating with like-minded Christians in other denominations, even when that meant crossing rifts as old as the Reformation itself. In keeping with the multitiered and transnational emergence of the religious conservatism that would shape the New Right, this development reflected and influenced similar trends beyond Brazil—an antiecumenist ecumenism, in other words, that became as global as the Christian Right itself.

We have already encountered certain hints of this. The overtures of José Lúcio de Araújo Corrêa are no doubt an example par excellence. Corrêa, an archconservative Catholic representing an organization that staunchly supported—and in some ways orchestrated—Mayer's and Sigaud's opposition to religious freedom and rapprochement with Protestants at Vatican II, reached out to create an alliance with Carl McIntire, whose ferocious anti-Catholicism should by rights have repelled the medievalesque and anti-Reformation TFP. (McIntire, we might note, named his own campaign and programming *The Twentieth Century Reformation Hour*, in oblique homage to Martin Luther himself.) Yet, though McIntire's own response may have lacked a certain verve, Corrêa was not alone in sublimating inherent contradictions—suggesting, that is, *togetherness* in antiecumenism.

Such togetherness, prickly and sensitive as it may have been, constituted a central plank in the construction of a national Christian Right in the United States, of course.[5] Paul Weyrich's devout Catholicism led him to join the Melkite Church—an orthodox church recognized by the Vatican—and abandon more mainstream Catholic congregations to what he considered modernist and ecumenist apostasy. Nevertheless, Weyrich had remarkably few qualms about building bridges with evangelicals. As noted in chapter 4, he prompted Jerry Falwell to create the Moral Majority, a momentous event in any history of the New Right. Even at more quotidian levels, Weyrich and his lieutenants eagerly cultivated such interdenominational cooperation. In 1987, for example, the Free Congress Foundation's annual report divulged the litany of triumphs achieved by its Catholic Center for Free Enterprise, Strong Defense, and Traditional Values in the previous year. Among these, the foundation noted the chumminess of its officers with evangelical mega-celebrity and New Right darling Pat Robertson. The Catholic Center's director, Angela Grimm, had appeared on Robertson's *700 Club* alongside another center personality, Michael Schwartz. Schwartz coauthored such conservative screeds as *AIDS and You*, which promoted the Catholic Center's argument that the epidemic was punishment for homosexuality. On Robertson's program, Schwartz and Grimm sought to elide the fissures militating against a pan-Christian, radically nativist neoconservatism. Catholicism, New Right patriotism, and evangelical fundamentalism, they suggested, could seamlessly cooperate, promulgating "a view that was at the same time supportive of the Pope and the United States."[6]

Nor were Weyrich and his associates alone in their adoption of ecumenist tactics to fight the "good" fight. The International Council of Christian Churches (ICCC) itself was founded precisely in order to combat the threat of theological modernism and particularly of ecumenism. In the 1950s, the organization's literature described its 1949 founding as a direct response to the inauguration of the World Council of Churches (WCC) a year earlier. The ICCC would provide "defense of the Gospel against modernism and liberalism as represented in the proposed World Council of Churches."[7] Yet just a decade later, ICCC leaders across the hemisphere had developed a language for defending an antiecumenist ecumenism of the Right, a network of fundamentalist, transnational, and interdenominational cooperation. The ICCC itself, of course, threatened to become something of a world church itself. Speaking at the Fourth Plenary Conference in Rio de Janeiro in 1958, American Council of Christian Churches (ACCC) president Harland J. O'Dell acknowledged the inherent tension and offered a subtle rebuttal. O'Dell denounced "modernism" and associated ecumenism, which "permits you to believe in whatever god you wish, thus destroying the true Christian faith." Yet O'Dell, himself a Baptist, warmly congratulated Presbyterian and Methodist fundamentalists, and those of "all other denominations" who had joined together in "fellowship" to defeat modernism. Moreover, against the fundamentalist contention that "we . . . need not fellowship with any other group of churches," O'Dell cited the legacy of "the missionary effort and a needed fellowship between organized churches [that] strengthens the cause of Christ." Critically for the ICCC, he essentially argued that one must adopt the tactics of one's enemy—that progressives' cooperation necessitated fundamentalist cooperation, however reluctant.[8] "Because of the modernistic apostate groups who control the old line denominations," O'Dell declared, "it is very important that we have an organization to represent us and our feelings in matters that . . . could threaten all of the churches" in the fundamentalist coalition.[9]

McIntire walked this contradictory line himself, sometimes crossing over into dangerously ecumenical-sounding affirmations. He publicly and privately made much of his friendship with fundamentalist leaders in other denominations, particularly Baptists, both in Brazil and in the United States. Writing to William Carey Taylor, a Southern Baptist missionary in Brazil, McIntire joked that he loved Baptists so much he had even married one; and he privately rejoiced, in a 1960 letter to an aide, that "the Baptists up here are in the fight now."[10] He and his agents, moreover, consistently recruited Baptist leaders in both countries, such that the Baptist pastor Adrião Bernardes served, paradoxically, on the Independent Board of Presbyterian Foreign Missions and became editor of the interdenominational publication *O fundamentalista*, supported by McIntire, Israel Gueiros, and their associates in Brazil.[11] (Bernardes graduated from Baylor in 1917 and served as McIntire's translator during his 1949 South American junket, when, to quote McIntire, Bernardes stuck "as close as a brother.")[12] During a 1960 visit to Brazil, McIntire gave a particularly revealing interview to a local journalist, presenting the ICCC as superordinate to denominational difference: "We did not come to Brazil as Baptists or Presbyterians, but as president of the International Council of Christian Churches."[13]

Speaking for the Latin American fundamentalists, Gueiros's brother-in-law Aggeu Vieira more or less defined antiecumenist ecumenism in a 1967 speech that sought to differentiate "false" from "true" ecumenism—the latter, to clarify, referring in Vieira's schematic to conservative cooperation *against* the ecumenical movement. Necessarily rather defensive, given the knife's edge on which this argument lay, Vieira went out of his way to heap vitriol on the latter. The speech recurred to what were by then well-worn stylistic and thematic trends in theological antimodernism. Progressive ecumenism meant "spiritual anarchy," a "doctrine of demons," and "a salad of the true and the false, the faithful with the infidel, the temple of God with the temple of idols, of God Himself with Satan." By contrast, he affirmed the desirability and necessity of linking arms with "genuinely evangelical denominations." Indeed, this was *precisely what the Latin American Alliance of Christian Churches (ALADIC) and the ICCC* intended to do. Laying out this complex position, Vieira declared, "It is thus that for us in the International Council of Christian Churches (ICCC) and the Latin American Alliance of Christian Churches (ALADIC), who only accept as ecumenism the *true* ecumenism, [true ecumenism] only includes those local, Baptist and Congregational Churches and others who profess, follow and preach the doctrines and fundamental principles of the Gospel of Our Lord Jesus Christ."[14]

The counterintuitive willingness to cooperate in the name of defeating cooperative efforts even superseded fundamentalists' rabid anti-Catholicism. Denunciation of "papism" had of course been the hallmark of Protestant Christianity long before the twentieth-century battle over modernism and ecumenism. This was particularly true in Brazil, where the dominance of the Catholic Church led Protestant Christians to adopt a particularly combative position, both before and after the late nineteenth-century triumphs of liberal anticlericalism. Indeed, as Émile Léonard pointed out in 1952, a great part of Brazilian Protestants' resistance to ecumenism (and of the success of Carl McIntire in Brazil) derived from the national legacy of "divisionism," including singularly ferocious anti-Catholicism and hatred of "unionism" among Protestants.[15] All the more surprising, then, the embrace of Catholic allies within the transnational milieus of the ICCC, the Confederation of Fundamentalist Evangelical Churches of Brazil, and the TFP. Renowned as an inveterate anti-Catholic bigot himself, McIntire denounced the Vatican in one moment while, in the next, corresponding with José Lúcio de Araújo Corrêa and promising a Jesuit colleague that conservatism bound them closer than denomination might, since "evangelical Protestantism is so much closer to Roman Catholicism than so-called liberal Protestantism is to the evangelical Protestantism."[16] Equally telling, McIntire maintained a long relationship of friendly, mutual promotion with Catholic conservative firebrand John T. Flynn. Flynn, an Old Right, anti–New Deal partisan of the America First Committee, must have been forgiven his Catholicism because he shared McIntire's vitriolic intransigence about modernism and the state. As opposed to ecumenism as he was to socialism, Flynn wrote that "we must stand resolutely against one more step. . . . Not one more surrender. Not one more compromise."[17] McIntire and the ICCC agreed wholeheartedly, all the while tempering such friendship and agreement with healthy doses of anti-Catholicism. While on the one hand, ICCC spokesman William Garman could denounce the Roman Catholic Church as one of the "three forces

[that] threaten the world today," on the other hand, McIntire himself seemed willing to make common cause with friends like Flynn in order to promote an earlier version of neoconservative hawkishness. The more important goal, it seemed to McIntire, was the discrediting and dismantling of ecumenist organizations like the Federal Council of Churches, whose pacifism, "if followed, would leave America limp in the presence of Russia's designs."[18]

II. "Superstitions and Idolatrous Practices": Antimodernism and the Details of Daily Practice

The cooperative antiecumenism that developed on the Right directly underscored a second characteristic of the nascent, transnational Christian conservatism: a staunch antimodernism, reacting against the perceived horrors of industrial, rationalized modernity but wedded, in its essence, to the nitty-gritty of liturgy and scriptural interpretation. That is, the rejection of modernism that bound together the TFP, the International Policy Forum (IPF), the Publishing House of the Assemblies of God in Brazil (CPAD), the ICCC, and even, significantly, key members of the Brazilian regime took as a core presumption the notion that the devil, so to speak, lay in the details. The *trappings* of mysticism, of morality, and of tradition struck each of these diverse conservative constituencies as the essential battleground where the struggle for divinely ordered hierarchy and inequality would play out. In a sense, the penchant for what fundamentalists in the United States called "that old-time religion" revolved around a broad, conservative consensus that the principal threats of modernity lay in the basics of everyday religious and moral practice, themselves safeguards against execrable rationalism.

Focus on materiality, on moral and liturgical rituals, has long characterized Christian connections to the spiritual and the supernatural. Indeed, as Diana Pasulka and Colleen McDannell have illuminated in the North American context, attachment to the material culture of the sacraments constituted a primary impediment to widespread acceptance of Catholic reform—something quite in keeping with a centuries-old proclivity for "magical mass-produced commodities" in American religious life.[19] This also applies, however, to non-American and certainly Brazilian Catholics, for whom changes to the liturgy and other rituals sparked furious protests. Perhaps more importantly, it also characterized the protests of evangelical conservatives, for whom doctrinal purism became the core of antimodernism and antiecumenism. Thus, somewhat paradoxically, an early ICCC resolution (1954) attacked the WCC on the grounds that a union of different faiths threatened the individual freedoms of its member churches, specifically the freedom to determine their own doctrinal and liturgical details. (The document did not, interestingly, address how the ICCC itself would avoid this pitfall.) The resolution stressed that doctrinal and practical details formed the backbone of the antimodernist, antiecumenist cause. The WCC—and ecumenism generally—jeopardized critical details that fundamentalists saw as the core of the faith: "Christ as presented in the old testament and preached by the apostles, a Christ who is truly god and truly man, who was born of a virgin, crucified for our sins and raised for our justification and who is coming again to judge the living and the dead." The resolution returned again and again to the idea that the principal problem with the WCC was that it imperiled these doctrinal imperatives.[20]

The ICCC document disqualified ecumenist leaders as "modernists in theology who question or deny precisely these basic doctrines of the Bible such as the deity of Christ, His Virgin Birth, His substitutionary and expiatory death, His bodily resurrection, and His glorious return." Moreover, doctrine's salvation lay in a symbiotic relation with the details of *practice*, the motions and materials of worship. At several points, the resolution denounced the "idolatry" of Catholics. More importantly, the threat to meaningful differences between denominationally specific customs sparked this opposition to ecumenism. In the words of the 1954 delegates at Philadelphia, "the future United Church, which is the goal of the so-called ecumenical movement," would destroy "creed" and "confession of faith" by forcing member worshipers to conform to either the meaningless rites of "Unitarians and liberals and neo-orthodox" or "on the other hand all the superstitions and idolatrous practices of the Roman Catholic and Eastern Orthodox Churches," or even the exotic formalities of the Greek Orthodox Church, including "idolatry, prayers to the saints and the virgin, and its Mass." Indicative of broader antirationalism bound up in this detailed, doctrinal, and practical antimodernism, the "World Church" was also accused of representing the rationalist threat presented by the "so-called Enlightenment in the 18th century."[21]

This attitude, in which modernism and ecumenism portended doom for time-honored, cherished doctrinal and practical precepts, united right-wing Catholics and Protestants across Brazil and the world. Brazilian Catholics, as we have seen, were on the forefront of objections to the liturgical changes proposed at Vatican II.[22] Indeed, the TFP, as a transnational organization, made this the vanguard of Catholic conservative resistance. For *tefepistas*, the visual and aural details of daily practice were the rock on which they would make their last and desperate stand against the Vatican and its progressives.

At the heart of such practice, of course, lay the Tridentine mass, whose ancient elements Mayer himself so staunchly defended during and after the
council. The *details*—priestly vestments, Latin, liturgical music, et cetera—
mattered most. Echoing Mayer's own precepts, one member put it thus in an
interview decades after the former's death:

> We have always rejected and will always reject the new Mass and all the
> proposals of the [Second Vatican] Council. That was an initiative of the
> communists who infiltrated God's clergy; all that's been proven already.
> In the Tridentine Rite, we could feel the presence of Our Lord, because
> everything in the tradition of the Church was based on Him. But in this
> modern Mass, you feel as if you're in a condominium board meeting. . . .
> It's absurd! It's a total mess, full of shouting, it seems like a Protestant ser-
> vice. All of the old beauty has been lost. It's sad, but I am sure it's even a
> sin to participate in the modern mass.[23]

The Tridentine mass provided but one denominational example when it
came to liturgical and ritual arch-fidelity. Prominent Brazilian Catholics
proved willing to reach across centuries of hatred and suspicion to unite with
Protestants in this regard. Ironically (given that liturgical and missal details
undergirded anti-Catholic and anti-Protestant prejudices), conservative
Christians, including Catholics, saw the defense of traditional practices per se
as common ground. In 1982, for example, as conservative evangelicals solidified their power in Brazil's media and political landscapes, some reactionary
Catholics applauded. Austregésilo de Athayde, long a voice of Catholic conservatism, saw emergent New Right Christians as allies, precisely because
they focused on morality, evangelization, and the coterminous maintenance
of traditional values and practices. After Nilson do Amaral Fanini's Maracanã
triumph, Athayde published an article in Fanini's own *Reencontro*, not only
lauding the Baptist preacher but also noting the uproar that had emerged
around threats to religious *practice*. "The moving spectacle that Maracanã offered to the Brazilian people," Athayde wrote, provided "a lesson to be duly
considered," in that spirituality took center stage, rejecting "distortions of
doctrine and audacious innovations in the theological field" alongside
changes to "the Latin mass, the traditionalism, and the liturgy." Himself a
Catholic, Athayde pointedly drew a contrast between Fanini and the national
Catholic hierarchy, accusing the latter of abandoning liturgical magisterium
for progressive politics. The bishops, wrote Athayde, had better follow Fanini's example, lest the Church rightly be eclipsed by Protestantism! The latter
eventuality, to Athayde's mind, would logically result from the "activity . . . of

their excellencies, the Brazilian bishops, no longer concerned with religious magisterium and instead with other, political directions."[24]

By the 1970s, even Brazilian intelligence forces, theretofore relatively unconcerned with Protestants, took note of the critical role played by detailed orthodoxy in motivating Christian conservatives regardless of denomination or nationality. Secret observers within the state had concluded, by this point, that the issue of daily practice and liturgical detail linked conservatives across denominations; indeed, the states' spies and enforcers shared the view that a global, Marxist conspiracy against traditional Christianity would make orthodox practice a primary target. According to a November 1981 National Intelligence Service (SNI) report on the WCC and its putative activities in Latin America, the problem with ecumenism went beyond its "Marxist perspective." At the core of righteous objections to it was the fact that it eschewed individual denominations' rituals of ages past and was "divorced from any religious orthodoxy."[25] Political police agents (from the Department of Political and Social Order, or DOPS) more pointedly claimed that the "purpose of the [ecumenical] movement" was the "DESTRUCTION OF CHRISTIAN PRINCIPLES, via the destruction of the Churches, for the implantation of a regime of leftist socialism. This will be obtained by the abatement of the Christian Faith, which has always been a bulkhead against materialist ideas." The agents clarified that such weakening of the faith would occur via "theological 'modernism,' which means the destruction of all the traditions of the Church, leading it into weakness."[26] These "traditions," then, were understood to be the pulsing heart of antimodernist antiecumenism, even by spies of the state, relative latecomers when it came to understanding historical Protestantism in Brazil. As if to demonstrate this hyperattentiveness to material and practical detail on the part of intelligence forces and their conservative allies, one reader of a classified 1976 intelligence report highlighted the sentence, "Certain groups, in Brazil and abroad, are radically opposed to liturgical renovation, even going so far as to consider new liturgy heretical."[27]

Notably for our purposes, the transnational organizations of the Right shared and promoted this perspective. For example, the World Anti-Communist League (WACL), via the Sociedade de Estudos Políticos, Econômicos e Sociais (SEPES), sponsored the speaking tour in Brazil of Polish priest Michal Poradowski, author of the 1976 volume *El marxismo en la teologia*. In Brazil, Poradowski would hold forth on Marxism's attacks not just on the Catholic Church but on Christianity generally. In a schematic for the priest's speeches, SEPES noted that he would address "Marxism against religion" and Marxists' "persecution of the Orthodox Church[,] ... of the Catholic Church[,] ... of all the Churches." Among the key points here would be a section entitled "Marxism within the Church," which had three subsections: "In Theology," "In the Catechism," and "In the Liturgy." Beyond simply dubbing theological progressivism a cover for Marxism, WACL activists believed it would seek to achieve its nefarious ends in the arenas of *detail*, of catechism and liturgical practice.[28] Indeed, SEPES's "Declaration of Principles" lobbed thinly veiled barbs at Christian progressives. The declaration's "religious dimension" insisted on "distinguishing between the church and men of the church, who may harm the church" by "infidelity" to its time-honored traditions, especially insofar as they yielded to "the temptation to secularize" Christian doctrine and practice.[29]

Paul Weyrich, meanwhile, could not have been clearer about the centrality of material and doctrinal detail and ritual, both privately and in his domestic and international activism. Raised a Roman Catholic, Weyrich abandoned the mainstream Church based on changes to the mass. According to a 1984 profile in Milwaukee's *Catholic Herald*, the Wisconsin native had become the darling of the Right in part because "he opposed many of the Latin rite's reforms."[30] As a first step, Weyrich formally joined the Melkite Catholic sect in the United States; but as a leader of the national New Right and as an international activist, he sought to focus attention on the importance of maintaining traditional religious exercises. The IPF-affiliated Catholic Center, by 1985, ran dozens of training conferences, its objective "to teach loyal Catholics how to effectively combat liberalism within the Church." According to the group's literature, that liberalism manifested in "problems" ranging "from moral to economic to liturgical questions."[31]

The mention of the moral was not incidental here. The details bedeviled by modernity did indeed center on liturgical and ritual details, but they relatedly encompassed a constellation of daily practices that were less religious than moral. In the next section, we shall explore the shared notion of the loss of the supernatural, a blight perceived by neoconservatives across the hemisphere; importantly, the absence of divine sensibilities was perceived by incipient New Right activists to have generated a visible, moral crisis. This perspective, shared by Weyrich and his ilk, created a transnational common ground with the TFP and other organizations seeking to explicitly link antimodern moralism with anticommunism, religious orthodoxy, and, eventually, free-market capitalism. As noted earlier, Weyrich made both his domestic and international foundations (the Free Congress Foundation, the Heritage Foundation, and the IPF) fonts of a morality-centric antimodernism—an ideological axis that linked, for example, Enrique Rueda and Claudionor de

Andrade. Rueda, a Catholic priest and leader within Weyrich's organizations, and Andrade, among the most famous of Pentecostal moralists and a celebrity of evangelical publishing giant CPAD, stood at the forefront of a massive 1980s campaign to demonize homosexuality. Their articles and books presented the rise of homosexuals as a hemispheric crisis and cemented an international narrative in which male homosexuality, especially in its newly visible, politicized form, both represented the apocalyptic immorality of the modern world and found just punishment in the advent of AIDS.[32]

CPAD, notably, would build on this legacy, growing into Latin America's largest single evangelical publishing outfit and, while doing so, championing the cause of doctrinal and moral orthodoxy. It was in the pages of CPAD's glossy *A Seara* that Pastor José Apolônio made the claim, noted in chapter 2, that the "biggest problem facing the evangelical family today" was an "avalanche of innovations, that is, the tendency toward change in doctrine and in customs . . . so much modernism."[33] CPAD's editors drew extensively on Brazilian and North American moralists, most often pastors who held forth about marriage, the family, and sexuality in ways that indicated hemispheric or even worldwide perspective. As we saw in chapter 4, this included North American celebrities like Billy Graham, David Wilkerson, and Jimmy Swaggart. But lesser-known pastors of U.S. and Brazilian extraction also got into the act.[34] In 1977, for example, *A Seara* republished "Free Love, Slave Love," in which Pastor José Maria de Nascimento Pereira denounced not only domestic immorality but a global threat that encompassed Erich Fromm, "the hippy philosophy," "slogans like 'make love, not war,'" Woodstock, and Jimmie Hendrix.[35]

Weyrich desired to transnationalize this model, in which everyday moral behavior, such as liturgical detail, became the bread and butter of antimodern reaction. Thus in 1988 he traveled to Argentina, where he argued that he had pioneered a movement, centered in morality, that sought *restoration* above all else. Weyrich waxed tutelary, dispensing advice for his counterparts outside the United States. This advice contained not only the fundaments of the New Right but specifically the instruction to "recuperate" proud, traditional, "great" nations. Weyrich told Bahía Blanca's *La Nueva Província* that he had pioneered the addition of "traditional values" to free enterprise–based, small-government conservatism. He went on to specify precisely what he meant by "traditional values," denouncing pornography, homosexuality, and "the true problem" of modernity: "the 'society of instant gratification,'" which meant that "the majority of problems reside in the idea that we should enjoy each pleasure immediately" and "we have seen . . . the failure to teach self-discipline to the young generations." Grouping the American Civil Liberties

Union, Michael Dukakis, and Students for a Democratic Society into this "true problem" category, Weyrich touted his own early stand for moralism, when he had opposed legislation relaxing the punishments for sodomy.[36]

The TFP, of course, shared this focus on moral detail as the space within which the battle for traditional culture and values would be fought—a penchant we have already seen exemplified, not least in the organization's policing of women's bodies.[37] Adherence to time-honored liturgical rituals and moralistic prohibitions, in other words, dovetailed in the organization's vision of medievalesque restoration, a goal espoused by each successive TFP chapter founded abroad. The TFP in Portugal outshone other chapters, going so far as to call its Lisbon headquarters the Reconquest Cultural Center. Yet the TFP in Brazil, alongside Sigaud and other archconservative Catholics, displayed overweening concern with a particular issue that lay precisely at the nexus of liturgy, ritual, and morality: priestly celibacy. Brazil's Catholic activists, leading the charge at Vatican II and afterward, focused on this issue with almost obsessive anxiety. In chapter 1, we saw these activists spearheading efforts to discredit reform within the Church, and doing so in ways that stressed details like liturgical attire. Celibacy, to Sigaud and others, was an issue, perhaps *the* issue, that epitomized such details, combining moral (or sexual) and ritual concerns. Writing to Plínio Corrêa de Oliveira in 1965, Sigaud ranked it among the highest of his concerns—right alongside religious freedom and the schema on the Church in the modern world.[38]

In fact, the retention of clerical abstention from sex lay so viscerally at the heart of traditionalist preoccupations that conservatives often listed it as the prime example of a crisis that they suspected progressives of fomenting. In a 1971 "working document" summarizing his arguments regarding the priesthood—an issue on which he opined strenuously at Vatican II and for decades thereafter—Sigaud appeared poised to advise the Synod of Bishops on what he saw as a critical intersection of sexuality and "secularization." The latter, he wrote, constituted a "crisis of identity" generated by the "socio-cultural transformation which has afflicted, in our days, Western human culture."[39] If, as noted earlier, he contended that modern materialism limited human consciousness to "observable and tangible things," this crisis was, to Sigaud, inextricably bound up with sex and celibacy. The latter had been a hotly contested question at Vatican II and remained a contentious issue for some elements within the Church—but by 1971 the pope and the synod had overwhelming indicated favorability to retaining the celibacy requirement.[40] Nevertheless, Sigaud's working document struck a note of moral crisis and railed against the "world of today . . . imprisoned by sex." In debate about priestly sexuality,

Sigaud discerned the tip of an iceberg of immorality, threatening even "marriage itself, whose indissolubility is contested." For Sigaud, such modernized sexual sensibilities constituted *the* place where humanity had most clearly lost its fear of the supernatural and come to focus exclusively on "observable and tangible things"—signally including the body, sex, and material gratification. He went on, in his advice, to quote Pope Paul VI's affirmation of celibacy and to (accurately, if redundantly) interpret the conclusions of Vatican II as upholding monastic abstention.[41]

Sigaud's lieutenants, particularly before and during Vatican II, echoed and even exceeded his own pronouncements on this topic. João Botelho, a Sigaud ally, wrote to Sigaud's secretary in 1965, deploring the council generally and lamenting any attempt to bring the Church in line with a modern world that was consumed with sexual deviance.[42] Botelho led Minas Gerais's Movement for a Christian World, founded in 1956 to coterminously "combat immorality" and communism via reinforcement of traditional values. As Heloisa Starling has illuminated, Botelho and Sigaud's lieutenant worked together in the Movement for a Christian World and in a group calling itself the Novos Inconfidentes. The latter collaborated with notorious Brazilian coup plotters to combine defense of the capitalist status quo with "defense of traditional moral values—Family, Religion, and Morality"—against a putative communist plot comprising "'destruction of the family,' sexual permissiveness, etc."[43] In his 1965 letter, Botelho reflected this ethos, complaining that the council would inevitably contravene traditionalist concerns for celibacy and sexual purity. As a resigned Botelho put it, "It is evident that the corruption of customs [in general] will impede celibacy."[44]

Celibacy featured prominently even in Sigaud's rage at Dom Pedro Casaldáliga, when, as we have seen, Sigaud accused the progressive bishop of communism via quotidian transgressions that robbed Catholic practice of mystery and magisterium. Conflated with outrage about Casaldáliga's multiple liturgical informalities, and among the first items Sigaud mentioned in his screed-like compendium of Casaldáliga's offenses, was the latter's opposition to celibacy. To Sigaud's mind, this offense pertained to the same order as direct insubordination: "Among the things [Dom Pedro] condemns is celibacy... the Magisterium of the Maximum Pontiff and that of the bishops."[45]

Celibacy featured centrally in the planning documents of the TFP activists who traveled to Rome, binding together the litany of issues I am discussing here: moral and liturgical detail, supernaturalism, magisterium and hierarchy, and anticommunism. Summing up the much-feared "Revolution" that the TFP, Mayer, and Sigaud sought to avert globally, Orlando Fedeli's notes to Sigaud complained of immoral "dances" and "fashions" and "neo-modernism" as of a piece with "society without classes, egalitarian church: and thus all that laicizes the priest, and the idea that the faithful might have an auto-priesthood—baptism, celibacy, secularization of the seminaries. More contact with the people." If these scattered notes did not make the point that celibacy and sundry other moral or sexual issues lay right alongside class warfare and modernism, Fedeli repeated these ideas with more precise articulation: "The Church should teach and honor the truths and virtues that the Revolution attacks [via], for example: abolition of priestly celibacy, of tonsure, secularization of priests, . . . and of cloisters."[46]

I have highlighted celibacy and moral and liturgical detail because this nexus of concerns demonstrates yet again the ways in which Brazil provided a special home for this brand of conservatism in this moment. Brazil's security forces, among other powerful elements of the regime, sympathized and some-times ardently concurred with the emergent Right's anxieties about ritual and moral minutiae. State spies, as well as Brazil's diplomatic establishment, dem-onstrated not only awareness of such anxieties but also firm support for the notion that the stylistic and moral trappings of "old-time religion" must be rescued. A 1982 army intelligence report argued that progressives, as part of a Marxist plot, had "rejected the historical traditions and grammatically correct interpretations of the Scriptures" that had defined Christianity across millennia. For many in the regime, liberation theology was just that simple; it consisted of an abandonment of the beautiful, practical *culture* of Christianity—including, but not limited to, priestly celibacy.[47] Military top brass also wrung their hands over a perceived laicization of priests, doctrine, morality, and liturgy. A 1981 special report—in some ways a compendium of intelligence on the Church—complained that Christianity and especially Ca-tholicism was "distancing itself from its traditional standards" via "religious innovations." The author listed the specific "distortions" of modernist, demo-cratized Christianity: "the liturgy[,] . . . the education of priests, the undue utilization of laypeople, the intervention in party politics, and . . . the aban-donment of celibacy."[48] To the generals, then, the liturgy and celibacy stood alongside democratization of the mass and even overt progressive politics as the principal threats posed by the "New Church."

This attitude toward the nitty-gritty of religious tradition proved wide-spread in other echelons of the regime, too, especially security forces, which made this a central platform of their already-noted support for conservatives (see chapter 1). The Air Force Intelligence Center objected to any tendency toward an abrogation of the Church's legacy in the realms of custom, ecclesiastical dress, morality, or even diplomatic convention, given that the Church was "many centuries old and the owner of an enviable tradition."[49] SNI operatives in Rio de Janeiro, sympathetic to the campaigns of Bishop Mayer and his followers in Campos, noted that "priests of this faction 'eject' from the churches women dressed in short skirts, with bared arms or pronounced décolletages"; these operatives also acknowledged, rather admiringly, that what was at issue was stylistic, doctrinal, and practical detail. Noting that conservatives like the Campos clergy traced their rites back to the Council of Trent, the SNI account referred to the "inflexibility of the traditionalists" with regard to "catechism . . . clothing, musical instruments, and the lyrics of profane music converted into holy songs."[50] An intelligence report on WACL, meanwhile, glibly cited Jesse Helms in 1975 on the ways in which Brazil and Hispanic South America had become final bastions for preserving Christianity's moral, spiritual, practical, and identitarian aspects, themselves the key to combating communism. The "internationalism" of Christian ecumenists and the United Nations would destroy "spiritual and group identity of the nations," based in "a moral dimension that orders and gives purpose to the daily lives of men." This could only compound global precarity, since "the United States had rejected its own national heritage," in which "our dominant cultures derive from . . . elements of Western civilization." The only hope, then, for the salvation of Christian codes of doctrine and "austere traditions of moral conduct" lay in the "robust process of religious awakening" occurring in the Protestant evangelization of South America.[51]

Attention to the quotidian particulars of tradition formed a pillar of regime support for conservatives in Brazil and outside it. As early as 1965, just as Vatican II ended, São Paulo DOPS agents informed their colleagues in the air force about the troubling abrogations of tradition they had surveilled in local churches—manifestations, the agents held, of a worldwide "cultural terrorism." These spies shared the TFP's global vision of the threat posed by changes to the liturgy, directly echoing TFP lionizations of the most reactionary of modern popes: Leo XIII, Pius X, and Pius XII.[52] Indeed, security forces' "general" support for the TFP, which I have elsewhere elaborated, lauded the organization as a global guarantor of continuity in what was perceived to be a liturgical and moral battle against communism and chaos.[53] A special report compiled for Justice Minister Armando Falcão in 1975 presented the TFP as a bulwark against noxious "reforms of ecclesiastical and liturgical laws . . . which seek to attack the principles of authority and hierarchy" alongside attempts to "introduce a relative morality . . . and favor class warfare."[54] For many in the regime, the "principles of authority and hierarchy" were best upheld by a now-familiar set of markers: priestly vestments, the Tridentine rite, and medieval (or at least classical) sacred music. On this last point, state spies were emphatic—the TFP stood on the forefront of defending the world's Catholic rituals from an onslaught of "modern" music. Public and clerical concern about this possibility had emerged during the council and before—even Brazil's progressive fathers felt the need to respond to fears that "the possibility of introducing profane and modern music in the churches" would convert "religious ceremonies into the spiritism of the *terreiro*," a reference to Afro-Brazilian religious spaces.[55] Federal police in Brazil, meanwhile, praised the TFP for fighting to sustain traditional music. "The Saint Pius X Choir, of the TFP," wrote one federal agent, "executes with the greatest technical and artistic perfection a varied repertoire of classical polyphony and Gregorian chant, with which the . . . ceremonies shine."[56] SNI agents in Rio de Janeiro went so far as to posit tradition as the antidote to communism in a 1973 report on "adverse propaganda." Summarizing the activity of "progressive sectors of the Church," they derided them as "clergy who long ago traded in the cross for the hammer and sickle and who prefer the Communist International to the traditional sacred hymns."[57] And in 1982, the Army Intelligence Center (CIE) execrated the "modernisms introduced" into the mass by progressives. At one rite, reported the scandalized spies, "there were various songs accompanied by a guitar, and the celebrant himself sang!"[58]

For some within Brazil's moralistic-authoritarian regime, support for the kind of conservative re-Christianization via tradition championed by WACL, Helms, Weyrich, and the TFP was quite personal. Generals and ministers alike focused, often passionately, on the details of the mass, on everyday moralism, and on the notion of restoring a glorious medieval past. In 1982, for example, the CIE railed against "modifying the liturgy and the catechism" to serve putative revolutionary goals and exalted an incident in which an army general publicly reacted against the "New Church" or "Popular Church." Army commandant Moacyr Pereira had interrupted a mass in Belo Horizonte, denouncing "the preaching of an 'ecumenism' that denies the basic principles of Catholicism." During the mass, "realized with so-called modernisms," Pereira stood, unbidden, and took the presiding priest to task: "You will stop this, because if not I am going to leave. You are even disrespecting the governor. . . . You are not behaving yourself in an appropriate fashion. So you will do us the favor of ceasing because if not I will leave. I cannot accept this. If you persist, we will leave and you will create a problem that will be your own responsibility. This is not my Church. My Church is the Church of everyone . . . that is my Church. It is the Church *that I traditionally know*."[59]

When the National Conference of Brazilian Bishops (CNBB) defended its pastors, declaring that Pereira did not "understand the affairs of the Church," a nationally syndicated newspaper article, addended and quoted by army intelligence officials, clarified precisely what was at issue: the familiar details, the sense of traditional knowing, referred to by Pereira, in all its minutiae. The addendum to the CIE report argued that if the CNBB could opine on politics and national security, then "surely they are giving the Army the right, for example, to demand the mass in Latin, and the cassock for priests."[60]

For Pereira, as for the TFP, this was, in no small part, about neomedieval-ism. The desire to preserve the details of the mass, and the moralities thought to pertain to a bygone age, was part of a broader conservative yearning for the glories of a premodern past. Explaining his inspiration for interrupting the mass, Pereira invoked Brazil's imperial and crusader past: "The sword and the cross have always walked together, in this country, ever since the Portu-guese caravels landed here." Pereira praised that "healthy part of the Catholic Church which . . . maintains the firm defense of the dominance of the spiri-tual over the material. That sees, in the missal and the Bible, the bases of reli-gion. That follows faithfully the serious and worthy orientation."[61] In this vein, Pereira echoed other eminent members of the regime who were equally given to romantic fantasies about the recuperation of a grand, medieval Luso-Brazilian past. Among these was Justice Minister Alfredo Buzaid, whom we have already encountered as a participant in WACL and affiliate of Condor functionary Carlo Barbieri Filho (see chapter 4). As I have elsewhere elabo-rated, Buzaid was a former Integralist, a leading exponent of the regime's moralistic anticommunism, and a friend and collaborator of Antônio Carlos Pacheco e Silva, who sought, like Buzaid, to transnationalize the work of anti-communist moralization.[62] Wont to praise the likes of Francisco Franco and Antônio Salazar, Buzaid likewise epitomized the strain of traditionalism within the regime that created fertile ground for the TFP's and WACL's neomedievalism. The justice minister lamented the transition "between the Middle Ages and the Renaissance, the former theocratic, bathed in spiritual-ity, and the latter anthropocentric, which is the point of origin for the most unbridled naturalism." According to Buzaid, "the mission of Portugal was to disseminate the religion of Christ in those lands where Mohammed had sown the seeds of Islam"; and "the virtue of Portugal consisted in tearing through the frontiers of progress without destroying the bonds of august tra-dition. [Portugal's] navigators set out to discover new worlds, conquering un-known seas; they were not moved by the mercenary spirit of conquest, or the obtaining of material riches, [but by] Christian faith."[63]

Buzaid and Pereira represent a certain kind of extreme in terms of their sustained and overweening reverence for the Middle Ages; but legions of Catholics were troubled by divergence from liturgy and sacerdotal practices seen as rooted in an ancient past. Within the regime, one constituency that shared this concern was the diplomatic establishment, where rejection of *progressismo* became the mandate of Brazil's foreign representatives, not least because of the government's concern with its international image, imperiled by episcopal human rights critiques. Yet celibacy, and more broadly the details of traditional morality and worship, also took center stage in Brazilian diplomatic assessments of Christianity's global status. Sympathy for traditionalists ran particularly high in the correspondence between Itamaraty and its outposts in Europe, especially at the Vatican. In the decades surrounding Vatican II, the diplomats poised to intervene (or not) in Brazilians' activities in Rome sided wholly with the TFP and its allies, and against progressives. This position, at least in part, depended on the penchant of the Brazilian ambassadors of this period for a material and cultural traditionalism that consisted in the details of daily and liturgical practice. Ambassador José Jobim (1968–73), though at times ambivalent about certain papal initiatives in this period, bridled almost obsessively when it came to celibacy. Fearing an "auto-demolition" of the Church, Jobim complained broadly of reforms and specified celibacy as a peculiarly nettling threat.[64] In 1970, Jobim wrote "Celibacy of Priests. Position assumed by the Holy Pope" in the subject line of one of his missives. The telegram maintained some semblance of dispassion on Dutch clerics' advocacy for priestly marriage, but Jobim rather revealed his partiality by defending "the tradition, across two millennia, of ecclesiastical celibacy, which is intimately linked to the evangelical mission of the Church [and] a disciplinary norm of the Western Catholic Church."[65] By the winter of 1970, in weekly report after weekly report, Jobim displayed further concern with this one particular but apparently very meaningful issue. Vatican II, to conservatives, boiled down precisely to issues like this—to quote Jobim, who made clear that he thought "partisan of celibacy" equated with "respected theological authority," the key disputes were "democratic and decentralized government of the church," "the necessity of accepting the irreversible phenomenon of marriage for priests; the priestly ordination of women."[66]

Jobim's focus on celibacy did not wholly exclude other particulars, from the liturgical to the moral. I alluded in chapter 1 to the way in which Itamaraty opposed changes in the rites of the Church, supporting Mayer's and Sigaud's dissidence at Vatican II. Like the conservative bishops, the ambassadors at the Vatican tended to see the reformists as engaged in a wholesale jettisoning of the doctrinal, ritual, and moral traditions of the Church, all rolled into one revolutionary effort, and this was apparent, truly unmistakable, during Jobim's tenure. With Jobim in office, formal and informal government support for Sigaud and his agenda became more overt, and clearly came from Brasília. Higher-ups in the regime had already expressed their admiration for Jobim's outrage about progressivism within the Church; for his part, Jobim—a devout Catholic—hoped that the Church would begin to contravene the tendencies he saw laid out by Vatican II, so as not to "continue to serve as a tool of subversion."[67] After Jobim wrote a compendious (fifty-page) report on the issue in January 1969, the minister himself assured the ambassador that his work constituted "one of the most important and constructive [reports] elaborated to date for this Embassy" and that it received "thorough examination" not only at Itamaraty but also by "his honor the President of the Republic."[68] The report, significantly for our purposes, took very much the same approach to the Church and the council that Sigaud and his allies at the council had outlined. As noted earlier, Jobim stressed priestly celibacy among several other issues; but this report, so highly praised in the halls of power in Brasília, *opened* by emphasizing a generalized emergency in Catholicism brought about by the suite of changes to which we have seen the Brazilian conservatives in Rome so strongly objecting. "I have been observing," Jobim began, "the crisis that has been shaking the Holy Roman Catholic and Apostolic Church, as well as the tension [this has occasioned] in relations between the Church and the Brazilian State." Jobim referred, with this last, to government authorities' growing hostility toward Brazilian prelates' progressivism and human rights activism—a problem for which he saw a clear root:

> At the chronological origin of the problem we find the realization of the Second Vatican Council, whose resolutions have produced a modernizing impulse that could be classified as revolutionary. To that initial factor today are added . . . innumerable others, like the crisis in priestly vocations; the excessive speed that many bishops, priests and laypeople seek to impose on liturgical reform; the rebelliousness on the part of the clergy against traditional disciplinary norms, including celibacy, probably motivated by the current liberalization of customs, the influence of the progress of science on human psychology, ethical relativism, and the pressure of a consumer society on the ancient standards of asceticism; and the growing autonomy of national episcopates in relation to the predominance . . . of the Roman Curia. These are just the exterior signs of a crisis that has long been spreading through the body of the Church.[69]

The foreign minister, for his part, not only "judged it indispensable to bring [this report] to the attention of the President of the Republic" but also underscored (in his reply to Jobim) the importance of sections in which Jobim addressed the government's breach with human rights–oriented Catholics, and in which he concluded that the Church was in "crisis" because of the liberalizations so anathema to Sigaud, Mayer, and Coetus Internationalis Patrum. In one passage highlighted by the minister, Jobim echoed the conservatives' equation of ecumenism with coterminous Marxism and the end of the Church: "Ecumenism does not seek only to establish a dialogue between the faithful, but also to establish a dialogue with non-believers (principally the Marxists) . . . by defending ecumenism the Church itself must inevitably suffer . . . , which explains the contestation of which [the Church] itself is the target on the part of its hierarchy, its clergy, and its faithful."[70]

Indeed, Jobim assiduously attacked Marxism alongside minutiae (liturgical, stylistic, and doctrinal changes, both actual and feared) because he saw them as inseparable.[71] Where Itamaraty itself fretted, in missives to Jobim, that Vatican II had opened the floodgates to clerical involvement in "temporal matters," Jobim responded with equal hand-wringing about the tendency among progressives to "condemn the rich," which he judged to be an error, if not outright blasphemy. Here he drew on long-standing anticommunist and Catholic traditions to champion inequality as organic and exempt from moral evaluation, directly challenging the notion that "it is easier for a camel to pass through the eye of a needle than for a rich person to enter the kingdom of heaven."[72] Perhaps most strikingly for the purposes of this chapter, Jobim judged Brazil to be the society on earth most poised to demonstrate the success of organic inequality (what Mayer called the "beauty of inequality") in response to communism, which he and his superiors discerned in progressive Christianity and its cultural accoutrements. Brazil, Jobim suggested, could prove the "society of the future" so long as it adhered to the kind of Catholicism outlined by Sigaud, Mayer, and the TFP—that is, so long as it steered clear of the doctrinal innovation, ecumenism, and "social justice" being suggested by reformers in the Church. Instead, the country should rely on "brotherhood in the Christian sense," which should generate a "society devoid of resentments."[73]

Sigaud, of course, had ferociously advocated for these ideas at the council; and so Jobim and Itamaraty sought to support him directly and indirectly. When, for example, the archbishop returned to Rome for a visit in 1970, the Foreign Ministry directed the ambassador to facilitate the success of Sigaud's mission: "Your excellency will kindly lend all the support you can to the illustrious visitor," particularly in Sigaud's "meeting with members of the Press."[74] This meeting served Sigaud's and the regime's purposes in terms of both denying rumors of torture in Brazil (what Jobim referred to, privately, as "isolated and explicable incidents")[75] and publicly promoting Catholic and anticommunist traditionalism. Hence Jobim responded with alacrity, arranging a press conference during which reporters laughed at the archbishop's rather shocking jokes about sexual torture and asked questions such as, "Why doesn't the Brazilian government shut the mouth of that Communist Bishop [Dom Hélder Câmara]?" Tellingly, Jobim sought both to support Sigaud's work and to cover up the Brazilian government's direct assistance to him. As Jobim wrote in a missive to the ministry about Sigaud's visit, "The Archbishop of Diamantina, to whom I lent every aid, in keeping with the instructions sent by Your Excellency, thought it would be better that such aid was given in the most discreet manner possible, so as not to compromise the impartial and spontaneous position he wished to assume in the face of public opinion."[76]

Ever conflating liturgical and moral change, Jobim railed against the progressive Catholics of the world. Among the "most serious" transgressions, he listed not only the "faithful taking the host in their own hands" during the mass but also the questioning of doctrinal items of faith (including the Immaculate Conception) and, in the same breath, "favoring birth control, divorce, and the moral acceptance of homosexual unions."[77] Jobim came back to the possibility of divorce legalization in Italy again and again as a topic of significance, personally and politically.[78] Other diplomatic staff at the Vatican shared this focus on quotidian morality and sexuality as arenas of concurrence with conservatives. During Vatican II itself, Ambassador Henrique de Souza Gomes represented Brazil; he survived the military coup of 1964, perhaps because of his remarkable capacity for diplomacy and adaptability (or perhaps because he explicitly expressed his support for the new regime).[79] Gomes, the most moderate of the ambassadors of this period, nevertheless admired the conservative Church fathers who, "conscious of the influence of the family on society[,] . . . considered the problem of matrimony and the family in the historical and cultural context of our time, and [showed] preoccupation with defending . . . the ethical principles which are the fundament of the family. Thus in the council hall condemnation was heard of divorce, of abortion, of infanticide, of sterilization."[80] Ten years later, Ambassador Antônio Borges Leal Castello Branco (1973–77) listed the "series of issues" that, to his mind, confronted the Church. Of the six "doctrinal points" he addressed, all were gendered or sexual: "a) certain aspects of sexual comportment; b) the voluntary interruption of pregnancy; c) the practice of birth control; d) priestly celibacy; e) the celebration of official rites for deceased non-Catholics; f) the ordination of women." Castello Branco admired the antimodern victories he saw taking shape on this front, not only in the efforts of Marcel Lefebvre but also in general resistance to the "pressures of this century."[81] Castello Branco's attitude on this issue was consistent, and not subtle: he championed "ethical and religious principles that the permissiveness of contemporary society, combined with the timidity of the Church in defending them, have been rendering indistinct, if not downright forgotten."[82]

III. The "So-Called Enlightenment": Conservatives and the Mourning of a World without Mystery

Conservatives made much of ritual detail because they saw awareness of divinity, the supernatural made palpable, bound up in such practices—and few things mattered more to conservatives across the hemisphere than the restoration of supernatural sensibilities. Objections to modernization, that is, revolved around a sense that rationalization, industrialization, and secularization represented part of a catastrophic attack on the mystical and the miraculous, indeed the divine itself. For several decades, scholars have critiqued binary notions of enchantment/disenchantment and observed the ways in which largely colonial "myths of secularization" coexist with sustained and resurgent contrary impulses.[83] In this section, I wish to demonstrate the role played by neoconservative Brazilians and their international counterparts in that sustenance and the revival, from a New Right perspective, of supernaturalism, or of the divine presence negating mundanity. Wringing their hands about a modernized world, execrating the Enlightenment and rationalism as excesses of modernity, rightists sought to fight "naturalism" and restore mystery and magisterium to everyday life . . . and to politics.

Brazil's Christian conservatives, Catholic and Protestant alike, mirrored the preoccupations of their counterparts abroad when it came to a perceived loss of the sense of the supernatural among everyday people as well as institutions. As we saw in chapter 1, Sigaud, Mayer, and the TFP sought to combat a perceived focus on "observable and tangible things" and to restore the "materialized and proletarianized masses" to an order in which "spirit and body, even in the middle of mundane necessities, should be ruled by dictates that derive from a supernatural purpose."[84] Conservative *crentes* (believers) shared this position, making much of international fundamentalist penchants for biblical literalism and esoteric ritual, from serpent-handling to speaking in tongues to exorcisms (which remain popular in Brazilian Pentecostalism).[85] As early as 1954, Israel Gueiros held forth on the evils of a "rationalistic philosophy" that would eliminate reverence for the divine and thus "harmonize" Christ and "Belial."[86] Nearly thirty years later, as evangelicals gained power and visibility, Abraão de Almeida held forth on the reasons ecumenism and progressive Christianity must be combatted, highlighting a supposed conspiracy to divest religion of its most fundamental property—a relationship with the cosmos. Attacking ecumenist Church leaders, Almeida wrote, "They are 'leaders' of *churches stripped of the heavenly vision*, and for this reason they seek to impose the new Babel. Because they do not have a message for the sinner, they appeal to political measures, demand collective solutions, even preaching armed social revolution. This is why the World Council of Churches has financed guerrilla movements, . . . facilitating communists' seizure of power."[87] According to conservatives, then, rationalism, the lack of "heavenly" perspective, both imputed to progressivism, existed in a directly proportional relationship with the encroachment of the apocalypse (Babel) and of violent, communist revolution.

The international organizations linking Brazilian rightists with allies abroad affirmed this perception that disenchantment, spawned by modernization, imperiled the Christian West. Gueiros's previously quoted denunciation of rationalism formed part of the speech he gave at the ICCC plenary meeting in Philadelphia. Addressing the delegates in English, Gueiros argued that the "dangerous doctrine" of progressive modernism had stripped not only Brazil but also the United States of the rightful sense of divine power and guidance. Instead, "people coming from pagan countries, people coming from uncultured countries, people coming even from backward lands, very close to savages," were "scandalized" by a nefarious "ministry of unbelief" that had set about destroying faith in the supernatural in the United States itself.[88] Indeed, Gueiros's point here became a common refrain of ICCC outposts the world over and of McIntire himself—in keeping with its fundamentalist tenor, the organization's principal articles of faith included the material reality of the supernatural and the miraculous. Vociferous belief in the virginity of Mary, the physicality of Christ's resurrection, and the palpable, burning reality of hell, among other elements, set ICCC members apart, in their own minds, from unbelievers ranging from non-Christians to the (in some ways worse) modernists of ecumenical progressivism. A late-1950s pamphlet entitled *What Is the Difference between the International Council of Christian Churches and the World Council of Churches?* made much of precisely these aspects of divine presence in the human world. The WCC's modernist relativism, argued the pamphlet, erred most egregiously when it came to the articles of faith in Christ's divinity and the more fantastical teachings of the Bible:

> The WCC cannot affirm its faith in the virgin birth of Christ, because many within its ranks completely reject this truth. But the ICCC can!
>
> The WCC cannot affirm its faith in the bodily or physical resurrection of Christ, because many of its leaders reject the actual physical resurrection of our Lord Jesus. But the ICCC can!
>
> The WCC cannot affirm its faith in the personal and visible return of Christ, because many within its circle deny and even ridicule this revealed truth. But the ICCC can!
>
> The WCC cannot refer to Heaven or Hell as places of habitation, because many of its leaders scorn such facts. But the ICCC can![89]

Rejecting "good works" as a route to salvation, the pamphlet disparaged progressive Christians' tendency to render the Kingdom of God as a "visible social order"—in other words, to render earthly that which should have been cosmological and to weave egalitarian, social justice–oriented mundanity into the rightly and righteously supernatural. The belief in hell as a physical "place of habitation" formed a core of Brazilian and global ICCC priorities. The February 1961 *Christian Beacon* (loudly lamenting what Pasulka has called a "loss of knowledge of the supernatural")[90] asked, "What Happened to Hell?" This article complained of progressive pastors who "personally [did] not believe in fire and brimstone hell" as a "geographical location." As the *Beacon* derisively concluded, "Hell in the past 20 years may not have frozen over, but according to the sermons of a good many ministers and to the relief of sinners, all, it has considerably cooled. The old-time hell of fire and brimstone is now a tormented state of mind. Death is a quiet transition into the hereafter where pray-as-you-go redemption makes eternity passé."[91] In Brazil, meanwhile, Émile Léonard observed "victory for the adversaries of the ecumenical World Council," who had joined their own antimodernism with that of McIntire himself. A poem in the conservative Presbyterian journal *O Puritano* satirized (with *Beacon*-like derision) a fictional modernist pastor whose moral transgressions matched his doctrinal disrespect for hell. The "consummate doctor," he permitted "smoking cigarettes, Cigars, or being a drinker," alongside movies on Sunday and "even dancing." The poem described the pastor as preaching the "Social Gospel" as a blasphemous "savior of all," and then: "And Hell? Ignore it! And the moral law? Without value."[92]

If the ICCC's supernaturalism, bound up in hell, the Immaculate Conception, and resurrection, revealed the more or less traditionally fundamentalist contours of the organization's doctrine, other, less classically fundamentalist and even Catholic conservatives also made such supernaturalism a hallmark of their activism.[93] Paul Weyrich, whom we have seen opting for the ritual comfort of the Melkite rite, rooted his philosophy in the need to reinfuse American and eventually global society not only with moralism and liturgical tradition but also with the sense of God's everyday presence. In Argentina, Weyrich warned that the problem with modernity lay in the replacement of theocentric with anthropocentric sensibilities, whereby "we make gods of our very selves." He told Argentine journalists that he and his allies struggled because "we believe that there is a force of the Creation that is much greater than we ourselves, and a personal God. . . . The recognition, or lack thereof, of that order which transcends us is the determinant factor." Weyrich stressed the everyday importance of "knowing our position with relation to the Creator" and "comprehend[ing] that all of Creation responds to having been invented and loved by an Other."[94] Back in the United States, in a roundtable that included Jerry Falwell, Weyrich waxed even more pointed on restoring supernatural sensibilities. As observed at the outset of this chapter, he blamed social (and sexual) disorder on the faltering of such sensibilities: the "declining influence of religion," excessive focus on "the here and now" at the expense of the "eternal picture," and "the absence of the recognition of God as having authority in all places." Weyrich held that conservative policies like school prayer might remedy these dire conditions in the United States and the world.[95]

Globally, WACL's relationship with Christianity varied, though the organization's meetings tended to be infused with a sense of God-given purpose. There was the affiliation with Unification Church, famous for Pastor Sun Myung Moon's proclamations about "God-denying forces such as communism."[96] Then, too, there were WACL associates' various appropriations of Christian righteousness, from affirming God's sanction for the group's paramilitary operations to anti-Semitic defense of "Christian culture." Presuming divine intervention on WACL's behalf was a commonplace of gatherings across the world.[97] In Brazil, SEPES directly articulated supernaturalism as an essential component of its mission. The group's promotional literature stressed the primacy of divine presence on earth. The pamphlet "What Is SEPES?" answered this question with various iterations of this message. SEPES was "an entity that affirms the existence of God and the transcendence of Man" and, as such, "rejects any and all materialist doctrine." Anticipating intensification of debates about creationism and biblical inerrancy, SEPES argued that earthly life revealed divine intervention both existentially and in terms of constituted authority. SEPES's publications could be quite philosophical on this point: "The universe, by its very nature, manifests the necessity of an Ordering and Creating Intelligence, God, from which it is distinct, just as the finite from the Infinite, just as created from Creator." Humans, while "of 'the world,'" must never lose sight of a plane "superior to 'the world'" or of a "superior nature" that was entirely spiritual. And perhaps most importantly, authority itself was an element of the divine made manifest on earth: "Society demands, to survive and develop itself, the existence of an authority and the cohesion of the social group. Thus authority enters into the plans of the very Author of nature, wherefore it must be affirmed that authority comes from God."[98]

Sigaud, Mayer, and their allies in the TFP placed themselves at the center of efforts to make precisely this point at and after the Second Vatican Council. As we saw in chapter 1, the Brazilian bishops and the activists they sponsored insisted that the divine physically inhabited the world, and that churchly magisterium rightly reminded humans of that fact. Sigaud's notes and letters from the council and afterward teemed with references to the significance of "mystery" and the need to resist the "temptation to temporalize the Church." To Sigaud's mind, mundanity threatened at every turn—as he wrote in a 1965 letter, "There is the great danger that we in the Council, wishing to be in the world and act in the world[,] will end up being of the world." Sigaud and other Coetus members made this point to increasing effect *after* Vatican II, such that by 1987 Jesuit scholar Avery Dulles would resist analyzing ecclesiastical divisions in terms of "progressive" versus "conservative." Instead, Dulles opted to refer to those with "a more humanistic and communitarian outlook" (i.e., progressives) facing off against a cohort that "had a remarkably supernaturalistic point of view" and who, following the lead of Sigaud, Mayer, and Lefebvre at the council, had made "mystery" a "kind of code word" in the decades thereafter. This latter group, by now more mainstream, included powerful insiders like Joseph Ratzinger who had taken up the cause of "God's holy mystery" in the wake of the council.[99]

The TFP, however, far outstripped Sigaud—who formally broke with the organization in 1970[100]—when it came to supernaturalism, especially as Plínio Corrêa de Oliveira succeeded in expanding his reach across Brazil, the hemisphere, and the Atlantic. The TFP in the United States, perhaps second only to the Brazilian variant in its eventual strength, epitomized the organization's fixation on the mystical and the otherworldly. The North American TFP, like that of Brazil, developed an extraordinary fascination with Our Lady of Fátima, stressing the miraculous nature of her apparition and naming its national campaign America Needs Fátima. Even here, the agency of Brazilian activists in the United States remained evident—the group's leading

Fátima scholar, Luíz Sérgio Solimeo, joined TFP Brazil in 1959 and as of 2018 taught "philosophy and history at the American TFP's Sedes Sapientiae Institute."[101] Yet Oliveira himself, and his eventual followers in the United States, went quite a bit further down the path of supernaturalism and the occult. In Brazil, subservience to Oliveira reached cultish levels, including veneration of the leader himself and of his mother, both by the rank and file and by an inner circle (the aforementioned "slaves of Dr. Plínio").[102] According to both the U.S. and Canadian TFP branches, North American *tefepistas* followed this extreme line, venerating Oliveira and his mother as quasi-saints and Oliveira himself as a miracle worker. Oliveira, his followers supposed, had a preternatural power, known as *thau*, to identify antimodern saintliness in certain individuals. Like the near worship of Oliveira and his mother, *thau* caused no small controversy, especially among critics of the TFP.[103] As one former member explained, "Dr. Plinio has the power to read a man's soul in order to determine if he possesses 'Tau,' the vocation and quality to fight the Revolution. He is even supposed to be able to make this determination from viewing a photograph. 'Tau' can be found only in males."[104] Yet the TFP in the United States felt strongly enough about this practice to defend it. A joint statement by the U.S. and Canadian chapters in 1989—prickling with defensiveness about the TFP's more unusual characteristics—characterized Oliveira's *thau* sensing as "supernatural assistance" to young members, helping weed out those unable to "reject . . . the general decadence, the moral abominations, and the crisis shaking the very Church of God in our days." The statement continued,

> For this reason, younger members of the TFP frequently ask Dr. Plínio to help them discern the present dispositions as well as the potential of this or that person with whom they are working and about whom they themselves have not yet formed an idea. This is necessary for various purposes. . . . TFP members living in other cities commonly send photographs to Dr. Plínio with the same intention: to verify whether or not a person has "thau." In other words, they ask Dr. Plinio if he discerns, by analyzing the person's physiognomy and bearing, the psychological features of an individual who rejects the present situation and is disposed to react.[105]

If the American TFP defended arcane supernaturalism even in the face of public scrutiny of such unorthodox practice, this must at least in part have stemmed from the assiduousness with which the Brazilian founding chapters courted allies in the United States (see chapter 4). Nowhere could that have been more evident than in the overtures mentioned earlier, whereby TFP leadership in Brazil sought common ground with Carl McIntire. As we have seen, José Lúcio de Araújo Corrêa thought to enlist McIntire's sympathies via shared identification in a "network of loyal patriots who got together to defend our menaced Christian Civilization." Looking more closely at the contours of that civilization, however, we can see that it consisted, to Corrêa's mind, precisely in the worldly presence of the supernatural—a sensibility he hoped McIntire would appreciate. In other words, Corrêa reasonably presumed that both men, Protestant and Catholic, had reason to object to the "rampant liberalism" and modernism of progressives, and to related "atheism" and communism. The basis of this objection was what Corrêa tellingly denounced as a coterminous deterioration of myth and of sanctity: "not only . . . an egalitarian revolution within the Church, but also . . . the implantation of atheism, disguised under the cover of *demythification, descralization*, and dealienation of the Church."[106] *Desacralização*—the very word used by Dom Fernando Arêas Rifan and scores of other traditionalists to refer to the Novus Ordo—thus lay at the core of what Corrêa presumed that he and McIntire might share. Despite their polarities, the two could agree that the loss of mystical sensibilities, of the mythical sense of the sacred in the everyday (be that the sense of hell or of *thau*), constituted a principal problem with modernity and modernists. This notion, as we shall see, was deeply bound up with another essential problem perceived by rightists—the threat to *hierarchy*.

Before discussing hierarchy itself, however, let us return to the Brazilian state and its affinity for neoconservatives. This arena—supernaturalism— might seem a surprising area for officials to take note of, much less weigh into. Yet the backchannels of the regime were full of support for right-wing mysticism and a religious sensibility that used ritual to preserve the literalism of a bygone age. Rio de Janeiro SNI agents, for example, confronted with Abraão de Almeida's complaint that ecumenists sought to divest the world of "heavenly vision," highlighted this passage as part of a report denouncing liberation theology and calling for the promotion of more "orthodox leaders" like Almeida.[107] Spies from the army, meanwhile, emphasized even more directly the idea that progressives sought to hollow out religion by ridding it of miracle and mystery. A list of the "false principles" of "TL" (shorthand for the hated liberation theology) argued that, to progressives, "salvation means political salvation" and not the saving of souls. More pointedly, the list claimed that "TL negates the supernatural origin and supernatural character of Christianity, making political liberation the central theme of the Gospel." TL, moreover, took "atheistic humanism" as its basis, "exaggerating" the human and doing so "outside the biblical contexts, where the sovereignty of God over us is much more emphasized." The army equated liberation theology with the "Death of God Movement" and with utter secularization—"a god who no longer transcends the world."[108]

For their part, the agents monitoring the increasingly explosive situation in Mayer's diocese in the 1970s and early 1980s sympathized with those in this "noble" region who had, in the SNI's words, "maintained their conservative position, opposed to the growing wave of innovations within the Church." These innovations, to SNI observers, "transformed the liturgy of the mass, in its essence, into a meaningless rite." The "essential points" had been lost, to wit: "the real, substantive presence of Our Lord Jesus Christ; the transformation of the bread and wine into the true body and blood of Christ; the mass as a true propitiatory sacrifice." The nitty-gritty of liturgy, in other words, mattered because the august majesty of the Church's supernatural power lay bound up in it. More broadly, SNI agents echoed conservative complaints about "assimilation to the spirit of the world" and the "dilution of spirituality" as problems linked to communism and, as we shall see, to a loss of essential and rightful, "necessary hierarchies."[109]

Observers in the regime's overt, formal establishment also voiced support for the supernatural as the fundament of liturgical and ecclesiastical power. Erstwhile justice minister Alfredo Buzaid, whose neomedievalism and involvement with WACL I have noted, prioritized the respiritualization of the world. This was so much the case that historian Rodolfo Costa Machado has used the word "spiritualize" to describe Buzaid's efforts to justify his participation in state terror, autocracy, and extreme capitalism.[110] Buzaid's neomedievalism itself, in fact, derived from his veneration of the Middle Ages as "an emphatically *theological* phase of history, in which the idea of the supernatural inspired civilization." Indeed, Buzaid and other sympathizers lamented modernity and modernization principally because the sense of an omnipresent divinity seemed lost. Hence he retroactively bemoaned the Renaissance, harbinger of the end of the pristine Middle Ages, precisely for its effects on supernaturalism: a "first step in the rupture between the natural world and the supernatural world. . . . A process of desacralization. . . . A first step toward proclaiming the banishment of God."[111] Ambassador José Jobim, meanwhile, though perhaps not as prolific as Buzaid when it came to championing the maintenance of medieval Christian supernaturalism, nevertheless did so in his communiqués with the Ministry of Foreign Relations. He replicated the complaints of fundamentalist Protestants when it came to the details—original sin, the reality of hell, the virgin birth—of progressives' perceived transgressions against taking the supernatural seriously.

Reporting on progressive Catholics' machinations, Jobim expressed shock and horror at new catechisms that considered "the possibility of negating the Immaculate Conception, original sin, the existence of angels."[112] Even Jobim's more moderate predecessor, Henrique de Souza Gomes, harped on the importance of "supernatural salvation" as a tenet that must be safeguarded from progressive reforms. Gomes made much of the encyclical *Mysterium Fidei* as a rebuke to liberalized, "elastic interpretation of the true sense of the Eucharist." The encyclical, he clarified, "reaffirms the real and *not symbolic* presence of Christ in the Eucharist."[113]

For Jobim as for others inside the regime and without, decided antirationalism was one key to this consistent invocation of the supernatural as a casualty of modernity. From Sigaud to the TFP to McIntire, Weyrich, and WACL, rightists saw science, rationalism, and especially naturalism as an enemy of the rightful world order they wished to see restored. Where Gueiros and the ICCC denounced "rationalistic philosophy" and "the so-called Enlightenment," Sigaud drafted a conciliar intervention designed to point out the rottenness of "the language of contemporary thought" in that it "favored existentialist phenomenology" as opposed to theocratically informed philosophy. Words like "naturalism" and "rationalism" appeared as epithets throughout rightist oeuvres, as in Sigaud's condemnation of the triad "opportunism, subjectivism and naturalism" or Mayer's warnings against "viscerally anti-Catholic naturalism."[114] Coetus's propaganda, meanwhile, referred derisively to a "Hobbes-Locke-Rousseau-French Revolution" philosophical line.[115] And when, in 1983, Mayer and Lefebvre crafted a joint statement to the pope— issued, notably, from Rio de Janeiro—they not only complained of a loss of the supernatural sense of transubstantiation in the mass but coupled this with a rebuke of the Enlightenment. Among the "errors contained in the documents of the Second Vatican Council," they wrote, was "a false notion of the rights of man," which, among other transgressions, appeared to favor religious freedom and fly in the face of the censures issued a century before by reactionary popes Pius IX and Leo XIII.[116]

As we saw in chapter 1, antirationalism tended to conflate science, sin, communism, and a materialistic politics of the body. Brazil's archconservative Catholic activists at Vatican II hoped to counter a "naturalism" that demystified and desanctified life and the human body, which must remain "mysterious." Communism, they argued, intended to mechanize knowledge and bodies themselves, as "the scientific method," fomenting "unregulated human passions," would guarantee communist "Revolution."[117] Jobim concurred, ardently criticizing Vatican II as a victory for modernity, sin, and somatic science, to the detriment of an older, better way. In 1969, the ambassador railed against the council's supposedly "modernizing" initiatives, calling them "revolutionary" in their implications for morality, ethics, and the privileging of "science" over age-old ecclesiastical wisdoms.[118] That same year, Brazilian chargé d'affaires Augusto Estellita Lima went so far as to identify a "crisis" in the relationship between science and the supernatural, which Vatican II had but worsened. Lamenting the "omission of the mediation of the Saints and the existence of angels" in the reformed Church, Lima referred to Pope Paul VI as "revolutionary," especially in relation to the conservative popes of the past, "Leo XIII, Pius XI, and Pius XII, who condemned modernism and manifested reservations about science." Lima called on the Vatican to recognize the antitraditional "crisis . . . in all the fields of human knowledge. In fact, today one can't really speak of scientific tradition, because of every ten scientists that have existed in the world, nine are contemporary."[119]

IV. "Man as the Good Lord Made Him, with a Solid Head and Robust Legs": Antimodernism, Neomedievalism, and the Transnational Mourning of Mythic Pasts

These hints at romanticization of the Middle Ages were no mere passing fancy on the part of Buzaid or Pereira. Rather, the various parties in the burgeoning, transnational Right shared a penchant for what we might call mythic pasts. Antimodernism, that is, logically depended on faith in the notion of a return to a better, simpler, more functional, holier time "before." These then, were early invocations, not of "Make America Great Again," but of "Make the West Great Again" or even "Make the World Great Again." That greatness, to neoconservative leaders, always entailed the restoration of a fully articulated—if only hazily understood—premodern world, including its social, religious, cultural, and economic systems. Scholars of the New Right in the United States have long covered this phenomenon—so much so that some debate has emerged about the legacy of consensus historians' equation of twentieth-century American conservatism with "a last-gasp attempt to recapture a mythical, pre-modern past."[120] Dan Carter's *Politics of Rage*, for example, understands "the origins of the new conservatism" via partisans' gaze "back through a romanticized filter toward a lost rural arcadia."[121] Yet this remains an exclusively North American historiography, one that presumes the national boundedness of neoconservatism and its romanticizing tendencies. In fact, nostalgia for a mythologized or glamorized past, be it cast as "old-time religion" or as medievalism, united rightists across denominations and nationalities in

ways that belie current explanations of the New Right as a movement generated by and largely limited to events and actors in the United States. In Brazil,
as in the United States, such nostalgias tempered or even transformed conservatives' visions of their political and social roles. Evangelicals, long given
to demanding freedom of conscience, found themselves harking back to bygone moralism and using their increasing influence in government to guarantee the sanctity of what, as we saw in chapter 2, they called "our territory."
Catholic conservatives, meanwhile, shared this moralism and coupled it with
dreams of reinvigorating medieval culture and theocracy.

To an extent, antimodernism itself, reactionary in its nature, determined
this tendency. Brazilian Protestant moralisms in the 1960s and thereafter presumed a proportional relationship between modernization, sinful media, and
the "wave of immorality" discussed in chapter 2; then, too, the desire for some
form of return was bound up in antimodern theological positions, which
sought the restoration of orthodox Christianities (rigidly doctrinal, putatively
neither political nor ecumenical). Beyond this, however, Christian conservatives mourned more general notions of a lost, ostensibly rosier past, in aesthetic as well as practical terms. Israel Gueiros, for example, publicly and
privately invoked the notion of a hemispheric golden age of Protestant evangelism, when—according to Gueiros—the United States had stood as a beacon of
Christian perfection for the rest of the world. That golden age, in the fundamentalist pastor's view, had fallen away. In a 1956 letter, Gueiros and his longtime collaborator Margaret Harden (herself a McIntire devotee) wrote of the
time, "many years ago," when Americans had possessed the "blessed Light of
the Gospel" and imparted it to Brazil—whereas now that Light had dimmed,
with America "departing from the faith by giving heed to seducing spirits."[122]
At the ICCC plenary in Philadelphia, Gueiros spoke even more pointedly,
harking back a century to recall the idealized past: "A hundred years ago this
country spread the Gospel all over the world through missions, and strong
churches were established to preach Christ and Him crucified to save sinners;
but modernism invaded this country, and but a very small number of faithful
men are left to face it."[123] This tone extended from leaders like Gueiros into
more local venues. As one letter to the editor of *A Seara* put it, "many readers"
thought the magazine was "in need of returning to years past" and now was
"just a shadow of those old issues."[124] Assemblies of God leader Joanyr de
Oliveira, meanwhile, recalled a past in which love and talk of it were simply
purer: "In the past, there was much talk of maternal love, filial love, fraternal
love. . . . Now, however, the 'love' which is most talked about is synonymous
with a practice in which physical attraction predominates."[125]

Weyrich, for his part, had made nostalgia his brand even before he founded the IPF.[126] He gestured toward a treasured past in the very name of his most famous creation—the Heritage Foundation—not to mention in his constant appeals to "traditional values" and the need to "recuperate the kind of country that made the United States a Great Nation." His book *The Next Conservatism*, coauthored with William S. Lind, coined the term "retroculture," described by the latter as "deliberately returning to past ways of thinking and of living [because] in terms of culture and morals, America from the Victorian age up through the 1950s was a far better place than America is today." The mythical or fantastical allure of so-called retroculture was not lost even on Lind and Weyrich, who invoked *Lord of the Rings* to argue that society "should look toward a world where, as Tolkien put it, there is less noise and more green."[127] Yet Weyrich's penchant for nostalgia also emerged in subtler forms, from the previously noted adoption of Melkite Catholicism to more secular rituals. To celebrate the tenth anniversary of the Committee for the Survival of a Free Congress (one of his early organizing gambits), Weyrich held an old-fashioned picnic at the National Capital Trolley Museum. The Americana-themed event, complete with a planned baseball game and congressional banjo accompaniment from the self-styled Capitol Hill Conservative Conservatory Band, did not offer alcoholic beverages—but it did feature Weyrich himself, complete with a conductor's costume, thanking the hundreds of gathered conservatives for their support.[128]

Catholics, of course, looked further back for a putative golden age of Christian power. While Protestants occasionally (and paradoxically) romanticized the Middle Ages, this was for the most part the terrain of Catholic conservatives, who glorified the medieval with relish and abandon.[129] Pioneering rightist individuals whom we have already met exemplified this tendency—not least Sigaud, whose revered "Medieval Man" we encountered in chapter 1, and Buzaid, whose previously noted fondness for medievalism encompassed his 1984 praise of an imagined premodern subjectivity, "natural man, man as the Good Lord made him, with a solid head and robust legs."[130] Like Mayer and Bishop Carlos Saboia Bandeira de Mello, who lamented the Renaissance as the death knell of European Latin, among other venerated customs, Buzaid used the language of "desacralization" to describe what had happened since the fifteenth century.[131] Doubtless, however, the example par excellence of medievalism as both inspiration and expression lay with the TFP, globally and in its national incarnations. Within Brazil, the TFP became famous for its medieval-inspired pageantry, complete with costumes, capes, banners, and parades. By the 1970s, the organization had drawn press attention for its recruitment of young inductees, who lived in communal, monastic dwellings and at least occasionally dressed in medieval costume. TFP's own institutional history observed with satisfaction the shock and confusion that such medieval dress caused in the organization's opponents.[132] The founder spoke constantly and glowingly of the Middle Ages, comparing himself and the TFP to crusaders: "In the Middle Ages," he wrote in 1971, "the crusaders spilled their blood to liberate the Sepulchre of our Lord Jesus Christ from the hands of the infidels, and to institute Christian Regnum in the Holy Land. This is our aim, our great ideal. We proceed toward a Catholic Civilization that will be born from the ruins of today's world, just like the medieval civilization that was born from the ruins of the Roman world."[133]

When Plínio Corrêa de Oliveira talked of "the world" in this sense, he made the transnational scope of this medievalesque vision explicit. The TFP's fetishistic preoccupation with a mythologized past became its most distinguishing characteristic on three continents. The North American TFP, across decades, has published paean after paean to the Middle Ages as a lost golden age. These include reprints of Oliveira originals, like the foregoing passage about crusaders and the advent of "Christian Civilization"; but the U.S. chapter broadcasts original pro-medieval propaganda to this day. In "The Middle Ages: An Explosion of Freedom, Creativity and Progress," for example, the TFP argued that whereas medieval "Christendom . . . spawned a surge of practical creativity that resulted in improvements in village life," this pinnacle of human history had met its end when "the despots of the 'enlightened' Renaissance . . . destroyed medieval cultural flourishing."[134] In a combined statement in 1989, the U.S. and Canadian TFPs displayed a defensive sensitivity to the "anti-medieval prejudice still affecting many people today." In an apparent attempt at pragmatism, the statement declared that

> the TFPs do not wish a mere return of the Middle Ages. However, they do believe that the ruling principles of that historic epoch—which are found in the Decalogue—*can and must be reestablished in society since they express the only proper order in human relations*. . . . Therefore, the restoration of the fundamental principles which inspired a temporal order in the Middle Ages, as well as their full blossoming in institutions of the highest perfection, is not a "dream" but *a goal to which no authentic Catholic truly confiding in God can cease to aspire.*[135]

Even José Lúcio de Araújo Corrêa's initial overture to Carl McIntire, designed to bridge not only borders but denominations, made much of the TFP's medievalism. Corrêa's letter glowed with pride in the TFP's "young militants in almost legendary campaigns," and especially the anachronistic pageantry that the organization had made its brand: "Putting on their scarlet capes, they go forth and raise high large red standards which have a golden lion with a cross in its midst—the symbol of a bold and noble struggle. . . . The TFP [has] the spirit of the crusaders . . . well aware they are engaged in a holy struggle for God and for Christian Civilization."[136] These "legendary campaigns," alongside public awareness of them, also spread beyond Brazil.

Beyond the TFP's various national leaderships, outside observers also took note of the aesthetic, ideological, and pedagogical penchant for a mythologized premodern past. Further safeguarding the TFP's conducive perch in dictatorial Brazil, an SNI comprehensive assessment of the group's activities lauded its medieval education of young people: "There exist . . . study commissions, each composed of 10 to 15 members, with two or three weekly meetings, to research and study historical and cultural themes. Among these, the commission specialized in the study of the Middle Ages stands out. It promotes parties, with medieval costumes, music, and games, with the objective of entertaining the youth and principally to awaken in them a taste for these historical themes."[137] Ambassador José Jobim, meanwhile, in a memo to Itamaraty titled "Relations between the Catholic Church and the Brazilian State," shared TFP's appreciation for the medieval. Describing the "medieval Church"—and comparing it favorably with the "modern Church" and especially the "Conciliar church"—Jobim wrote that, "dominated by the spirit of victory, the triumphant [medieval] Church saw itself realizing temporally its redemptive mission [via] the conquest of the Holy Land via the collective action, in a communion of blood, of the Catholic Knights."[138]

Brazilian and U.S. journalists took the TFP's bait, in that they responded precisely to the sensational medieval-inspired pageantry of youthful TFP representatives.[139] In the United States, the *Washington Post* portrayed the group as a bizarre cult with a focus on medieval flair and costumery. In a 1974 article entitled "The Brotherhood," correspondent Uli Schmetzer seemed unable to tear his eyes from the "grey sleeveless capes," "intricate tapestries," "red-caped 'knights' wearing black bonnets," the "flag of a yellow lion with flickering tongue," and the way in which Oliveira himself was "slightly flushed with pleasure in showing the treasures [of his order]. 'I want these men to live with tradition around them.'"[140] The *New York Times* reported that the group had offices in California and New York and "seemed to adhere to a kind of medieval philosophy."[141] When the TFP acquired additional property in suburban New York in 1979, *Church and State*—the newspaper of Americans United for Separation of Church and State—titled its coverage "Bringing

Back the Middle Ages." The paper warned of a new "North American beach-head for an avowedly fascist, medieval Roman Catholic organization head-quartered in Brazil."[142] These sources, of course, treated TFP medievalism as exotic and even dangerous; yet the retrospective outlook of the organization and its leaders gained enough visibility to draw the attention of other groups with similarly misty visions of the medieval past. During and after the Second Vatican Council, Sigaud and his TFP operatives in Rome corresponded with various medievalesque and self-styled chivalric orders, from the Knights of Malta, to the U.S.-based Blue Army, to the rather more esoteric L'Ordre des Chevaliers de Notre Dame, which described itself as a "movement of con-temporary knights," with French and U.S. chapters and links to the arch-traditionalist Society of Saint Pius X.[143]

The desire to connect with a chivalric legacy was, of course, no coinci-dence, as the mythic past(s) envisioned by the pioneers of the New Right also encompassed a preoccupation with nobility, hierarchy, and aristocracy. This ranged from personal obsession with nobility and lineage to reverence for the structural hierarchies of an imagined past, the "legitimate inequali-ties" that Mayer so prized. Beyond cavorting in medieval-inspired attire, arch-conservatives in Brazil and the United States were wont to see themselves as the restorationist heirs to a rightful temporal and ecclesiastical nobility whose potency had been lost to modernization. The TFP once again led the pack in this regard, as evidenced by the eventual publication of *Nobility and Analo-gous Traditional Elites.* The book, published in English, Spanish, Portuguese, Italian, and French and promoted by the TFPs worldwide, remains Oliveira's latter-day magnum opus and a call to arms for reinstating the heritable nobil-ity to which Oliveira himself and his compatriots laid claim. The TFPs have historically revered Pope Pius XII as an exponent of such restoration, but they were not alone in prizing this form of antidemocratic change. Praising *Nobility and Analogous Traditional Elites,* Paul Weyrich lamented the lack of a North American aristocratic legacy. "Sadly, most American elites are now de-voted to self-interest, not to service, which is one reason why affairs here go so badly," he wrote in endorsement. "Your book may help reawaken people to the realization that we need and can have an elite devoted to service."[144] Wey-rich collaborator Morton Blackwell actually wrote the preface to the English translation of *Nobility,* declaring that the need for the titular nobility tran-scended national and denominational boundaries. Blackwell described him-self as "an Episcopalian married to a Southern Baptist," indicating the need for conservative Christians of all stripes to unite against the "deadly leveling tendencies of modern times." The critical question, to Blackwell's mind, was,

"What are the duties and responsibilities of people ... born to high status?" In response, he asserted that "good elites are legitimate, desirable and necessary" and that for this reason he himself had become part of the effort to transnationalize a conservatism that recognized this fact. While he had found most foreigners "hopeless," he lauded the TFP as "impressive," noting its monarchism and adding that "they could be likened to a medieval religious order. They stand opposed to much that has occurred in modern times, which they consider to have commenced at the end of the middle ages, a not unreasonable view."[145]

Other U.S. traditionalists likewise advocated European-style aristocracy, glorifying an ersatz past of medieval peace and prosperity ensured by heritable rulership. After the canonization of the Hapsburg emperor Charles I of Austria and Charles IV of Hungary, for example, the *Remnant* (a far-right U.S. Catholic newspaper) printed the analysis of British Catholic leader James Bogle. *Remnant* editors exhorted readers (American and British) not to forget the "last Catholic King" and to make of him a symbol of the lamentable "sacrifice of the old Catholic order on the altar of Godless democracy by the thugs of the New World Order." Bogle himself penned a romantic description of "Blessed Emperor Charles," a relic of the rightful order of the premodern world, doomed to suffer in modernity. Bogle's fascination with the pageantry of ancient and medieval culture dovetailed with his arguments for reviving it. He trilled over the "moving sight" of "members of various chivalric orders" gathered for the beatification beneath medievalesque tapestries, and the "old Austrian nobility ... superbly elegant and many of them stunningly beautiful in that blonde Teutonic manner." The point bound up in this aesthetic fetishism was the rightfulness of looking "back to the days of the political and economic distributism of the Holy Roman Empire with its famous patchwork of baronies, counties, duchies, principalities and kingdoms," which Bogle equated with "federalism and political self-determination."[146]

V. A Neoliberal Nobility: Hierarchalism, Private Property, and the Capitalistic New Right

Not for nothing did Bogle champion the supposed "self-determination" of this bygone paradise; the conflation of mythic pasts, hierarchalism, and unfettered or unregulated freedoms also became a hallmark of the transnational New Right. It was here that cultural traditionalism met the sometimes contradictory neoliberalism that has characterized renewed conservatism from the 1970s until today. This brings us to perhaps the most puzzling conundrum that has confronted scholars of the Right in recent decades: How do social and religious conservatism make sense in combination with what has come to be thought of as economic "conservatism" (that is, the revival of deregulated capitalism after labor strife and the Great Depression discredited it in certain venues)? Despite many years' worth of investigation, this question continues to stymie analysts, some of whom have, understandably, taken this conflation for granted rather than interrogating it.[147] In fact, the early champions of what would become the transnational New Right championed a platform that embraced these incongruous pillars by drawing on the hallmarks we have explored thus far—doctrinal rigidity, antimodern moralism, rather starry-eyed nostalgia, and anticommunism. To Oliveira, McIntire, Falwell, Weyrich, Mayer, and their supporters, the core component of their conservatism was a hierarchalism based in the notion of a "rightful order" that holistically encompassed religion, morality, property tenure, political organization, and social stratification. Their individual and collective excurses reveal an incipient neoliberalism, foregrounding anticommunism, opposition to an expanded state ("big government"), and fundamental faith in the interrelated tenets of private property, individual self-reliance, and the rightness of unequal income and wealth distribution.[148] In a sense, these religious conservatives met more classically defined neoconservatives halfway. Whereas the latter camp—dominated by nonfundamentalists and featuring prominent Jewish intellectuals like Irving Kristol, Norman Podhoretz, and Leo Strauss[149]—did not necessarily seek religious revival, its ideologues could easily agree with Weyrich, Oliveira, and McIntire, who likewise insisted that religious hierarchy was the only reliable guarantee of other, rightful orders. As Kristol unerringly put it in his critique of the welfare state, "The three pillars of modern conservatism are religion, nationalism, and economic growth. Of these, religion is easily the most important *because it is the only power that, in the longer term, can shape people's characters and regulate motivation."*[150]

Returning briefly to Oliveira's *Nobility and Analogous Traditional Elites*, we find traces of the ways in which the fascination with a mythologized past, conceived of as more orderly, more moral, and more righteously religious, was bound up with neoconservative opposition to equality of rights, of income, and of wealth distribution. Opposing Christian progressives' "preferential option for the poor," Oliveira began by proposing a "preferential option for the Nobility," as "the situation of the impoverished noble is more poignant than that of a poor man in the street." This might seem near-hallucinatory whimsy to the unsympathetic reader, but Oliveira explained himself—at length—via recourse to an updated medievalist organicism. "Today's radically egalitarian populism," its evils punctuated by "technological progress," "neopagan 'democratism,'" and disrespect for hereditary wealth and authority, flew in the face of the *"pulchrum"* of a previous time, when moral, economic, and cultural order had been guaranteed by specific hierarchies—by "traditional elites based . . . upon aptitudes and virtues transmitted through genetic continuity." Cultural traditionalism, including "virtue, culture, style and education," alongside "chivalrousness" and "holy intransigence," had ensured the rightful order of the Middle Ages—an order dependent on Oliveira's most insistent value: "traditional Catholic doctrine," which "proclaims the legitimacy and even the necessity of just and proportional inequalities among men." By preserving morality and Catholic traditionalism, in other words, bygone nobles had created the most perfect of societies, "an authentic national representation that faithfully mirrored social organicity" by *containing* the energies of the masses, mitigating popular participation in politics and the economy, "maintaining the distinction of classes," and creating a seigniorial paradise founded on those inequalities, to the benefit of all.[151]

The breakdown of feudalism, the "sensuality" of the French Revolution, the "paganization" of modern nobility, and the resultant "radically egalitarian populism" of the twentieth-century welfare state must, in Oliveira's view, be corrected by a return to the hierarchies (cultural, religious, moral, and economic) capped and held in place by traditional nobility.[152] Oliveira waxed romantic on this front, via express comparisons to the Crusades, but he also sought to make his work practical and explicitly transnational. He applied his theories directly to the United States, where, he admitted, "we will not attempt to find . . . a medieval military nobility" but where, nevertheless, elites could be found who might lead the new, reactionary era. Interestingly, Oliveira named two women, apparently because they were major benefactors of the TFP. Regardless of their largesse, these oil heiresses represented not only the kind of Republicans fomenting a Reagan Revolution in the United States—they were, from Oliveira's perspective, allies in the fight to restore traditional elites and traditional hierarchies.[153] The idea, that is, was to leave the rule of populace and polity to wealthy and powerful individuals like these, and not to meddlesome democratic, egalitarian, or pluralistic political systems or interest groups.[154] In Brazil, of course, the elite analogue would be those who, like Oliveira himself, claimed the "great planters . . . similar to feudal lords" among their ancestors.[155]

Mayer's and Sigaud's promotion of this retrospective hierarchalism rivaled Oliveira's, especially in the years when they worked together to defeat progressive efforts at reform within the Catholic Church. The bishop of Campos, as we have seen, expounded on the putative, unsung "beauty of inequality," and particularly on the idea that inequality should in no way be disrupted by public intervention. In perhaps their most widely disseminated cooperative effort, the three coauthored *Agrarian Reform: A Question of Conscience*, a 1961 book designed to vanquish efforts at such reform. The book made the case both for hereditary seigniorial hierarchies *and* for the notion that these stemmed not only from divine ordination but also from the individual, capitalistic, and entrepreneurial virtue of the ruling class. The liege lord of the *fazenda* (estate or plantation) appeared as a benevolent, organic authority, rightfully in power by dint of his thrifty hard work, responsibility, and charitable outlook:

> Lord of land acquired through arduous labor and honored by a legitimate hereditary succession, [the *fazendeiro*] did not content himself with culling from them, lazily, that which was strictly necessary for his subsistence and that of his own [family]. On the contrary, moved by a desire to augment the general well-being and to promote culture, he aspired to the full utilization of the font of wealth which he had in his hands.... Dedicated day by day to the management of rural labor, the landowner, associated with the manual laborers in the task of taking from the soil the resources by which others might live, was truly a "father," a "*patrão*" from whose goods and whose action all received food, shelter, clothes, and the means of saving each according to his situation and his collaboration.[156]

Even before the book's publication, Sigaud and Mayer championed hierarchy for hierarchy's sake within and outside the Church. Among the papers that TFP operatives prepared for Sigaud's use at Vatican II was one containing the contention, common in their circles, that democracy itself was incompatible with an orderly, holy society. "An example of the modern errors," read the draft prepared for Sigaud to present to Cardinal Tardini, is that "democracy is the only form of government [and] that even ... the Church and its style of life should be democratized."[157] Worse still, the results of "this sense of democracy" construed threats to desired inequalities and related tenure of capital: "Obedience is no longer permissible [and] private property no longer corresponds to the status of Western life."[158] Sigaud brought this perspective to Coetus Internationalis Patrum, seeking to firm up the argument that hierarchy, humility, and obedience were interrelated virtues threatened by proposed reforms. Coetus documents authored by Sigaud throughout the council argued, for example, against episcopal collegiality, as "where this spirit of so-called collegiality reigns, obedience in fact disappears."[159] Likewise, he outlined

Coetus's positions against Schema 13, on the basis that "the Church's traditional doctrines" on "intrinsic hierarchies" (including those between men and women) did not appear firmly enough in the document.[160] To Sigaud and his collaborators, these intrinsic hierarchies were absolutely fundamental, even cosmologically so: as his "point for reflection" put it, "Obedience and Hierarchy here meet their worth and importance: oneness with Christ and collaboration in the redemption of the world."[161]

Warning, as ever, against communism, Mayer wrote a pastoral letter in 1961 to denounce statism, the West's "big," overweening governments that usurped the rightful role of the Church. (Here he included all government-sponsored redistributive efforts but took aim principally, we must presume, at Cuba.) Writing against such overstepping "public powers," Mayer recurred to the tried-and-true Catholic conservative tenet that poverty must be addressed privately—"charity" alone, he insisted, should be applied to the long-standing "social question." Yet the bishop also made clear that the impetus to, as he put it, "do something useful for the poor" did *not* mean eliminating hierarchy and inequality. Instead, Mayer quickly recurred to his habitual railing against "destruction . . . of the social hierarchy" and resultant "complete egalitarianism." In some sense, this egalitarianism was communism's principal offense, in Mayer's eyes: "By dint of being egalitarian it destroys the right to inherit, the family, private property, social elites, and tradition."[162] Mayer's letter, among other declarations of his ideology, joined Catholic notions of charity with New Right emphasis on individual responsibility and behavior as the salve for the world's necessary (and in some sense desirable) ills. When the bishop exalted the "exercise of Christian virtues," he meant that these would operate in concert, such that morality, obedience, humility, and respect for private property, for tradition, and for rightful authority would restore desired order to the world. Invoking the teachings of antimodernists Leo XIII and Pius XII, Mayer wrote that "youth and children . . . should be educated in the spirit of hierarchy. . . . Without that spirit, the exercise of the virtues of obedience and humility, which are indispensable to amicable social coexistence, is practically impossible."[163]

Mayer's and other rightists' moralism—the "traditional values" Weyrich so proudly claimed to have brought to the renovated Right's platform—thus went beyond morality for morality's or tradition's sake. Rather, the traditionalist rationale dovetailed with the idea that moralism itself would foster and preserve what would become tenets of neoconservative policy-making: rightful inequalities and a concomitant emphasis on individuals' own behavior as the reason for their (deserved) fates in this world and the next. These tenets seamlessly merged faith-related or ecclesiastical hierarchies with the material hierarchies of class and of capitalism, but they were certainly explicit about the inclusion of the latter. SEPES, the Brazilian WACL affiliate led by Carlo Barbieri Filho, introduced these concepts in its propaganda, affirming that the Church must be respected as "Mother and Master," its "hierarchical structure" guaranteeing its "spiritual authority." As noted, the group insisted on the felt presence of a God that would order the world—and that order included socioeconomic inequality, which was humanity's default: "By its nature, society is organically structured into small social groupings, defined in their areas and attributions, endowed with the necessary autonomy for the achievement of their own distinctive objectives."[164] Mayer concurred, contending that the battle against secularism and for hierarchy and tradition would preserve this "organic" structure and win the war against social unrest: "Strengthening of faith, the indispensable reform of behavior, and other means of a spiritual order [are] necessary so that the inquietude provoked by the modern lay economy may be eliminated."[165]

Even when not openly advocating Oliveira's literal restoration of feudalism, exponents of neoconservatism across the hemisphere demonstrated a multifaceted antistatism, ranging from anticommunist to utterly free-market, but always denouncing regulation and the growth of the state. While some scholars bind this element of modern conservatism to reaction against the United States' New Deal, Brazil's Right complicates this view, since opposition to "big government" appeared as part and parcel of the religiously inflected traditionalism that we have seen drawing Brazilian ultramontane Catholics to their Protestant counterparts in Brazil and abroad. This was perhaps nowhere more evident than in Brazilians' organizing of conservative forces before and at Vatican II. In the text he drafted in preparation for Sigaud's role at the council, Orlando Fedeli included a section called "Statification and the New Age," in which he argued that the state, in its modern, burgeoning form, represented the greatest threat to humanity and to a prized bygone order. Temporal authority must abate in favor of religious and aristocratic authority, according to Fedeli's talking points: "To explain the breakdown at which society has arrived, look to the additional action of the State [which] is much broader than it ought to be normally. . . . The greatest part of the problems can only be resolved by the reform of behavior, and therefore, because this cannot be obtained with religion, the base of temporal order is in the Christianization of Society and *not* in the multiplication of laws and of state institutions."[166] In other words, the crisis—as ever—was moral and religious, and not only must be resolved but also must deal with the fast-growing problem of interventionist and overreaching governments. Later, Fedeli would simultaneously rail against "statification" and the faltering of individual responsibility, complaining about the "intervention of the State in areas that, normally, are the purview of individual initiative and that of social groups." He also amended his previous assertions about the "re-Christianization of Society" to read "the re-Christianization of *individuals*." Big government, then, was the enemy of social order and must be combatted by the restoration of self-reliance and religiously imposed morality.[167]

If Oliveira, Sigaud, and Mayer drew on older Catholic ways of thinking about charity, hierarchy, and opposition to public aid, McIntire and his Brazilian allies repackaged this message in, ironically, more ecumenical terms. From their beginnings in the 1940s, McIntire's North American and international organizations championed not only anticommunism but an anti-institution stance that ranged from opposing global ecumenical organizations to denouncing limitations on what the ACCC called "economic freedom and private enterprise." As early as 1943, McIntire's church called on fundamentalists to "use every legitimate Christian means" to defend free enterprise from impending state intervention.[168] McIntire's adherents in the United States and abroad exchanged copies of his 1945 book *Rise of the Tyrant: Controlled Economy versus Free Enterprise.*[169] Even those who disagreed with McIntire's more cantankerous moral positions put faith in his leadership against internationalism, ecumenism, and government intervention. As the Seattle businessman and libertarian maven James W. Clise wrote to McIntire in 1959, "I . . . agree wholeheartedly with your exposure of the godless perfidy . . . of the UN and UNESCO." Clise congratulated McIntire with particular warmth on his exposure of those who "have espoused the use of force (government) to achieve Christian aims that can only be reached through personal and voluntary understanding and sacrifice."[170] By the time of its plenary in Rio de Janeiro, the ICCC had built up a myth of self-making around McIntire, turning moderate Presbyterians' expulsion(s) of him into a story of virtuous bootstraps-pulling. As Baptist reverend Robert T. Ketcham, then president of the ACCC, told the gathered delegates, McIntire represented the spirit of "men all over the United States" who, rather than accepting unwarranted regulation, "take joyfully the spoiling of their goods" in order to maintain their freedom. McIntire's story served as a legendary parable of a man who, "rather than bow to the dictation of apostate leaders, . . . walked out of a beautiful $275,000 building, constructed a board tabernacle a few blocks away, and is still worshipping there today."[171]

Israel Gueiros propounded this combination of hierarchalism and radical individualism, publicly and privately, both in Brazil and abroad. For much of his life, he remained a sort of anchor figure of the ICCC and its Latin American subsidiary, ALADIC. Speaking for the latter in 1978, he praised the political and economic measures by which Augusto Pinochet had made "Chile . . . the nation with the happiest people in the world and the most enthusiastic about their government." Gueiros not only told *O Estado de S. Paulo* that ecumenist progressives were communists but based this contention in the deeper belief that Christianity prized hierarchy and distinction over cooperation and collectivism: "Christianity is deeply exclusivist," he said, and thus diametrically opposed to the religious and cultural "amalgamation" proposed by "communist leaders" in Brazil and elsewhere. (Gueiros named Martin Luther King Jr., Dom Hélder Câmara, and, in a show of extremism, Billy Graham.)[172] Early in his transnational career, Gueiros collaborated with McIntire as well as with other Brazilian and U.S. fundamentalists on a "Declaration of Faith and Principles," which made clear the ways in which these men's faith mandated a vision of the world in which people, not institutions, were responsible for their welfare. This meant not only their spiritual welfare but also their material well-being, including basic necessities like shelter and nourishment. Echoing Mayer's thinking discussed earlier, the document insisted that humans were sinners first and bodies second ("we believe in the complete depravation of human nature") and should focus their efforts on salvation rather than any material concerns. "The Kingdom of God," said Gueiros, "is not eating nor drinking, but . . . peace and joy in the Holy Spirit." As a result, human organizations (governments, but especially churches) should abandon social justice in favor of collective and individual pursuit of betterment via "the traditional faith in the Word of God." In other words—to quote a draft sent by Gueiros to McIntire in June 1950—"We will combat the so-called Social Gospel, because we understand that the principal mission of the Church is not to divide fortune among men (Luke 12:14), but to preach the Gospel of Grace; and because we believe that, if sinners seek FIRST the Kingdom of God and His righteousness, ALL things will be added unto them (Mat. 6:3), including better social conditions." Individuals, in other words, must rely on their *own* faith and ingenuity to guarantee personal, spiritual-cum-material well-being—and "better social conditions," far from a collective project, would serve as the reward (and the evidence) of the righteous search for divine favor. Gueiros shared this declaration with McIntire's aide Margaret Harden, then sent it to the man himself in New Jersey. McIntire enthusiastically praised Gueiros's work. "I do praise God for it," he wrote, adding, "Mrs. McIntire and I have read it carefully together." In a rare display of largesse, the generally tight-pursed McIntire responded to Gueiro's draft by sending US$200 to help disseminate the message.[173]

Of course, this evangelical penchant for individualistic, spiritual self-reliance that would foster economic well-being emerged most strongly in the gospel of wealth, or prosperity gospel, perhaps more widespread among Brazilian evangelicals than it is even in the United States. As eminent historian of Brazilian evangelism Paul Freston pointed out nearly a quarter century ago, a glaring correlation coupled ascendant evangelicals' prosperity theology with "neoliberal apologism." Certainly this was the case with, for example, Baptist preacher Fausto Rocha, who preached that the faithful would be rewarded, but not by the welfare state ("total statification," to use Rocha's terminology). Rather, they should look to Matthew 25:21: "Well done, good and faithful servant: thou hast been faithful over a few things, I will set thee over many things."[174] Strikingly, Brazilian evangelicals drew directly on North American preachers to make this case. While North American televangelists like Jimmy Swaggart, Pat Robertson, and Rex Humbard brought the prosperity gospel into Brazilian homes on popular programs, right-wing evangelical publications also emphasized this message domestically. CPAD, not surprisingly, took the lead here, as in a translated passage from *A Seara*, wherein U.S. radio personality and psychologist Clyde Narramore equated, in the most familiar of terms, poverty with "laziness" and success with a combination of work and divine favor. In 1987, as the wave of Reaganomics crested in the United States, Narramore championed the thriftiness and hard work bred of living in a "free country." Narramore's guide to "economic security" concluded, "Surely we have all heard the popular refrain that says 'God helps those who help themselves.' This is in large part true. God never approves of laziness."[175]

Weyrich continually made the point that campaigns against regulation and campaigns for re-Christianization must go hand in hand. The IPF proudly announced that it had gained support from the Center for International Private Enterprise, a division of the U.S. Chamber of Commerce that sponsored the IPF's 1988 training program in Argentina. Yet Weyrich carefully differentiated his vision from that of other deregulationists, emphasizing that he and his allies wished to restore an organicist social order in which putatively over-inflated government would be obviated by individual *morality*, often sexual morality. Weyrich, having deplored the "declining influence of religion" and the supernatural, went on to slightly chastise his "libertarian friends." In an interview with *Policy Review*, Weyrich condemned cohabitation before marriage, explaining that the renewal of traditional moral codes set him apart from libertarian allies, who presumably would not opine on such moral issues: "Our libertarian friends don't understand that private actions have public consequences. We need to *restigmatize* this kind of behavior. I don't know whether laws prohibiting it will in fact do much good, but we cannot tolerate the attitude that living together without the benefit of matrimony is just as good as being married; it is not."[176] In the same interview, Weyrich collaborator Midge Decter—a neoconservative heroine in her own right (albeit of a slightly different stripe) and a Heritage Foundation board member—provided a more pointed example of just how traditional morality must provide the ultimate neoliberal security.[177] Deriding both welfare itself and the "black community" leaders who supposedly propounded it, Decter argued that "if you actually look at these little girls, you see they would be having babies even if there were no welfare programs. . . . What I am saying is beginning to be recognized in the black community, where black leaders are at least commencing to acknowledge that *what is needed is not a new government program, but a new ethos—one in which these little girls will be encouraged to keep their knees together until they grow up and find husbands.*"[178]

The IPF reemphasized this deregulation-via-moralism approach in its mission statements and promotional literature. As we have seen, Weyrich told international observers that his organizations "were the first to add the concept of 'traditional values' to that equation"—that is, to the political and strategic formula of "limited government, free enterprise, strong national defense, and traditional values."[179] The IPF in particular sought to transnationalize this "equation." As a statement of organizational guiding principles reiterated, the group's constant use of terms like "pro-freedom" had a specific meaning, which linked "free enterprise" to antistatist belief that welfare states with strong government were the natural enemies of God: "The International Policy Forum believes in limited government and, thus, limited taxation. Too much government intervention strangles the freedoms and erodes the security of the citizens of any country. IPF believes in the right to free enterprise, guaranteeing each person's liberty to pursue economic prosperity. We believe that our rights are God-given, not government-given. God-given rights include traditional family moral values. These values are often undermined by governments, by secular humanism in education, and the breakup of the family through various social programs."[180]

VI. Brazil: "Confusing Freedom with Equality"— Nurturing Neoliberalism?

Weyrich and his allies in the United States expressed increasing frustration with the Reagan administration, "concluding," to quote the *Conservative Digest*, "that they must leave the president and his supporters behind to fulfill the bright promise of 1980 themselves."[181] In dictatorial Brazil, meanwhile, conservative activists felt themselves to be working in a friendlier milieu; the idea that traditional hierarchies, especially religious hierarchies, were precisely what was at stake in the culture wars had gained powerful adherence within the halls of power. I have elsewhere outlined the ways that such culture wars lay at the heart of dictatorial visions of the Cold War in Brazil.[182] Yet it is important to recognize that powerful individuals and agencies within the authoritarian state stood staunchly by the side of those conservatives who perceived individualism and traditionalist authority to be under attack and would see them reaffirmed. Security forces quite clearly recognized this "problem," albeit more from the point of view of anticommunism than from that of proto-neoliberalism. Police officials denounced progressive Catholics and Protestants alike as aggressors who sought to eliminate timeless, necessary structures and forms of authority. When it came to Vatican II, in fact, government spy agencies in Brazil nearly unanimously interpreted the council as a perilous forum where communists and progressives strategically sought to strip the Church of its mysteries and hierarchies. In part, this stemmed from these agencies' observation of challenges to intrainstitutional power and to the meaning of the Church and the supernatural in the world. In a secret 1973 memorandum, spies in Belo Horizonte observed,

> It is a fact that the Clergy, after the Second Vatican Council, is engaged in changing the image of the Church and, consequently, the image of Christ. Until the Second Vatican Council, the mentality reigned in which Christ was a severe God, always attentive to the sins of humanity in order to punish it. On the other hand, the Church was closed in its acts and prayers, austere, seldom or never communicative with its followers. After the Council, there were many innovations meant to make the Church accessible to the faithful . . . even if that meant that a New Church was configured and even if these innovations were susceptible to the following observations: (a) MORE NATURAL, . . . tending even toward fanaticism; (b) MORE SECULARIZING, since the opening has made possible greater participation of laypeople in the life of the Church.[183]

Of note in this passage are the agents' disdain for a popular Church, which many feared to be a communist stratagem; their wariness of the secularization they felt Vatican II portended; and, perhaps most importantly, the idea that such dangers were bound up in the loss of earthly and celestial hierarchies— the loss, that is, of a rightfully severe and unforgiving God, of an "austere" and unfriendly Church, and of a laity that had no right or expectation of participation in the Church's practice or governance.

On this last point, security forces took pains to side with conservatives, emphasizing again and again that any modifications to the hierarchies within the Church must be resisted. A 1982 report from the Rio de Janeiro SNI sympathized with Mayer on a number of points and articulated the threat posed by the "laicization of the church" and especially the impending "lack of definition between the common parish priest and the Church hierarchy."[184] Likewise, in dialogue with the Belo Horizonte agents just quoted, SNI officials in Brasília described the "current" of the clergy that they sought to promote: "Conservatives," they wrote, "(a) from an ideological point of view support, in Brazil, in a general way, the orientation of the Government; (b) consider in the first place spiritual values, and only after that material values; (c) tenaciously oppose communism and its manifestations . . . (e) *follow the orientation of the official texts of the Church and rigorously observe obedience to the Church. Therefore, they are known, as well, by the name of 'papalists.' They adhere to hierarchical obedience and traditional ecclesiastical discipline.*"[185] Vatican II, then, and especially progressive efforts within and around it, appeared to police eyes as communist-inspired tactics *based in threats to Church hierarchies*. At least part of this fear lay in state functionaries' equation of egalitarianism with indiscipline and lack of "obedience." To be sure, that fear was in one sense incompatible with neoliberals' championing (at least rhetorically) of "equal opportunity" and of the putatively temporary indiscipline of unregulated markets. Yet given that conservatives promoted hierarchy as the inevitable, divinely sanctioned outcome of competition and talent, that foe of communist subversives, security forces' and Christian conservatives' hierarchalism in a sense dovetailed quite closely with emergent free-market doctrines.[186] The conservatives, considered friends of the regime, gained that dubious honor by dint of their ferocious anticommunism, bound up in their minds and those of the Brazilian security state with maintenance of strict verticality within the Church, from the pope down to the laity. Little wonder, then, that the Porto Alegre SNI looked with scorn and suspicion on those who wished the pope to make state visits "as a simple Bishop and not as the chief trustee of the Church." Indeed, this report made separate mention of liberation theology's tendency toward increased autonomy for priests, a major source of debate in the mid-century Church. Secretly observing John Paul II's visit to Brazil in 1980, the agents noted that such autonomy, with its disruption of the vertical channels of power within the Church, "might deform the orientations of the Second Vatican Council and produce misleading and harmful results."[187]

These fearsome representatives of dictatorship—a dictatorship that saw progressive Christians as a principal enemy—thus considered ecclesiastical and supernatural hierarchy as critical Cold War issues. Moreover, they staunchly supported conservatives, Brazilian and otherwise. If, however, Mayer's "legitimate inequalities" encompassed such positional gradients—those between parishioner, priest, bishop, and pope—they also included more mundane disparities. On this point, too, security forces concurred—that is, the state's most dangerous agents made plain that they understood the secularization-dehierarchalization dyad to extend to issues of class and wealth. This attitude appeared with representative clarity in the special report prepared by federal police deputy Jesuan de Paula Xavier for the minister of justice in 1975. Agreeing with the TFP, Xavier affirmed that "progressismo" represented "a mentality dominated by the uncontained desire [for] reinterpretation of dogma and scripture, reform of the ecclesiastical and liturgical laws, adjusting the Church, thus, to what is 'modern' (in a pejorative sense)." And here the assessor made a key clarification—what was "modern" meant most particularly the *jettisoning of rightful hierarchies, within and outside the church*: "This mentality has concretized itself, in Brazil, via two movements: *The liturgical*, in which the intention is to attack the principles of authority and hierarchy and substitute the true Christian asceticism with a communitarian pity; and *Ação Católica*, in which the principles of authority and hierarchy are denied, moral relativism is followed, and the harmonic inequality between social classes is rejected and a struggle between them is favored."[188] The "principles of authority and hierarchy," then, must be depended on to guarantee "harmonic inequality" between classes, such that relativism did not foment questioning of either the moral or the material status quo.

An army intelligence report epitomized this vision of religious and socio-economic hierarchy threatened by progressive Christianity. Blaming Vatican II for "unleashing a strong prejudice against vertical theology and traditional theism" and obviating the everyday sense of God's supernatural transcendence in the world, the CIE insisted that such "Liberation Theology has been (and remains) the tool used" for "penetration by the USSR" in the Americas. The report went further, however, construing liberation theology as ideologically suspect and elucidating the agents' affinity for the hierarchical traditionalism of conservatives in terms of a sort of basic neoliberal philosophy of individualism. Ecclesiastical hierarchy provided a guarantee of the rightful order and class structure of society, in which individuals recognized their place and accepted what Mayer called "legitimate inequalities": "The message of Liberation Theology," read this 1982 report, consisted of "false principles," attacking the rightful existence of "class distinction" and affirming instead a world in which society, and not individuals, would be responsible

for everyone's well-being: "Society (and not man) should change to a structure that permits that [false] 'equality.' . . . Sin and blame are basically social
problems, and not individual ones. In this way, individual responsibility for
sin disappears and the point of reference for conversion stops being the heart
of man. . . . The Bible becomes the source of motivation for class warfare. . . .
*Liberation theology confuses freedom with equality, swearing that all lack of equal-
ity is wrong and unjust in and of itself. In this way, God's will in creating differences
[among individuals] is discarded.*"[189]

This focus on venerable hierarchies transcended, in security forces' estimation, Catholicism. For example, the progressive North American Presbyterian Richard Shaull seemed a threat precisely because he advocated
mitigating extant hierarchies within Protestant churches. Shaull, according to
police, was a "preacher of modernism and the needlessness of ethical principles to guide life, which identifies his atheist and materialist spirit. Founder of
a modernist school, [he] preaches the needlessness of ecclesiastical organization." Moral abandon, subversion, and the diminution of ecclesiastical hierarchies, then, represented linked threats, as much to the SNI as to Christian
conservatives themselves.[190]

Homing in on threats to hierarchy, articulated in moral, ecclesiastical, and
material terms, as a central problem, security forces perhaps got some of their
information from Brazil's official representatives in Rome. These officials, at
least, seem to have shared much of the conservative trepidation about threats
to traditional hierarchies. Over the course of the 1960s and 1970s, devout
Catholics served as Brazil's ambassadors, varying in their degrees of conservatism (and occasionally displaying some openness to reform) but generally
contemplating Vatican II and especially progressives with reserve if not outright alarm. As Ambassador José Jobim put it in his diplomatic missives, the
latter were the "least level-headed sectors of Catholicism," "partisans of revolution" who had created a situation in which "the Church finds itself today in
an hour of inquietude and—one could even say self-destruction!"[191] Jobim's
successor Antônio Castello Branco denounced the "notorious relaxation in
the area of morality and customs," blaming the zeitgeist and the weakness
that reform had putatively introduced into the Church. When it came to "sexual morality," Castello Branco condemned modern "permissiveness" and the
"timidity of the Church" in enforcing time-honored precepts.[192] To the ambassador, this conflated problem of "timidity" and "permissiveness" derived
from threats to hierarchy within the Church. Disapproving of suggested miti-
gations of Church hierarchy (which would contravene "religious and historic
fundaments" by, for example, allowing bishops to join cardinals in choosing

the pope), the ambassador directly addressed the issues of papal and centralized authority, and the ancient structures of ecclesiastical power.

> The Church . . . ought to be one, holy, and Catholic. Contrary to the theories diffused in the last few years about the democratic origin of the Church's authority, about the role of the Pope, about the autonomy of local Churches, the Holy Year of 1975 emphasized [that] the organic and hierarchical structure of the Church should be preserved intact—which structure is given to us by the Scriptures, by Tradition, and by the Magisterium—and in particular, the primacy of the Pope, felt and desired by all the Church as the Master, Supreme Pastor, and Sanctifier.[193]

Indeed, Castello Branco—like at least one other ambassador in this period—more or less openly approved of Marcel Lefebvre, at least in diplomatic correspondence. The ambassador referred to the French renegade in 1977 as "a European . . . whose contentious arguments correspond, essentially, to the causes of the malaise that afflicts a considerable portion of the pre-Conciliar Catholic generations." Distinguishing these right-wing arguments from "the other contestation," that of progressives, Castello Branco declared categorically that the latter was, "in [his] view, much more serious, because more diffuse and less open and forthright." In other words, Itamaraty, or at least its representative in Rome, preferred Lefebvre's understandable, conservative "malaise" to the far more threatening, conspiratorial machinations of leftist Catholics.[194]

VII. "The Persecution Which He Has Endured Is as Severe as Any I Know": The Transnational Right as Underdog

I do not wish to suggest that Brazil's security forces, nor much less its diplomatic corps, were monolithic; certainly they did not seamlessly promote neoliberalism or even its embryonic forms. Rather, within a diverse and often chaotic authoritarian state, there were powerful forces advocating for something akin to a religious neoliberalism, then being promoted by anticommunist Christians from Sigaud to McIntire to Weyrich to Gueiros. Far greater consistency, however, characterized these conservative actors when it came to one particular characteristic: the sense of themselves as persecuted, as the underdogs. This dynamic will surely be familiar to contemporary readers, who may see echoes of this combative stance in the petulant attitudes and arguments of a Jair Bolsonaro, a Donald Trump, an Alex Jones, a Movimento Brasil Livre, and other manifestations of today's Right. Indeed, recent scholarship has noted the persecution complex as a contemporary "broader and growing trend in political discourse as it emerges from certain branches of right-wing political Christianity."[195] Yet this "trend" dates back far beyond the current U.S. debate about ersatz "religious freedom" or the "War on Christmas" (and Christians); and in fact it transcends the United States. Predominant Catholicism made minoritarian status—and anxiety—the rule for Brazil's historic Pentecostals, who, as sociologist Ricardo Mariano has pointed out, were able as early as the 1989 presidential election to "reenact an old syndrome of persecution" in order to encourage voting against the "communist" Workers' Party.[196] Such a syndrome was truly "old" at that time—not only by dint of Protestants' long-term precarity in Catholic Brazil, but because persecution had served as a mantra for hemispheric conservatives, who consistently cast themselves as the victims of mass culture, rather than its arbiters and beneficiaries. In Brazil, this extended beyond the complaints of Protestants about their lack of religious freedom vis-à-vis Catholics. Protestants and Catholics alike were united in their sense of themselves as *losing* a great battle against the devil, modern culture, and secularization.[197]

Carl McIntire nearly perfected this art, feeling, feigning, or manipulating what one scholar has called his "exaggerated persecution anxieties."[198] McIntire forever presented himself and his lieutenants as victims, not of their own cantankerous and personalistic divisiveness, but of a world bent on conspiracy against them. Whereas McIntire's acolytes in Brazil and elsewhere lionized him, as we saw in chapter 4, as a "an ever-lit shining torch," his adversaries and erstwhile coreligionists tended to see him in very different light—as an antagonist who skillfully "exploited" the tensions in Latin American churches and whose allies (including Gueiros) "festered like a thorn in the flesh of the seminary, the mission, and the Church."[199] McIntire adopted the language of combat, casting himself and his allies as embattled heroes in a desperate struggle against a more powerful foe. As he wrote to a budding Brazilian ally in 1959, "We are in a terrific worldwide struggle to preserve our historic Christian faith."[200] Margaret Harden, a sort of secretary-cum-missionary whom McIntire maintained in Brazil, wrote to him to plead for more support in their "open warfare" against other Presbyterians, which she represented as a losing battle: "I believe more than ever that we need a good man from the states to take over here and lead this fight, for fight it must be, and open warfare, from now on. I have conscientiously done all I could do, but it is all too little."[201] Such allies were quick to laud McIntire as the put-upon, tenacious hero of their against-the-odds struggle. ALADIC founder and sometime secretary Rafael Camacho, a conservative Presbyterian from São Paulo, testified about his "hard fight against modernism" but ceded the greater honor to

McIntire, whose "fight . . . has been very hard, since, as is well known, it is the noble American nation where modernism has its headquarters."[202] When McIntire found himself, in the late 1960s, at odds with members of his own ACCC, Camacho insisted that the Collingswood preacher was once again the victim: "Now I am praying [for you] more and more. You have my sympathy in this time of struggle. . . . I know you had many enemies outside of the fundamental movement, but I never thought that those men you considered your friends were undermining your work . . . behind the scenes."[203]

Israel Gueiros himself preached unceasingly against doctrinal modernism and ecumenism—even when his perceived antagonists remained quite far from either—praising those who, like him, execrated "tolerance." Yet, often in the same breath, Gueiros complained of the *lack* of tolerance shown him, McIntire, and their belligerent allies. In 1950, for example, Gueiros wrote to a like-minded pastor, José da Silva, congratulating him on the "polemical" tone he had taken against "'tolerant' modernists," but warning him that fierce persecution was their collective lot: "The fire . . . is going to be raised against you because you dared to defend the great leader of the defense of sound doctrine of the Gospel of Christ, Rev. Carl McIntire."[204] Gueiros's warning came informed by his and McIntire's shared conviction that they suffered such victimhood together. As McIntire wrote to Keith Altig, a Grace Brethren missionary in Belém, in 1957, "Dr. Gueiros has really suffered. The persecution which he has endured is as severe as any I know. The Presbyterian Church in the USA has simply done everything in its power to turn everybody against Gueiros."[205] As early as 1950, when McIntire and Gueiros had scarce begun their collaboration, McIntire made a note of "the story of the severe persecution which he has been receiving"—a fact to be used, no doubt, for propagandistic, among other, purposes.[206]

Even Brazilian evangelicals not directly affiliated with McIntire adopted this stance, born at least in part of Brazilian Protestants' long-standing position as a religious minority and resultant truculence vis-à-vis Catholics. Yet by 1986, Brazilian Protestant conservatives saw themselves as put-upon gladiators in an all-out battle to save the democratizing nation from "groups of women, Indians, the black community, various associations and even homosexuals [who] are entirely mobilized to successfully send representatives to the constitutional assembly." *Crentes*, then, putatively ever on the back foot (in reality, this was certainly less the case at this moment than ever before), would thus need "men committed to fighting like true prophets of God in the Congress."[207] Hewing to the well-trodden ground of moral panic, conservative Protestant battle cries from this period suggested that morality and indeed

Christian culture faced extinction in the face of political and cultural assaults. In keeping with this attitude, they adopted the language of war and besiegement: "the battle against abortion" and the "war against pornography"; the "struggle against the legalization of gambling," and the need for "constant vigilance to avoid the subversion of order."[208] As one 1986 call titled "Say No to Divorce" would have it, "women's rights" threatened Christian culture entirely, "in an epoch in which women are abdicating their traditional functions." The piece went on to decry "an unprecedented attack on Christian marriage.... Films and magazines proclaim women's rights and treat adultery like romance.... These weapons of war are flying over the Christian family [in an] unrelenting combat."[209]

By 2014, veteran scholars of Brazilian Pentecostalism Joanildo Burity and Maria das Dores Campos Machado would conclude that one way of understanding Protestant ascendancy in Brazilian politics was the perceived need "to resist besiegement by social movements, discrimination by the media, and the continuing privilege enjoyed by the Catholic Church."[210] So-called lifestyle defense, then, certainly played a role in the rise of politicized evangelicalism in Brazil. Yet Catholics, too, participated in the discourse of the put-upon, forging an identitarian space in which conservative Christianity generally could be seen as embattled and fighting for its very survival against waves of cultural depredation. In the United States, Weyrich was unceasing in his efforts to present his brand of renewed conservatism as a nick-of-time reaction to the onslaught of civil rights, sexual revolution, and postwar growth of the welfare state. He narrated his career as one premised on the fundamental weakness of the Right in the face of an onslaught of left-wing organizing, both domestically and internationally. The task, to hear him tell it, was to "keep the ship from sinking as fast as it was" while being forced to "play on the turf of the liberals."[211] As we saw in chapter 4, his IPF synthesized this challenge in "The Problem: Our Lack of Solidarity." Weyrich and his allies also infused this putatively disadvantaged positionality with a note of the mystical and the apocalyptic, similar to the tones struck by Plínio Corrêa de Oliveira in his theorizations of the age-old, inimical "Revolution." Ronald Reagan's conservatism, to Weyrich, fell far short of the desired mark—hence in 1984 he wrote in the archconservative Catholic magazine the *Remnant* of his own and his like-minded coreligionists' dire position when it came to saving the United States and traditional culture. "We see all around us," said Weyrich, "the forces of darkness which attack and seek to destroy any force for good in Washington.... The Pharisees of Christ's age are still with us." Invoking the notion—shared, as we saw in chapter 2, by Brazilian Protestants—of

Christians as hamstrung by their own moral righteousness, Weyrich recounted how a "friend" had brought this to his attention as the source of their disadvantage: "We could not prevail against the forces of evil because they play by different rules than we, as Christians, must play by."[212]

Such ideas dovetailed quite closely with a broader sense of Christian renewal responding to the changes of the 1960s—a diffuse, moralistic reaction. In Brazil, the idea of Christianity as outmatched by modern, antireligious foes likewise took the form of an amply distributed moral panic, whose contours I have elsewhere discussed, particularly insofar as they granted structure to dictatorial anticommunism. Even at the height of countersubversive dictatorial violence, Catholic conservatives shrilly pronounced the moral doom of Brazil and of Christendom at the hands of atheistic communism and its "useful innocent" collaborators.[213] The TFP, however, took these diffuse ideas and made them specific to the organization itself, creating a narrative in which persecution of *tefepistas* and their leader made *them* (despite their closeness to the authoritarian regime) the victims. As João Camilo de Oliveira Torres pointed out in his 1962 *History of Religious Ideas in Brazil*, conservative integrists had long discerned a "catastrophic nature of history,"[214] and no one perhaps did this better than Plínio Corrêa de Oliveira. Oliveira's magnum opus, *Revolution and Counterrevolution*, presented Catholics like him as embattled, locked in combat with an eternal, multifarious, satanic, disembodied forced known as "the Revolution." Even as the book's introduction acknowledged that in Brazil, "statistically speaking, the situation of Catholics is excellent," it warned of a mysterious, "terrible blow against the Bride of Christ"—an evil force, "impalpable and subtle, and as penetrating as a powerful and fearful radiation." This force—Oliveira dubbed it "the Revolution"—"exerts its undefined but overwhelming sway, producing symptoms of tragic grandeur."[215]

Presuming itself the West's principal defender against this overwhelming foe, the TFP naturally assumed a combat-ready stance and expected to be attacked. Nonetheless, when attacks (or even questions) arrived, the organization's leadership loudly decried a conspiracy against it. Across decades, Oliveira and his acolytes complained that they had been singled out as targets of well-directed, subversive calumny. By the 1980s, in fact, the TFP had begun to assign ordinal numbers to the supposed waves of "estrondos publicitários" (publicity blitzes) marshaled against it.[216] In 1975, amid a spike in suspicion of the TFP's secretiveness and its recruitment of youths, the organization decried a "fast-moving publicity attack. Multiple calumnies ... as if born as one from the earth, in the far corners of the country, were diffused for numerous press outfits. . . . Thus was configured the first publicity blitz against the TFP on a national scale."[217] Ten years later, the organization would mark the "XI estrondo publicitário," further evidence of the organization's perceived besiegement by the media, politicians, and the public.[218] Notwithstanding his decades-long run as a regular columnist for *Folha de S. Paulo*, Oliveira and other TFP leaders published a years-long series of combative texts whose titles reveal their self-positioning as the persecuted: "The TFP in Legitimate Self-Defense"; *The TFP's Refutation of a Frustrated Attack* (in two volumes); and "After the Failure of Ten Publicity Blitzes, an Extraordinary Attempt to 'Implode' the TFP."[219] The organization's history of itself presented this as a David and Goliath story: "The TFP, with the minimal means, achieves maximal results. . . . Certain sectors of the media industry engage in cyclical campaigns against the TFP, and with maximal means, fail to obtain results."[220] This attitude transcended Brazil, spreading to international chapters. In Chile, the TFP claimed it had weathered "persecution and vengefulness . . . accompanied by constant defamatory invective on the part of the demo-Christian and socialist-communist press."[221]

The various TFPs promoted this vision of the organization as besieged and beleaguered across decades; and accompanied by Sigaud and Mayer, *tefepistas* at Vatican II propagated the notion of conservatism as underdog. Amid dire pronouncements about the Revolution's penetration of the clergy—consistent with conservative reactions to progressive Catholicism—the Brazilian proponents of curial conservatism insisted that the situation was critical, the power of the Revolution fearsome, and their own position shaky. In a draft of a letter to the pope on this subject, Sigaud emphasized the need for a war footing: "The Church must organize on a global level a *systematic fight against the Revolution*." This was necessary because the Revolution had infiltrated the clergy and Christians across the world, just as, Sigaud observed, "paganism" had plagued the medieval Church.[222] Among the observations made by Sigaud and the TFP in response to the initial summons to the council was a similarly apocalyptic pronouncement, with an added note of complaint: the allegation that the crisis had gone so far as to produce systematic discrimination against such conservatives as remained within the hierarchy. Commenting on "the life of the Church in Brazil and in the world," this document decried "a great internal weakening, a profound penetration of the errors of a spirit of worldliness," and "alongside this . . . an impressive silence of the Bishops, an active collaboration of many members of the Clergy in the work of the Revolution. Instead of fighting openly against the Revolution, many members of the Hierarchy block good priests and good laypeople from fighting. Priests who are worthy of the episcopate are not promoted because they are antirevolutionary."[223]

Perhaps these exponents of Brazil's Catholic Right were able to see them-selves this way because they enjoyed a cozy relationship with Brazil's conspiracy-minded, anticommunist police state. More likely, though, that relationship produced mutually reinforcing affirmations of the perceived difficulty of con-servative anticommunists' position. Whatever the case, powerful state agents in dictatorial Brazil certainly shared the view that the Right, particularly the Catholic Right but also evangelicals, battled against the odds. This view was particularly prevalent among security forces, who focused on the progres-sive clergy once other sectors of opposition activism and opposition to the regime had been brutally eradicated. Discerning, among change-minded Catholics, a massive communist conspiracy, state spies engaged in frequent hand-wringing about the supposed powerlessness of conservative religious leaders and groups, whom reports described in glowing terms, only to be-moan their "adverse" circumstances. Foreshadowing a long-term rallying cry of the contemporary Right, SNI agents in Rio de Janeiro in 1982 sought to explain why "the activities of the clergy known as traditionalist, a rightist seg-ment of the Catholic clergy, are so little known"—and came up with liberal media conspiracy as the answer. "The usurpation, by the forces of the Left, of the means of dissemination and of communication," they argued, must be responsible for a plot to discredit traditionalist clerics, especially those whose "doctrinal positions ... predate the Second Vatican Council." The SNI re-ported extensively on the crisis of authority precipitated by Bishop Mayer's refusal to implement post–Vatican II reforms, especially when it came to celebration of the mass and tolerance for "liberties" among the congregants. Indeed, state spies observing Mayer's diocese used the term "Holy War" to describe the dispute between the bishop and the Vatican. The SNI lion-ized the former and lamented his relative impotence. Whereas Mayer faith-fully maintained "a very clear position against the modifications introduced, by the Council, in the Church's traditions," he and other conservatives had their backs against the wall, struggling against nefarious "innovations within the Church." These holdouts had what SNI agents judged to be "solid doctrine" behind them, yet could not prevail against subversive leftists who "always find a voice in their defense among the Episcopal hierarchy." Echoing the conservatives of Campos and like-minded traditionalists, SNI agents felt that progressive "innovations" were likely to amalgamate racial, moral, and cultural threats to the Church's centuries of patriarchal power. In nearly the same breath, they denounced progressive designs to institute "a Quilombo Mass, to the rhythms of Candomblé," alongside religious policies "favorable to the Pill."[224]

If Mayer enjoyed the sympathy of the military regime's enforcers, they likewise admired Sigaud as something of an anticommunist martyr. As the archbishop of Diamantina ratcheted up his condemnations of liberation theology and of particular prelates in Brazil's hierarchy, federal agents decried a conspiracy of "all sorts of pressures to silence the voice of [Sigaud] who denounces communist infiltration in the Catholic Church." Sigaud's censures not only of individual bishops (particularly Dom Aloísio Lorscheider and Dom Pedro Casaldáliga) but of the CNBB as a whole seemed to SNI observers the actions not only of an ally but of an embattled champion of anticommunism—a victim of the unfair fight against conservatives. "On another front," a report from SNI headquarters contended, "the CNBB, in a totally factious position, freely permits public manifestations of bishops either accusing D. Sigaud or openly taking a position against the government, without the least reprimand or warning against those bishops." The report feared that "in these conditions, the attitude taken by the CNBB and by *progressista* bishops . . . will force . . . Dom Sigaud into silence"—and added that the same might happen to Mayer, based on his efforts to combat "Marxist infiltration in the Church." Reflecting the general attitude of persecution, the report concluded that "the angst of prelates who, condemning the machinations of the leftist clergy, which controls the CNBB, feel themselves powerless to reaction, is well-known."[225] Such references to "machinations" and the like reflected the firm conviction that Sigaud himself had been the victim of the very "war" that security forces thought themselves to be fighting. As Ministry of Education and Culture spies put it in a report titled "The Evolution of Subversion," because "Dom Sigaud decried communist infiltration in the clergy, he has been massacred and neutralized by intense psychological tactics."[226] Once again, José Jobim brought this attitude to the diplomatic core. As Itamaraty's representative at the Vatican, Jobim clearly frowned on the changes proposed at Vatican II and sympathized with conservatives. Calling conservative Church fathers "the responsible elements . . . concluding that the Church needs to urgently take heed" and keep itself from becoming a "tool of subversion," Jobim echoed anxieties about an apparent plot to exclude such "elements" from positions of visibility and power. "It is revealing to note," he commented darkly, "that prelates like Dom Geraldo Proença Sigaud, Archbishop of Diamantina, and Dom Antônio de Castro Mayer, Bishop of Campos . . . whose conservative positions are well-known, do not occupy any positions within the CNBB."[227]

As we have seen, such friendliness to Mayer, to Sigaud, and to Catholic conservatism more generally did not preclude regime insiders' broad embrace of the rise of politicized archconservatism within Brazil's burgeoning evangelical communities. Here, too, security forces not only expressed support for reactionaries but saw their conservative friends in the Protestant churches as put upon, waging an unlikely and difficult battle against a common, subversive foe. Basing, as noted in chapter 2, their knowledge of *progressismo* on *Mensageiro da Paz* and other reactionary or fundamentalist sources, authorities replicated those sources' own sense of themselves as harassed and beset by, for example, the putatively omnipresent "tentacles" of the reviled WCC.[228] The very 1981 SNI summary that sought to provide an "initial" introduction to any agents who somehow had missed the recent developments lamented the "inexistence of strong orthodox leadership" within Protestants' ranks. Their desire for such leadership, they wrote, ran up against a major, "diffused," international conspiracy of financially endowed, well-placed, progressive ecumenists, led by "the WCC and the 'progressista' wing of the Catholic Church in the Americas. . . . Here and there one hears words of protest and mistrust [of progressivism], immediately shut down by the economic power of groups interested in carrying forward ecumenism."[229] Likewise, a later report from the same agency listed the fundamentalists Gueiros, Fanini, Abraão de Almeida, and José dos Reis Pereira among the regime's conservative allies but complained that unlike progressives, "they do not have ample financial resources, nor the open support of Catholic priests engaged in 'Theology of Liberation.'"[230]

Conclusion

Interestingly enough, scholarship has long echoed this tendency to see the Right as, if not persecuted, certainly weak, disorganized, and unlikely to succeed. In some ways this surely stems from broader academic neglect of studying and historicizing right-wing actors and movements—a neglect that, to quote Gilberto Calil, "leads to the false conclusion that the Right is fragile, poorly organized, and merely reactive."[231] Yet even when scholars have taken up conservatism, there has been a propensity to presume that actors like those we have seen articulating the common ground of a transnational and transdenominational religious conservatism in fact lacked precisely that articulation. Indeed, as political theorist Corey Robin writes in his 2011 endeavor to excavate an essence of modern conservatism, this presumption of weakness, disunity, and negligibility goes so far among scholars that "many continue to believe the differences on the right are so great it would be impossible to say anything about the right."[232] Particularly in international contexts, analyses of Christian conservative activists describe them as "without much experience" in organizing, outmaneuvered by progressive opponents, and unable to effectively formulate strategies and messaging.[233] While this was no doubt true in certain of the cases scrutinized by insightful scholars of conservatism, it seems worth reconsidering this notion in light of the assiduous efforts to foster and share tactics and experience demonstrated by individuals like Weyrich and Oliveira and organizations like the TFP and Coetus.

Ironically, perhaps, conservative activists did not always see themselves this way—they could, even in the midst of a general tendency to self-identify as weak and put upon, celebrate their own initiatives as a "movement" and even as propitious successes in an otherwise dark battle. Thus even as they positioned themselves as bound to suffer the effects of a grand conspiracy orchestrated by Judaism, Masons, communists, and Satan himself, Brazil's conservative Catholics celebrated moments of hope during Vatican II. Before the council, Sigaud's eventual ally Bishop Carlos Saboia Bandeira de Mello wrote a pastoral letter announcing the meeting to his flock. The bishop jubilantly projected a conservative "renewal" of the Church: "The Council will be the point of departure for a renovation of the Sacred Gospel in the whole world. Do you perceive this? Reflect upon it with us: renewal of the Sacred Gospel! Is it not true that the Gospel is forgotten in the modern epoch?"[234] Such jubilation on the part of conservatives cropped up from time to time throughout the 1960s. As late as 1965, Sigaud wrote to Plínio Corrêa de Oliveira about their doomed effort to gain a formal place for Coetus at the council, what they referred to as an "officialization of the minority."[235] The failure to achieve this signaled yet more adversity to both Sigaud and Oliveira, on whose efforts council leadership frowned because of their vitriolic and divisive tone.[236] Yet Sigaud mused that perhaps the reason that officials did *not* approve such a role for Coetus was that it was *gaining* momentum: "Perhaps the results of the Third Session showed the efficiency of our work [in marshaling opposition] and called attention down upon [Coetus]?"[237]

This tempered optimism, the idea that conservatives might at least delay the tide of immoral, antitraditional, godless, modernistic, and even communist innovation, survived for a brief time. Particularly as the Second Vatican Council drew to a close, its legacy seemed uncertain, as much to the Church fathers themselves as to observers. At the Brazilian embassy in Vatican City, Henrique de Souza Gomes demonstrated not only an awareness of the conservative efforts spearheaded by his countrymen but also a sense that, as of 1964, those efforts had borne fruit. Gomes referred, in a January missive, to the "unexpected opposition" that had emerged to challenge progressive efforts at the council, and concluded that, "generally, . . . the second session lacked that revolutionary impulse that . . . characterized the first part of the Council."[238]

Time and space, however, would not be kind to these glimmerings of hope—which, it bears noting, do not appear among contemporary Protestants. As the decades wore on, outrage about progressive Catholicism grew more entrenched and drove some Catholics—notably Mayer, Lefebvre, and Weyrich—out of the arms of their beloved Roman Church. Among Protestant conservatives, meanwhile, the sense of moral and spiritual crisis, of a losing battle against Satan, communism, and secularization, also gained momentum, leading eventually to the kinds of alliances we have seen here. Links between Jerry Falwell and Paul Weyrich, or between Weyrich and the TFP; the TFP's overtures toward the fierily anti-Catholic McIntire; the adherence by religious conservatives to international and nondenominational organizations like WACL, CAL, and the IPF—all of these drew fuel from the discourses of these men, whose pronouncements and correspondence brimmed with the language of fear, calamity, and decline. The sense of embattlement formed one impetus to draw together—and when they drew together, such actors agreed on a common agenda that we can now recognize as the platform of a religious Right that transcends nation-states and denominations. That platform included, from its early days, the issues and anxieties I have examined in this book: an antimodernism that fleshed out its sense of the "modern" by opposing communism, ecumenism, secularization, and the loss of moral order, and the perceived besiegement of traditional hierarchies and inequalities rooted in worldly and supernatural, rightful disparities. Herein lay the roots of the bitter, vitriolic Right of today, which derides human rights, globalism, international cooperation, social movements, and redistributive justice as conspiracies. It must come, given the foregoing evidence, as little surprise that there is so much correspondence between that Right in Brazil, where partisans simultaneously rejoice in the victory of Jair Bolsonaro and bemoan his perceived victimization by a shadowy "establishment," and in the United States, where the narrative of right-wing suffering, from Brett Kavanagh to Donald Trump, has never been stronger, nor more generative of policies designed to combat precisely the changes we have seen opposed by the embryonic transnational Right delineated in this book.

Notes

Abbreviations Used in the Notes

ACMSP	Arquivo da Cúria Metropolitana de São Paulo
ACRSP	Arquivo da Casa das Redentoristas, São Paulo
AHPI	Arquivo Histórico do Palácio do Itamaraty
AMAD	Arquivo da Mitra Arquidiocesana de Diamantina
AN/COREG	Arquivo Nacional, Coordenação Regional no Distrito Federal
CENIMAR	Centro de Informações de Marinha
CIE	Centro de Informações do Exército
CISA	Centro de Informações da Aeronáutica
FDS	Fundo Dom Sigaud
JE	*Jornal Evangélico*
LOCW	Library of Congress, Manuscripts Division, Paul Weyrich Papers
MRE	Ministro das Relações Exteriores
OE	*O Estandarte*
PTSM	Princeton Theological Seminary Library, Carl McIntire Collection
SCE	Seção de Correspondência Especial
SNI	Serviço Nacional de Informações
SNI/AC	Agência Central
SNI/APA	Agência Porto Alegre
SNI/ARJ	Agência Rio de Janeiro
SNI/ASP	Agência Regional de São Paulo
UOJWC	University of Oregon Knight Library, James W. Clise Papers

Introduction

1. Unless otherwise noted, translations are my own. Thaïs Bilenky, "Fã de Olavo de Carvalho, assessor internacional de Bolsonaro ecoa cartilha da nova direita," *Folha de S. Paulo*, 6 January 2019, https://www1.folha.uol.com.br/mundo/2019/01/fa-de-olavo-de-carvalho -assessor-internacional-de-bolsonaro-ecoa-cartilha-da-nova-direita.shtml; "Luiz Philippe de Orleans e Bragança: 'Olavo de Carvalho tem uma função cívica,'" Jovem Pan, 6 May 2019, https://jovempan.uol.com.br/programas/panico/luiz-philippe-de-orleans-e-braganca -olavo-de-carvalho-tem-uma-funcao-civica.html; João Fellet, "Monarquistas ocupam cargos em Brasília e reabilitam grupo católico ultraconservador," BBC News Brasil, 4 April 2019, https://www.bbc.com/portuguese/brasil-47728267.

2. Previously, Alves had declared that "girls will be princesses and boys will be princes," a response to the so-called ideology of gender, a right-wing construction of gender studies and gender freedom as a conspiracy designed to actively repress conventional gender expression among children.

3. Amanda Mars, "Bolsonaro ganha de Trump apoio para OCDE, aceno à OTAN e um banho de ideologia," *El País*, 19 March 2019, https://brasil.elpais.com/brasil/2019/03/19/politica/1553011412_470388.html.

4. Paulo Coelho, "'Quem quiser vir ao Brasil fazer sexo com mulher, fique à vontade,' diz Bolsonaro," Pragmatismo Político, 26 April 2019, https://www.pragmatismopolitico.com.br/2019/04/jair-bolsonaro-brasil-paraiso-gay.html.

5. Weeks later, Bolsonaro would remove the original tweet from his feed. "Após postar vídeo com pornografia, Bolsonaro pergunta o que é 'golden shower,'" G1 Política, 6 March 2019, https://g1.globo.com/politica/noticia/2019/03/06/apos-postar-video-com-pornografia-bolsonaro-pergunta-o-que-e-golden-shower.ghtml; Ricardo Senra, "Bolsonaro apaga tuíte do 'golden shower' após revelação de ação no STF," *Época Negócios*, 21 March 2019, https://epocanegocios.globo.com/Brasil/noticia/2019/03/bolsonaro-apaga-tuite-do-golden-shower-apos-revelacao-de-acao-no-stf.html.

6. Fernando Trisotto, "Não é só o diesel! 6 atos pouco liberais do governo Bolsonaro," *Gazeta do Povo*, 15 April 2019, https://www.gazetadopovo.com.br/republica/bolsonaro-liberal-diesel-promessa-campanha-economia/; "É possível consertar decisão de Bolsonaro, diz Guedes após intervenção na Petrobras," *Gazeta do Povo*, 14 April 2019, https://www.gazetadopovo.com.br/republica/paulo-guedes-consertar-decisao-bolsonaro-diesel/.

7. Angela Boldrini, "MBL abre dissidência virtual e critica atuação de Bolsonaro nas redes sociais," *Folha de S. Paulo*, 13 March 2019, https://www1.folha.uol.com.br/poder/2019/03/mbl-abre-dissidencia-virtual-e-critica-atuacao-de-bolsonaro-nas-redes-sociais.shtml.

8. "What Conservatives Think of Ronald Reagan," *Policy Review* 27 (1984): 19; "Thunder from the Right," *Conservative Digest*, May 1984, LOCW.

9. "What Conservatives Think," 19. On the term "entitlement programs" as a conservative buzzword, see John Makin and Norman Ornstein, *Debt and Taxes* (New York: Random House, 1994), 224; Katherine S. Van Wormer and Rosemary Link, *Social Welfare Policy for a Sustainable Future* (London: SAGE, 2016), 164; and Hendrik Hertzberg, "Sense of Entitlement," *New Yorker*, 8 April 2013.

10. "Bolsonaro propõe salário mínimo sem aumento real e veta concurso público em 2020," *El País*, 15 April 2019, https://brasil.elpais.com/brasil/2019/04/16/politica/1555371819_186058.html; "Bolsonaro decreta fim das faculdades de Filosofia e Sociologia: 'Objetivo é focar em áreas que gerem retorno imediato,'" Revista Forum, 26 April 2019, https://www.revistaforum.com.br/bolsonaro-decreta-fim-das-faculdades-de-filosofia-e-sociologia-objetivo-e-focar-em-areas-que-gerem-retorno-imediato/; Cláudio Ângelo, "Brazil's Government Freezes Nearly Half of Its Science Spending," *Nature*, 8 April 2019, https://www.nature.com/articles/d41586-019-01079-9.

11. "Promulgada emenda constitucional do teto dos gastos públicos," Câmara dos Deputados (Brazil), 15 December 2016, https://www2.camara.leg.br/camaranoticias/noticias/ECONOMIA/521413-PROMULGADA-EMENDA-CONSTITUCIONAL-DO-TETO-DOS-GASTOS-PUBLICOS.html.

12. Henrique Mota, "Brasil: Nenhum Paraíso para pessoas LGBT," Medium, 24 January 2019, https://medium.com/@henriquemota/brasil-nenhum-para%C3%ADso-para-pessoas-lgbt-e48d652a270b; Sam Cowie, "Violent Deaths of LGBT People in Brazil Hit All-Time High," *Guardian*, 22 January 2018.

13. "'Feliz é a nação cujo Deus é o Senhor,' diz Dilma a evangélicos," Reuters, 8 August 2014, https://br.reuters.com/article/domesticNews/idBRKBNoG81S620140808.

14. Cristián Parker, "Religious Pluralism and New Political Identities in Latin America," *Latin American Perspectives* 43, no. 3 (2016): 22.

15. Anna Virgínia Baloussier, "Com ideais conservadores, bancada católica ocupa posições estratégicas na Câmara," *Folha de S. Paulo*, 24 December 2017, https://www1.folha .uol.com.br/poder/2017/12/1945831-com-objetivos-conservadores-bancada-catolica -ocupa-posicoes-estrategicas-na-camara.shtml. See also Magalí Nascimento da Cunha, "Bancada evangélica tem católicos como aliados em pautas homofóbicas, diz pesquisadora," interview by Helder Lima, Opera Mundi, 29 April 2015, https://operamundi.uol.com .br/samuel/40266/bancada-evangelica-tem-catolicos-como-aliados-em-pautas-homo fobicas-diz-pesquisadora.

16. Martin Durham and Margaret Power, eds., *New Perspectives on the Transnational Right* (New York: Palgrave Macmillan, 2016); Luc van Dongen, Stéphanie Roulin, and Giles Scott Smith, eds., *Transnational Anti-communism and the Cold War: Agents, Activities, Networks* (Basingstoke, UK: Palgrave Macmillan, 2014); Ernesto Bohoslavsky, "La historia transnacional de las derechas argentinas en el siglo XX: ¿Qué sabemos y qué podríamos saber?," *Páginas* 10, no. 24 (2018): 10–33.

17. "Tercer Colóquio Pensar las Derechas en América Latina" Universidade Federal de Minas Gerais, Belo Horizonte, 2018; Camila Rocha, "'Menos Marx, mais Mises': Uma gênese da nova direita brasileira" (PhD diss., Universidade de São Paulo, 2018); Gizele Zanotto, "A TFP em foco na academia," *Anais do XXVI Simpósio Nacional de História* (2011).

18. Darren Dochuk, "Revival on the Right: Making Sense of the Conservative Movement in Post–World War II American History," *History Compass* 4, no. 5 (2006): 975–99; Dochuk, *From Bible Belt to Sunbelt: Plain-Folk Religion, Grassroots Politics, and the Rise of Evangelical Conservatism* (New York: Norton, 2011); Daniel Bell, ed., *The Radical Right* (London: Routledge, 2017); Lisa McGirr, *Suburban Warriors: The Origins of the New American Right* (Princeton, NJ: Princeton University Press, 2001); Matthew D. Lassiter, *The Silent Majority: Suburban Politics in the Sunbelt South* (Princeton, NJ: Princeton University Press, 2006); Kathleen Belew, *Bring the War Home: The White Power Movement and Paramilitary America* (Cambridge, MA: Harvard University Press, 2019); Daniel T. Rodgers, *Age of Fracture* (Cambridge, MA: Belknap Press of Harvard University Press, 2011).

19. Much more research is needed on the relationship between Protestantism and blackness in Brazil, as eminent Brazilianist John Burdick has pointed out. That said, most extant scholarship concludes that evangelical leaders and congregants in Brazil have avoided confronting problems of race and racism, more or less keeping pace with the rest of Brazilian society. This remains generally true despite the fact that lay evangelicals identify as Afro-descended at a higher rate than the general population. Even neo-Pentecostals' attacks on Afro-Brazilian religion have been interpreted by scholars as "heterophobia" rather than racism—a conclusion that is surely complicated by the longer history of persecuting Afro-Brazilian religions, not to mention by the "syncretistic" practices and proselytization in southern Africa by Brazil's Igreja Universal do Reino de Deus (Universal Church of the Kingdom of God, IURD), a prominent neo-Pentecostal church. Recent research indicates a further complication: Brazilian evangelical congregants may generally support antiracist policies (such as affirmative action), but their leadership and evangelical politicians have

taken much more conservative stances that do not reflect the attitudes of their constituencies. In the United States, by contrast, fundamentalist segregationists and more moderate evangelical white voters, pastors, and politicians resolved their differences on the form and severity of racism before turning, broadly, against civil rights and the Democratic Party. See John Burdick, *The Color of Sound: Race, Religion, and Music in Brazil* (New York: New York University Press, 2013), 9, 176; Valdir Pede, Everton Santos, and Margarete Fagundes Nunes, "Política, religião e etnicidade: Relações e deslocamento de fronteiras," *Revista Sociedade e Estado* 26, no. 2 (2011): 277–300; Regina Novaes and Maria da Graça Floriano, *O Negro Evangélico*, special edition, Comunicações do ISER (Rio de Janeiro: Instituto de Estudos da Religião, 1985), 73; Amy Erica Smith, *Religion and Brazilian Democracy: Mobilizing the People of God* (Cambridge: Cambridge University Press, 2019), 67, 154; Daniel K. Williams, *God's Own Party: The Making of the Christian Right* (Oxford: Oxford University Press, 2012), 69–88; Ari Oro, "Neopentecostais e Afro-brasileiros: Quem vencerá esta guerra?," *Debates do NER* 1, no. 1 (1996): 31; and Paul Freston, "The Universal Church of the Kingdom of God: A Brazilian Church Finds Success in Southern Africa," *Journal of Religion in Africa* 35, no. 1 (2005): 41.

20. Dochuk, "Revival on the Right," 991n5.

21. Rodgers, *Age of Fracture*, 166, 169; Dan T. Carter, *The Politics of Rage: George Wallace, the Origins of the New Conservatism, and the Transformation of American Politics* (Baton Rouge: Louisiana State University Press, 2008), 315–16.

22. "O liberalismo é condemnado [*sic*] pela Igreja," *Acção*, 10 November 1936, 1, ACMSP, pasta Correspondência de Dom José Maurício da Rocha.

23. "O liberalismo é condemnado"; Archbishop of São Paulo to José Maurício da Rocha, 10 November 1940, ACMSP.

24. José Maurício da Rocha, "Carta Pastoral sobre o áureo jubileu sacerdotal do Santo Padre Pio XII," 1949, ACRSP, Box 262.852(81); José Maurício da Rocha, "O dever dos Brasileiros em Ordem à Futura Carta Constitucional," in *Pelo Brasil* (São Paulo: Typografia Paulista, 1933), 46–63.

25. Carl McIntire (1906–2002) was a pioneer of North American fundamentalism and founder of the Bible Presbyterian Church, the International Council of Christian Churches, and the American Council of Christian Churches, among other institutions.

26. Literature elaborating the rise of liberationist currents among Catholics and Protestants in Brazil is too abundant to list here. For a recent treatment of progressive evangelicals in Brazil's postdictatorship period—by which time they were decidedly the minority in evangelical politics—see Fernando Coelho Costa, "Evangélicos progressistas: Uma experiência política no período de abertura democrática no Brasil," *Revista Interdisciplinar em Cultura e Sociedade* 4 (2018): 545–56.

27. Elizete da Silva, *Protestantismo ecumênico e a realidade brasileira: Evangélicos progressistas em Feira de Santana* (Feira de Santana: UEFS, 2010), 213.

Chapter One

1. Helio Damante, "Bispo defende latim e batina," *O Estado de S. Paulo*, 29 Septmber 1964.

2. "Bispo defende (AINDA!) latim e batina," *O Conciliábulo* 33 (14 October 1964): 1, ACRSP.

3. José Leme Alves de Oliveira, "Santa Missa em sufrágio da alma de Dom José Maurício da Rocha—45 anos de falecimento," *Fratres in Unum* (blog), 20 November 2014, https://fratresinunum.com/2014/11/20/missa-em-sufragio-da-alma-de-dom-jose-mauricio-da-rocha-45-anos-de-falecimento/.

4. Dom Geraldo Proença Sigaud (1909–99) was bishop of Jacarezinho, Paraná, and later archbishop of Diamantina, Minas Gerais; Dom Antônio Castro Mayer (1904–91) was the bishop of Campos, Rio de Janeiro, from 1949 to 1981.

5. French archbishop Marcel Lefebvre (1904–91) was the most celebrated of Catholic traditionalists and founder of the Society of Saint Pius X.

6. Antônio de Castro Mayer and Marcel Lefebvre, "Open Letter to the Pope: Episcopal Manifesto," reprinted in the *Remnant*, 15 January 1984, http://www.remnantnewspaper.com/Archives/archive-2005-0831-lefebvre.htm.

7. Plínio Corrêa de Oliveira (1908–95) was a Brazilian intellectual and longtime Catholic activist.

8. Secondary literature to date has proved durably ambivalent about the role of the Brazilian clerics at Vatican II and afterward. Generally, scholars have focused on European conservative prelates at the council; even Brazilian sources have stopped short of granting Sigaud and Mayer leading roles as activists. See, for example, Daniele Menozzi, "El Anticoncilio (1966–84)," in *La recepción del Vaticano II* (Madrid: Cristiandad, 1987), 385–413; Melissa J. Wilde, *Vatican II: A Sociological Analysis of Religious Change* (Princeton, NJ: Princeton University Press, 2007); Rodrigo Coppe Caldeira, "Bispos conservadores brasileiros no Concílio Vaticano II (1962–65): D. Geraldo de Proença Sigaud e D. Antônio de Castro Mayer," *Horizonte* 9, no. 24 (2011): 1010–29; Marcos Paulo dos Reis Quadros, "O conservadorismo católico na política brasileira: Considerações sobre as atividades da TFP ontem e hoje," *Estudos de Sociologia* 18, no. 34 (2013): 193–208; Giuseppe Alberigo and Joseph Komonchak, eds., *The History of Vatican II*, vol. 3, *The Mature Council, Second Period and Intersession, September 1963–September 1964* (Maryknoll, NY: Orbis Books, 2000); Rodrigo Coppe Caldeira, *Os baluartes da tradição: O conservadorismo católico brasileiro no concílio Vaticano II* (Curitiba, Brazil: Editora CRV, 2011); Luc Perrin, "Il 'Coetus Internationalis Patrum' e la minoranza conciliare," in *L'evento e le decisioni: Studi sulle dinamiche del concilio Vaticano II*, ed. Maria Teresa Fattori and Alberto Melloni (Bologna: Il Mulino, 1997), 173–87; Luiz J. Baraúna, "Brasil," in *A Igreja Latino-Americana às vésperas do Concílio: História do Concílio Ecumênico Vaticano II*, ed. José Oscar Beozzo (São Paulo: Edições Paulinas, 1993), 146–77; José Oscar Beozzo, *A Igreja do Brasil no Concílio Vaticano II, 1959–1965* (São Paulo: Edições Paulinas, 2005); and Antônio de Araújo, "Católicos e política nos anos 60: Uma aproximação lexical," in *Religião e cidadania: Protagonistas, motivações e dinâmicas sociais no contexto ibérico*, ed. Antônio Matos Ferreira and João Miguel Almeida (Lisbon: Centro de Estudos de História Religiosa, Universidade Católica Portuguesa, 2011), 132.

9. David Allen White, *The Mouth of the Lion: Bishop Antônio de Castro Mayer and the Last Catholic Diocese* (Kansas City, MO: Angelus, 1993), 243.

10. Michael Cuneo, *The Smoke of Satan: Conservative and Traditionalist Dissent in Contemporary American Catholicism* (Oxford: Oxford University Press, 1997); Michael Cuneo, "The Vengeful Virgin: Case Studies in Contemporary American Catholic Apocalypticism," in *Millennium, Messiahs, and Mayhem: Contemporary Apocalyptic Movements*, ed. T. Robbins

and S. J. Palmer (New York: Routledge, 1997), 175–95; Massimo Faggioli, *Sorting Out Catholicism: A Brief History of the New Ecclesial Movements*, trans. Demerio S. Yocum (Collegeville, MN: Liturgical, 2014).

11. Geraldo de Proença Sigaud, Antônio de Castro Mayer, and Plinio Corrêa de Oliveira, *Reforma agrária: Questão de consciência* (São Paulo: Vera Cruz, 1962), ii.

12. Benjamin A. Cowan, *Securing Sex: Morality and Repression in the Making of Cold War Brazil* (Chapel Hill: University of North Carolina Press, 2016), chapter 2.

13. Scholars have reinterpreted secularization and secularism as convenient mythologies of colonialism and of liberal democracy. I thus refer here to discourses of secularization, or fears of secularism, nominally agnostic liberalism, or disenchantment. See Talal Asad, *Formations of the Secular: Christianity, Islam, Modernity* (Stanford, CA: Stanford University Press, 2003); and Fenella Cannell, "The Anthropology of Secularism," *Annual Review of Anthropology* 39 (2010): 85–100.

14. Geraldo de Proença Sigaud, "Sacrosancti Concilium Vaticanum, Sessio IV: De Libertate Religiosa," 21 September 1965, AMAD, Caixa 83.

15. Alberigo and Komonchak, *History of Vatican II*; Beozzo, *A Igreja do Brasil*; Caldeira, *Os baluartes da tradição*; Perrin, "Il 'Coetus Internationalis Patrum'"; Henri Fesquet, *The Drama of Vatican II*, trans. Bernard Murchland (New York: Random House, 1967).

16. Several sources have suggested that right-wing Catholics were caught off guard and failed to organize effectively at Vatican II. See, in particular, Wilde, *Vatican II*. My research suggests that, at the very least, right-wing mobilization was quickly forthcoming, if not planned in advance.

17. Bernardo [Peate?] to Dom Geraldo Proença Sigaud, n.d., ACRSP, FDS, Pasta "Concílio Ecumenico Vat. II—D. Sigaud—Consagração do mundo a N. Senhora." See also Benjamin Cowan, "The 'Beauty of Inequality' and the Mythos of the Medieval: Brazil and the Forging of Global Catholic Traditionalism," *Luso-Brazilian Review* 56 (2019): 105–29.

18. Cássio to Sigaud, 22 October 1965, ACRSP, FDS; Lydia Magon Villar to Sigaud, 1 September 1965, ACRSP, FDS.

19. Carlos P. (Probst) to Sigaud, 10 September 1963, ACRSP, FDS; José M. F. Collaço to Sigaud, 7 July 1965, ACRSP, FDS.

20. See Cowan, "'Beauty of Inequality.'"

21. "Organização," handwritten note, 1965[?], AMAD, Caixa 83.

22. "Salesmes France—13 August '65—Mons. Sigaud," 13 August 1965, AMAD, Caixa 85.

23. Geraldo de Proença Sigaud, invitation template, 2 October 1964, AMAD, Caixa 79.

24. Sigaud to Plínio Corrêa de Oliveira, 1 September 1965, AMAD, Caixa 79.

25. Sigaud to Dom Antônio Castro Mayer, 3 September 1965, AMAD, Caixa 79.

26. Sigaud to Vasco Leitão da Cunha, 2 September 1965, AMAD, Caixa 79.

27. TFP, *Um homem, uma obra, uma gesta: Homenagem das TFPs a Plínio Corrêa de Oliveira* (São Paulo: Edições Brasil de Amanhã, 1989), 30; Rodrigo Coppe Caldeira, "Em defesa da Ação Católica: Plínio Corrêa de Oliveira, um baluarte da tradição," *Revista Brasileira de História das Religiões* 6 (2013): 104–5; Gizele Zanotto, "É o caos!!! A luta anti agro reformista de Plínio Corrêa de Oliveira" (MA thesis, Universidade Federal de Santa Catarina, 2003), 43.

28. Sigaud to Oliveira, 1 September 1965; Sigaud to Dom Antônio de Castro Mayer, 3 September 1965, AMAD, Caixa 79. Rodrigo Coppe Caldeira details some of this coopera-

tion in a fascinating article on the subject, though he does not go so far as to note the intimacy of this collaboration and Sigaud's direct appeals for advice and direction. See Rodrigo Coppe Caldeira, "D. Geraldo de Proença Sigaud e as direitas católicas contra as inovações do Concílio Vaticano II," *Nuevo Mundo Mundos Nuevos*, 27 April 2016, http://nuevomundo .revues.org/68896.

29. See Cowan, "'Beauty of Inequality.'"

30. Fernando Furquim de Almeida to Sigaud, 12 December 1963, ACRSP, FDS.

31. Sigaud to Henrique Barbosa Chaves, 2 September 1965, AMAD, Caixa 79; Sigaud to Oliveira, 1 September 1965.

32. Sigaud to Cunha, 2 September 1965, emphasis added.

33. "Atuação da TFP e de Dr. Plinio no Concílio Vaticano II. Um profeta no Concílio," *O Príncipe dos Cruzados*, accessed 1 October 2016, http://www.oprincipedoscruzados .com.br/2015/06/atuacao-da-tfp-e-de-drplinio-no.html.

34. Marcel Lefebvre, *Do liberalismo à apostasia: A tragédia conciliar*, trans. Ildefonso Albano Filho (Rio de Janeiro: Permanência, 1991), 101.

35. Fesquet, *Drama of Vatican II*, 619.

36. "Luiz Nazareno Teixeira de Assumpção Filho," *Catolicismo*, February 2009.

37. Roberto de Mattei, *The Crusader of the 20th Century: Plinio Corrêa de Oliveira* (Leominster, UK: Gracewing, 1998), 192n32.

38. "Atuação da TFP."

39. Sigaud's apparent unwillingness to go along with this plan proved portentous: in 1970 he would officially distance himself from TFP. He remained staunchly anticommunist and culturally traditionalist, in a sense agreeing with his former allies in everything except their tactics and their disobedience vis-à-vis the pope. Cowan, "'Beauty of Inequality'"; "D. Geraldo Sigaud e a TFP: Comunicado de imprensa," *Catolicismo* 239 (November 1970): 8; Mattei, *Crusader*, 77.

40. Wilde, *Vatican II*; Perrin, "Il 'Coetus Internationalis Patrum'"; Beozzo, *A Igreja do Brasil*, 88.

41. "Comitatus Episcopalis Internationalis," 28 May 1965, AMAD, Caixa 83, Pasta "II Concílio Vaticano—Outras Conferências."

42. Draft response to Tardini, n.d., ACRSP, FDS, Pasta "Posicionamento sobre diversos esquemas a serem votados."

43. Sigaud to Oliveira, 1 September 1965.

44. Many scholars have treated papal and European Catholics' responses to modernity, especially in the context of corporatism and fascism. Seminal works include Giovanni Miccoli, "Chiesa e società in Italia fra Ottocento e Novecento," in *Fra mito della cristianità e secolarizzazione* (Casale Monferrato, Italy: Marietti, 1985), 21–92; and Daniele Menozzi, *La Chiesa cattolica e la secolarizzacione* (Turin: Einaudi, 1993).

45. Sigaud to Oliveira, 1 September 1965.

46. James Chappel, *Catholic Modern: The Challenge of Totalitarianism and the Remaking of the Church* (Cambridge, MA: Harvard University Press, 2018), 26–29.

47. Maurícios Severo de Souza, "A relação entre Igreja e Estado no Brasil do século XIX nas páginas d'*O Novo Mundo* (1870–79)," *Sacrilegens* 10, no. 2 (2013): 59; Edgar da Silva Gomes, "Um Embate ideológico: Estado-Igreja no crepúsculo do século XIX no Brasil," *Reveleteo*, no. 2 (2007): 2.

48. José de Oliveira Vianna, *Populações meridionais do Brasil: História, organização, psicologia, Vol. 1* (Niteroi, RJ: Editora Itatiaia, 1987), 76.

49. Everardo Backeuser, *A sedução do comunismo* (Rio de Janeiro: Centro Dom Vital, 1933), 47.

50. Tânia Salem, "Do Centro Dom Vital à Universidade católica," in *Universidades e instituições científicas no Rio de Janeiro*, ed. Simon Schwartzman (Brasília: CNPq, 1982), 97. See also Wellington Teodoro da Silva, "Catolicismo militante na primeira metade do século XX brasileiro," *História Revista* 13, no. 2 (2008): 557.

51. Plínio Salgado, *Conceito Cristão da Democracia* (São Paulo: Editora Presença, 1945), 9, 17, 25.

52. Giulio Folena, *Escravos do Profeta* (São Paulo: EMW Editores, 1987); John T. Armour, "TFP: A Dangerous Cult," *Angelus*, July 1983, n.p.; "Heralds of the Gospel," Fish Eaters, https://fisheaters.com/forums/showthread.php?tid=23830&pid=306230; White, *Mouth of the Lion*, 181–82.

53. Cowan, "'Beauty of Inequality.'"

54. Heloisa Maria Murgel Starling, *Os senhores das gerais: Os Novos Inconfidentes e o Golpe Militar de 1964* (Petrópolis, Brazil: Vozes, 1986), 236. See also Maristela Proença Sigaud to Geraldo Proença Sigaud, n.d., AMAD, FDS.

55. Geraldo Proença Sigaud, "Sínodo Episcopal: A respeito do Sacerdócio Ministerial: Esboço de argumentos que se discutirá na segunda reunião geral," 1973[?], AMAD, Caixa 79.

56. Antônio de Castro Mayer, *Carta pastoral sobre problemas do apostolado moderno, contendo um catecismo de verdades oportunas que se opõem a erros contemporâneos*, 2nd ed. (Campos, Brazil: Boa Imprensa, 1953), 75, 79, 85.

57. "Animadversiones criticae in textum reemendatum," 28 May 1965, AMAD, Caixa 83; "Salesmes France."

58. Sigaud, "Sacrosancti Concilium Vaticanum, Sessio IV."

59. Carlos Eduardo Saboia Bandeira de Mello, *Carta Pastoral Sôbre o Concílio Vaticano II* (Petrópolis, Brazil: Vozes, 1961), 9.

60. To quote the encyclical, "Now, we have to meet the Rationalists, true children and inheritors of the older heretics, who, trusting in the turn to their own way of thinking, have rejected even the scraps and remnants of Christian belief which had been handed down to them. They deny that there is any such thing as revelation or inspiration, or Holy Scripture at all." Pope Leo XIII, "Providentissimus Deus," 18 November 1893, http://w2.vatican.va/content/leo-xiii/en/encyclicals/documents/hf_l-xiii_enc_18111893_providentissimus-deus.html. Ulrich Lehner's recent *Catholic Enlightenment* joins a body of scholarship that illustrates how complex the relationship between Catholicism, Catholics, and the Enlightenment has been. Even Sigaud's and Mayer's rejection of it cannot be called "wholesale"—yet their opposition to "naturalism" and adherence to a Maritainesque Thomism stands in stark contrast to the subjects investigated by Lehner or the "fraternal" reformists and Christian Democrats studied by James Chappel. Ulrich Lehner, *The Catholic Enlightenment: The Forgotten History of a Global Movement* (Oxford: Oxford University Press, 2016).

61. Draft response to Tardini.

62. David Kertzer, *The Popes against the Jews: The Vatican's Role in the Rise of Modern Antisemitism* (New York: Knopf, 2001).

63. Draft response to Tardini.

64. João Botelho to Caio [de Castro], n.d., AMAD, Caixa 79; "Appel Angoisse au Saint-Pere et aux Peres Conciliaires," 25 October 1964, AMAD, Caixa 85.

65. Draft response to Tardini.

66. It is worth noting that progressives did *not* seek a secularized or rationalized world, nor a Church stripped of supernaturalism. Indeed, faith in everyday divinity is what inspired some reform-minded leaders' luminous visions of ecumenism, the early Church, and the role of the laity, among other topics. Dom Hélder's own mysticism was expressed across the course of his life, including at the council. See Jean-Marie Laurier, "Dom Hélder Câmara e o Concílio Vaticano II," *Contemplação* 1 (2010), http://fajopa.com/contemplacao/index.php/contemplacao/article/view/2. This was known to conservatives and lent the debates, serious as they were, an air of mutual respect and even affection. See Sigaud to Dom Hélder Câmara, n.d., ACRSP, FDS, Pasta "Concílio Ecumenico Vat. II—D. Sigaud—Carta ao Santo Padre e seus rascunhos."

67. Draft response to Tardini; Orlando Fedeli, "Desigualdade & igualdade: Considerações sobre um mito," Montfort Associação Cultural, accessed 1 September 2018, http://www.montfort.org.br/bra/veritas/religiao/desigualdade/.

68. Plínio Corrêa de Oliveira, *Nobility and Analogous Traditional Elites in the Allocutions of Pius XII: A Theme Illuminating American Social History* (York, PA: Hamilton, 1993), 25, 44.

69. Geraldo Proença Sigaud, lecture, Escola de Aperfeiçoamento de Oficiais, 20 August 1968; "D. Sigaud diz que eleição de D. Hélder foi um Golpe," *Última Hora*, 21 August 1968, 3.

70. "Rascunho," n.d., ACRSP, FDS, Pasta "Concílio Ecumenico Vat. II—D. Sigaud—Carta ao Santo Padre e seus rascunhos"; draft response to Tardini, 10, 19.

71. Alfredo Moreira da Silva Júnior, "Catolicismo, poder e tradição: Um estudo sobre as ações do conservadorismo católico brasileiro durante o bispado de D. Geraldo Sigaud em Jacarezinho (1947–61)" (MA thesis, Universidade Estadual Paulista Júlio de Mesquita Filho, 2006), 44.

72. Geraldo de Proença Sigaud, "Pastoral de Saudação," São Paulo[?], 1947, 7–8, ACRSP.

73. Mayer, *Carta pastoral*, 94.

74. Mayer, Intervention, n.d., reprinted in "Boletim," 24 September 1965, ACRSP, Fundo Hipólito, 005.3/148.

75. The quotations in this section's title are from Mayer, *Carta pastoral*, 88–89.

76. See, for example, William D. Dinges, "Roman Catholic Traditionalism," in *America's Alternative Religions*, ed. Timothy Miller (Albany: State University of New York Press, 1995), 101–7; Manuel Victor J. Sapitula, "The Formation and Maintenance of Traditionalist Catholicism: A Preliminary Sociological Appraisal of the Society of St. Pius X," *Philippine Social Sciences Review* 62, no. 2 (2010): 315–43; Cuneo, *Smoke of Satan*, 90–93; and James Hitchcock, *Catholicism and Modernity: Confrontation or Capitulation?* (New York: Seabury Press, 1979), 13–14.

77. José Jobim to MRE/José Magalhães Pinto, 27 January 1969, Secreto. No. 45, 8–9, 17–18, AHPI, emphasis added. Previous masses mandated reception of the host on the tongue from a kneeling position.

78. On postconciliar traditionalists and the presence of the sacred in Catholic material culture, see Diana Walsh Pasulka, *Heaven Can Wait: Purgatory in Catholic Devotional and Popular*

Culture (Oxford: Oxford University Press, 2015); and Colleen McDannell, *Material Christianity: Religion and Popular Culture in America* (New Haven, CT: Yale University Press, 1998).

79. Sigaud to Ernesto Geisel, 30 March 1977, AN/COREG, Fundo SNIG, AC-ACE -104214-77-002.

80. Sigaud to Geisel, 30 March 1977.

81. Sigaud to Geisel, 30 March 1977; Sigaud to [Antônio] Azeredo da Silveira, AHPI, SCE, Caixa 234, Número maço 600.1 (B46). Sigaud sent a version of this letter to various authorities, including Geisel, Foreign Minister Antônio Francisco Azeredo da Silveira, and the papal nuncio in Brazil.

82. Orlando Fedeli, handwritten note, 1963[?], ACRSP, FDS, Pasta "Concílio Ecumenico Vat. II—D. Sigaud—Carta ao Santo Padre e seus rascunhos."

83. SNI/ASP, "Informação no 1480/SNI/ASP," 28 November 1968, AN/COREG, Fundo SNIG, ASP-ACE-9411-81.

84. Mayer to Sigaud, n.d., ACRSP, FDS, emphasis added.

85. Mayer, *Carta pastoral*, 15, 19; Antônio de Castro Mayer, *Prevenindo os diocesanos contra os ardis da seita comunista*, 2nd ed. (São Paulo: Vera Cruz, 1961), 11.

86. Mayer, *Carta pastoral*, 50–53.

87. "Nomen Episcopi," 1965[?], ACRSP, FDS, Pasta "Posicionamento sobre diverso esquemas a serem votados."

88. Mayer, quoted in Ralph Wiltgen, "As Vantagens do Latim na Liturgia São Muitas—Diz Dom Antônio de Castro Mayer, Bispo de Campos," *Informações Verbo Divino*, 7 November 1962.

89. Draft response to Tardini, 10, 19.

90. Mayer, *Carta pastoral*, 79.

91. Mayer, *Prevenindo*, 24.

92. Mayer to Przyklenk, 9 September 1970, ACRSP, 209.1/132, emphasis added.

93. Coetus Internationalis Patrum, "Exc.me Pater," 3 December 1965, ACRSP, Fundo "Petro," 050.2/173[?].

94. D. José Mauricio da Rocha, *Sobre o áurea jubilêu Sacerdotal do Santo Padre Pio XII* (1949), ACRSP, Box 262.852(81), 81.

95. Gomes to A. B. L. Castello Branco, 11 October 1965, AHPI, Pasta Vaticano Ofícios Set–Dez 1965; Gomes to Vasco Tristão Leitão da Cunha, 27 November 1965, AHPI, Pasta Ofícios Set–Dez 1965.

96. José Antônio Pedriali, *Guerreiros da Virgem: A vida secreta na TFP* (São Paulo: EMW, 1985), 20, 37, 59; José Pedriali, interview by author, 16–17 June 2012, Londrina, Paraná, Brazil.

97. "Miracema Conflagrada," *Jornal do Brasil*, 26 July 1978, Caderno B, 4; "Em Miracema, hoje, procissão de jovens contra o vigário," *O Globo*, 30 July 1978, 19.

98. "Miracema insiste em ir ao Papa contra o Padre," *O Fluminense*, 25 July 1978, 7.

99. Gilson Rebello, "Uma cidade em pé de guerra contra o padre Olavo," *Jornal da Tarde*, 18 August 1978, 7.

100. "Miracema Conflagrada."

101. Vera de Vives, column, *O Fluminense*, 5 August 1978, 8; "Jovens de Miracema não desfilaram contra o padre," *O Globo*, 31 July 1978, 13.

102. Cowan, *Securing Sex*; Benjamin A. Cowan, "TFP: A Family Affair," paper presented at 2nd International Symposium "Brazil: From Dictatorship to Democracy," Brown University, 7 April 2017.

103. DSI/MJ, "Encaminhamento No. 284/78/DSI/MJ," 13 September 1978, 29, AN/COREG, Fundo DSI/MJ, BR-AN-RIO-TT-0-MCP-PRO-1469.

104. CISA, "Campanha Contra a Sociedade Brasileira de Defesa da Tradição Família e Propriedade (TFP)," 16 September 1975, AN/COREG, Fundo CISA BR-AN-BSB-VAZ-098-0003.

105. Sigaud to Cunha, 29 August 1965, AMAD, Caixa 79.

106. Sérgio Henrique da Costa Rodrigues, "Entre a cruz e a espada: Relações diplomáticas entre a ditadura militar brasileira e o Vaticano (1964–77)" (MA thesis, Universidade Federal do Rio de Janeiro, 2006), 66.

107. Gomes to Juracy Magalhães, 26 July 1966, Ofício Secreto No. 207, AHPI, Pasta Ofícios Secretos 1965–1966.

108. Gomes to A. B. L. Castello Branco, 30 September 1965, AHPI, Pasta Ofícios Set–Dez 1965.

109. Augusto Estellita Lima to MRE/Gibson Barbosa, 1969, Ofício 363, AHPI, Pasta Ofícios Ago/Dez 1969.

110. SNI, "Infiltração Comunista na Igreja Católica," 13 October 1970, AN/COREG, Fundo SNIG, AC-ACE-CNF-23177-70.

111. Ministério do Exército, "Relatório Especial de Informações no. 02/81," 30 December 1981, AN/COREG, Fundo SNIG, ASP-ACE-12368-82-001.

112. CIE, "Secreto. No. 629," and CIE, "Secreto. No. 630,"17-20, 12 December 1967, AN/COREG Fundo SNIG, BR-AN-BSB-IE-002-012.

113. Divisão de Segurança e Informação do Ministério de Educação e Cultura, "Encaminhamento no. 013/10099/79/10/DSI/MEC," 15 August 1979, AN/COREG, Fundo CISA, BR-AN-BSB-AA1-MPL-102.

114. CISA, Subchefia de Operações e Informações, "Comitê do PCB," 29 September 1967, AN/COREG, Fundo CISA, BR-AN-BSB-VAZ-050A-0168; CISA, "Informação no. 257/QG-4," 24 October 1966, AN/COREG, Fundo CISA, BR-A-BSB-VAZ-041A-0160.

115. DSI/MJ, "Relatório Especial de Informação no. 03/78," 11 July 1978, AN/COREG, Fundo DSI-MJ, BR-RJANRIO-TT-0-MCP-AVU-0047-D001.

116. SNI/AC, "Correntes e Linhas do Clero," 30 August 1973, AN/COREG, Fundo SNIG, DI-ACE-65577-73.

117. SNI/AC, "VII Semana de Reflexão Teológica," 14 July 1975, AN/COREG, Fundo CISA BR-AN-BSB-VAZ-017-0088; SNI/AC, "Documento de Informações no. 88/40/AC/73," 25 July 1973, AN/COREG, Fundo PF, BR-DFANBSB-Z4-SNA-0002.

118. SNI/ARJ, "Informação no. 116/43/ARJ/82," 30 September 1982, AN/COREG, Fundo SNIG, ARJ-ACE-7010-82.

119. Pedro Cândido Ferreira Filho, "Levantamento do Vale do Jequitinhonha," 22 August 1971, AN/COREG, Fundo SNIG, AC-ACE-75297-74.

120. Adido do Exército junto à Embaixada do Brasil na Venezuela, "Informações Necessárias do Mês de Março de 1977," 14 March 1977, AN/COREG, Fundo CIEX, BR-DFANBSB-Z4-REX-IBR-0051.

121. CISA, "Encaminhamento no. 08/QG-4," 5 March 1968, AN/COREG, Fundo CISA, BR-AN-BSB-VAZ-019-0034.

122. DSI/MJ, "Informação no. 364/78/DSI/MJ," 2 May 1978, AN/COREG, Fundo DSI-MJ, BR-AN-RIO-TT-0-MCP-PRO-1284.

123. CISA, "O Papa, o episcopado brasileiro, e a reforma agrária," 17 March 1980, AN/COREG, Fundo CISA, BR-AN-BSB-VAZ-079-0031.

124. Ministério do Exército, "Relatório Especial de Informações no. 10/82," 25 October 1982, AN/COREG, Fundo SNIG, AC-ACE-38078-83.

125. CISA, "Informe no. 044 /85-I/A2-III COMAR," 8 April 1985, AN/COREG, Fundo CISA, BR-AN-BSB-VAZ-0841-0070. In the document, the agents appear to have been quoting their informants in Campos.

126. SNI/ARJ, "Apreciação Sintética sobre Campos," 13 November 1975, AN/COREG, Fundo SNIG, ARJ-ACE-9909-83.

127. SNI/ARJ, "Informação 034/19/ARJ/82," 10 November 1982, AN/COREG, ARJ-ACE-7198-82. The security establishments' affinities, which developed through surveillance of Catholic activists and support for Sigaud and Mayer, extended to Marcel Lefebvre, who would become a key face of global Catholic traditionalism. Following the lead of the Brazilian clerics, Brazilian spies saw Lefebvre as a right-minded ally in the fight against the "new positions of the Church, infiltrated by international communism." DSI/MJ, "Encaminhamento no. 259/76/DSI/MJ," 30 July 1976, AN/COREG, Fundo DSI/MJ, BR-RJANRIO-TT-0-MCP-AVU-0228-d001; SNI/Agência Fortaleza, "Informação no. 333/116/AFZ/76," 13 October 1976, AN/COREG, Fundo SNIG, AFZ-ACE-1615-82.

128. CISA, "Encaminhamento no. 0027/CISA," 6 February 1974, AN/COREG, BR-AN-BSB-VAZ-118-0015.

129. Polícia Militar do Estado do Paraná, "Informe no. 024," 26 March 1976, AN/COREG, BR-AN-BSB-ZD-013-008.

130. Jobim to MRE, 14 July 1970, AHPI, Setor Secreto, Caixa 03, Vaticano/Washington, Ofícios Recebidos 1969/70.

131. Jobim to MRE, 14 July 1970.

132. Ana Maria Koch, "Cruzada pela democracia: Militantes católicos no Brasil republicano," *Revista Brasileira de História* 33, no. 66 (2013): 288–93.

133. Fundação Getúlio Vargas, Centro de Pesquisa e Documentação de História Contemporânea do Brasil, Acervo Juarez Távora, JT-33F.

134. "Dom Sigaud apóia ação do govêrno," *O Estado de S. Paulo*, 14 September 1968, 6. See also untitled news clipping, n.d., ACRSP, FDS, 209.2/268.

135. Carlos Luís Guedes, *Tinha que ser Minas* (Rio de Janeiro: Nova Frontera, 1979), 141.

136. "D. Sigaud diz que eleição," 3.

137. "Bishop Antônio de Castro Mayer," Society of Saint Pius X, originally published in the *Angelus*, July 1991, http://sspx.org/en/bishop-antonio-de-castro-mayer.

138. SNI/ARJ, "Informação no. 074/19/ARJ/84," 11 July 1984, AN/COREG, Fundo SNIG, ARJ-ACE-7198-82-MF-ALT-2.

139. Dom Fernando Rifan, interview by author, 4 May 2015, Campos dos Goytacazes, Rio de Janeiro.

140. "Missa no Mosteiro de São Bento—Fratres in Unum entrevista Padre Jonas dos Santos Lisboa, da Administração Apostólica," *Fratres in Unum* (blog), 5 October 2008, https://fratresinunum.com/2008/10/05/missa-no-mosteiro-de-sao-bento-fratres-in-unum-entrevista-padre-jonas-dos-santos-lisboa-da-administracao-apostolica/, emphasis added.

141. Griff Ruby, *The Resurrection of the Roman Catholic Church: A Guide to the Traditional Catholic Movement* (self-pub., iUniverse, 2002), 102.

142. "About Us," *Remnant*, accessed 12 April 2019, https://remnantnewspaper.com/web/index.php/about-us.

143. Michael J. Matt, "Old Mass/Old Faith, New Mass/New Faith," *Remnant*, 9 October 2015, https://remnantnewspaper.com/web/index.php/component/k2/item/2067-old-mass-old-faith-new-mass-new-faith.

144. Michael J. Matt and John Vennari, "On Rome and the Society of St. Pius X: A Joint Statement from The Remnant and Catholic Family News," 28 February 2006, http://www.remnantnewspaper.com/Archives/archive-2006-0228-cfn-remnant.htm.

145. Bernard Fellay, "What Catholics Need Know" (speech, Kansas City, MO, 10 November 2004), http://sspx.org/en/what-catholics-need-know.

146. Priests of Campos Brazil, *Catholic, Apostolic, and Roman* (Kansas City, MO: Angelus, 2005), back cover.

147. "Bishop Antônio de Castro Mayer."

148. Michel Gleize, "The State of Necessity: Part 1 of 2," *Courrier de Rome*, July–August 2008, https://fsspx.org/en/state-necessity; "Qui Sommes Nous?," *Courrier de Rome*, https://www.courrierderome.org/, accessed 12 August 2019.

149. John Vennari, "A Bishop Speaks" (speech, Kansas City, MO, 16 October 2010), http://op54rosary.ning.com/profiles/blogs/a-bishop-speaks-at-the-council-the-defense-of-tradition-by-john-v.

150. Quoted in Bernard Tissier de Mallerais, *Marcel Lefebvre: The Biography*, trans. Brian Sudlow (Kansas City, MO: Angelus, 2004), 291.

151. Marcel Lefebvre, "Recalling Why He Resisted: Letter to Friends and Benefactors," 21 August 1975, http://www.remnantnewspaper.com/Archives/archive-2006-0215-lefebvre-1975.htm.

152. Lefebvre, *Do liberalismo*, 101.

153. Mayer and Lefebvre, "Open Letter to the Pope."

154. Quoted in Ruby, *Resurrection*, 172–79.

155. Ruby, 180, 190, 223.

156. David Allen White, "The Conversion of Dr. David Allen White," https://www.olrl.org/stories/drwhite.shtml, accessed 12 August 2019.

157. White, *Mouth of the Lion*, 44.

158. White, 30.

159. White, 79, 83, 243.

Chapter Two

1. Joá Caitano, "Um doente condenado à morte," *A Seara*, May–June 1969, 31.

2. See chapter 5.

3. See, for example, Maria Tereza Gonzaga Alves, "Conteúdos ideológicos da nova direita no município de São Paulo: Análise de surveys," *Opinião Pública* 6, no. 2 (2000): 187–225.

4. Elizete da Silva, *Protestantismo ecumênico e a realidade brasileira: Evangélicos progressistas em Feira de Santana* (Feira de Santana: UEFS, 2010), 213, 217.

5. R. Andrew Chesnut, *Born Again in Brazil: The Pentecostal Boom and the Pathogens of Poverty* (New Brunswick, NJ: Rutgers University Press, 1997); N. Ivette Feliciano, "Politics,

Pentecostals, and Democratic Consolidation," 3 July 2005, https://people.carleton.edu /~amontero/Ivette%20Feliciano.pdf; Paul Freston, *Evangélicos na política brasileira: História ambígua e desafio ético* (Curitiba, Brazil: Encontrão, 1994).

6. See the discussions of Fanini, Figueiredo, and Sarney later in this chapter.

7. "Moral em decadência: Está repercutindo em todo o país o pronunciamento de deputado federal, denunciando imoralidade nos meios de comunicação," *Mensageiro da Paz* (August 1988), 3; Costa Ferreira, *Discurso na comissão de soberania e dos direitos e garantias do homem e da mulher* (Brasília: Senado Federal, 1987), 88.

8. Quoted in Antônio Flávio Pierucci, "Representantes de Deus em Brasília: A Bancada Evangélica na Constituinte," *Ciências Sociais Hoje* 11 (1989): 114, 126.

9. Mala Htun's arguments about the fates of the Catholic Church in Argentina, Chile, and Brazil, compelling as they are, do not take into account the complicating and complicated role played by evangelical allies of the Brazilian regime. Mala Htun, *Sex and the State: Abortion, Divorce, and the Family under Latin American Dictatorships and Democracies* (Cambridge: Cambridge University Press, 2003).

10. In an interview with Elisa Marconi, Magali Cunha dates the rise of evangelical access to broadcasting power to an alliance with the Sarney administration. Magali Cunha, "O poder evangélico," *Revista Giz*, 12 May 2016, http://revistagiz.sinprosp.org.br/?p=6531.

11. Benjamin A. Cowan, *Securing Sex: Morality and Repression in the Making of Cold War Brazil* (Chapel Hill: University of North Carolina Press, 2016).

12. Lysâneas Maciel (1926–99), lawyer, federal deputy, and major activist for redemocratization, was among the most famous of these.

13. Even recent scholarship—despite the ascendancy of conservative evangelicals in Brazil—has continued to associate fundamentalism with eschewal of politics. According to Elizete da Silva, "A conservative protestant would tend toward pietism and fundamentalism . . . avoiding 'dirtying his/her hands with the things of the world,' especially politics." Da Silva, *Protestantismo ecumênico*, 35.

14. "Onde estão as virtudes?," *Mensageiro da Paz*, 1–15 January 1961, 1.

15. Vandir Henrique da Silva, "A Igreja no Mundo," *Mensageiro da Paz* 47, no. 3 (1977): 7.

16. Brazilians of all faiths (or lack thereof) use the word *crentes* (believers) to refer broadly to evangelicals.

17. Reginaldo de Souza, "Não é tempo de brincar de ser crente," *Mensageiro da Paz*, June 1990, 5; Geziel Gomes, "Doutrina e Costumes," *Mensageiro da Paz*, 1–15 July 1977, 2. See also Benjamin A. Cowan, "'Nosso Terreno': Crise Moral, Política Evangélica e a Formação da 'Nova Direita' Brasileira," *Varia História* 30, no. 52 (2014).

18. See, for example, Abraão de Almeida, "Igreja e Política: É lícito às lideranças religiosas envolveram-se em luta de classe?," *Mensageiro da Paz*, July 1980, 4; and Orlando Ferraz, "Reivindicações dentro da lei," *OE*, 15 October 1968, 1.

19. "Guerra aos vícios," *Igreja Metodista do Brasil*, 19 October 1969, 1.

20. Joanyr de Oliveira, "Nós, a política e o parlamento," *Mensageiro da Paz* 1083 (1978): 2.

21. Daniel Astério, "Os nossos na política," *OE*, March 1983, 8. *O Estandarte* is the official journal of the Independent Presbyterian Church of Brazil, which broke with the Presbyterian Church of Brazil in 1903.

22. Joanyr de Oliveira, "Joanyr de Oliveira," *Jovem Cristão* 15 (1983): 9. Even at this juncture, however, the spokesmen of the Assemblies of God more firmly denounced the politi-

cal involvement of *left*-wing religious figures (those influenced by liberation theology). *Mensageiro* warned, "Transforming pulpits into political grandstands, or substituting the Good News of Salvation for revolutionary 'slogans,' is the same thing as turning firefighters into arsonists." Religious leaders were meant to quash leftist political sentiment, not tolerate or—unthinkably worse—encourage it. Almeida, "Igreja e Política," 4.

23. "Ainda sobre estudantes," *Jornal Batista*, 21 April 1968, 3.

24. Jost Ohler, "Agradar Gregos e Troianos: Possibilidades e Limítes do Jornal Evangélico," *JE*, 1–15 January 1975, 5; editorial, *JE*, 16–31 January 1975, 3.

25. Edson Dourado, "Onde Está Sara, Tua Mulher?," *Mensageiro da Paz*, May 1977, 11.

26. "Moral em Decadência," *Mensageiro da Paz*, August 1980, 3.

27. Joanyr de Oliveira, "Coluna do Diretor," *Mensageiro da Paz* 47, no. 9 (1977): 2.

28. "Conferências de Vida Abundante," advertisement, *Mensageiro da Paz*, March 1977, 16. Fonseca served as an infamously homophobic federal deputy (2006–14).

29. Gerson Correia de Lacerda, "Reformed Worship in Brazil," in *Christian Worship in Reformed Churches Past and Present*, ed. Lukas Vischer (Grand Rapids: Eerdmans, 2003), 241.

30. Abel Amaral Camargo, "Televisão X Vida Cristã," *Aleluia*, December 1974, 3.

31. "A Morte da Modestia," *O Presbiteriano Conservador*, July 1976, 3; "A mulher virtuosa," *O Presbiteriano Conservador*, July 1976, 11.

32. "A Crise Moral dos Nossos Dias," *Revista da Mocidade*, September–December 1969, 2; "Sexo e Sexualidade," *Revista da Mocidade*, September–December 1969, 6; "Família em Perigo," *Revista da Mocidade*, September–December 1969, 10.

33. For a fuller introduction to Fanini (1932–2009), see chapter 4.

34. Nilson do Amaral Fanini, "Evangelizemos," *Reencontro*, July 1977, 7.

35. Nilson do Amaral Fanini, "Deus Salve o Brasil" (reprinted speech), *Reencontro*, January 1984, 4–5; Nilson do Amaral Fanini, "Nosso Relacionamento com Deus," *Reencontro*, April–June 1984, 5.

36. Delcyr de Souza Lima, editorial, *Reencontro*, August 1983, 3, emphasis added.

37. João Bernardes da Silva, "Clamor ao coração dos que podem cooperar com Reencontro," *Reencontro*, April–June 1984, 7.

38. "Sobre a empresa," accessed 14 July 2013, https://www.cpad.com.br/institucional/sobre-a-empresa; Claiton Ivan Pommerening, *A Obra da salvação* (Rio de Janeiro: CPAD, 2017), 117.

39. Nels Lawrence Olson, *O lar ideal* (Rio de Janeiro: CPAD, 1983), 11. See Cowan, *Securing Sex*, on moral panic in earlier moments of the Brazilian dictatorship.

40. Olsen, *O lar ideal*, 93.

41. Abraão de Almeida, "O jovem na sociedade de consumo," *Jovem Cristão*, January–March 1979, 10–11; Gilberto Velho, "Becker, Goofman e a antropologia no Brasil," *Sociologia* 38 (2002): 9–17.

42. Geremias do Couto, "Menores delinqüentes: O desafio do século," *Jovem Cristão*, July–December 1979, 44.

43. "Paixões infames," *Jovem Cristão*, January–March 1980, 3.

44. Claudionor Corrêa de Andrade, *Há esperança para os homossexuais!* (Rio de Janeiro: CPAD, 1987), 9, 14, 18, 63, 65, 71, 74–75, 87.

45. "Modernismo," *O Obreiro*, October–December 1977, 30.

46. Isvaldino dos Santos, "Entrevista: Pastor José Apolônio," *A Seara*, January 1983, 9, emphasis added.

47. See, for example, Claudionor de Andrade, "A família cristã frente à permissividade atual," *A Seara*, March 1987, 7.

48. Daniel T. Rodgers, *Age of Fracture* (Cambridge, MA: Belknap Press of Harvard University Press, 2011), 145, 171.

49. "Fuja dos laços de Satã," *A Seara*, April 1969, 29; Boaventura P. Souza, "Apostasia, corrupção, e vaidade têm passé livre," *A Seara*, April 1969, 23.

50. Quoted in Astério, "Os Nossos," 8.

51. Joanyr de Oliveira, "Coluna do Diretor," 2.

52. "Informação," *Mensageiro da Paz*, January 1980, 13.

53. Pierucci, "Representantes." There were 559 delegates in total.

54. "Informação," *Mensageiro da Paz* 47, no. 3 (1977): 16.

55. Joanyr de Oliveira, "Nós, a política," 2.

56. Nemuel Kessler, "Os nossos candidatos à constituinte," *A Seara*, July 1986, 22.

57. Nemuel Kessler, "Preservemos a moral e os bons costumes," *A Seara*, May 1986, 19, emphasis added.

58. Arolde de Oliveira, *Atividades Parlamentares: Pronunciamentos do Deputado* (Brasília: Câmara dos Deputados, Coordenação de Publicacões, 1983), 5.

59. José dos Reis Pereira, "Orações pela convenção," *Jornal Batista*, 3 January 1988, 3, emphasis added.

60. José dos Reis Pereira, "Um conselho editorial," 4 October 1988, 1; Pereira, "Orações."

61. One need look no further than Jair Bolsonaro himself, who famously declared, "I am prejudiced, and very proud of it." "Jair Bolsonaro," *Revista Época*, 2 July 2011. Social media further exhibits sundry pronouncements about conservative identity in Brazil, including various Facebook, Instagram, and Twitter accounts dedicated to "Orgulho de Ser Conservador." (See, for example, https://www.facebook.com/brennokFF/.) As blogger Liziê Moz Correa put it in the heady days of 2015, as impeachment loomed, "Yes, we are conservative. And with pride." Liziê Moz Correa, "Conservadores, Com Orgulho," Direitas Já!, 22 April 2015, https://direitasja.com.br/2015/04/22/conservadores-com-orgulho/. Also see Felipe Moura Brasil, "Por que eu, brasileiro, sou um conservador," *Veja*, 8 February 2017, http://veja.abril.com.br/blog/felipe-moura-brasil/artigo-por-que-eu-brasileiro-sou-um-conservador/.

62. José dos Reis Pereira, "Ponto Final," *Jornal Batista*, 24 April 1988, 3, emphasis added.

63. See Benjamin A. Cowan, "'Nonreligious Activities': Sex, Anticommunism, and Progressive Christianity in the Late Cold War," in *Gender, Sexuality, and the Cold War: A Global Perspective*, ed. Philip E. Muehlenbeck (Nashville, TN: Vanderbilt University Press, 2017), 68–87. On ecumenism and Richard Shaull's progressive theology as the spark of controversy and crisis in the Presbyterian Church of Brazil, see João Dias de Araújo, *Inquisição Sem Fogueiras* (Rio de Janeiro: Instituto Superior de Estudos da Religião, 1982), 31, 40–41.

64. The WCC arose in 1948 out of ecumenical movements and has historically promoted progressive theology, social justice initiatives, and left-wing political and social programs. It has sparked decades of controversy, drawing the ire of anticommunists, Christian conservatives, and some more moderate critics who allege that the WCC shows favoritism toward left-wing governments. In Brazil, the WCC's most famous adherents included Paulo Freire and Richard Shaull, both known for their pronounced progressivism and their use of Marxist scholarship to construct a Christian social justice agenda. See Andrew J. Kirkendall, *Paulo*

Freire and the Cold War Politics of Literacy (Chapel Hill: University of North Carolina Press, 2010); and Christian Smith, *The Emergence of Liberation Theology: Radical Religion and Social Movement Theory* (Chicago: University of Chicago Press, 1991), 31. It bears mentioning, too, that accusations of "Marxism" against Brazil's Christian Left failed to discern the nuance and variety of positions among progressives. Many, if not most, of the country's rank-and-file and prominent protestant progressives *rejected* Marxism for the same reasons that conservatives did—its presumed incompatibility with godliness. Long taxed as a Marxist himself, João Dias de Araújo in fact criticized the "extremes" of social conscientiousness on the Left and re-marked that Marxism "transforms Man into an object without a soul." Quoted in Da Silva, *Protestantismo ecumênico*, 123–24. By 2007, he would amend this position somewhat, but remain committed to a non-Marxist way forward: "The values of the Kingdom of God will triumph, but we can work together [with communists]." João Dias de Araújo, interview by Elizete da Silva, 6 January 2007, quoted in Da Silva, *Protestantismo ecumênico*, 125. See also Da Silva (196–97) on evangelical progressives' ambivalent cooperation with Marxists like Francisco Julião, whose own Marxism stopped short of open attacks on the faithful.

65. A. P. Vasconcellos, "Ecumenismo: Uma Solução Religiosa?," *Mensageiro da Paz*, May 1980, 1–2.

66. Abraão de Almeida, "Para onde caminha o ecumenismo massificado?," *O Obreiro*, October–December 1977, 28.

67. On the linkage with sexuality, see Cowan, "'Nonreligious Activities.'"

68. Daniel Augusto Schmidt, "O protestantismo brasileiro: Entre a colaboração e a re-sistência no período da Ditadura Civil e Militar (1964–74)" (PhD diss., Universidade Metodista de São Paulo, 2015), 204–7; Valdir Gonzalez Paixão Junior, "Poder, memória e repressão: A Igreja Presbiteriana do Brasil no período da ditadura militar (1966–78)," *Bauru* 2, no. 2 (2014): 20–40; Zwinglio Motta Dias, *Memórias ecumênicas protestantes—Os protestantes e a ditadura: Colaboração e resistência* (Rio de Janeiro: Koinoinia, 2014); "Dossiê: O protestantismo e o regime militar no Brasil," *Mnemosine* 5, special ed. (2014); Araújo, *Inquisição Sem Fogueiras*; Lyndon de Araújo Santos, "O púlpito, a praça e o palanque: Os evangélicos e o regime militar brasileiro," in *A Ditadura em debate: Estado e Sociedade nos anos do autoritarismo*, ed. Adriano de Freixo and Oswaldo Munteal Filho (Rio de Janeiro: Contraponto, 2005), 151–82; Michael Löwy, *The War of Gods: Religion and Politics in Latin America* (London: Verso, 1996); Paulo Julião da Silva, "O alinhamento protestante ao Golpe Militar e a repressão aos 'crentes subversivos,'" *História e-História* 1, no. 1 (2009): 1–16; Saulo Baptista, *Pentecostais e neopentecostais na política brasileira: Um estudo sobre a cultura política, estado e atores coletivos religiosos no Brasil* (São Paulo: Annablume, 2009).

69. *Brasil Presbiteriano*, May–June 1974, 1; Araújo, *Inquisição Sem Fogueiras*, 31; Leonildo Silveira Campos, "Protestantes na primeira fase do regime militar brasileiro: Atos e retórica da Igreja Presbiteriana Independente (1964–69)," *Estudos de Religião* 16, no. 23 (2002): 116.

70. See, for example, Gilberto Moreira, "Autoridade: Um fator de equilíbrio," *A Seara*, November 1984, 13.

71. Joanyr de Oliveira, "Coluna do Diretor," 2.

72. Editorial, *Jornal Batista*, 5 April 1964, 1.

73. "A Morte do Estudante," *Jornal Batista*, 4 April 1968, 3; "A Prisão dos Padres," *Jornal Batista*, 22 December 1968, 3. See also João Reis Perreira, "Bispo Guerrilheiro," *Jornal Batista*, 8 February 1981, 2.

74. Oswald Smith, "O Anticristo," *Mensageiro da Paz*, July 1980, 12.

75. Alceu Moreira Pinto, "Na Seara Alheia: Mestres do Engano," *O Presbiteriano Conservador*, November–December 1964, 3.

76. "A vitória da democrácia," *O Presbiteriano Conservador*, April–May 1964, 3.

77. Araújo, *Inquisição Sem Fogueiras*, 65. As Leonildo Campos (among others) has noted, evangelicals also served the regime as bureaucratic functionaries in various capacities. For example, Reverend Sérgio Paulo Freddi took over the São Paulo Special Counsel's office; another pastor took the choir of his Brasília church to sing at the presidential palace for Christmas. Campos, "Protestantes," 125–26.

78. Guilhermino Cunha, *Comemoração do dia do diplomata* (Rio de Janeiro: Escola Superior de Guerra, 1980).

79. Cowan, *Securing Sex*.

80. Guilhermino Cunha, Rubem Alberto Gado, and Marina Therezinha Dias, "Juventude Brasileira—Realidade e Perspectivas: A Família Brasileira," 1980, 7, 13, 37, Escola Superior de Guerra Biblioteca General Codeiro de Farias TG-CE-I-85/Gr.3.

81. Guilhermino Cunha, *Os Elementos Subjetivos do Desenvolvimento Nacional* (1980), Escola Superior de Guerra Biblioteca General Codeiro de Farias TE-80/C.PSICOS.T.177.

82. Arolde de Oliveira, *Atividades Parlamentares*, 15.

83. Nilson Fanini, "A qualidade de vida como fator de fortalecimento do poder nacional, compreendendo os seus aspectos ecológicos, o crescimento descontrolado das cidades e seus consequentes problemas relativos à habitação e a estrutura familiar," 1981, 10, Escola Superior de Guerra Biblioteca General Codeiro de Farias TE-81/C.PSICOS.T.17A.

84. "Governo concede canal 13 de Televisão ao Pastor Fanini," *Reencontro*, January 1984, 1.

85. Arolde de Oliveira, *Atividades Parlamentares*, 5.

86. Pierucci, "Representantes," 111.

87. Nilson Dimarzio, "Censura Censurada," *Jornal Batista*, 18 September 1988, 3.

88. Alberto Blanco de Oliveira, "Liberdade sem Anarquia," *Jornal Batista*, 24 January 1988, 4.

89. Fanini, "Evangelizemos," 7.

90. "Moral em Decadência," 3.

91. Andrade, *Há esperança*, 93. See also Kessler, "Preservemos," 19.

92. Magali Cunha has pointed to the Sarney government as a point of origin for this process; in fact, the relationship originated earlier, in the Figueiredo regime. Cunha, "O poder evangélico."

93. See, for example, CENIMAR, "Congresso Mundial Batista de Evangelismo urbano," 23 August 1983, AN/COREG, Fundo SNIG, AC-ACE-36617-83.

94. SNI/ARJ, "Ação do Conselho Mundial das Igrejas (CMI) na América Latina e no Brasil," 15 November 1981, AN/COREG, Fundo SNIG, ARJ-ACE-5437-81; SNI/APA, "A Posição da Igreja Católica Apostólica Romana em Relação às Demais Religiões ou Seitas," 18 January 1978, AN/COREG, Fundo SNIG, G0052619-1982.

95. Samuel Escobar, "O Cristão e a política," *O Obreiro*, October–December 1977, 20–22.

96. Joanyr de Oliveira, "Legalização do aborto," *Mensageiro da Paz*, March 1981, 13.

97. I use "brethren" advisedly here; I was able to find few examples of women writing or speaking in these venues.

98. "Brazilian Churchmen Speak at Services," *Washington Post*, 14 January 1946, 11.

99. Israel Gueiros to Margaret Harden, 20 October 1951, PTSMCMC, box 18, file 47.

100. Paul Everett Pierson, *A Younger Church in Search of Maturity: Presbyterianism in Brazil from 1910 to 1959* (San Antonio, TX: Trinity University Press, 1974), 209.

101. SNI/AC, "Cisão entre protestantes no Brasil," 3 September 1982, AN/COREG, Fundo SNIG, AC-ACE-27301-82.

102. Araújo, *Inquisição Sem Fogueiras*; Pierson, *Younger Church*.

103. SNI/ARJ, "O Mensageiro da Paz," 26 November 1985, AN/COREG, C0125039.

104. Abraão de Almeida, "A Ameaça Ecumênica," appendix A in SNI/ARJ, "Ação do Conselho."

105. SNI/AC, "Paulo Maciel de Almeida," 22 September 1980, AN/COREG, AC-ACE -11453-80.

106. SNI/ARJ, "Divisão entre protestantes no Brasil," 23 August 1982, AN/COREG, ASP-ACE-12582-82; SNI/AC, "Cisão entre protestantes."

107. SNI, "O Centrão na Assemblía Nacional Constituinte," 14 April 1988, AN/COREG, DI-ACE-65605-88.

108. SNI/AC, "Avaliação do grau de confiabilidade de parlamentares do paraná e Santa Catarina no sentido de atuarem em defesa dos interesses de nosso órgão," 31 July 1987, AN/ COREG, no. 071754-1987; SNI/Curitiba, "Repercussão e consequencias no Paraná e Santa Catarina da provavel instituição do Voto Distrital Misto para a eleição dos deputados federais e estaduais em Nov 90," 28 August 1987, AN/COREG, N0071353-1987.

109. CIE, "Situação nos campos militar, político, e psicossocial," 31 December 1986, AN/ COREG, AC-ACE-61207-87.

110. "Confidencial: Confederação Evangélica do Brasil," 3 November 1987, 5, AN/ COREG, Fundo SNIG, AC-ACE-68632-88; SNI/AC, "Bloco Parlamentar Evangélico— Apoio irrestrito ao Presidente Sarney," 5 June 1987, 9, 26, 27, AN/COREG, AC-ACE-63733-87-001 For Antunes's ideas about the antidiscrimination statute, see Pierucci, "Representantes," 114.

111. Interestingly, authorities noted that Dias was black but quickly distinguished him from other, more activist Afro-descended politicians: "He is black, but the racial issue does not make up his discourse. His principal commitments are to the family and moral traditions." SNI/AC, "Bloco Parlamentar Evangélico," 31, 46.

112. Renato Cavallera, "Líderes evangélicos do Brasil irão fazer homenagem a José Sarney e Dilma Rousseff durante encontro," GospelMais, 20 September 2011, https://noticias .gospelmais.com.br/evangelicos-homenagem-sarney-dilma-rousseff-encontro-25350 .html.

113. Igo Losso, "O importante trabalho desenvolvido por 'Reencontro' sob a liderança do Pastor Nilson Fanini" (speech, Brasília, 17 October 1980) (Brasília: Coordenação de Publicações, 1981), addendum.

114. See Alexandre Brasil Fonseca, *Evangélicos e Mídia no Brasil* (São Paulo: Bragança Paulista, 2003), 63; Aramis Millarch, "Política e fé na busca de prefixos," *Estado do Paraná*, 13 May 1989, 3; and Alexander Fajardo, "A Atuação dos Evangélicos no rádio brasileiro" (MA thesis, Universidade Metodista de São Paulo, 2011), 134–35.

115. "Uma Obra Meritória," *Reencontro*, special ed., 20 January 1979, 4.

116. Figueiredo, quoted in "Presidente aponta evangelho como 'Guia Seguro,'" *Reencontro*, September 1982, 3.

117. SNI/ARJ, "Sétimo Aniversário de Reencontro: Obras Sociais e Educacionais," 21 July 1982, AN/COREG, ARJ-ACE-6621-82.

118. Arolde de Oliveira, "O Reencontro e o Presidente," *Reencontro*, September 1982, 8.

119. Austregésilo de Athayde, "Espiritualidade e Política," *Jornal do Comércio*, 1 September 1982.

120. "Governo concede canal 13 de televisão ao Pastor Fanini," *Reencontro*, January 1984, 1.

121. "O Novo tempo do povo evangélico," *Reencontro*, January 1984, 2.

122. "Governo João Figueiredo," March–April 1982, Arquivo Nacional, Acervo Secretaria de Imprensa e Divulgação, DX/VID.0085 (VHS #219).

123. SNI/AC, "Bloco Parlamentar Evangélico," 3, 9, 26; Baptista, *Pentecostais*; Freston, *Evangélicos na política brasileira*.

124. SNI/AC, "Bloco Parlamentar Evangélico."

125. "Confidencial: Confederação Evangélica do Brasil," 5.

126. "Câmara vai investigar evangélico que trocou voto por verba federal," *Jornal do Brasil*, 9 August 1988, 2; "Evangélicos trocam votos por vantagens," *Jornal do Brasil*, 7 August 1988, 1.

127. Teodomiro Braga, "A constituição segundo os evangélicos," *Jornal do Brasil*, 7 August 1988, B4.

128. Freston, *Evangélicos na política brasileira*, 80.

129. Fonseca holds that Sarney distributed broadcasting rights to those who supported his presidency. Fonseca, *Evangélicos*, 62. Also see Jamenson Amaro Schneider, "Evangélicos de costas para o povo," *JE*, 21 February–12 March 1988, 13; and "Deputado Evangélico, autor da emenda de cinco anos para Sarney, recebe críticas da Igreja," *JE*, June 1988, 5.

130. See, for example, Millarch, "Política e fé," 3. See also João Antônio de Souza Mascarenhas, *A tríplice conexão: Machismo, conservadorismo político, falso moralismo* (Rio de Janeiro: Planeta Gay Books), 48–50.

131. Cristiano Paixão, quoted in André Gonçalves, "Só 6 parlamentares do PR," *Gazeta do Povo*, 4 May 2008.

132. "Vitória na Constituinte," *Jornal Batista*, 24 July 1988, 1; Salatiel de Carvalho, quoted in Fonseca, *Evangélicos*, 63.

133. "Fanini e a Nova Republica," *Aconteceu no Mundo Evangélico*, January 1986, 2.

134. Arolde de Oliveira, "O Reencontro e o Presidente," 8.

135. Oliveira, "O Reencontro e o Presidente," 8.

136. The complicated politics of the Figueiredo-Neves-Sarney transition eventually meant a break between Figueiredo and Sarney, particularly when the latter assumed the presidency. Nevertheless, Sarney's savvy politics could not erase the record of his cooperation with the military regime. Popular chants against Sarney's inauguration—"Diretas já! Sarney não dá!" (Direct elections now! Sarney won't work!)—suggested Sarney represented a continuation of the military years.

Chapter Three

1. "Mercadores da Fé: Os evangelistas eletrônicos em questão," supplement to *Aconteceu no Mundo Evangélico* (hereafter *Aconteceu*) 65 (April 1988), 2.

2. "Mercadores da Fé," 8.

3. "Mercadores da Fé," 8, emphasis added. On the Maracanã prayer meeting, see chapter 2.

4. Scott Mainwaring, *Igreja catolica e a politica no Brasil (1916–1985)* (São Paulo: Brasiliense, 1989); Kenneth P. Serbin, *Secret Dialogues: Church-State Relations, Torture, and Social Justice in Authoritarian Brazil* (Pittsburgh, PA: University of Pittsburg Press, 2000); Kevin Neuhouser, "The Radicalization of the Brazilian Catholic Church in Comparative Perspective," *American Sociological Review* 54, no. 2 (1989): 233–44.

5. Elizete da Silva, *Protestantismo ecumênico e a realidade brasileira: Evangélicos progressistas em Feira de Santana* (Feira de Santana: UEFS, 2010), 213; Michael Löwy, *The War of Gods: Religion and Politics in Latin America* (London: Verso, 1996); Paul Freston, *Evangélicos na política brasileira: História ambígua e desafio ético* (Curitiba, Brazil: Encontrão, 1994); Amy Erica Smith, *Religion and Brazilian Democracy: Mobilizing the People of God* (Cambridge: Cambridge University Press, 2019).

6. Virginia Garrard-Burnett, *Terror in the Land of the Holy Spirit: Guatemala under General Efraín Ríos Montt, 1982–1983* (Oxford: Oxford University Press, 2010); David Stoll, *Is Latin America Turning Protestant? The Politics of Evangelical Growth* (Berkeley: University of California Press, 1990); Angela M. Lahr, *Millennial Dreams and Apocalyptic Nightmares: The Cold War Origins of Political Evangelicalism* (Oxford: Oxford University Press, 2007); Löwy, *War of the Gods*; Virginia Garrard-Burnett and David Stoll, *Rethinking Protestantism in Latin America* (Philadelphia: Temple University Press, 1993); Paul Freston, ed., *Evangelical Christianity and Democracy in Latin America* (Oxford: Oxford University Press, 2008).

7. Lyndon de Araújo Santos, "O púlpito, a praça e o palanque: Os evangélicos e o regime militar brasileiro," in *A Ditadura em debate: Estado e Sociedade nos anos do autoritarismo*, ed. Adriano de Freixo and Oswaldo Munteal Filho (Rio de Janeiro: Contraponto, 2005), 151–82.

8. See Löwy, *War of the Gods*, 68, 79, 109; Zwinglio Motta Dias, *Memórias ecumênicas protestantes—Os protestantes e a ditadura: Colaboração e resistência* (Rio de Janeiro: Koinoinia, 2014); and Michael Löwy, *A jaula de aço: Max Weber e o marxismo weberiano* (São Paulo: Boitempo, 2014).

9. Gessé Moraes de Araújo, "Nossas Famílias," *OE*, 31 May 1984, 2.

10. "Comentário do *Credo Social da Igreja Metodista*," *Em Marcha*, October–December 1981, 53.

11. "Comentário," 53.

12. *Flâmula Juvenil*, September–December 1981, 24.

13. "O Juvenil Perante Questões de Hoje," *Flâmula Juvenil*, July–September 1981, 18.

14. Lutherans and Methodists ordained women pastors in the 1980s; the Independent Presbyterian Church of Brazil invited women pastors from the United States to minister in Brazil as early as 1987 but did not ordain its own *pastoras* until 1999. As of this writing, the Igreja Presbiteriana do Brasil still did not recognize women pastors.

15. Jorge Bertolaso Stella, "A Mulher e o Mundo," *Revista Alvorada*, May–August 1970, 4–5.

16. Christina Toledo, "A Igreja Viva," *Folha de Londrina*, 3 February 1984.

17. "A vez do Leitor," *OE*, October 1987, 3.

18. "Trabalho de Recuperação de Prostitutas nos EUA," *Aconteceu*, January 1986, 7.

19. Assir Pereira, "A Palavra do Presidente," *OE*, March 1988, 16.

20. Pereira, 16.

21. Gustavo Gomes da Costa Santos, "Mobilizações homossexuais e estado no Brasil: São Paulo (1978–2004)," *Revista Brasileira de Ciências Sociais* 22, no. 63 (2007): 121–35.

22. *Sangue Novo* (Rio de Janeiro: ABIA, [1988?]), 18–19.

23. "Eleições Conseguiu [*sic*] Preocupar até a IPB," *Aconteceu*, November 1982, 4.

24. "Finalmente, a revelação do que é TFP," *JE*, 15–28 February 1975, 4.

25. "Eleições Conseguiu," 4.

26. "Os Batistas e o Filme Proibido," *Aconteceu*, January 1986, 5.

27. André Delaqua, "'A mensagem oculta do Rock,' Uma pequena exposição," *Jornal Batista*, 31 January 1988, 2.

28. On the moralism of progressive Catholics, see Benjamin A. Cowan, *Securing Sex: Morality and Repression in the Making of Cold War Brazil* (Chapel Hill: University of North Carolina Press, 2016).

29. The Conservative Presbyterian Church, or IPC, was formed in 1940 as a separate denomination opposed to the doctrinal and cultural liberalizations of more mainstream Presbyterians.

30. Claude E. Welch Jr., "Mobilizing Morality: The World Council of Churches and Its Program to Combat Racism, 1969–1994," *Human Rights Quarterly* 23, no. 4 (2001): 863–910. Much of the controversy surrounding the WCC stemmed from decisions taken in the 1970s to support African militants and to combat racism via alliance with opposition groups in Zimbabwe-Rhodesia and South Africa.

31. "Atos oficiais da Igreja: Mesa Administrativa," *OE*, 15 January 1962, 4. The IPIB did not formally join the WCC until 2008, but *O Estandarte* exhibited a favorable stance toward the organization from the 1960s onward. The Brazilian Anglican Church joined in 1966.

32. "Ecumenismo," *Igreja Metodista do Brasil*, 16 August 1970, 1.

33. Rudolfo Kunde, "Delegação Ecumênica negocia paz na América," *JE*, June 1988, 11.

34. Da Silva, *Protestantismo ecumênico*; Zwinglio Motta Dias, *Memórias Ecumênicas Protestantes*; João Dias de Araújo, *Inquisição Sem Fogueiras* (Rio de Janeiro: Instituto Superior de Estudos da Religião, 1982); Rudolf von Sinner, Elias Wolff, and Carlos Gilberto Bock, *Vidas Ecumênicas: Testemunhas do ecumenismo no Brasil* (Porto Alegre, Brazil: Padre Reus, 2006); Daniel Augusto Schmidt, "O protestantismo brasileiro: Entre a colaboração e a resistência no período da Ditadura Civil e Militar (1964–74)" (PhD diss., Universidade Metodista de São Paulo, 2015).

35. "O Ecumenismo é Irreversível," *Aconteceu*, April 1988, 4.

36. See "Deputado Evangélico Ataca a CNBB," *Aconteceu*, February 1986, 6.

37. Brahim José Málaque, "Entre a Cruz e a Espada," *OE*, 31 March 1964, 4; "O País Tem Novo Presidente," *OE*, 15–30 April 1964, 2; Daily Resende França, "Dom Jorge, a Revolução Armada e os Apelos da Paz," *OE*, 15 March 1968, 1.

38. Nelson Aves Barroso, "Violência e Tortura," *OE*, October 1987, 16; Roberto Vicente Cruz Tehmudo Lessa, "Juventude Pós 64," *OE*, October 1987, 7.

39. "Esquadrão em Julgamento," *JE*, 15 November 1971, 1.

40. "Geisel falou à nação: O Brasil será um país diferente," *JE*, 1–15 February 1975; "Meditação: Responsabilidade política dos cristãos," *JE*, 15–31 March 1975, 3.

41. A. Maedsche, "Chile: Uma Esperança?," *JE*, 1 March 1972, 16.

42. Editorial, *Aconteceu*, November 1982, 2; "Argentinos Condenam Violência" and "Hiber Conteris Continua Preso," *Aconteceu*, January 1983, 4; "Metodistas Chilenos Contra a Violência do Regime Militar," *Aconteceu*, January 1986, 3.

43. "Cassação Anulada," *Aconteceu*, January 1986, 5. Wright belonged to the Igreja Presbiteriana Unida (United Presbyterian Church), founded in 1978 to protest the conservative administration of the IPB.

44. See chapter 2.

45. "Os Batistas e o Filme," 5.

46. Lessa, "Juventude Pós 64," 7.

47. Editorial, *JE*, 16–31 January 1975, 3.

48. Though Ernesto Geisel was Brazil's first Protestant president, scholars have concluded that little can be made of his personal Lutheranism. He may have offered some Lutheran practitioners an opportunity to identify with the head of state; but he remained relatively distant from the Church and appears to have shared the security community's suspicion of his own coreligionists when it came to "leftist infiltration." Rudolf von Sinner, *The Churches and Democracy in Brazil: Towards a Public Theology Focused on Citizenship* (Eugene, OR: Wipf and Stock, 2012), 212–13; Mala Htun, *Sex and the State: Abortion, Divorce, and the Family under Latin American Dictatorships and Democracies* (Cambridge: Cambridge University Press, 2003); Hans-Jürgen Prien, *Christianity in Latin America* (Leiden: Brill, 2013), 467.

49. See, for example, "Luteranos Processados pela UDR," *Aconteceu*, June 1988, 4. Catholic progressives also criticized knee-jerk anticommunism. Tristão de Athayde, "Demagogia ou Realismo?," *Jornal do Brasil*, 12 January 1973, 6; "A Serviço do Erotismo," *O São Paulo*, 22 July 1972, 3.

50. "O mundo em que vivemos," *Flámula Juvenil*, September–December 1981, 24.

51. Odair Mateus, "Lute pela vida!," *OE*, 31 March 1983, 10.

52. "Primeiro de Maio: Festa ou Protesto?," *JE*, 1–15 May 1975, 1; "Estados Unidos: Corporificação do Imperialismo Capitalista," *JE*, June 1988, 16; "Agrotóxicos," *JE*, 21 February–12 March 1988, 8.

53. "1975: Um ano só para ELAS," *JE*, 15–28 February 1975, 5; "Um basta à submissão," *JE*, 15–28 February 1975, 5.

54. See chapter 2.

55. F. Freytag, "Jornal Mais Político," *JE*, 21 February–12 March 1988, 2.

56. As early as 1968, an army intelligence report warned of the danger posed by the Cuban liberationist pastor Sérgio Arce Martínez—who had studied at Princeton and stood accused of guerrilla activity. CIE, "Frente Religioso—Movimento Camilo Torres," 23 April 1968, AN/COREG, Fundo CISA, BR-AN-BSB-VAZ-054-01130. Accusations against domestic evangelicals appeared in the late 1960s and early 1970s. See, for example, SNI/ARJ, "Informação no. 08316/73," 30 November 1973, AN/COREG, Fundo SNIG, AC-ACE-64728-73; and Humberto de Souza Mello to Office of the President, 7 November 1969, AN/COREG, BR-DFANBSB-AAJ-IPM-09510.

57. SNI/ARJ, "Atividades da Igreja Protestante no Brasil," 4 September 1979, AN/COREG, Co013160-1979.

58. SNI/ASP, "Atividade de Grupos Religiosos," 28 October 1980, AN/COREG, ASP-ACE-4837-80.

59. Comando do II Exército, "Relatório Periódico de Informações no. 10/84," 31 October 1984, 25, AN/COREG, ASP-ACE-16489-84.

60. Comando do II Exército, 23.

61. SNI/ARJ, "Informação no. 08316/73."

62. SNI/APA, "Atividades de Grupos Religiosos," 30 April 1984, 4, AN/COREG, APA-ACE-8612-84.

63. SNI/APA, 32.

64. SNI/APA, "Informação no. 049/119/APA/81," 30 November 1981, AN/COREG, APA-ACE-3674-81.

65. SNI/APA, "Atividades de Grupos Religiosos," 30.

66. SNI/APA, 9–10.

67. SNI/ARJ, "Ação do Conselho Mundial das Igrejas (CMI) na América Latina e no Brasil," 15 November 1981, AN/COREG, Fundo SNIG, ARJ-ACE-5437-81.

68. Ample documentation, memoirs, and scholarly work attest to this persecution. See chapter 2, nn. 72–73.

69. Benjamin A. Cowan, "'Nonreligious Activities': Sex, Anticommunism, and Progressive Christianity in the Late Cold War," in *Gender, Sexuality, and the Cold War: A Global Perspective*, ed. Philip E. Muehlenbeck (Nashville, TN: Vanderbilt University Press, 2017), 68–87.

70. SNI/ARJ, "Infão no. 121/320/ARJ/79," 10 August 1979, AN/COREG, ARJ-ACE-1111-79.

71. SNI/ARJ, "Divisão entre os protestantes no Brasil," 23 August 1982, 4, AN/COREG, ASP-ACE-12582-82. See also SNI/AC, "Cisão entre protestantes no Brasil," 3 September 1982, AN/COREG, AC-ACE-27301-82.

72. CENIMAR, "Informe no. 1937," 9 November 1965, 11, AN/COREG, BR-AN-RIO -55-0-MCP-PRO-0022.

73. SNI/AC, "Atividades de elementos-evangélicos ligados à atividade comunista," 29 April 1969, 4, AN/COREG, Fundo SNIG, AC-ACE-1857-69.

74. "Elementos da Igreja Presbiteriana do Brasil cujos nomes por atuações dentro da Igreja merecem investigação," n.d., Arquivo Público de São Paulo, Pasta OP 1398 do Arquivo do DOPS de São Paulo, quoted in Schmidt, "O protestantismo brasileiro," 236.

75. SNI, "Atividades da Igreja Protestante no Brasil, Federação Nacional de Igrejas Protestantes," 10 October 1979, AN/COREG, Fundo SNIG, C0015738 (1979).

76. Kerr is a world-famous scientist and geneticist who also happens to be Methodist. As a youth he led programs at the Central Methodist Church of Piracicaba. José Geraldo Magalhães, "EECSN Warwick Estevam Kerr," Igreja Metodista, 20 September 2013, http://www.metodista.org.br/eecsn-warwick-estevam-kerr.

77. DSI/MT (Ministério de Transportes), "Conselho Mundial de Igrejas, CMI ou WCC," September 1981, AN/COREG, A0127917-1981.

78. Secretaria da Segurança Pública do Estado do Rio Grande do Sul, Divisão Central de Informações, "Infiltração Comunista na Igreja Luterana," 12 March 1970, AN/COREG, APA-ACE-10864-85.

79. See, for example, Secretaria da Segurança Pública do Estado do Rio Grande do Sul, Divisão Central de Informações, "Infiltração"; DSI/MT, "Conselho Mundial"; SNI/AC, "Atividades do Conselho Mundial de Igrejas (CMI) e Centro Ecumênico de Documentação e Informação (CEDI)," 23 May 1986, AN/COREG, C0028484 (1980).

80. SNI/ASP, "Informe no. 2416/116/ASP/82," 16 August 1983, AN/COREG, AGO-ACE-3081-82; CISA, "HUGO ASMANN," 31 May 1981, AN/COREG, BR-AN-BSB-VAZ-024-0190; SNI/AC, "Universidade Metodista de Pracicaba (UNIMEP)," 29 July 1981, AN/COREG, A0182485-1981.

81. In an impressive dissection of one document from the period, Schmidt concludes that a list of names must have been furnished by Presbyterians themselves. This seems likely for the document in question, though the language of such documents was in many ways shared by security forces as they gained a sense of their allies and enemies within Protestant Brazil. Schmidt, "O protestantismo brasileiro," 251.

82. SNI/ARJ, "Ação do Conselho," 1.

83. SNI/ARJ, "Informação no. 116/43/ARJ/82," 30 September 1982, 3, AN/COREG, Fundo SNIG, ARJ-ACE-7010-82.

84. CIE, "Informação no. 1407/S-102-S3-CIE," 17 December 1973, 176, AN/COREG, BR-DFANBSB-Z4-DPN-ENI-0106.

85. SNI/AC ao Chefe do SNI, 2 July 1979, AN/COREG, A0025380 (1979).

86. CISA, Rio de Janeiro, "Informação 121/320/ARJ/79," n.d., AN/COREG, Fundo SNIG, A0074305-1980.

87. SNI/ARJ, "Centro Ecumenico de Documentação e Informação—CEDI," 16 November 1984, AN/COREG, Fundo SNIG, C0114455-1984; SNI/ARJ, "Infão no. 121/320/ ARJ/79."

88. SNI/ASP, "Informe no. 2416/116/ASP/82," 16.

89. DSI/MRE, "Ligações no Processo Subversivo," 1 February 1982, AN/COREG, Fundo SNIG, AC-ACE-22066-82.

90. "Entregues 2 códigos," *O Estado de S. Paulo*, 8 May 1969, 4; Silas Luiz de Souza, "O respeito à lei e à ordem: Presbiterianos e o governo militar no Brasil (1964–85)" (PhD diss., Universidade Estadual Paulista, 2013), 149; Licínio Leal Barbosa, "Benjamin Moraes: Traços para o Perfil da sua Vida e Obra," *Revista da Faculdade de Direito da UFG* 5, no. 1–2 (1981): xiii. Some have suggested that Moraes even played a role in elaborating the notorious Institutional Act Number 5. See Zwinglio Motta Dias, *Memórias Ecumênicas Protestantes*, 44.

91. DSI/MJ, "Informação no. 845/75/DSI/MJ," 10 December 1975, AN/COREG, Fundo SNIG, AC-ACE-70069-74. Moraes, the first leader of the Presbyterian Church's youth program, did work with ecumenists, including Waldo César, with whom Moraes founded the liberal-minded Department of Church and Society of the Evangelical Confederation of Brazil (CEB). Araújo, *Inquisição Sem Fogueiras*, 45.

92. SNI/ARJ, "Infão no. 121/320/ARJ/79."

93. SNI/ARJ, "Divisão entre os protestantes"; SNI/AC, "Cisão entre protestantes"; "Elementos da Igreja Presbiteriana do Brasil."

94. Jobim to MRE, Confidencial no. 29, 27 January 1970, AHPI, SCE, Caixa 138; José Jobim to MRE, "Urgente-Confidencial," 17 April 1970, AHPI, SCE, Caixa 138.

95. José Jobim to MRE, 30 November 1970, AHPI, SCE, Caixa 98.

96. SNI/AC ao Chefe do SNI, 2 July 1979.

97. SNI/ARJ, "Ação do Conselho," 7.

98. SNI/AC, "Atividades do Conselho Mundial de Igrejas (CMI)."

99. SNI/ARJ, "Centro Ecumenico de Documentação e Informação—CEDI."

100. SNI/ARJ, "Ação do Conselho."

101. CIE, "Teologia da Libertação," 21 December 1982, 13–14, ASP-ACE-13399-83.

102. Ernest W. Lefever, "Backward, Christian Soldiers! The Politics of the World Council of Churches," *National Interest* 14 (1988/1989): 72–82.

103. Kenneth A. Briggs, "Aid for Guerrillas Splits Church Unit," *New York Times*, 3 January 1979; Darril Hudson, "The World Council of Churches and Racism in Southern Africa," *International Journal* 34, no. 3 (1979): 485.

104. SNI/ARJ, "Centro Ecumenico de Documentação e Informação—CEDI." On Brazilian relations with independence movements in Africa, see Jerry Dávila, *Hotel Trópico: Brazil and the Challenge of African Decolonization, 1950–1980* (Durham, NC: Duke University Press, 2010).

105. Serbin, *Secret Dialogues.*

106. Faustino Teixeira and Zwinglio Motta Dias, *Ecumenismo e Diálogo Inter-Religioso: A Arte do Possível* (Aparecida, Brazil: Santuário, 2008).

107. Comando do II Exército, "Relatório Periódico de Informações no. 10/84," 23.

108. Adrian Hastings, "The Christian Churches and Liberation Movements in Southern Africa," *African Affairs* 80, no. 320 (1981): 351.

109. See, for example, Centro de Informações do Exterior, "Atividades Subversivas no Brasil," 19 November 1970, AN/COREG, BR-AN-BSB-IE-005-009.

110. SNI, "Ligações do American Friends Service Committee (AFSC) com a Comissão de Justiça e Paz," 7 March 1980, AN/COREG, Fundo SNIG, C0024168 (1980).

111. SNI/APA, "Reunião do Conselho Nacional de Igrejas Cristãs do Brasil," 13 December 1985, AN/COREG, G0131544-1985.

112. SNI/APA, "Atividades de Grupos Religiosos."

113. CISA, "Informação no. 049 D9/CISA-BR," 4 April 1977, AN/COREG, BR-AN-BSB-VAZ-064A-0137.

114. CISA, "Jornal Subversivo 'Contacto,'" 15 June 1967, AN/COREG, BR-AN-BSB-VAZ-089-0122; SNI/ASP, "Movimento Evangélico do PMDB," 26 February 1988, AN/COREG, ASP-ACE-20041-88.

115. CENIMAR, "Atuação de Orgãos Internacionais de Ideologia Marxista," 5 January 1970, AN/COREG, Fundo SNI, AC-ACE-10452-70.

116. CIE, "Frente Religioso—Movimento Camilo Torres."

117. Araújo, quoted in Da Silva, *Protestantismo ecumênico*, 122. On evangelical conservatives' veneration of traditional hierarchy, see chapter 2; on Catholics', see chapter 1.

118. SNI/ARJ, "Informação 034/19/ARJ/82," 10 November 1982, 5, ARJ-ACE-7198-82.

119. Ministério do Exército, "Relatório Especial de Informações no. 02/81," 30 December 1981, 31, AN/COREG, Fundo SNIG, ASP-ACE-12368-82-001.

120. SNI/APA, "Atividades de Grupos Religiosos," 28–29.

121. SNI/APA, 32.

122. SNI/ARJ, "Informação no. 116/43/ARJ/82," 3.

123. Humberto de Souza Mello, "Extrato de Prontuário," n.d. [1969?], AN/COREG, Fundo IPM, BR-DFANBSB-AAJ-IPM-0950.

124. CENIMAR, "Informe no. 1937"; Departamento de Ordem Política e Social, Divisão de Informações, "Pedido de Busca no. 635/70," 4 November 1970, 154, Arquivo Público do Estado do Rio de Janeiro, Fundo Polícias Políticas, Setor Secreto, Pasta 79. See Cowan, *Securing Sex*, chapter 4.

125. Ministério da Aeronáutica, "Atividades de Dom Sebastião Baggio, Núncio Apostólico do Brasil," 18 September 1967, AN/COREG, Fundo CISA, BR-AN-BSB-VAZ-054-0180.

126. *Boletim* (conciliar record of Dom Walmor Battú Wichrowski), 24 September 1965, ACRSP, Fundo Hipólito, 005.3/148.

127. *Boletim*, no. 6 (22 September 1965), and *Boletim*, no. 9 (27 September 1965), ACRSP, Fundo "Petro," 050.2/250.

128. Heitor de Souza Gomes to Leitão da Cunha, 30 October 1965, AHPI, Pasta Ofícios Set-Dez 1965.

129. A. B. L. Castello Branco, "Informação Global Anual," 8 March 1977, AHPI, Caixa 228, Numero maço 600 (F5), Assuntos Políticos: Vaticano, Maio de 1974.

130. CISA, "Encaminhamento no. 0027/CISA," 6 February 1974, AN/COREG, BR-AN-BSB-VAZ-118-0015. See chapter 4.

131. Gouvêa Mendonça and Abraão de Almeida both refer to McIntire or his International Council of Christian Churches as orchestrating the creation of CIEF. Antônio Gouvêa Mendonça, "O protestantismo no Brasil e suas encruzilhadas," *Revista USP* 67 (2005): 58; Abraão de Almeida, *Teologia Contemporânea* (Rio de Janeiro: CPAD, 2014), 45. In 1981 William "Bill" LeRoy was its executive secretary. SNI/ARJ, "Ação do Conselho."

132. SNI/ASP, "Informe no. 3048/119/ASP/81," 11 December 1981, 8, AN/COREG, Fundo SNIG, ASP-ACE-9645-81; Paul Everett Pierson, *A Younger Church in Search of Maturity: Presbyterianism in Brazil from 1910 to 1959* (San Antonio: Trinity University Press, 1974), 211; Raimundo C. Barreto Jr., "O Movimento Ecumênico e o Surgimento da Responsabilidade Social no Protestantismo Brasileiro," *Numen* 13, no. 1–2 (2010): 273–323.

133. Invitation to the biannual CIEF national congress, São Paulo, 7 November 1981, appendix B in SNI/ARJ, "Ação do Conselho."

134. *Confederação de Igrejas Evangélicas Fundamentalistas do Brasil* (São Paulo: Excelsus, 1974), 3. The "faith once delivered to the saints" is drawn from Jude 3.

135. *Confederação*, 3.

136. SNI/ASP, "Informe no. 3048/119/ASP/81," 2.

137. SNI/ARJ, "Ação do Conselho." See also chapter 4.

138. "A história do surgimento e da ascensão da bancada evangélica na política," *Pragmatismo político*, 30 January 2016, https://www.pragmatismopolitico.com.br/2016/01/a-historia-do-surgimento-e-da-ascensao-da-bancada-evangelica-na-politica.html.

Chapter Four

1. "Brazilian Nilson Fanini Dies at 77," *Baptist Press*, 21 September 2009, http://www.bpnews.net/31304/brazilian-nilson-fanini-dies-at-77.

2. Nilson Fanini, "Evangelizemos," *Reencontro*, 20 July 1977.

3. SNI/APA, "Atividades de Grupos Religiosos," 30 April 1984, 4, AN/COREG, APA-ACE-8612-84.

4. CENIMAR, "Congresso Mundial Batista de Evangelismo urbano," 23 August 1983, AN/COREG, Fundo SNIG, AC-ACE-36617-83. The legacy of these international pastoral allies would vary in the decades to come. Denton Lotz, for example, followed Fanini to Cuba and later cited such visits as the reasons he and others were accused of anti-Americanism (following which the Southern Baptists of the United States left the Baptist World Alliance). John Bisagno, however, once noted for his introduction of rock music to Baptist worship, supported the fundamentalist ascendancy in the Southern Baptist Convention in the late 1990s

and as of 2014 wrote editorials condemning same-sex marriage. "Victors and Victims of the Fundamentalist Takeover of the SBC," *Mainstream Messenger*, July 1999, http://www .mainstreambaptists.org/mob/victors&.htm; John Bisagno, "The Issue of Homosexuality," *Baptist Messenger*, 21 January 2014, https://www.baptistmessenger.com/first-person-the -issue-of-homosexuality/.

5. As Rodrigo Jurucê Mattos Gonçalves, among others, has shown, the military dictatorship itself depended on ideological and personal continuity with older iterations of the Right, particularly integralists. In a sense, the regime's coup plotters, its administrators, and its nongovernmental supporters laid the groundwork for a national conservative power base that rejected modernity and rationalism, despised the French Revolution, sought to shore up traditional hierarchies, and saw modern Brazilian society as a "triumph of the profane." Adolpho Crippa, "A nova problemática dos direitos humanos," *Convivium* 5 (1973): 108–9, quoted in Rodrigo Jurucê Mattos Gonçalves, *História Fetichista: O aparelho de hegemonia filosófico Instituto Brasileiro de Filosofia Convivium (1964–1985)* (Goiânia, Brazil: Universidade Estadual do Oeste do Paraná, 2017), 190. See also Benjamin A. Cowan, *Securing Sex: Morality and Repression in the Making of Cold War Brazil* (Chapel Hill: University of North Carolina Press, 2016); Gilberto Grassi Calil, *Integralismo e hegemonia burguesa: A intervenção do PRP na política brasileira (1945– 1965)* (Cascável, Brazil: UNIOESTE, 2010); and Gilberto Grassi Calil, *O integralismo no pós- guerra: A formação do PRP (1945–1950)* (Porto Alegre, Brazil: EDIPUCRS, 2001).

6. Joanyr de Oliveira, editorial, *A Seara*, October 1977, 2.

7. José Maria Nascimento Pereira, "Amor livre, amor escravo," *A Seara*, October 1977, 16.

8. Pereira, 16.

9. Cowan, *Securing Sex*.

10. Jonathan D. James, *McDonaldisation, Masala McGospel and Om Economics: Televangelism in Contemporary India* (New Delhi: SAGE, 2010), 51.

11. "Ministério do Jimmy Swaggart no Brasil," Sociedade Bíblica de Brasil, accessed 8 March 2018, http://www.sbb.org.br/hotsites/biblia-de-estudo-do-expositor/ministerio-de -jimmy-swaggart-no-brasil/.

12. "Nosso obreiro," *O Obreiro*, October–December 1987, 1.

13. David Wilkerson, "Um Muro de Fogo Protegerá a Família," trans. Donald Stamps, *A Seara*, May 1986, 6.

14. Wilkerson, 6.

15. "Entrevista: Billy Graham," *A Seara*, October 1983, 2.

16. Claudionor de Andrade, *A Mensagem Oculta do Rock* (Rio de Janeiro: CPAD, 1986); Claudionor de Andrade, "Musica, Cultura, Igreja," *A Seara*, July 1986, 16.

17. Nemuel Kessler, "Preservemos a Moral e os Bons Costumes," *A Seara*, May 1986, 10.

18. Clyde M. Narramore, "Segurança Econômica no Lar," *A Seara*, June 1987, 10.

19. Peggy Musgrave, "Mulheres no Cenáculo," trans. Miguel Vaz, *A Seara*, January 1987, 16.

20. Arlene M. Sánchez Walsh and Eric Dean Patterson, "Latino Pentecostalism: Globalized Christianity and the United States," in *The Future of Pentecostalism in the United States*, ed. Eric Patterson and Edmund John Rybarczyk (Lanham, MD: Lexington Books, 2007), 76–77; R. G. Robins, *Pentecostalism in America* (Santa Barbara, CA: ABC-CLIO, 2010), 126.

21. Carl McIntire, *The Struggle for South America* (Collingswood, NJ: Christian Beacon, 1954[?]), 31.

22. Geziel Gomes, "Doutrina e Costumes," *Mensageiro da Paz*, 1–15 July 1977, 2; Adroaldo José Silva Almeida, "'Pelo Senhor, marchamos': Os evangélicos e a ditadura militar no Brasil (1964–1985)," (PhD diss., Universidade Federal Fluminense, 2016), 139. A decade and a half later, Gomes would join other evangelical celebrities in "bringing the downtown of Rio de Janeiro to a halt" during a massive march to demonstrate the bloc's strength. "Evangélicos Superam no Rio 'Diretas Já,'" *Reencontro*, March 1992, 1.

23. "Missions," *Mensageiro da Paz*, June 1980; Geziel Gomes, "Que a América Latina Escute a Voz de Deus," *Mensageiro da Paz*, March 1980, 3.

24. "FTE Focus: Committee for the Survival of a Free Congress," *Free the Eagle*, 5 May 1984, 3.

25. Daniel K. Williams, *God's Own Party: The Making of the Christian Right* (Oxford: Oxford University Press, 2012), 135. By 1987, Weyrich's Free Congress Foundation (via its Catholic Center) was sponsoring interfaith cooperation in the name of fighting homosexuality—and doing so in so exalted an *evangelical* forum as *The 700 Club*. Free Congress Research and Education Foundation (FCF), *1987 Annual Report*, LOCW, Box 17.

26. Williams, *God's Own Party*, 174.

27. "What Conservatives Think of Ronald Reagan," *Policy Review* 27 (1984): 19; "Women Spokesmen Training Conference," in FCF, *Annual Report, 1983*, 25, LOCW, Box 13, Folder 3; "Sex and God in American Politics," *Policy Review* 29 (Summer 1984): 11; "Interview with Paul Weyrich," *Forerunner*, September 1984, 10; Paul Weyrich, "Thoughts at Easter," *Remnant*, 30 April 1984, 6.

28. On Enrique T. Rueda's 1982 *Homosexual Network* (in some sense Weyrich's project as much as it was Rueda's) as a key event in "launching the New Right's anti-gay campaign," see Jean Hardisty, *Mobilizing Resentment: Conservative Resurgence from the John Birch Society to the Promise Keepers* (Boston: Beacon, 2000), 101.

29. "The Five Minute Report," 22 January 1988, LOCW, Box 17; "Women Spokesmen Training Conference."

30. "The Morality of Political Action," in FCF, *Annual Report, 1983*, 36.

31. "The Catholic Center," in FCF, *Annual Report, 1983*, 33.

32. "International Policy Forum Prospectus, 1984–1985," n.d., LOCW, Box 13.

33. "International Policy Forum Prospectus."

34. "International Policy Forum Prospectus."

35. "International Policy Forum Prospectus."

36. "International Policy Forum Prospectus." On Shoff and the KKK, see Ross Bellant, *The Coors Connection: How Coors Family Philanthropy Undermines Democratic Pluralism* (Cambridge, MA: Political Research, 1999), 38. IPF literature described Shoff as "a great fighter for freedom all over the world; particularly in Central America, where he assists the freedom fighters of Nicaragua." IPF, "The Short Forum," December 1988, LOCW, Box 17.

37. Meeting minutes, International Policy Forum, Executive Committee Meeting, 14 January 1988, LOCW, Box 17; program, IPF Board of Governors Meeting, 2–4 July 1988, LOCW, Box 17; IPF, "The Short Forum," 19 February 1988, LOCW, Box 17; "The Five Minute Report," 22 January 1988.

38. IPF, "The Short Forum," 30 September 1988, LOCW, Box 17.

39. Instituto de Estudios Contemporâneos and IPF, "Tecnicas de Campaña y Organización Política," 1988(?) LOCW, Box 17.

40. Program, IPF Board of Governors meeting, 2–4 July 1988.

41. Program, IPF "Understanding Politics Conference, Córdoba, August 26–28, 1988," LOCW, Box 17.

42. IPF, "The Short Forum," 30 September 1988.

43. "Paul Weyrich: El conservadorismo norteamericano, una revolución inconclusa?," *La voz del interior* (Córdoba), 12 September 1988, 3; "The Five Minute Report," 23 September 1988, LOCW, Box 17; "The Five Minute Report," 7 October 1988, LOCW, Box 17.

44. "El movimiento conservador norteamericano en la opinión de Paul M. Weyrich," *La Nueva Província* (Bahía Blanca), 6 October 1988, Ideas y Imágenes Section, 2–3; Luís Álvarez Primo, *El movimiento conservador norteamericano en la opinión de Paul M. Weyrich* (Buenos Aires: Fundación Adolfo Alsina, [1988?]), emphasis added.

45. Sam Zakhem, U.S. ambassador to Bahrain, to secretary of state, telegram, 18 October 1987, LOCW, Box 17.

46. "Mourning the Death of Paul M. Weyrich," American Society for the Defense of Tradition, Family and Property, December 19, 2008, http://www.tfp.org/mourning-the-death -of-paul-m-weyrich/.

47. "Norte-americanos fazem conferências," *Catolicismo*, December 1986; TFP, *Um homem, uma obra, uma gesta: Homenagem das TFPs a Plínio Corrêa de Oliveira* (São Paulo: Edições Brasil de Amanhã, 1989), 350, 444.

48. *Catolicismo*, October 1988 (clipping), LOCW, Box 17, emphasis added.

49. Morton Blackwell, interview by Margaret Power, 7 August 2009, 6. Power's interview with Blackwell is one of a kind—I thank her for creating and for allowing me to consult this invaluable source.

50. Blackwell, 7.

51. Margaret Power, "Transnational, Conservative, Catholic, and Anti-Communist: Tradition, Family, and Property (TFP)," in *New Perspectives on the Transnational Right*, edited by Margaret Power and Martin Durham (New York: Palgrave Macmillan, 2010), 98.

52. Plínio Corrêa de Oliveira, "A importância do fator religioso nos rumos de um bloco-chave de países: A América Latina," *Catolicismo*, June 1985, 3.

53. "Ao leitor," *Catolicismo*, June 1985, 2.

54. "Carlos Eduardo Schaffer—Former Guest Speaker at the Leadership Institute," Leadership Institute, accessed 21 March 2018, https://leadershipinstitute.org/training/contact .cfm?FacultyID=679589; *Crusade*, November/December 2002, 2.

55. His Facebook profile claimed he was the group's deputy chairman. Carlos Eduardo Schaffer, Facebook profile, accessed 21 March 2018, https://www.facebook.com/ceschaffer. The TFP's German chapter, still attracting participants as of 2018, now has links to the national, developing Christian Right, in the form of the Alternative for Germany party. See Andrea Althoff, "Right-Wing Populism and Religion in Germany: Conservative Christians and the Alternative for Germany (AfD)" (unpublished paper shared with the author, 15 February 2018), 20.

56. "TFP participa de Congresso mundial anticomunista nas Filipinas," *Catolicismo*, August 1971. The TFP sent Marcos Ribeiro Dantas to represent Plínio Corrêa de Oliveira at the fifth plenary congress of the World Anti-Communist League (see later in this chapter). Dantas frequently traveled as Oliveira's representative, sometimes accompanying José Lúcio de Araújo Corrêa.

57. "TFP participa do II 'National Wanderer Forum' e do 'Wanderer Youth Forum,'" *Catolicismo*, July 1966; Abel de Oliveira Campos Filho, *Meio século de epopéia anticomunista* (São Paulo: Editora Vera Cruz, 1980).

58. "Enviado da TFP faz conferências em vinte cidades, no Canadá," *Catolicismo*, March 1971.

59. Markku Ruotsila, *Fighting Fundamentalist: Carl McIntire and the Politicization of American Fundamentalism* (Oxford: Oxford University Press, 2015); John Fea, "Carl McIntire: From Fundamentalist Presbyterian to Presbyterian Fundamentalist," *American Presbyterian* 72, no. 4 (1994): 253–68; Heather Hendershot, "God's Angriest Man: Carl McIntire, Cold War Fundamentalism, and Right-Wing Broadcasting," *American Quarterly* 59, no. 2 (2007): 373–96. Daniel K. Williams (*God's Own Party*, 39) argues that, facing the relative calm of Southern fundamentalism and anticommunism before World War II, McIntire successfully inflamed Southern fundamentalists, touting the "gravity of the internal communist danger and the necessity of supporting right-wing anticommunist politicians."

60. José Lúcio de Araújo Corrêa to Carl McIntire, 30 May 1974, PTSM, Box 37; "Brazilian Society for the Defense of Tradition, Family, and Property," pamphlet, 1974, PTSM, Box 37.

61. Ruth Trato to José Lúcio de Araújo Corrêa, 10 July 1974, PTSM, Box 33. I was unable to find any evidence that Corrêa or any other *tefepista* ever attended a meeting of the ICCC or ALADIC.

62. TFP, *Um homem, uma obra*, 307, 351.

63. "Getting Back to Basics: 2006 TFP National Conference," American Society for the Defense of Tradition, Family and Property, 5 October 2006, http://www.tfp.org/getting -back-to-basics-2006-tfp-national-conference/.

64. "Today, June 10, Is the Birthday of a Great Man," *America Needs Fatima Blog*, 10 June 2009, http://americaneedsfatima.blogspot.com/2009/06/today-june-10-is-birthday -of-great-man.html.

65. Giulio Folena, letter, *Folha da Manhã*, 14 March 1985; Giulio Folena, *Escravos do Profeta* (São Paulo: EMW Editores, 1987).

66. American Society for the Defense of Tradition, Family and Property and the Canadian Society for the Defense of Tradition, Family and Property, *Let the Other Side Also Be Heard: The TFPs' Defense against Fidelity's Onslaught* (Pleasantville, NY: TFP, 1989), 88; "Presentazione di Alleanza Cattolica," Alleanza Cattolica, 1 December 2017, http:// alleanzacattolica.org/presentation-ac/.

67. "Qui sommes-nous?," Lecture et Tradition, accessed 29 March 2018, http://lecture-et -tradition.info/qui-sommes-nous.

68. William Martin, *With God on Our Side: The Rise of the Religious Right in America* (New York: Broadway Books, 2005), 113.

69. "Revolução e Contrarevolução: Elevação de Pensamento—Eficácia na Ação," *Catolicismo*, April 1999, http://www.pliniocorreadeoliveira.info/BIO_199904_RCRrepercussoes .htm.

70. *Journal*, April 1999, 2–3, https://www.summit.org/archives/journal/1999-04-Summit -Journal.pdf.

71. Pierre Abramovici, "The World Anti-Communist League: Origins, Structures, and Activities," in *Transnational Anti-communism and the Cold War: Agents, Activities, Networks*, ed. Luc van Dongen, Stéphanie Roulin, and Giles Scott Smith (Basingstoke, UK: Palgrave

Macmillan, 2014), 118–24; Adrian Hänni, "A Global Crusade against Communism: The Cercle in the 'Second Sold War,'" in Van Dongen, Roulin, and Smith, *Transnational Anticommunism*, 164; John Lee Anderson and Scott Anderson, *Inside the League: The Shocking Exposé of How Terrorists, Nazis, and Latin American Death Squads Have Infiltrated the World Anti-Communist League* (New York: Dodd Mead, 1986), 74, 109, 152, 183; "News and Facts," *Réplica*, March 1973, 34; Jorge Prieto Laurens, "A Crusader for Liberty and Democracy Dies," *Réplica*, April 1973, 17. See also Fernando López, *The Feathers of Condor: Transnational State Terrorism, Exiles and Civilian Anticommunism in South America* (Newcastle upon Tyne: Cambridge Scholars, 2016), 286; and Bill Weinberg, *Homage to Chiapas: The New Indigenous Struggles in Mexico* (London: Verso, 2002), 354.

72. Power, "Transnational, Conservative, Catholic," 98; See *Catolicismo*, August 1971; *Catolicismo*, October 1971.

73. Adolpho Corrêa de Sá e Benevides, memorandum, 10 October 1974, AN/COREG, BR-DFANBSB-Z4-DPN-PES-VIS-0076.

74. Divisão de Segurança e Informação do Ministério das Relações Exteriores, "Informação no. DSI/195," 18 January 1974, 16, AN/COREG, BR-DFANBSB-Z4-DPN-ENI-0044-edit2.

75. Abramovici, "World Anti-Communist League," 119; Rodrigo Patto Sá Motta, *Em guarda contra o "perigo vermelho": O anticomunismo no Brasil, 1917–1964* (São Paulo: Perspectiva, 2002), 144.

76. Rubens Valente, "Célula anticomunista atuou no Brasil durante a ditadura," *Folha de S. Paulo*, 15 November 2009, http://www1.folha.uol.com.br/fsp/brasil/fc1511200911.htm; Rodolpho Costa Machado, "Alfredo Buzaid e a contrarrevolução burguesa de 1964" (MA thesis, Pontifícia Universidade Católica de São Paulo, 2015), 18. Mercedes Jansa, "Garzón reúne más datos de Pinochet," *El Periódico de Catalunya*, 4 December 1998.

77. Anderson and Anderson, *Inside the League*, 141.

78. Barbieri to Armando Falcão, 5 March 1975, AN/COREG, BR-AN-RIO-TT-0-MCP-PRO-0405; DSI/MRE, "Informação No. DSI/195"; TFP, *Um homem, uma obra*, 196; Costa Machado, "Alfredo Buzaid," 217; DSI/MRE, "Informação para o ministro Souto Maior," 20 May 1974, 3, AN/COREG, BR-DFANBSB-Z4-DPN-PES-VIS-0076-edit.

79. DSI/MRE, "Secreto-Urgente," 13 May 1976, AN/COREG, AC-ACE-97161-76.

80. CISA, "Encaminhamento no. 0027/CISA," 6 February 1974, AN/COREG, BR-AN-BSB-VAZ-118-0015.

81. DSI/MRE, "Informação para o ministro Souto Maior," 4.

82. *Sepes Boletim*, n.d. 42, AN/COREG, BR-DFANBSB-Z4-DPN-ENI-0044-edit.

83. "Relatório Confidencial de Informações," 6 March 1975[?], AN/COREG, BR-AN-RIO-TT-0-MCP-PRO-0405; "Liga Encerra Congresso," *O Estado de S. Paulo*, 26 April 1975, 4.

84. SNI/ASP, "Participação de ativistas políticos brasileiros em reuniões internacionais de caráter anti-comunista na República da China, em ago 87," n.d., AN/COREG, ASP-ACE-19806-87.

85. In the immediate aftermath of dictatorship, Brazil's government retained many of the power brokers of the military regime. An amnesty law prevented prosecutions of atrocity perpetrators; a truth commission did not emerge until 2014.

86. Cowan, *Securing Sex*; Benjamin A. Cowan, "TFP: A Family Affair," paper presented at 2nd International Symposium "Brazil: From Dictatorship to Democracy," Brown University, 7 April 2017.

87. SNI/ASP, "Informação no. 1480/SNI/ASP," 28 November 1968, 3, AN/COREG, Fundo SNIG, ASP-ACE-9411-81.

88. Jesuan de Paula Xavier, "Informação no. 227/19/AC/75," 31 July 1975, AN/COREG, Fundo DSI/MJ, BR-AN-RIO-TT-0-MCP-PRO-0439.

89. SNI/ASP, "Revista Hora Presente; Revista Permanência," 12 August 1974, AN/COREG, ASP-ACE-6015-81.

90. SNI/ASP, "Informe no. 3048/119/ASP/81," 11 December 1981, AN/COREG, Fundo SNIG, ASP-ACE-9645-81.

91. SNI/ARJ, "Ação do Conselho Mundial das Igrejas (CMI) na América Latina e no Brasil," 15 November 1981, AN/COREG, Fundo SNIG, ARJ-ACE-5437-81.

92. Oliver Villar and Drew Cottle, *Cocaine, Death Squads, and the War on Terror: U.S. Imperialism and Class Struggle in Colombia* (New York: Monthly Review Press, 2014), 42–43; Anderson and Anderson, *Inside the League*, 72, 138–41.

93. SNI/AC, "Documento de Informações no. 0327/19/AC/74," 8 April 1974, 97, AN/COREG, Fundo SNIG, BR-DFANBSB-Z4-DPN-ENI-0106.

94. Chip Berlet, "McCain Advised Ultra-Right Group Tied to Death Squads," Huffington Post, November 7, 2008, updated May 25, 2011, https://www.huffingtonpost.com/chip-berlet/mccain-advised-ultra-righ_b_132612.html.

95. DSI/MJ, "Elemento Detido no Congresso da Liga Anti-Comunista Mundial," 28 April 1975, AN/COREG, AC-ACE-82502-75.

96. DSI/MRE, "Informação para o ministro Souto Maior," 3–4; MRE to Brazilian embassy in Asunción, 30 March 1973, 34, AN/COREG, BR-DFANBSB-Z4-DPN-ENI-0044-edit2.

97. DSI/MRE, "Secreto-Urgente," 4.

98. Costa Machado, "Alfredo Buzaid," 220; Elio Gaspari, *A Ditadura Escancarada* (Rio de Janeiro: Companhia das Letras, 2002), 20.

99. Barbieri to Falcão, 5 March 1975.

100. American embassy in Brasília to American embassy in Santiago, Chile, cable, 3 September 1975, https://www.wikileaks.org/plusd/cables/1975BRASIL07678_b.html.

101. Fernando de Alencar to MRE, 29 May 1979, 8–16, AN/COREG, BR-DFANBSB-Z4-DPN-ENI-0044-edit; DSI/MRE, "Informe no. 36/185," 25 September 1985, 5, AN/COREG, BR-DFANBSB-Z4-DPN-ENI-0044-edit.

102. Ralph Lord Roy, *Apostles of Discord: A Study of Organized Bigotry and Disruption on the Fringes of Protestantism* (Boston: Beacon, 1953), ix.

103. James Rorty, "The Wreckers: *Apostles of Discord*, by Ralph Lord Roy," *Commentary*, 1 November 1953, https://www.commentarymagazine.com/articles/apostles-of-discord-by-ralph-lord-roy/.

104. Ruotsila, *Fighting Fundamentalist*, 2.

105. McIntire to Kenneth Kinney, 19 April 1950, PTSM, Box 254.

106. News clipping, 6 May 1954[?], FBI Communism and Religion File, 98, https://ia801809.us.archive.org/11/items/foia_Communism-Religion-1/Communism-Religion-1.pdf.

107. J. Edgar Hoover to [redacted], 9 June 1954, FBI Communism and Religion File, 78, https://ia801809.us.archive.org/11/items/foia_Communism-Religion-1/Communism -Religion-1.pdf.

108. International Council of Christian Churches, "4th Plenary Congress, August 12–21, 1958, Petrópolis, Brazil," program, materials from 4th Plenary Congress of ICCC, obtained via Inter-Library Loan from Columbia University Library.

109. Émile-G. Léonard, "O Protestantismo Brasileiro: Estudo de eclesiologia e de história social (VII)," *Revista de História* 11 (1951–52): 178–79.

110. Elizete da Silva, *Protestantismo ecumênico e a realidade brasileira: Evangélicos progres-sistas em Feira de Santana* (Feira de Santana: UEFS, 2010), 36–37.

111. McIntire to Geronimo Gueiros, 15 September 1949, PTSM, Box 38.

112. McIntire to Israel Gueiros, 6 October 1949, PTSM, Box 27.

113. McIntire to Israel Gueiros, 20 September 1949, PTSM Box 27.

114. Gladys Titzck Rhoads and Nancy Titzck Anderson, *McIntire: Defender of Faith and Freedom* (Maitland, FL: Xulon, 2012), 451.

115. Carl McIntire, "Crise do Protestantismo no Plano Universal," n.d., PTSM, Box 315; Israel Gueiros, "Resoluções do 7° Congresso Plenário da ALADIC," 15–22 July 1967, PTSM, Box 315; "Resolução n° 15: Um Aviso aos Governos Latino-Americanos," 22 July 1967, PTSM, Box 315; McIntire to "My Dear Brethren in Christ," 12 May 1967, PTSM, Box 315; Gueiros to McIntire, 4 July 1967, PTSM, Box 315.

116. Aggeu Vieira, "Rev. Carl McIntire, a Trench against Communism," July 1967, PTSMC, Box 315.

117. Roderick Carneiro de Mello, special report, "Attack on Presbyterianism in Brazil," 24 October 1956, PTSM, Box 33.

118. Antônio Gouvêa Mendonça, "O protestantismo no Brasil e suas encruzilhadas," *Revista USP* 67 (2005): 58.

119. Harden to McIntire, 8 November 1964, PTSM, Box 20; untitled program, Primeira Igreja Presbiteriana Conservadora de São Paulo, 25 September 1976, PTSM, Box 33; Trato to Correa, 10 July 1974; Ruth Trato to Arlindo Pereira, 7 May 1968, PTSM, Box 33.

120. Abraão de Almeida, *Teologia Contemporânea* (Rio de Janeiro: CPAD, 2014), n.p. Almeida later sought to export the gospel to the United States, helping, among other things, to translate the New International Version of the Bible into Portuguese. "Entrevista com o pastor e teólogo Abraão de Almeida," Centro Apologético Cristão de Pesquisas, accessed 17 September 2018, http://www.cacp.org.br/entrevista-com-o-pastor-e-teologo-abraao-de -almeida/.

121. McIntire to Ernesto Geisel, 1 April 1978, PTSM, Box 33.

122. SNI/AC, "Cisão Entre Protestantes no Brasil," 3 September 1982, AN/COREG, AC -ACE-27301-82.

123. SNI/AC, "Informe no. 098/19/AC/81," 21 August 1981, AN/COREG, AC-ACE -18733-81.

124. Estado Maior do Exército, "Informe no. 061-22.1," 22 May 1981, AN/COREG, AC -ACE-16196-81.

125. SNI, Agência Salvador, "Informe no. 0039/16/ASV/81," 27 March 1981, AN/ COREG, ASV-ACE-1445-81.

126. McIntire, *Struggle for South America*, 27, 31, 35, 48.

Chapter Five

1. Draft response to Tardini, n.d., ACRSP, FDS, Pasta "Posicionamento sobre diversos esquemas a serem votados," 3.

2. Jean Hardisty, *Mobilizing Resentment: Conservative Resurgence from the John Birch Society to the Promise Keepers* (Boston: Beacon, 2000), 102.

3. "Sex and God in American Politics," *Policy Review* 29 (Summer 1984): 11. In this, Weyrich reflected the emergent Christian Right's focus on education as a focal battlefield, and a broad attack on public schools at the heart of religious conservatives' organizing strategy. Seth Dowland, *Family Values and the Rise of the Christian Right* (Philadelphia: University of Pennsylvania Press, 2015), 80; Andrew Hartman, *A War for the Soul of America: A History of the Culture Wars* (Chicago: University of Chicago Press, 2015), 72–73.

4. Andrea Muehlebach insightfully identifies a recent Venn diagram between social Catholicism and neoliberalism; what I wish to point out is that the foundations of such commonalities date back at least to Weyrich and his cohort, who represent one in a series of cycles of response to perceived periods of economic redistribution and moral permissiveness. Andrea Muehlebach, *The Moral Neoliberal: Welfare and Citizenship in Italy* (Chicago: University of Chicago Press, 2012).

5. Daniel K. Williams, *God's Own Party: The Making of the Christian Right* (Oxford: Oxford University Press, 2012), 119; Lisa McGirr, *Suburban Warriors: The Origins of the New American Right* (Princeton, NJ: Princeton University Press, 2001), 233; Deal W. Hudson, *Onward, Christian Soldiers: The Growing Political Power of Catholics and Evangelicals in the United States* (New York: Threshold, 2008), 126–27.

6. Free Congress Foundation, *1987 Annual Report*, LOCW, Box 17.

7. Invitation to the Fourth Plenary Congress of the ICCC, Rio de Janeiro, 1958, obtained via Inter-Library Loan from Columbia University Library.

8. This argument would reappear again and again in conservative and neoconservative arguments for everything from torture (putatively justified by subversives' terrorist tactics) to other forms of alliance—including Weyrich's International Policy Forum. "International Policy Forum Prospectus, 1984–1985," n.d., LOCW, Box 13.

9. "Message from Dr. Harland J. O'Dell," in program, "4th Plenary Congress, August 12–21, 1958, Petrópolis, Brazil," obtained via Inter-Library Loan from Columbia University Library.

10. McIntire to W. C. Taylor, 27 June 1950, PTSM, Box 38; McIntire to Harden, 8 August 1960, PTSM, Box 20.

11. See "Information on Teams" (n.d.) and "The Brazilian Mission: Fundamental—Espiritual—Premilenial," n.d., PTSM, Box 38; E. W. Kerr to McIntire, 3 December 1952, PTSM, Box 38; Ronn Spargur, "Biographical Facts about Dr. Kenneth R. Kinney," press release, 8 June 1960, PTSM, Box 314.

12. Carl McIntire, *The Struggle for South America* (Collingswood, NJ: Christian Beacon, 1954[?]), 28. Bernardes would later serve as a federal deputy for the military regime's ARENA (Aliança Renovadora Nacional) party.

13. McIntire to Joseph Brown, 19 July 1960, PTSM, Box 33.

14. Aggeu Vieira, "Ecumenismo, o falso e o verdadeiro," speech, Recife, Brazil, 15[?] July 1967, PTSM, Box 315.

15. Émile-G. Léonard, "O Protestantismo brasileiro: Estudo de eclesiologia e de história social (VII)," *Revista de História* 11 (1951–52): 178–79.

16. McIntire to Warren Lilly, 26 December 1950, PTSM, Box 71, Folder RC-Correspondence to 1950, quoted in Markku Ruotsila, *Fighting Fundamentalist: Carl McIntire and the Politicization of American Fundamentalism* (Oxford: Oxford University Press, 2015), 107.

17. John T. Flynn, *The Road Ahead* (New York: Devin Adair, 1949), 108, 153.

18. *Presenting: An International Council of Christian Churches* (American Council of Christian Churches, 1948), obtained via Inter-Library Loan from Columbia University Library.

19. Colleen McDannell, *Material Christianity: Religion and Popular Culture in America* (New Haven, CT: Yale University Press, 1998), 7; Diana Walsh Pasulka, Heaven Can Wait: Purgatory in Catholic Devotional and Popular Culture (Oxford: Oxford University Press, 2015).

20. ICCC, "The So-Called Ecumenical Movement and the World Council of Churches," pamphlet, 1954, obtained via Inter-Library Loan from Columbia University Library.

21. ICCC, "The So-Called Ecumenical Movement."

22. See chapter 1.

23. Marcos Paulo dos Reis Quadros, "O conservadorismo católico na política brasileira: Considerações sobre as atividades da TFP ontem e hoje," *Estudos de Sociologia* 18, no. 34 (2013): 198.

24. Austregésilo de Athayde, "Espiritualidade e Política," *Reencontro*, September 1982, 3; SNI/ARJ, "Sétimo Aniversário de Reencontro: Obras Sociais e Educacionais," 21 July 1982, AN/COREG, ARJ-ACE-6621-82.

25. SNI/ARJ, "Ação do Conselho Mundial das Igrejas (CMI) na América Latina e no Brasil," 15 November 1981, AN/COREG, Fundo SNIG, ARJ-ACE-5437-81.

26. "Elementos da Igreja Presbiteriana do Brasil cujos nomes por atuações dentro da Igreja merecem investigação," n.d., Arquivo do DOPS de São Paulo, Arquivo Público do Estado de São Paulo, Pasta OP 1398, reproduced in Daniel Augusto Schmidt, "O protestantismo brasileiro: Entre a colaboração e a resistência no período da Ditadura Civil e Militar (1964–74)" (PhD diss., Universidade Metodista de São Paulo, 2015), anexo B.

27. SNI/AC, memorandum, 28 April 1976, AN/COREG, AC-ACE-90907-76.

28. "Planos das Conferências do Pe. Dr. Miguel Poradowski no Brasil—Agosto de 1975," n.d., AN/COREG, BR-DFANBSB-Z4-DPN-ENI-0044-edit, 39–41.

29. SEPES, "O que é a SEPES?," n.d., pamphlet, AN/COREG, BR-AN-RIO-TT-0-MCP-PRO -0405-edit.

30. "Racine-Born Weyrich Learned Organizing Value from Liberals," *Catholic Herald* (Milwaukee), 2 August 1984.

31. Free Congress Foundation, *Annual Report, 1985*, LOCW, Box 13.

32. Enrique Rueda, *The Homosexual Network: Private Lives and Public Policy* (New York: Devin Adair, 1986); Claudionor Corrêa de Andrade, *Há esperança para os homossexuais!* (Rio de Janeiro: CPAD, 1987). Andrade's book made direct reference to the United States as a place where, on the one hand, churches had begun to accept gays and, on the other, AIDS justly punished them; Rueda, meanwhile, cited São Paulo as a center of gay life.

33. Isvaldino dos Santos, "Entrevista: Pastor José Apolônio," *A Seara*, January 1983, 9.

34. Bartlett Petersen, "Eu Creio, Senhor!," *A Seara*, March 1987, 30; Clyde M. Narramore, "Segurança Econômica no Lar," *A Seara*, June 1987, 10; G. Raymond Carlson, "Alcoolismo: Um jogo mortal," *A Seara*, November 1983, 1.

35. José Maria Nascimento Pereira, "Amor Livre, Amor Escravo," *A Seara*, October 1977, 16.

36. "El movimiento conservador norteamericano en la opinión de Paul M. Weyrich," *La Nueva Província* (Bahía Blanca, Argentina), 6 October 1988, Ideas y Imágenes Section, 2–3.

37. See chapter 1.

38. Sigaud to Plínio Corrêa de Oliveira, 1 September 1965, AMAD, Caixa 79.

39. Geraldo Proença Sigaud, "Sínodo Episcopal: A respeito do Sacerdôcio Ministerial: Esboço de argumentos que se discutirá na segunda reunião geral," 1971[?], AMAD, Caixa 79.

40. Kimba Allie Tichenor, *Religious Crisis and Civic Transformation: How Conflicts over Gender and Sexuality Changed the West German Catholic Church* (Waltham, MA: Brandeis, 2016), 52–53.

41. Sigaud, "Sínodo Episcopal."

42. João Botelho to Caio [de Castro], 23 November 1965, AMAD, Caixa 79.

43. Heloisa Maria Murgel Starling, *Os senhores das gerais: Os Novos Inconfidentes e o Golpe Militar de 1964* (Petrópolis, Brazil: Vozes, 1986), 216–17.

44. Botelho to Caio [de Castro], 23 November 1965.

45. Sigaud to Ernesto Geisel, 30 March 1977, AN/COREG, Fundo SNIG, AC-ACE-104214-77-002.

46. Draft response to Tardini, 15a.

47. CIE, "Teologia da Libertação," 21 December 1982, 9, AN/COREG, ASP-ACE-13399-83.

48. Ministério do Exército, "Relatório Especial de Informações no. 02/81," 30 December 1981, AN/COREG, Fundo SNIG, ASP-ACE-12368-82-001.

49. Ministério da Aeronáutica, "Atividades de Dom Sebastião Baggio, Núncio Apostólico do Brasil," 18 September 1967, AN/COREG, Fundo CISA, BR-AN-BSB-VAZ-054-0180.

50. SNI/ARJ, "Atividades de Grupos Religiosos," 5 November 1982, 9, AN/COREG, Fundo SNIG, ARJ-ACE-7140-82.

51. *Sepes Boletim*, n.d., 42, AN/COREG, BR-DFANBSB-Z4-DPN-ENI-0044-edit.

52. CISA, "Análise da situação na area Religiosa Católica de S. Paulo," 20 July 1965, AN/COREG, BR-AN-BSB-VAZ-042-0116. In his much-cited 1891 encyclical *Rerum Novarum*, for example, Leo XIII counseled, "No matter what changes may occur in forms of government, there will ever be differences and inequalities of condition. . . . Society cannot exist or be conceived of without them." Leo XIII, "Rerum Novarum," 15 May 1891, http://www.vatican.va/content/leo-xiii/en/encyclicals/documents/hf_l-xiii_enc_15051891_rerum-novarum.html.

53. Benjamin A. Cowan, *Securing Sex: Morality and Repression in the Making of Cold War Brazil* (Chapel Hill: University of North Carolina Press, 2016).

54. Jesuan de Paula Xavier, "Informação no. 227/19/AC/75," 31 July 1975, 1–2, AN/COREG, Fundo DSI/MJ, BR-AN-RIO-TT-0-MCP-PRO-0439.

55. Angela Copsche, letter to *O Estado de S. Paulo*, quoted in *O Conciliábulo*, 17 October 1964, ACRSP.

56. Xavier, "Informação no. 227/19/AC/75," 5.

57. SNI/ARJ, "Informação no. 08316/73," 30 November 1973, 2, AN/COREG, Fundo SNIG, AC-ACE-64728-73.

58. Ministério do Exército, "Relatório Especial de Informações no. 10/82," 25 October 1982, AN/COREG, Fundo SNIG, AC-ACE-38078-83.

59. Ministério do Exército, emphasis added.

60. "Sentadinhos, heim?," *Tribuna do Ceará* (Fortaleza, Brazil), 29 September 1982, appended to Ministério do Exército, "Relatório Especial de Informações no. 10/82."

61. Ministério do Exército, "Relatório Especial de Informações no. 10/82."

62. Cowan, *Securing Sex.*

63. Alfredo Buzaid, *Camões e o renascimento* (São Paulo: Saraiva, 1984), quoted in Rodolpho Costa Machado, "Alfredo Buzaid e a contrarrevolução burguesa de 1964" (MA thesis, Pontifícia Universidade Católica de São Paulo, 2015), 528.

64. Jobim to MRE, 15 October 1970, AHPI, Pasta Ofícios, Vaticano, 1970 (02); José Jobim to MRE/José Magalhães Pinto, 27 January 1969 (Secreto. No. 45), 7, AHPI, SCE, Ofícios, Embaixadas, Moscou a Washington, Ano: 1969/70, Caixa 98. Ironically, Jobim himself would eventually fall victim to the military regime. In 1979, a week after attending the presidential inauguration of General João Figueiredo, Jobim was disappeared, tortured, and murdered by the state. Hellen Guimarães, "Diplomata foi morto pela ditadura antes de denunciar corrupção no regime, confirma nova certidão," *Época*, 12 September 2018, https://epoca.globo.com/diplomata-foi-morto-pela-ditadura-antes-de-denunciar-corrupcao-no-regime-confirma-nova-certidao-23089585.

65. Jobim to MRE, 13 February 1970, AHPI, Pasta Ofícios, Vaticano, 1970 (01).

66. See, for example, Jobim to MRE, 17 July 1970, AHPI, Pasta Ofícios, Vaticano, 1970 (02); Jobim to MRE, 6 August 1970, AHPI, Pasta Ofícios, Vaticano, 1970 (02); Jobim to MRE, 24 September 1970, AHPI, Pasta Ofícios, Vaticano, 1970 (02); Jobim to MRE, 7 January 1971, AHPI, Pasta Ofícios, Vaticano, 1971 (01).

67. Jobim to MRE, 23 April 1970, 1, AHPI, SCE, Telegramas Recebidos/Expedidos, Embaixadas Taipé a Viena (1969/70), Caixa 112.

68. MRE to Jobim, 12 February 1969, AHPI, SCE, Telegramas Recebidos/Expedidos, Embaixadas Taipé a Viena (1969/70), Caixa 112.

69. Jobim to MRE, 27 January 1969, 1–2.

70. Jobim to MRE, 27 January 1969, 50; MRE to Jobim, 12 February 1969.

71. See chapter 1.

72. Jobim to MRE, 30 November 1970, AHPI, SCE, Ofícios, Embaixadas, Moscou a Washington, Ano: 1969/70, Caixa 98. The "eye of the needle" reference is from Matthew 19:23–26, often invoked in debates about liberation theology and Christian reorientation in favor of the poor.

73. MRE to Jobim, 9 November 1969, AHPI, SCE, Confidencial, Telegramas Recebidos e expedidos, Embaixadas, Varsóvia a Wellington, Ano: 1969, Caixa 409; Jobim to MRE, 30 November 1970.

74. MRE to Jobim, 27 June 1970, AHPI, SCE, Telegramas Recebidos e expedidos, Caixa 415.

75. Jobim to MRE, 27 January 1969, 47.

76. Jobim to MRE, 14 July 1970, AHPI, SCE, Ofícios, Embaixadas, Moscou a Washington, Ano: 1969/70, Caixa 98.

77. Jobim to MRE, 27 January 1969, 19.

78. See, for example, Jobim to MRE, 24 February 1969, AHPI, SCE, Confidencial, Ofícios Recebidos, Embaixadas, Vaticano (68/70), Viena (47/59), Ano 1947/70, Caixa 138.

79. Henrique Souza Gomes to MRE, 6 April 1964, AHPI, Pasta Vaticano Ofícios Janeiro–Abril 1964. According to historian Sérgio Rodrigues, Gomes was the *only* diplomat to ex-

press such support. Sérgio Henrique da Costa Rodrigues, "Tensão e diálogo: Relações diplomáticas entre a Ditadura Militar brasileira e o Estado do Vaticano" (paper presented at ANPUH [Associação Nacional de História], Londrina, Brazil, 2005), 2.

80. Gomes to Castello Branco, 11 October 1965, AHPI, Pasta Vaticano Ofícios Set–Dez 1965.

81. A. B. L. Castello Branco, "Informação Global Anual," 8 March 1977, 1, AHPI, Caixa 228, Numero maço 600 (F5), Assuntos Políticos: Vaticano, Maio de 1974.

82. A. B. L. Castello Branco, "Informação Global de 1975," 8 April 1976, AHPI, Caixa 228.

83. José Casanova, "Religion Challenging the Myth of Secular Democracy," in *Religion in the 21st Century: Challenges and Transformations*, ed. Lisbet Christoffersen and Margit Warburg (London: Taylor and Francis, 2016), 19–36; Talal Asad, *Formations of the Secular: Christianity, Islam, Modernity* (Stanford, CA: Stanford University Press, 2003); Fenella Cannell, "The Anthropology of Secularism," *Annual Review of Anthropology* 39 (2010): 85–100.

84. Sigaud, "Sínodo Episcopal"; Geraldo Sigaud, "Sacrosancti Concilium Vaticanum, Sessio IV. De Libertate Religiosa," 21 September 1965, AMAD, Caixa 83; Carlos Eduardo Saboia Bandeira de Mello, *Carta Pastoral Sôbre o Concílio Vaticano II* (Petrópolis, Brazil: Vozes, 1961), 9.

85. Margane Laure Reina, "Pentecostalismo e questão racial no Brasil: Desafios e possibilidades do ser negro na igreja evangélica," *Plural* 24, no. 2 (2017): 253–75.

86. Israel Gueiros, "Liberty and the Historic Christian Faith," speech, 5 August 1954, Philadelphia, PA, PTSM, Box 18, File 28.

87. "Ameaça Ecumênica," *Mensageiro da Paz*, September 1981, 12–13, emphasis added.

88. Gueiros, "Liberty."

89. English Consultative Committee of the ICCC, *What Is the Difference between the International Council of Christian Churches and the World Council of Churches?* (London: ICCC, 1958[?]), 5.

90. Pasulka, *Heaven Can Wait*, 29.

91. "What Happened to Hell?," *Christian Beacon*, 2 February 1961, 4.

92. *O Puritano*, 10 May 1950, quoted in Léonard, "O Protestantismo Brasileiro," 180. See also R. J. Ryle, "Is There a Hell?," *Christian Beacon*, 3 August 1961, 3.

93. The ICCC's focus on the virginity of Mary can be seen in some ways as ironic, given the tensions surrounding veneration of Mary that divided and continue to divide Protestants and Catholics. Yet McIntire himself insisted that even the linguistic details mattered on this front. Contemplating the "substitution of the term *young woman* for *virgin* in Isaiah 7:14," McIntire argued that "to break the force of the predictive nature of this passage in Isaiah in such a way is inexcusable." Ralph Lord Roy, *Apostles of Discord: A Study of Organized Bigotry and Disruption on the Fringes of Protestantism* (Boston: Beacon, 1953), 205.

94. "El movimiento conservador norteamericano."

95. "Sex and God in American Politics," 11.

96. Fred Clarkson, "Moon's Law: God Is Phasing Out Democracy," *Covert Action Information Bulletin* 27 (1987): 35.

97. On God's intervention in and sanction for WACL leaders Alfredo Stroessner and John Singlaub, see, for example, John Lee Anderson and Scott Anderson, *Inside the League: The Shocking Exposé of How Terrorists, Nazis, and Latin American Death Squads Have Infiltrated the World Anti-Communist League* (New York: Dodd Mead, 1986), 141; and Charles R. Babcock, "Dallas Hosts Anti-Communist League," *Washington Post*, 17 September 1985.

98. SEPES, "O que é a SEPES?," 5, 7.

99. Avery Dulles, "The Reception of Vatican II at the Extraordinary Synod of 1985," in *The Reception of Vatican II*, ed. Giuseppe Alberigo, Jean-Pierre Jossua, and Joseph A. Komonchak (Washington, DC: Catholic University of America Press, 1987), 353.

100. Roberto de Mattei, *The Crusader of the 20th Century: Plinio Corrêa de Oliveira* (Leominster, UK: Gracewing, 1998), 44n48.

101. "Author: Luíz Sérgio Solimeo," TFP Student Action, accessed, 13 June 2018, https://www.tfpstudentaction.org/authors/luis-sergio-solimeo; Luíz Sérgio Solimeo, *Fátima: A Message More Urgent than Ever* (Spring Grove, PA: TFP, 2008); Antônio Augusto Borelli and John R. Spann, *Our Lady of Fatima: Prophecies of Tragedy or Hope?* (n.p.: TFP, 1985).

102. Giulio Folena, *Escravos do Profeta* (São Paulo: EMW Editores, 1987); John T. Armour, "TFP: A Dangerous Cult," *Angelus*, July 1983, n.p.; "Heralds of the Gospel," Fish Eaters, accessed 13 June 2018, https://fisheaters.com/forums/showthread.php?tid=23830&pid=306230.

103. David Allen White, *The Mouth of the Lion: Bishop Antônio de Castro Mayer and the Last Catholic Diocese* (Kansas City, MO: Angelus, 1993), 181–82.

104. Armour, "TFP."

105. American Society for the Defense of Tradition, Family and Property and the Canadian Society for the Defense of Tradition, Family and Property, *Let the Other Side Also Be Heard: The TFPs' Defense against Fidelity's Onslaught* (Pleasantville, NY: TFP, 1989), 55.

106. José Lúcio de Araújo Corrêa to Carl McIntire, 30 May 1974, PTSM, Box 37, emphasis added.

107. SNI/ARJ, "Ação do Conselho."

108. CIE, "Teologia da Libertação," 10–11.

109. SNI/ARJ, "Informação 034/19/ARJ/82," 10 November 1982, AN/COREG, ARJ-ACE-7198-82.

110. Costa Machado, "Alfredo Buzaid," 11, 739–40.

111. Alfredo Buzaid, *Da Conjuntura Política Nacional* (Brasília: Departamento de Imprensa Nacional, 1972), 13; Alfredo Buzaid, *Humanismo Político* (Brasília: Departamento de Imprensa Nacional, 1973), 19.

112. Jobim to MRE, 27 January 1969.

113. Henrique Souza Gomes to MRE, 11 September 1965, AHPI, Pasta Vaticano, Telegr. 1965–66, 372F.

114. "Boletim no. 9," 27 September 1965, ACRSP, 050.2/250; Antônio de Castro Mayer, *Carta pastoral sobre problemas do apostolado moderno, contendo um catecismo de verdades oportunas que se opõem a erros contemporâneos*, 2nd ed. (Campos, Brazil: Boa Imprensa, 1953).

115. "Comitatus Episcopalis Internationalis," 28 May 1965, AMAD, Caixa 83, Pasta "II Concílio Vaticano—Outras Conferências."

116. Marcel Lefebvre and Antônio de Castro Mayer to Pope John Paul II, 21 November 1983, http://archives.sspx.org/archbishop_lefebvre/1983_open_letter_to_pope_episcopal_manifesto_ab_lefebvre-bp_de_castro_mayer.htm.

117. Draft response to Tardini.

118. Jobim to MRE, 27 January 1969.

119. Augusto Estellita Lima to MRE, 6 November 1969, AHPI, Pasta Ofícios, Vaticano, 1971 (02).

120. Examples, as Dochuk points out, can be found in Daniel Bell, ed., *The Radical Right* (London: Routledge, 2017); Richard Hofstadter, *The Paranoid Style in American Politics* (New York: Vintage, 2008); and Seymour Martin Lipset and Earl Raab, *The Politics of Unreason: Right-Wing Extremism in America, 1790–1970* (New York: Harper and Row, 1970). Darren Dochuk, "Revival on the Right: Making Sense of the Conservative Moment in Post–World War II American History," *History Compass* 4, no. 5 (2006): 991n5.

121. Dan T. Carter, *The Politics of Rage: George Wallace, the Origins of the New Conservatism, and the Transformation of American Politics* (Baton Rouge: Louisiana State University Press, 2008), 315–16. See also Ann Burlein, *Lift High the Cross: Where White Supremacy and the Christian Right Converge* (Durham, NC: Duke University Press, 2002).

122. Israel Gueiros and Margaret Harden, "News and Notes concerning the National Presbyterian Seminary in Recife, Brazil," 16 April 1956, PTSM, Box 18.

123. Gueiros, "Liberty."

124. Luiz Costa, letter to the editor, *A Seara*, April 1987, 2.

125. Joanyr de Oliveira, editorial, *A Seara*, October 1987, 2.

126. Media scholar Anna Williams credits Weyrich, among others, with innovating a "narrative that appeals to a nostalgia for a lost, patriarchal, segregated past while simultaneously promising its return." Anna Williams, "Conservative Media Activism: The Free Congress Foundation and National Empowerment Television," in *Media, Culture, and the Religious Right*, ed. Linda Kintz and Julia Lesage (Minneapolis: University of Minnesota Press, 1998), 281.

127. Paul M. Weyrich and William S. Lind, *The Next Conservatism* (South Bend, IN: St. Augustine's, 2009), 47, 50, 79; William S. Lind, "The Next Conservatism: Applying Retroculture," traditionalRIGHT, 30 August 2016, https://www.traditionalright.com/the-next -conservatism-applying-retroculture/.

128. Mary Jordan, "The Conservatives Have a Picnic," *Washington Post*, 27 June 1984, F9.

129. If this was not exactly clear in (Anglican) Lind's call for a Tolkienesque pastoralism, it clearly appeared, for example, in the pastoral nationalism of R. J. Rushdoony, a pioneer of the New Right who might have rivaled McIntire if things had gone the former's way. Rushdoony prefigured "retroculture" and like nostalgias by lauding the U.S. War of Independence as a "Protestant restoration of feudalism." Michael J. McVicar, *Christian Reconstruction: R. J. Rushdoony and American Religious Conservatism* (Chapel Hill: University of North Carolina Press, 2015), 87–88, 125. As Bruce Schulman's masterful *The Seventies* makes clear, that was the decade in which nostalgia for the "traditional southern lifestyle" of bucolic lords and their fiefdoms became an article less of Confederate pride than of American patriotism. Bruce J. Schulman, *The Seventies: The Great Shift in American Culture, Society, and Politics* (Cambridge, MA: Da Capo, 2002), 102.

130. Buzaid, *Camões*, 29. See also Werner Sombart, *The Quintessence of Capitalism: A Study of the History and Psychology of the Modern Business Man* (New York: Dutton, 1915), 13.

131. Carlos Saboia Bandeira de Mello, *Sôbre a Missa Comunitária* (Petrópolis: Vozes, 1963); Buzaid, *Humanismo Político*, 19; Buzaid, *Camões*, 56.

132. Benjamin A. Cowan, "TFP: A Family Affair," paper presented at 2nd International Symposium "Brazil: From Dictatorship to Democracy," Brown University, 7 April 2017; TFP, *Um homem, uma obra, uma gesta: Homenagem das TFPs a Plínio Corrêa de Oliveira* (São Paulo: Edições Brasil de Amanhã, 1989), 96.

133. Plínio Corrêa de Oliveira, "A cruzada do século XX," *Catolicismo*, January 1971, http://www.pliniocorreadeoliveira.info/1971_241_CAT_A_Cruzada_do_S%C3%A9culo_20.htm.

134. Luis Dufaur, "The Middle Ages: An Explosion of Freedom, Creativity and Progress," American Society for the Defense of Tradition, Family and Property, 31 December 2014, http://www.tfp.org/the-middle-ages-an-explosion-of-freedom-creativity-and-progress/. See also Plínio Corrêa de Oliveira, "Why Saturday Is Dedicated to Our Lady," American Society for the Defense of Tradition, Family and Property, 31 March 2018, http://www.tfp.org/why-saturday-is-dedicated-to-our-lady/.

135. American Society for the Defense of Tradition, Family and Property and the Canadian Society for the Defense of Tradition, Family and Property, *Let the Other Side*, 8, emphasis added.

136. Corrêa to McIntire, 30 May 1974.

137. Xavier, "Informação no. 227/19/AC/75," 11.

138. Jobim to MRE, 27 January 1969, 9.

139. For Brazilian examples, see Cowan, "TFP: A Family Affair"; "Miracema quer tudo apurado," *O Fluminense*, 26 July 1978, 5; and "Jovens de Miracema não desfilaram contra o padre," *O Globo*, 31 July 1978, 13.

140. Uli Schmetzer, "The Brotherhood," *Washington Post*, 6 January 1974, B3.

141. "A 'Phenomenon' Called TFP," *New York Times*, 17 December 1978, WC7.

142. Marc Corelli, "Bringing Back the Middle Ages," *Church and State* 32, no. 7 (1979): 19.

143. "At a Call to Chivalry Camp: 'The Most Beautiful Adventure Is Ours,'" American Society for the Defense of Tradition, Family and Property, 9 July 2005, http://www.tfp.org/at-a-call-to-chivalry-camp-qthe-most-beautiful-adventure-is-oursq/; "Príncipes do Brasil na Ordem de Malta," *Catolicismo*, December 2002, http://catolicismo.com.br/materia/materia.cfm/idmat/386/mes/Dezembro2002; Alfred W. Williams to Sigaud, 15 July 1967, ACRSP, FDS; Dom M.-Gérard Lafond to Sigaud, 25 March 1964, "Un initiative de laics," AMAD, Caixa 85; "The Historical Ordre," Blackfriar.org, http://blackfriar.org/ordre/historicalordreT2.htm, consulted 21 September 2020.

144. "What They Say about *Nobility and Analogous Traditional Elites in the Allocutions of Pius XII*," Nobility and Analogous Traditional Elites, accessed 18 April 2018, http://www.nobility.org/what-they-say-2/.

145. Morton Blackwell, preface to Plínio Corrêa de Oliveira, *Nobility and Analogous Traditional Elites in the Allocutions of Pius XII: A Theme Illuminating American Social History* (York, PA: Hamilton, 1993), xii–xxv.

146. James Bogle, "The Beatification of Europe's Heart," *Remnant*, accessed 28 April 2018, https://www.remnantnewspaper.com/Archives/archive-2005-1015-beatification_of_europe.htm.

147. Stephen J. Andes, for example, presents the fusion of "non-economic values" and "economic interest" as a spontaneous and hence inexplicable conflation. Stephen J. C. Andes, *The Vatican and Catholic Activism in Mexico and Chile: The Politics of Transnational Catholicism, 1920–1940* (Oxford: Oxford University Press, 2014), 31. In an example of more nuanced wrestling with this issue, Maria das Dores Campos Machado and Joanildo Burity contend that Pentecostals have historically accepted some parts of neoliberalism (entrepreneurship, individual responsibility) while retaining a peculiar and selective statism. Maria das Dores Campos Machado and Joanildo Burity, "A Ascensão Política dos Pente-

costais no Brasil na Avaliação de Líderes Religiosos," *Revista de Ciências Sociais* 57, no. 3 (2014): 611.

148. Following Angus Burgin, I use "neoliberalism" to mean a revival of laissez-faire liberalism, whose conceptual relationship to the past changed over the course of the twentieth century, but which by the late Cold War can be said to have generally favored deregulation, privatization, and increasingly rationalized, moralistic narratives of self-reliance and "limited government." Angus Burgin, *The Great Persuasion: Reinventing Free Markets since the Depression* (Cambridge, MA: Harvard University Press, 2015). See also Johanna Bockman, *Markets in the Name of Socialism: The Left-Wing Origins of Neoliberalism* (Stanford, CA: Stanford University Press, 2011).

149. Murray Friedman, *The Neoconservative Revolution: Jewish Intellectuals and the Shaping of Public Policy* (Cambridge: Cambridge University Press, 2006).

150. Irving Kristol, *The Neoconservative Persuasion* (New York: Basic Books, 2011), 293.

151. Plínio Corrêa de Oliveira, *Nobility*, 6, 10, 18, 25, 28, 35, 37, 44, 71, 80, 94.

152. Oliveira, 25.

153. A former Brazilian TFP member told me that the Tattons became "the biggest financial supporters of TFP," donating money and large tracts of land for institutional headquarters in the United States. José Lúcio de Araújo Corrêa, email to author, 4 February 2019.

154. Plínio Corrêa de Oliveira, *Nobility*, 134, 143; "Generous Dedication from Donors and TFP Members," *Crusade*, July/August 2013, 7; Christine Carroll, "The Texas 100: Survey Results," *Texas Monthly*, September 1992.

155. Plínio Corrêa de Oliveira, *Nobility*, 343–64.

156. Geraldo de Proença Sigaud, Antônio de Castro Mayer, and Plinio Corrêa de Oliveira, *Reforma agrária: Questão de consciência* (São Paulo: Vera Cruz, 1962), 15.

157. Fascinatingly, while certain archtraditionalists (like those of the TFP or the Society of Saint Pius X) could champion an end to democracy as the means of preserving rightful hierarchy, other neoconservatives presented themselves and their commitment to deregulation as *itself* the truest form of democracy, designed to preserve hierarchies organically (based on markets and inherent, individual qualities).

158. Draft response to Tardini, 7.

159. "Venerabilis Pater," 2 November 1964, ACRSP, Fundo Petro, 050.2/171.

160. Coetus Internationalis Patrum to "Exc.me Pater," 3 December 1965, ACRSP, Fundo Petro, 050.2/17[5].

161. "Apontamentos para reflexão," n.d., ACRSP, FDS.

162. Antônio de Castro Mayer, *Prevenindo os diocesanos contra os ardis da seita comunista*, 2nd ed. (São Paulo: Vera Cruz, 1961), 18.

163. Antônio de Castro Mayer, *Prevenindo os diocesanos*, 28.

164. SEPES, "O que é a SEPES?"

165. Mayer, *Prevenindo*, 20.

166. "Rascunho," n.d., ACRSP, FDS, Pasta "Concílio Ecumenico Vat. II—D. Sigaud—Carta ao Santo Padre e seus rascunhos," 18.

167. Draft response to Tardini, 19.

168. Markku Ruotsila, "Carl McIntire and the Fundamentalist Origins of the Christian Right," *Church History* 81, no. 2 (2012): 384–85.

169. J. W. Clise to Howard Pew, 17 March 1958, UOJWC, Box 5.

170. J. W. Clise to McIntire, 1 July 1959, UOJWC, Box 5.

171. Robert T. Ketchum, "Greetings!," in *Presenting*, 6.

172. "Criticada orientação da Igreja," *O Estado de S. Paulo*, 9 March 1978, 6.

173. "Declaration of Faith and Principles," draft, 1950[?], PTSM, Box 18, File 27; McIntire to Gueiros, 15 June 1950, PTSM, Box 18, File 27.

174. Paul Freston, *Evangélicos na política brasileira: História ambígua e desafio ético* (Curitiba, Brazil: Encontrão, 1994), 82. Freston argues that the Brazilian evangelical Right of this moment should *not* be compared with the New Right of the United States; but as my work and that of others demonstrates, there was significant room for comparison. See Antônio Flávio Pierucci, "Representantes de Deus em Brasília: A Bancada Evangélica na Constituinte," *Ciências Sociais Hoje* 11 (1989): 120.

175. Narramore, "Segurança Econômica no Lar," 10.

176. "Sex and God in American Politics," 15.

177. Lee Edwards, *Leading the Way: The Story of Ed Feulner and the Heritage Foundation* (New York: Crown, 2013), n.p.

178. "Sex and God in American Politics," 23.

179. "El movimiento conservador norteamericano," 2–3.

180. "International Policy Forum Prospectus, 1984–1985," 2.

181. "Thunder from the Right," *Conservative Digest*, May 1984.

182. Cowan, *Securing Sex*.

183. Secretaria de Estado de Segurança Pública de Minas Gerais to SNI/ABH, 25 January 1973, AN/COREG, DI-ACE-65577-73, emphasis in the original.

184. SNI/ARJ, "Informação 034/19/ARJ/82."

185. SNI/AC, "Correntes e Linhas do Clero," 30 August 1973, AN/COREG, Fundo SNIG, DI-ACE-65577-73, emphasis added.

186. Indeed, this relationship might be traced back at least as far as Pope Leo XIII, whose seminal *Rerum Novarum* (1891) in some sense attempted to harmonize Catholic teaching and modern capitalism—much as neoconservative Christians a century later would attempt to create logics for promoting neoliberal capitalism. Though rightly celebrated for its denunciations of "the hardheartedness of employers and the greed of unchecked competition," and often presented as Leo XIII's vision of a nationalist, modern state as a solution to the "social question," the 1891 encyclical also contained nuggets of something else: a mainstream Catholic anticommunism that, as surely as it formed the basis for European social democracies, fomented antistatist championing of inequality itself. Indeed, it is possible to read *Rerum Novarum* as rather decidedly *anti*state: to quote the document, "There is no need to bring in the State." Anticipating later anticommunisms by accusing socialists of promoting state intrusion into parenting and moral matters, *Rerum Novarum* perhaps most notably argued that redistribution, by violating private property, would impoverish all by derailing "natural" aptitudes: "And in addition to injustice, it is only too evident what an upset and disturbance there would be in all classes, and to how intolerable and hateful a slavery citizens would be subjected. The door would be thrown open to envy, to mutual invective, and to discord; *the sources of wealth themselves would run dry, for no one would have any interest in exerting his talents or his industry; and that ideal equality about which they entertain pleasant dreams would be in reality the levelling down of all to a like condition of misery and*

degradation." Leo XIII, "Rerum Novarum," emphasis added. On *Rerum Novarum* and capitalism, see Muehlebach, *Moral Neoliberal*, 79, 86, 95.

187. SNI/APA, "Visita do Papa João Paulo II," 11 July 1980, AN/COREG, APA-ACE-1521-80.

188. Jesuan de Paula Xavier to Armando Falção, 31 July 1975, 4–5, AN/COREG, BR-AN-RIO-TT-0-MCP-PRO-0439-edit, emphasis original.

189. CIE, "Teologia da Libertação," 11–12, emphasis added.

190. "Modernismo," in Schmidt, "O Protestantismo brasileiro," anexo B.

191. Jobim to MRE, 15 October 1970; Jobim, Ofício no. 280, n.d., AHPI, MDB Cidade do Vaticano, Ofícios Dez 1968; Jobim to MRE, 27 January 1969.

192. Castello Branco, "Informação Global de 1975." Even ambassador Henrique Souza Gomes, appointed before the 1964 coup, sympathized with Lefebvre and with the partisans of Pius XII during the council. Henrique de Souza Gomes to MRE, 12 March 1964, AHPI, Pasta Vaticano, Cartas Telegr. 1963–1965, 03735; Henrique de Souza Gomes to MRE, 10 June 1963, AHPI, Pasta Vaticano, Cartas Telegr. 1963–1965, 03735.

193. Castello Branco, "Informação Global de 1975."

194. Castello Branco, "Informação Global Anual," 2–4.

195. Elizabeth A. Castelli, "Persecution Complexes: Identity Politics and the 'War on Christians,'" *differences* 18, no. 3 (2007): 154. Earlier analyses of the Christian Right in the United States did pick up on something like this—what scholars in the 1980s referred to as "lifestyle defense." To quote Allison Calhoun-Brown, "Lifestyle defense theory holds that . . . evangelicals perceive a threat to the integrity of their way of life, they seek to have congruity between their beliefs and public policies." Allison Calhoun-Brown, "Still Seeing in Black and White: Racial Challenges for the Christian Right," in *Sojourners in the Wilderness: The Christian Right in Comparative Perspective*, ed. Corwin Smidt and James Penning (Lanham, MD: Rowman and Littlefield, 1997), 117. See also Louise J. Lorentzen, "Evangelical Life Style Concerns Expressed in Political Action," *Sociological Analysis* 41, no. 2 (1980): 146.

196. Ricardo Mariano, "Pentecostais e política no Brasil," *Ciência e Religião*, 10 May 2005, http://www.comciencia.br/dossies-1-72/reportagens/2005/05/13.shtml.

197. In the North Atlantic context, Corey Robin configures this within the frame of monarcho-Christian antimodernity, where "the conservative not only opposes the left; he also believes that the left has been in the driver's seat since, depending on who's counting, the French Revolution or the Reformation." Corey Robin, *The Reactionary Mind: Conservatism from Edmund Burke to Sarah Palin* (Oxford: Oxford University Press, 2011), 23.

198. Heather Hendershot, "God's Angriest Man: Carl McIntire, Cold War Fundamentalism, and Right-Wing Broadcasting," *American Quarterly* 59, no. 2 (2007): 380.

199. Paul Everett Pierson, *A Younger Church in Search of Maturity: Presbyterianism in Brazil from 1910 to 1959* (San Antonio, TX: Trinity University Press, 1974), 207, 210.

200. McIntire to Mr. and Mrs. Gerson de Campos Kerr, 31 August 1959, PTSM, Box 33.

201. Harden to McIntire, 27 March 1952, PTSM, Box 20.

202. Rafael Camacho, "The Twentieth Century Reformation in Brazil," speech, n.d., PTSM, Box 33.

203. Camacho to McIntire, 23 January 1969, PTSM, Box 33.

204. Gueiros to José da Silva, 14 February 1950, PTSM, Box 18.

205. McIntire to Keith Altig, 14 March 1957, PTSM, Box 33.

206. Gueiros to McIntire, 31 March 1950, PTSM, Box 18.

207. "Os rumos da constituinte," *Mensageiro da Paz*, September 1986, 14.

208. Nemuel Kessler, "Os nossos candidatos à constituinte," *A Seara*, July 1986, 4.

209. Breda Savittiere, "Diga Não ao Divórcio," *Mensageiro da Paz*, July 1986, 11.

210. Machado and Burity, "A Ascensão Política dos Pentecostais," 614.

211. "Paul Weyrich," *Forerunner*, September 1984, 10.

212. Paul Weyrich, "Thoughts at Easter," *Remnant*, 30 April 1984, 6.

213. Cowan, *Securing Sex*.

214. João Camilo de Oliveira Torres, *História das idéias religiosas no Brasil: A Igreja e a sociedade brasileira* (São Paulo: Grijalbo, 1968), 219.

215. Plínio Corrêa de Oliveira, introduction to *Revolução e Contrarrevolução* (São Paulo: Retornarei, 2002), 1.

216. Plínio Corrêa de Oliveira, "Sobranceira e serena, a TFP enfrenta o XI estrondo publicitário," *Folha de S. Paulo*, 26 March 1985, 7.

217. TFP, *Um homem, uma obra*, 83.

218. Oliveira, "Sobranceira e serena."

219. "A TFP em legítima defesa," *Folha de S. Paulo*, 30 May 1975, https://www.plinio correadeoliveira.info/MAN%2075-05-21%20A%20TFP%20em.htm; *Refutação da TFP a uma investida frustrada*, 2 vols. (São Paulo: TFP, 1984); TFP, *Um homem, uma obra*, 2.

220. TFP, *Um homem, uma obra*, 78.

221. TFP, 340.

222. "Reverentissime Domine," draft, n.d., ACRSP, FDS, "Concílio Ecumenico Vat. II—D. Sigaud—Carta ao Santo Padre e seus rascunhos."

223. Draft response to Tardini, 1.

224. SNI/ARJ, "Informação 040/19/ARJ/1984," 21 September 1983, AN/COREG, ARJ-ACE-7198-82-MF-ALT-1; SNI/ARJ, "Informação 034/19/ARJ/82"; SNI/ARJ, "Atividades de Grupos Religiosos."

225. SNI/AC, "Atividades da Esquerda Clerical," 24 May 1977, 2–3, AN/COREG, AC-ACE-109394-78-edit.

226. DSI/MEC, "Encaminhamento no 013/10099/79/10/DSI/MEC," 15 August 1979, AN/COREG, Fundo CISA, BR-AN-BSB-AA1-MPL-102.

227. Jobim to MRE, 27 January 1969.

228. A. P. Vasconcellos, "Ecumenismo: Uma Solução Religiosa?," *Mensageiro da Paz*, May 1980, 1–2.

229. SNI/ARJ, "Ação do Conselho," 3.

230. SNI/AC, "Cisão Entre Protestantes no Brasil," 3 September 1982, 2, AN/COREG, AC-ACE-27301-82.

231. Gilberto Grassi Calil, Preface to *História Fetichista: O aparelho de hegemonia filosófico Instituto Brasileiro de Filosofia Convivium (1964–1985)*, by Rodrigo Jurucê Mattos Gonçalves (Goiânia, Brazil: Universidade Estadual do Oeste do Paraná, 2017), 16.

232. Robin, *Reactionary Mind*, 35.

233. Melissa J. Wilde, *Vatican II: A Sociological Analysis of Religious Change* (Princeton, NJ: Princeton University Press, 2007), 4; Doris Buss and Didi Hermann, *Globalizing Family Values: The Christian Right in International Politics* (Minneapolis: University of Minnesota Press, 2003), 41.

234. Mello, *Carta Pastoral*, 13.

235. Sigaud to Oliveira, 1 September 1965.

236. Cicognani to Carli, 11 August 1965, AMAD, Caixa 79.

237. Sigaud to Oliveira, 1 September 1965.

238. Gomes to MRE, 21 January 1964, AHPI, Pasta Vaticano, Cartas Telegr. 1963–1965, 03735.

Index

Primo, Luís Álvarez, 150
private property, 14–15, 19, 33, 38–39, 59, 155, 173–74
"The Problem: Our Lack of Solidarity", 146
progressive Christianity, surveillance of, 45–46, 50, 111, 114–15
progressives, 5, 14–15, 17, 32, 35–36, 57, 61, 76–77; advocating for ecumenism, 14, 106–7; and anticommunism, 109; as irreligious, 112–14; Jobim on, 193, 203–4; and moralism, 50, 104–5; opposition to, 7, 14, 45, 63, 78, 83, 86–88, 99, 128–29, 212, *See also* Protestant progressives
prosperity gospel, 218–19
Protestantism, 60, 73, 100, 165–66, 179, 206, *See also* Conservative Protestants
Protestant Left, 14, 99–101, 111
Protestant progressives, 83, 98, 101, 103, 107, 111–17
Protestant Right, 83, 131, 136, 227
protests, 42–43, 79
Protocols of the Elders of Zion, 11, 31, 41, *See also* anti-Semitism
Przyklenk, João Batista, 40
Publishing House of the Assemblies of God in Brazil (CPAD), 69–70, 185

racism, 110, 129, 239–40n19
Ramalho, Jether Pereira, 117
Rangel, Licínio, 57
rationalism, 30, 32, 175, 197, 204
Ratzinger, Joseph, 200
Reagan, Ronald, 4, 110, 145, 148, 150, 165
Reencontro, 68–69, 90, 92, 135, 182
Reforma agrária, 18, 214
religion: and leftist political parties, 5, *See also* Christian Right
religious freedom, 27, 30, 34, 132, 176
"Religious Question" controversy, 27
religious Right, 13, 62–63, 235
the *Remnant*, 54–55
Rerum Novarum (Leo XIII), 280–81n186
Revista da Mocidade, 68
Ribeiro, Boanerges, 78–79, 116
Rifan, Dom Fernando Arêas, 53, 55, 202

Rio de Janeiro, 47, 49, 84, 86, 91, 100, 112–15, 118, 189, 202, 222
Robertson, Pat, 75, 139, 141–42, 177, 219
Roberts, Oral, 75, 141–42
Robin, Corey, 233, 281n197
Rocha, Dom José Maurício da, 10–11, 13, 16–17, 19, 41
Rocha, Fausto, 219
Rodgers, Daniel, 9
Rousseff, Dilma, 5, 89
Ruby, Griff, 54
Rueda, Enrique, 145, 184–85, 272n32
Ruff, Howard J., 144–45
Ruffini, Ernesto, 132

Saint Pius X Choir, 190
Salem, Tânia, 28
Salgado, Plínio, 12, 19, 28
Salvation Army, 84, 124
Santos, Theophilo de Azeredo, 164
São Paulo, 3, 34, 100, 112, 115–16
Sarney, José, 75, 89, 93–95, 142, 256n136
Schaffer, Carlos Eduardo, 153, 266n55
Schlafly, Fred, 157, 159
Schlafly, Phyllis, 145, 148, 157
Schmetzer, Uli, 209
Schneider, Sílvio, 126
Schwartz, Michael, 177
Schwarz, Fred, 145, 149
Second Vatican Council, 10, 44–46, 49–50, 136–37, 195–96, 205, 221, 223–24, 234–35, 242n16; and celibacy, 27, 186–87, 192; *De Libertate Religiosa*, 19–20, 30, 131–32; and ecumenism, 37, 45–47, 50, 106; and Mayer, 17–18, 25, 40, 58, 131–32, 192, 204, 230; resistance to, 35, 47, 58–59, 173, 181, 192; and Rocha, 12–13, 16–17; Schema XIII, 24, 27, 215; and Sigaud, 18–20, 22, 25, 29–30, 33, 186–87, 192, 194–95, 214, 216–17, 230, 234; and supernaturalism, 50, 204, 223, *See also* liturgical traditionalism; worship
secularism, 5, 11, 14–15, 242n13
secularization, 18, 29–30, 50, 175, 196, 203, 242n13; opposition to, 27, 34–35, 223